"The interfacing of the Christian Gospel and Islam triggers conversations in most countries I travel, as political, social, and religious issues raise concerns over how these faith-driven convictions can live together. Dr. Wahba's invaluable service is in his laying out the basic factors, historically, the intertwining of faith and politics and in their respective core beliefs. This is a must-read for those seeking to understand these two major and global faiths."

Brian C. Stiller, global ambassador for the World Evangelical Alliance and president emeritus at Tyndale University

"Wafik Wahba's *Global Christianity and Islam* is a comprehensive work that briefly and objectively covers the encounter between Christianity and Islam on different dimensions, in particular the theological differences. It is a must-read for any scholar who needs an introductory work on Christian-Islamic comparative studies."

Hesham Shehab, founder of Messiah for Muslims and Salam Christian Fellowship

"In our fragmented and polarized world, mutual respect and understanding between Muslims and Christians are more important than ever. To navigate the terrain where they encounter one another, you could not hope for a more trustworthy interpreter than Wafik Wahba. Fair, balanced, sympathetic, patient, irenic, concise, and clear—this is an indispensable guide for all who travel the frontiers of Christian-Muslim relations."

Kenneth R. Ross, professor of theology and dean of postgraduate studies at Zomba Theological University in Malawi

"In this breathtaking study of global Christianity and Islam, Wafik W. Wahba delivers a sweeping account of the history, politics, and beliefs of Christianity and Islam as global religions. As an Egyptian Christian who teaches in North America, Wahba is uniquely positioned to tell this story, and he does so to great effect. This is a 'must-read' for any Christian who wants to think better about Islam today."

John A. Vissers, professor of systematic theology at Knox College, University of Toronto

"In this sweeping, masterful study of Christian-Muslim interactions spanning thirteen centuries, Wafik W. Wahba provides a compelling analysis of the impact of historical developments, sociopolitical dynamics, and religious beliefs on past and current Christian-Muslim relations globally. Wahba is an eminently qualified guide in this exploration, a distinguished, Arabic-speaking theologian who, for thirty years, has studied and taught Christian-Muslim relations all over the globe. This is a meticulously researched, scholarly text, yet also highly readable and accessible to anyone seeking greater understanding of the world's two largest religions. Wahba's respectful, irenic tone beautifully embodies the book's stated aim—to better understand and communicate with the religious other and find a path to a peaceful future."

Janet Clark, dean emerita at Tyndale University in Ontario, Canada

"This is the book I want for an overview into Islam's interaction with Christianity through the centuries followed by contemporary insights into current beliefs and practices. My interest is piqued based on the logical and informative organization of the historical features in lockstep eras as well as how the Muslim world regards its mission and agenda in the twenty-first century. This is bundled in the trusted knowledge through personal and academic experience by Wahba and the superb writing style which endears itself to students in their quest to grasp its relevance."

Mark A. Lamport, professor at Grand Canyon University and Colorado Christian University

WAFIK W.
WAHBA

GLOBAL CHRISTIANITY AND ISLAM

EXPLORING
HISTORY, POLITICS,
AND BELIEFS

An imprint of InterVarsity Press
Downers Grove, Illinois

InterVarsity Press
P.O. Box 1400 | Downers Grove, IL 60515-1426
ivpress.com | email@ivpress.com

©2025 by Wafik W. Wahba

All rights reserved. No part of this book may be reproduced in any form without written permission from InterVarsity Press.

InterVarsity Press® is the publishing division of InterVarsity Christian Fellowship/USA®. For more information, visit intervarsity.org.

All Scripture quotations, unless otherwise indicated, are taken from The Holy Bible, New International Version®, NIV®. Copyright © 1973, 1978, 1984, 2011 by Biblica, Inc.™ Used by permission of Zondervan. All rights reserved worldwide. www.zondervan.com. The "NIV" and "New International Version" are trademarks registered in the United States Patent and Trademark Office by Biblica, Inc.™

The publisher cannot verify the accuracy or functionality of website URLs used in this book beyond the date of publication.

Cover design: David Fassett
Interior design: Daniel van Loon

ISBN 978-0-8308-5195-9 (print) | ISBN 978-0-8308-8852-8 (digital)

Printed in the United States of America ∞

Library of Congress Cataloging-in-Publication Data
Names: Wahba, Wafik, author.
Title: Global Christianity and Islam : exploring history, politics, and
   beliefs / Wafik Wahba.
Description: Downers Grove, IL : IVP Academic, [2025] | Includes
   bibliographical references and index.
Identifiers: LCCN 2024034063 (print) | LCCN 2024034064 (ebook) | ISBN
   9780830851959 (print) | ISBN 9780830888528 (digital)
Subjects: LCSH: Christianity and other religions–Islam–History. |
   Islam–Relations–Christianity–History. | BISAC: RELIGION / Comparative
   Religion | RELIGION / Ecumenism & Interfaith
Classification: LCC BP172 .W2343 2025 (print) | LCC BP172 (ebook) | DDC
   297.2/83–dc23/eng/20240808
LC record available at https://lccn.loc.gov/2024034063
LC ebook record available at https://lccn.loc.gov/2024034064

To my wife, Wafaa

My son Ramy and his wife, Liz

My son Mark

And granddaughter Mimi

*With my deepest gratitude for
their support, prayers, love, and encouragement*

CONTENTS

Acknowledgments ix

Introduction xi

PART ONE

HISTORICAL DEVELOPMENTS AND ENCOUNTERS | 1

1 The First Five Hundred Years of Christianity 3
2 Byzantine Christendom and the Early Islamic Caliphates (500–1000) 13
3 Christianity and Islam During the Middle Ages (1000–1500) 44
4 Christianity and Islam in the Age of Discovery (1500–1750) 83
5 Christianity and Islam in the Modern Age (1750–1910) 115

PART TWO

RELIGION AND POLITICS | 145

6 Historical Developments and Political Interactions (1910–2020) 147
7 Religion and Politics in Contemporary World Contexts 198

PART THREE

RELIGIOUS BELIEFS | 223

8 God: Absolute, Relational 225
9 Jesus Christ: A Prophet 254
10 Jesus Christ: The Savior 280
11 Humanity and Salvation 302
12 Community: The Ummah and the Church 314

General Index 333

ACKNOWLEDGMENTS

I AM DEEPLY GRATEFUL for the community of family, friends, and colleagues who supported me with their love, encouragement, prayers, and valuable comments. I would like to thank Tyndale University for its continuous support through the research and writing of this book. I am deeply grateful to the former dean of Tyndale Seminary, Dr. Janet Clark, and the current dean, Dr. Arnold Neufeldt-Fast, for their continuous support and encouragement. I am also grateful for the support of former presidents Dr. Brian Stiller and Dr. Gary Nelson as well as the current president, Dr. Marjory Kerr, and Provost Beth Green for their vision and leadership in supporting Tyndale faculty to engage in scholarship for the sake of the academy and the church.

I am deeply grateful for my faculty colleagues Professors Dennis Ngien, Ron Kydd, and Ian Gentles, who took the time to read various chapters of the manuscript and provide invaluable feedback. My gratitude to Wesley Huff and Mark Wahba for reading and editing the manuscript.

I am grateful to the libraries of Tyndale University, the University of Toronto, Northwestern University, and the University of Chicago for their professional and timely support of my research.

I am grateful to the many academic institutions that provided me with the opportunity to teach and lead seminars on Christianity and Islam and Christian-Muslim relations globally, which enhanced and influenced my research and writing: North Central College, Naperville, IL; Wheaton College, Wheaton, IL; Garrett Evangelical Theological Seminary, Evanston, IL; Lutheran Theological Seminary and McCormick Theological Seminary, Chicago; Fuller Theological Seminary, Pasadena, CA; Regent College, Vancouver, BC; Calgary University, Alberta; McMaster University,

Hamilton, Ontario; Internationale Hochschule, Bad Liebenzell, Germany; Edinburgh University, Scotland; South American Theological Seminary, Londrina, Brazil; Evangelical Theological Seminary, Cairo, Egypt; Evangelical Theological Seminary, Jakarta, Indonesia; Singapore Bible College, Singapore; Evangelical Theological Seminary, Kuala Lumpur, Malysia; South Asia Institute for Advanced Christian Studies, Bangalore, India; African Enterprise, Pietermaritzburg, South Africa; and Lusaka University, Zambia; along with many academic institutions and centers in Egypt, Lebanon, Tunisia, Algeria, and Morocco.

I am grateful for the opportunity to present and lead workshops on Christianity and Islam at various international conferences such as the Lausanne Forum on World Evangelization, Pattaya, Thailand; World Council of Churches interfaith dialogue in Bossey and Geneva, Switzerland; All Africa Council of Churches, Nairobi, Kenya; Middle East Council of Churches and Middle East Evangelical Association, Aya Napa, Cyprus; and The Islamic University of North America, Chicago, to mention a few. I am also grateful for the opportunity to engage with many Christian and Muslim scholars and colleagues globally, who inspired the writing of this book.

I am deeply grateful to IVP Academic for their continuous support throughout the process of editing and publishing the manuscript. I am grateful to Dr. Jon Boyd, associate publisher and academic editorial director of IVP Academic, and Rebecca Carhart, associate academic editor of IVP Academic, along with the editing and the graphic design teams for their outstanding work in the editing and publishing of the book.

I want to express my heartfelt gratitude for my family, who has faithfully and patiently supported me with their love, prayers, and encouragement during the many years of research and writing. Above all, I give thanks to the Lord, who sustained me through this long journey. To him be all glory, honor, and praise.

INTRODUCTION

CHRISTIANITY AND ISLAM DOMINATE the global scene with over four billion adherents, more than half of the world's population. It is expected that the number of Christians and Muslims will continue to grow in the twenty-first century and that both religions will gain converts from among other religious traditions. Meanwhile, advancements in communication technology through various means of social media and unprecedented access to physical mobility provide new levels of interaction among the world population, which in turn advances the spread of Christianity and Islam globally. The message of the Christian faith is being communicated around the clock in various languages through social media to millions of people worldwide. Islam is also gaining new ground in every continent through social media, migration, and economic advantages. While the number of Muslims has tripled in Europe and North America during the last three decades, thousands of Muslims are turning to Christianity in the Middle East and North Africa.[1] Hardly a day passes without a reference to the impact of Christian and Islamic worldviews on politics, economics, and social interactions.

Religious identity and aspirations prove to be as powerful and appealing to people as political affiliations. Continuous turmoil in the Middle East and in other parts of the world is persistently affirming this reality. The renewed sense of religious identity is resulting in new religious affinities that transcend national borders and ethnicities. There is a cluster of integrated issues that one needs to explore to reach a wide-ranging understanding of the current dynamics in Christian-Muslim interactions globally. This book

---

[1] Samples of current Muslim population: France, 9 percent (4.5 million); England, 8 percent (4.6 million); US, 5 percent? (15 million?).

provides a comprehensive overview of Christianity and Islam that covers three interrelated areas: historical developments and encounters, the influence of religion on politics, and religious beliefs and worldviews. Exploring the variant narratives that shaped and continue to shape both Christianity and Islam is crucial to understanding current trends in Christian-Muslim interactions and their impact on future relations between the two communities globally.

Part One: Historical Developments and Encounters

Christian and Muslim communities have coexisted in many parts of the world for thirteen centuries. The history of coexistence and interaction between the two religious communities is long and rich, carrying many layers of memories and events. Some memories are painful and discouraging; others are hopeful and promising. Lessons learned from times of accommodation and coexistence as well as times of conflict, misunderstanding, and hostility offer a framework for understanding current sociopolitical dynamics and their future impact. Learning from historical events can help us to avoid repeating the mistakes of the past.

Christianity and Islam developed differently through history, resulting in each religious tradition's current cultural outlook. They emerged in different cultural contexts and had various means of expansion through the centuries. Christianity emerged in the Hellenistic culture of the Roman Empire, while Islam appeared in seventh-century Arabia. The early spread of Christianity was driven by preaching a gospel of forgiveness and reconciliation, while the remarkable lifestyle of early Christians attracted others to explore the new faith.

Despite enduring significant times of persecution, Christians were able to survive and transform the Roman Empire from within. For most of its history, the spread of the Christian faith came through missions activities. However, when Christianity became the official religion of the Byzantine Empire in the fourth century, the church's mission and the state's ambitions for control intertwined. By the ninth century and in response to the sweeping expansion of Islam, certain measures of forced Christianization were implemented in Europe. The Christianization of the New World took place in the context of colonization, starting from the fifteenth century, while the nineteenth century witnessed a noteworthy era of Christian missions to the whole world.

The early expansion of Islam during the seventh and eighth centuries was achieved through major military battles that toppled both the Byzantine and the Persian Empires while incorporating significant geographical territories across the ancient world. In later times, trade played a significant role in the expansion of Islam into Africa and Asia. Inviting people to embrace the faith (*da'wa*) resulted in converting millions around the globe. Migration, business, and trade also played a remarkable role in incorporating large territories and people into Islam.

By the eighth century, the Islamic empire had come into its golden era of scientific and social advancements, while Christians and Jews were major players in the advancement of society. The Islamic caliphate (empire) emerged victorious militarily in defeating both the Crusaders in the eleventh and twelves centuries and the Mongols in the thirteenth century. However, the Islamic empire was not able to maintain a steady progress in social and cultural development due to tendencies toward conservatism in its sociopolitical structure, which restricted non-Muslims from contributing to the advancement of society. Thoughtful consideration of such historical developments affirms the notion that social and cultural advances come about through collaborative efforts regardless of one's religious tradition. When people are treated equally and given the opportunity to achieve their potential, society at large flourishes and advances. To the contrary, when people are restricted and marginalized, society suffers. Perceiving the "other" as a threat often results in mistrust and conflicts, while embracing the other usually results in better coexistence and enrichment. Examining patterns of intellectual cooperation between Christians and Muslims during the same era provides hope for better coexistence. Cooperation, not war, is ultimately a better way of coexistence.

The dominance of Islam over large parts of the ancient world, combined with the spread of Christianity across Europe by the turn of the millennium, triggered the notion of Western Christianity in the modern era. Historically speaking, however, Christians living under Islam in western Asia, the Middle East, and North Africa enjoyed majority status until the twelfth century. That Islam dominated over large swaths of the world from India to Spain did not result in the Islamization of indigenous Christians living across this vast territory instantly. The process of Islamization, and sometimes Arabization, in those regions resulted in majority-Muslim status only in the fourteenth century. Simultaneously, it must be noted that for almost a millennium, between the seventh and the sixteenth centuries, the Islamic empire (caliphate) challenged the very existence of Christian Europe. Only after the modernization of Europe and the collapse of the Ottoman Empire did Christianity start to gain influence on the world scene.

The current cultural outlook of Western Christianity was primarily shaped by the era of discovery (sixteenth century) and modernization (eighteenth century), while the global expansion of Christianity is credited to the significant missionary movement of the nineteenth and twentieth centuries. Southern Christianity, which is the dominant form of Christianity today, might differ in its historical development and cultural outlook from that of Western Christianity. Themes addressed in this study have been chosen carefully from among hundreds of historical events and encounters, and they serve as building blocks that help us navigate the historical and political developments of Christianity and Islam, leading into current interactions and perceptions. Historical analysis is not simply the study of the past; it is an explanation of the present.

Part Two: Religion and Politics

As the number of Muslims and Christians continues to grow globally, it is expected that their political orientation will continue to influence the sociopolitical and economic systems around the world. In theory, Christianity and Islam have different views on the role of religion in politics. However, both religions have used religious rhetoric, beliefs, and symbols to influence political decisions. While the starting point of Christianity involved the separation of religion and state, Islam affirms *deen wa dawlah* (religion and state) as an inseparable identity. Jesus' words "My kingdom is not of this world" inspired early Christians to endure persecution from the state, and various Christian theologians through the centuries have reaffirmed the separation of the spheres of church and state. However, starting from the Byzantine and European models of Christendom, the church's mission became entangled with the political agenda and the ambitions of the state. Even with the secularization of the West, the Christian ethos continued to influence the drive for democratic systems and the standards of human rights in many Western nations. It is safe to say that the Christian ethos still influences the sociocultural life in the West to some extent.

Affirming that Islam encompasses religion and politics, Islamic societies had different experiences with secularization. While some measures of secularization have been implemented (many Islamic societies are now considered semisecular), the notion of a secularized society is not fully embraced. Even today, many are not able to distinguish between secularized Western societies and Christianity. Political decisions and interactions with the West are sometimes perceived from the lens of an Islamic-Christian struggle over world resources and territories. Some Muslims even perceive the Western agenda as a deliberate offense against Muslims and Islam.

While many moderate Muslims accept some form of secularized political structure where politics and religion are kept apart, others consider such separation a deviation from Islam itself, which should encompass all of life: the social, economic, and political spheres. In general, Islam envisions a community, *ummah*, where Islamic principles are implemented in every sphere of life. Exploring trends of political Islamism provides a better understanding of the current structure of governing adopted by several Muslim nations. A comprehensive survey of the sociopolitical developments of various Islamic communities around the world provides wide-ranging perspective on the current state of Islamic nations globally along with the status of Christians living in these territories.

Part Three: Religious Beliefs

Patterns of interaction between Christian and Muslim communities around the globe suggest that religious orientation is key to people's perceptions of the other as well as the way they interpret the world around them. There seems to be a high level of confusion today about the beliefs of Islam and Muslims as well as Christian history, beliefs, and tradition. Some Muslims, for example, are concerned that Christians exhibit in their beliefs and behavior a lifestyle that is not compatible with what the Qur'an perceives as the true worship of God and a godly lifestyle. Believing in the deity of Christ and a trinitarian God, for instance, is blasphemous according to Islam.

Exploring key religious beliefs facilitates a better understanding of the core values of each religious tradition, which influence perceptions and attitudes toward the other. A major focus of this book is to create an opportunity for better ways of communication by clarifying the core Islamic and Christian beliefs that influence people's actions and attitudes toward the other. One key theological topic to be explored is the absoluteness and relatedness of God. While Christianity emphasizes a personal relationship with God through the life and salvific work of Jesus Christ, Islam perceives the sovereignty of God through his laws and the words of the Qur'an. This leads to differing views of the person and work of Jesus Christ. Other key topics such as human nature as well as the concept of the Islamic *ummah* or community and how it relates to the church will be explored. Revealed scriptures along with their interpretations provide a framework for the community to live and interact. Religious orientation influences attitudes toward others, and people's beliefs and ways of worship often lead to certain actions.

Exploring these interrelated themes of the historical development of Christianity and Islam, the relation between religious beliefs and praxis, and their impact on sociopolitical systems and structures can provide a framework for establishing better relations between Christians and Muslims in the twenty-first century while enabling the Christian community to become increasingly conversant as they engage in witness among Muslims. There are varying Christian perceptions of Islam and Muslims as well as varying Islamic perceptions of Christianity and Christians. Such perceptions are shaped by experiences and encounters. This book addresses both religious traditions from a general framework, with the understanding that Christianity and Islam are each highly diverse in religious and cultural outlook. It must be noted that religious experiences differ from one culture to the other, and the lived faith of a group of Christians or Muslims varies significantly.

In the global context of today, we need to be well informed about the realities that are shaping the future of our societies. Christian-Muslim interactions are vital in determining relationships among countries and communities around the globe in the twenty-first century. This study reflects over twenty-five years of teaching on these topics in various world contexts as well as frequent conversation among Christians and Muslims in over thirty countries, representing various religious and cultural settings. My hope and prayer is that this study will provide an effective tool for the academy and the church to better understand the current religious dynamics that are shaping the future of our societies.

PART ONE
HISTORICAL DEVELOPMENTS AND ENCOUNTERS

Christianity and Islam experienced different historical developments, resulting in the current sociocultural outlook of each religious tradition. They emerged in different cultural contexts and had various patterns of expansions through the centuries. The following chapters will cover the historical developments of both Christianity and Islam, presenting a comprehensive survey of major historical events that shaped the Christian and Islamic traditions, highlighting main encounters between Christianity and Islam during the last thirteen centuries. The history of Christian-Muslim encounters provides a significant framework for understanding current global events, with the hope of attaining better means of interaction between the followers of the two religions, avoiding the mistakes of the past and highlighting positive encounters between the two communities.

1

THE FIRST FIVE HUNDRED YEARS OF CHRISTIANITY

CHRISTIANITY WAS BORN in the multicultural context of the Greco-Roman world of the first century and was the dominant religion in what is today the Middle East, North Africa, and southern Europe during the first seven centuries. Even with the geographical dominance of Islam over two-thirds of the Christian world of the seventh century, Christians under Islamic rule continued to hold majority status until the twelfth century around the Mediterranean basin.

EARLY SPREAD

The spread of the Christian faith into the ancient world surrounding the Mediterranean occurred simultaneously in multiple areas and not only in Europe. Along with the early disciples of Christ, many Christian leaders and merchants spread the new faith to various urban centers across the Roman Empire. By the close of the first century, Christianity became a noticeable religion that attracted the educated and elites as well as the poor and marginalized, incorporating the various strata of the Roman society in church communities. Early Christianity was transcultural, embracing various cultural identities within its fellowship. Contrary to the common belief at the time that higher moral life was something attained only by philosophers and those who allowed reasoning to shape their minds, early Christians proved to the world that all people could attain such high moral standards. Christians were able to communicate the message of the gospel effectively to a multitude of cultural and religious groups not through coercive means but through their living faith and sacrificial lifestyle, winning them the respect of others in a world of great cultural and religious diversity.

Several other factors contributed to the spread of Christianity during the early centuries before Islam, trade and persecution among them. Christian merchants from Syriac, Armenian, and Coptic backgrounds played a significant role in spreading the gospel to Africa, India, and central Asia. As early as the third century, the Syriac church (Iran and Iraq) sent missionaries to India. There is a reference to Christians living in Bactria (Afghanistan) around the year 200. An eighth-century Syriac text known as *The Chronicle of the Seer* gives a glimpse of the connection between the Syriac and Indian churches in the last half of the third century.[1] Reports from fifth-century Syriac church synods list churches for several cities along the Silk Road. Many of these major cities are located in modern Uzbekistan, Turkmenistan, Tajikistan, and Afghanistan.

By the third century, Christianity was well rooted in Egypt, not only in the cosmopolitan city of Alexandria but as far as Nag Hammadi, about five hundred miles to the south. Christians in Egypt counted for the largest Christian community in the Roman Empire during the third and fourth centuries, with an estimated Christian population of 16 percent.[2] Missionaries were sent from Egypt to eastern Libya, Nubia, the Sudan, Ethiopia, Yemen, India, and Persia. During the fourth and fifth centuries, the missionary outreach of the Copts reached to Gaul (France) and Britain.[3] The Monastery of St. Maurice, an Egyptian Roman official, near modern Geneva is a reminder of these early missionary activities by the Egyptian church.[4]

By the end of the fourth century, the population of the city of Antioch (one of the early cities associated with Christianity; see Acts 13) was about half a million, and half of the inhabitants were Christian. The gospel

---

[1] G. A. Williamson, *The History of the Church from Christ to Constantine* (New York: Barnes and Noble, 1965).
[2] Rodney Stark, *The Rise of Christianity* (Princeton, NJ: Princeton University Press, 1996), 13.
[3] It must be noted that Christianity reached Gaul (France) in the late first and early second century.
[4] Kenneth Cragg, *The Arab Christian: A History in the Middle East* (Louisville: Westminster John Knox, 1991), 177. St. Maurice was part of a Roman legion serving in Switzerland. The legion included a medical team where people such as St. Verena from Upper Egypt were sent to attend to the health needs of the Swiss and educate them on new methods of hygiene.

spread from Asia Minor (Turkey) to Armenia in the north. After sporadic times of persecution, the king of Armenia became a Christian, the first king to accept Christianity, and in turn Armenia became the first Christian nation two decades before Constantine, the first Roman emperor, decriminalized Christianity in the Roman Empire in 313.[5]

By the close of the fourth century, Christianity reached most of southern Europe, major parts of the Middle East and North Africa, Nubia, and Ethiopia as well as India. During the early centuries of Christianity, the Christian faith spread in a sophisticated multicultural world of various religions and cultures by introducing a gospel of peace and reconciliation that engaged the minds and hearts of people, not through waging wars on these communities and forcing them to accept the faith. The spread of Christianity during this time occurred despite or even because of severe persecution that claimed hundreds of thousands of Christian lives across the Roman Empire.

Early Christianity is credited with articulating and defending the Christian faith by formulating various statements of faith or creeds. The renowned schools of thought that flourished in major urban areas such Alexandria, Egypt, Antioch, Asia Minor, and Carthage, Tunisia, played an instrumental role in educating Christian leaders while producing major theological work on the basics of the Christian faith that are still in use by the global church today. The remarkable spiritual movement of monasticism that originated in Upper Egypt has influenced Christian spirituality all through the history of Christianity. The movement was instrumental in spreading the Christian faith across Europe and other parts of the world, while monasteries played an instrumental role in preserving biblical texts and manuscripts.

Transforming a Powerful Empire

Christianity transformed Greco-Roman culture in a remarkably short period of time. It started and flourished in urban centers and from there moved to influence the countryside. It is estimated that by the end of the first century there were churches in fifty urban cities in the Roman Empire, most of them in Asia Minor, Syria, Egypt, North Africa, and southern Europe, primarily Greece and Italy. By the third century, Christianity witnessed

---

[5]Dale T. Irvin and Scott W. Sunquist, *History of the World Christian Movement* (New York: Orbis Books, 2001), 113. It must be noted that Constantine merely decriminalized Christianity in 313, marking the "era of peace with the church." However, Emperor Flavius Theodosius I (379–393) was the first Roman emperor to declare Christianity the state religion of the Roman Empire.

significant increase in North Africa, Ethiopia, Spain, Gaul (France), and Germany. It is estimated that Christians formed more than 10 percent of the total population of the empire by the end of the third century.[6]

The remarkable increase in the number of Christians even before Christianity was made the official religion of the state is indicative of the noteworthy transformation that took place in the Roman Empire as a whole. The exemplary lifestyle of the early Christians won them the respect of the larger Roman society. While they lived like strangers and sojourners, they were faithful citizens who abided by the law and even rose above the obligations of the law. Closely related to the values the gospel affirmed was the moral character Christians demonstrated in their daily lives. It was the extraordinary exemplary life of Christians that attracted others to the faith. Christians set up schools and hospitals to educate and treat people while attending to the needs of the community at large, not only Christians. They extended unconditional love to those who hated them and harassed them. Their sacrificial lives and witness to the faith they had in Christ presented a new hope for the people around them. They were able to transform the social strata of the community, where rich and poor, masters and slaves, men and women were all part of the new community.

The transformation of society did not occur through coercive laws of the new religion, and they did not use armies to conquer territories and bring them under the banner of Christianity; such a practice is foreign to the model of the kingdom that Jesus exhibits through his life, teaching, and sacrificial death on the cross. The kingdom of God that Jesus preached is about forgiveness and healed relationships. Christian influence on society during the first three centuries was quite remarkable considering the powerful political structure of the Roman Empire, with its massive pagan worship and its mechanism of enforcing harsh laws.

Institutionalized Christianity

The conversion of Constantine to Christianity ushered in a new era in the life and ministry of the church. After enduring persecution for three centuries, Christians were finally given the freedom to practice their faith without the fear of being tortured. By the first decade of the fourth century, Roman

---

[6]Stark, *Rise of Christianity*, 7.

emperors put an end to the persecution of Christians. Christianity became the official religion of the empire in 392, ushering in the era of Byzantine Christendom, a form of institutionalized Christianity. (The Christendom model in Europe started in the eighth century and lasted in the West for over a thousand years.) Constantinople, named after the emperor, was built on the site of the small city of Byzantium and was dedicated as the capital of the Christian world in 330. The new capital reflected the magnificent power of the new empire replacing Rome, which was associated with the political and religious systems of the old Roman Empire. From the fourth to the eighth century, Christianity was primarily associated with the eastern side of the empire, not with Rome. Constantinople was the first Christian metropolitan capital city and continued to occupy this role until the end of the first millennium, when it was replaced by Rome. Byzantium, however, continued to be the most significant metropolitan city until its fall to the Ottoman Turks in 1453.

The institutionalization of Christianity in the fourth century had significant ramifications for the sociocultural development of Christianity. Christianity became the official religion of the state. Imperial coins bore the name of Christ, and the imperial army incorporated Christian symbols on their shields. The state built churches and magnificent cathedrals. Public buildings and monuments were decorated with Christian symbols. As persecution of Christians subsided, the lifestyle of Christians was not any different from the rest of the Roman citizens. Gone were the days when Christians were known for their dedicated and sacrificial Christian life; they just lived and behaved like everybody else. As Stephen Neill writes, "Faith became superficial, and was identified with the acceptance of dogmatic teachings rather than with a radical change of inner being."[7]

The impact of the emperor's toleration of Christianity was far-reaching. As Christianity became the privileged faith, clergy were supported by the government and were exempt from imperial taxes. This brought with it a new form of imperial domination. The emperor's approval became necessary for episcopal appointments in major sees. Bishops who were recipients of imperial funds were dragged into supporting or blessing political decisions and were asked to advise the emperor in matters of war and politics beyond their initial callings.[8]

---

[7] Stephen Neill, *A History of Christian Missions*, 2nd ed. (New York: Penguin, 1986), 41.
[8] For more details on the role of Constantine in Christianizing the Roman Empire, see Ramsay MacMullen, *Christianizing the Roman Empire (A.D. 100–400)* (New Haven, CT: Yale University Press, 1984).

One issue usually associated with Constantine's endorsement of the Christian faith is whether such a move was a help or a hindrance to the life and ministry of the church. One might initially think that with Constantine's conversion and the empire's full acceptance of the faith, finally Christians were able to worship freely and flourish. However, a deeper look at the context of such political change discloses a completely different picture. According to studies done by Rodney Stark, Robert Wilken, Roger S. Bagnall, and others, the number of Christians in the Roman Empire increased drastically in spite of persecution (or perhaps because of persecution) during the second half of the third century.[9] Stark argues that by the year 300 the number of Christians was over 10 percent of the total population, or more than six million out of the estimated population of sixty million. This significant increase from only 2 percent fifty years earlier (the year 250) made it impossible for the Roman authorities to continue their policy of persecuting Christians. It became clear to authorities that persecuting Christians during the rule of Emperor Diocletian in 303 and his successor, Emperor Galerius, in 305 had failed to force Christians to support state polices and religious practices. As a result, by 311 Emperor Galerius switched tactics, exempting Christians from worshiping the Roman gods provided that they prayed to their own God for the safety and protection of the Roman Empire.[10]

In light of this background, Emperor Constantine's Edict of Milan two years later was not out of the ordinary. Rather, it was simply a continuation of a new state policy of embracing a prevailing movement rather than wasting time and energy fighting it. Because of the exemplary lifestyle of Christians and their faithful support of the well-being of all citizens in the Roman Empire, it was imperative for the state to embrace the Christian God as one among others in the pantheon of gods worshiped across the empire. While Constantine's move to establish Christianity as the official religion of the state contributed significantly to the well-being of Christians and the

---

[9] Robert L. Wilken, *The Christians as the Romans Saw Them* (New Haven, CT: Yale University Press, 1984), and Stark, *Rise of Christianity*. Both writers present compelling arguments on the significant increase in the number of Christians during the third century of Christianity. Bagnall presents similarly astonishing findings about the number of Christians in Egypt during the third and fourth centuries. He argues that in the year 280 Egypt's population was 13.5 percent Christian, while in the Roman Empire Christians were at 5.4 percent; he also argues that in 315, the number of Christians in Egypt increased to 18 percent, while in the Roman Empire as a whole it increased to 17.4 percent. See Roger S. Bagnall, "Religious Conversion and Onomastic Change in Early Byzantine Egypt," *Bulletin of the American Society of Papyrologists* 19 (1982): 105-24.
[10] Stark, *Rise of Christianity*, 3-13.

organizational structure of the church, the reality was that by the end of the third century Christianity had already become a very powerful force within the Roman Empire, one that necessitated such a move. The resilient presence of Christians required a different treatment from the state, which came in the form of official recognition of the Christian faith as a state religion.

Byzantine Christendom: Setting the Stage for Islamic Advancement

Understanding the Byzantine model of Christendom explains the religious and political context at the time when Islam appeared in the seventh century and why the Muslim armies were able to sack significant parts of the Byzantine Empire with relative ease. It also points to several issues regarding the impact of this new arrangement on the life of the church and Christians during that period.

When Christianity was declared the official religion of the Roman Empire in the late fourth century, the relationship between the church and the state entered a new phase. Under this new arrangement, the state not only supported the church but also interfered in its business. Constantine's top priority was to keep the empire powerful and united, and one of his main concerns was the unity of the Christian churches. If the Christian faith was to serve as the unifying religion of the empire, Christianity had to be a unified system, whichever teaching it might hold.[11] Thus, while the issue of church unity was not new in the time of Constantine, decisions on theological matters were perceived as crucial for the unity of the church and ultimately for the unity of the empire. Accordingly, the emperor invited church leaders to settle their differences and to defend the Christian beliefs against heresies. During the fourth and fifth centuries, several ecumenical councils were held to discuss a host of theological issues. The nature and person of Christ were at the center of these theological debates. Through these ecumenical councils, the church was able to express its belief in and understanding of Christ, the Trinity, and other major doctrines. The outcomes of ecumenical councils were usually expressed in a statement of faith or creed. The first and probably the most well-known of such statements of faith is the Nicene Creed of 325.

---

[11]See Maureen A. Tilley, trans., *Donatist Martyr Stories: The Church in Conflict in Roman North Africa* (Liverpool: Liverpool University Press, 1996); also W. H. C. Frend, *The Donatist Church: A Movement of Protest in Roman North Africa* (Oxford: Clarendon, 1952).

Before Constantine, the only means bishops had to enforce church discipline was excommunicating the other party. With imperial power interfering in church decisions, church discipline could be carried out by force. Imperial troops took responsibility for suppressing any movement that would have disturbed the peace of the empire. Those who opposed the Nicene Creed were sent into exile. Church leaders of North Africa known as Donatists were also arrested and sent into exile.[12] Imperial involvement in church affairs resulted in intensified divisions and hatred among church leaders and Christian communities. Christians who disagreed with the majority decision were finding themselves for the first time being persecuted by the Christian state that was supposed to protect them.

The imperial hope for unity among Christians was never achieved. To the contrary, divisions between leading theological schools intensified, and bishops started competing over prestigious seats. By the fifth century, the leading theological schools, in Alexandria and Antioch, produced different theological stances on the relationship between the divinity and the humanity of Christ, prompting the imperial court to call for another ecumenical council to settle the disputes. The Council of Chalcedon (the fourth ecumenical council) met in 451 with the hope of resolving these theological differences.[13] The outcomes of the council were rejected by the Egyptian, Armenian, and some Syrian churches, resulting in the first major division in the church. Meanwhile, using Greek to formulate statements of faith was completely foreign to the Latin-speaking Christians of North Africa and southern Europe. Accordingly, the church in the Latin world (Rome and North Africa) was not enthusiastically involved in the early ecumenical councils.

---

[12]The North African church was one of the largest Christian communities in the Roman Empire, with over seven hundred bishoprics at the beginning of the fourth century. The Donatists were concerned about allowing Christian leaders who previously denied the faith during the time of persecution to participate in any leadership role. They regarded any sacraments practiced by traitors of the faith to be invalid. Other leaders argued against such strict roles and were willing to forgive the traitors if they repented. Several councils were held to resolve the issue. The councils ruled against the Donatists, a decision that was backed by imperial power. The conflict between these two parties resulted in two churches in North Africa, Catholics and Donatists, with each having its own senior bishop. The Donatist controversy dragged on for another three centuries and was only resolved by the near disappearance of the church in North Africa centuries later under Islamic rule. It must be stated that the disappearance of the North African church started before the coming of Islam and was also due to the various attacks by the Vandals during the sixth century, which resulted in the destruction of Rome as well as several major urban centers in North Africa, forcing many Christians to flee to Spain and southern Italy.

[13]The second ecumenical council was held in Constantinople in 381, while the third ecumenical council was held in Ephesus in 431.

Power Struggles

The interference of the imperial court in the church's life resulted in power struggles among the leading churches. While Antioch and Alexandria were known for their outstanding theological schools, prominent theologians, and endless theological debates, Constantinople and Rome represented political power and authority. By the beginning of the fifth century, political tensions between Constantinople and Rome were obvious. Rome could no longer boast a prominent imperial presence, a status that had drastically shifted to Constantinople, but it was the city that gave the empire its previous glory and prestige. By the mid-fifth century, several church decrees, backed by imperial approval, indicated that the bishop of Rome occupied a place of special authority within the churches of the empire. Similar statements came out of the Council of Chalcedon, establishing the authority of the bishop of Constantinople over the rest on the eastern side of the empire. The impact of such political moves proved to be detrimental to the overall relationship between churches in the region, keeping in mind that neither Rome nor Constantinople had produced any significant theological work at the time.[14]

The Christian state of Byzantium was supposed to protect the Christians and the clergy, but to the contrary, those who opposed the state were persecuted, harassed, and sent into exile. While many Christians saw this new arrangement as a great victory for the church and for the cause of Christ, others were deeply concerned about the interference of the state in ecclesiastical issues. Christians in Egypt, Syria, North Africa, and parts of southern Europe suffered persecution and were harassed by the Byzantine Empire; for them, the church-state partnership simply represented another form of imperial oppression, one masked in Christian garb. The Byzantine model of Christendom was a mixture of blessing and disaster for the church. On one hand, it supported Christians and helped the church to survive, but on the other, it was responsible for intensifying church divisions and weakening the church's unity, creating major factions among Christians. By the seventh century, Christians were fighting Christians and even persecuting other Christians with the support of the state. The Byzantine model of Christendom had dire consequences for the church. When Muslim armies

---

[14]Harold Allen Drake, *Constantine and the Bishops: The Politics of Intolerance* (Baltimore, MD: Johns Hopkins University Press, 2000).

marched into Syria, Mesopotamia, Egypt, and North Africa in the seventh century, they were able to sack these nations with relative ease because the church was weak and divided. These majority-Christian nations at the time were weary of three centuries of constant conflict and persecution inflicted by Byzantium. Meanwhile, decades of fighting between the Byzantine and Persian empires exhausted their abilities to defend themselves, and major territories under their domain were easily sacked by the Muslim armies before the close of the seventh century.

Conclusion

Worldwide Christianity today is indeed in debt to its eastern roots around the Mediterranean. Early Christians lived a remarkable lifestyle that was shocking to the surrounding pagan culture, and their unconditional love and service won them the respect of the larger community. The early Christians were able to transform the highly sophisticated Roman Empire not by force but by preaching a gospel of peace and reconciliation while exhibiting a lifestyle that truly reflected the ethos of the gospel. The spread of the Christian faith during this era occurred through winning the hearts and minds of people, not through wars and invasions. From its inception, Christianity was characterized by significant aspiration for education, demonstrated in the early Christian schools of thought, accompanied by a desire for strong spirituality, expressed in the monastic movement. The early Christians who endured inconceivable persecution were able to keep the unity of the church community and to protect its integrity.

By the fourth century, Christianity became the official religion of the Roman Empire, ushering in the era of Byzantium Christianity. Christian ethos and religious beliefs dominated the cultural and social life around the Mediterranean. The conversion of the Roman imperial order brought dramatic changes in Christianity. Imperial interference in ecclesiastical matters to keep the unity of the church while maintaining a unified empire politically resulted in significant divisions and hostilities among Christians and church leaders across the region. By the time Islam appeared in the seventh century, Christians were fighting Christians, and their divisions resulted in the sacking of their territories by Muslim armies with relative ease.

2

BYZANTINE CHRISTENDOM AND THE EARLY ISLAMIC CALIPHATES (500–1000)

Starting from the seventh century, the history of Christianity was linked to that of Islam. The new monotheistic religion that erupted from Arabia in the seventh century, combined with significant military strength, would challenge the core theological beliefs of Christianity and its very existence for centuries to come. Within four decades after the death of Islam's Prophet Muhammad, the founder of the new religion, Arab forces toppled the Persian Empire and shook the Byzantine Empire to its core, bringing two-thirds of the world's Christian inhabitants under the rule of Islam. Islamic domination over two-thirds of the eastern Roman Empire by the seventh century further weakened the power of Byzantium and prompted southern Europe to use every measure, including military force, to stop the advancement of Muslim invaders. Rome in turn emerged as the most important center for church life in Europe.

Christianity expanded in Europe beyond its traditional base around the Mediterranean. Christian missionaries, primarily monks and nuns from Irish and Anglo-Saxon backgrounds, spread the Christian faith into northern Europe. During this period, the Franks in the south became the most powerful political power in Europe. The coronation of Charlemagne as holy Roman emperor in the year 800 marked a new beginning in the history of Christianity in Europe. Charlemagne became the first political figure to represent the emerging Christian Europe in contrast to the ailing eastern Roman see out of Constantinople. Charlemagne's ascension into power was not welcomed by Byzantium. By the ninth century, missionaries were sent from Constantinople to the Bulgars and the Slavs in eastern Europe. By the tenth century, Greek missionaries spread the Christian faith into Russia and most of eastern Europe.

The Rise of Islam

Islam, which originated in Arabia, emerged into the world scene of the seventh century when the Persian and Roman empires were the dominant forces across the region. The people of Arabia lived on the borders of these great empires for centuries without being absorbed by either of them. In fact, the land of Arabia was never occupied by any foreign power. The parched desert nature of the land and the lack of major natural resources did not attract outsiders. The Arabs called their homeland Jazerat Al-Arab ("the island of the Arabs"). Although Arabia is not actually an island, it seemed an island to its people and to those around it. This is not to suggest that Arabs lived in isolation; to the contrary, the Arabs were active traders and warriors who always boasted about their bravery and power. Nehemiah makes a reference to "Geshem the Arab" as one of the leaders appointed to rule over Jerusalem during exile in the fifth century BC (Neh 2:19). The Arabs, however, were a people on the move; the majorities were Bedouins or nomads, who constantly had to move from one place to another searching for suitable pastures for their flocks. Across this massive desert land, a few small urban centers were established around the trade generated by caravans. Arab merchants were instrumental in moving goods to the markets of Egypt, Syria, Persia, Yemen, and Ethiopia. In contrast to other major urban civilizations around the Mediterranean, the aridity of the desert did not allow the Arabs to build any enduring civilization or to form a centralized government. Poetry made up their social and cultural life, and there is no record of Arabic literature before the seventh century.

Before Islam, polytheism dominated the religious landscape in Arabia, where Arabs worshiped a host of different gods and goddesses. Scattered Christian and Jewish communities were also part of this multifaith context. According to Arab tradition, the Ka'ba, one of the most significant houses of worship in Arabia, hosted more than 360 images of gods and goddesses, including statues for Jesus and Mary. For centuries before Islam, the different Arab tribes used to come for an annual pilgrimage to the Ka'ba, located in the city of Mecca, a practice that continued after Islam but was given Islamic religious meaning and practice.

In 570, Prophet Muhammad was born into this Arabian context of Mecca. After receiving what are recorded in the Qur'an as revelations from the angel Gabriel, he invited his fellow Meccans to abandon their polytheistic beliefs and to submit to and worship God alone (the word *Islam* means "to submit"). The message of Islam attracted few followers in Mecca, however; the majority rejected the new faith and saw in Prophet Muhammad's new teaching a direct threat to their status and economic gains from the revenues generated by pilgrimage to the Ka'ba. Fearing for his life, Prophet Muhammad fled from Mecca to Medina in 622, the year of immigration (*hijra*), which marks the beginning of the Islamic calendar. In Medina, Prophet Muhammad gathered large crowds of followers, establishing the first Muslim community. The Muslim community gained strength through a series of attacks on caravans and other neighboring communities.[1] In the Medina period (622–630) Muslims won significant victories against various Arab tribes and the Jews. In less than three years, Prophet Muhammad was able to establish his role not only as a religious leader but also as a judge and a warrior among the Muslim community of Medina. He returned to Mecca in 630, and Muslims under the military leadership of Prophet Muhammad were able to capture the city and institute Islam as its religion. By the time of Prophet Muhammad's death in 632, Islam was established as the unifying force in most of western Arabia.[2]

---

[1]Using the raiding system known in Arabic as *ghazawat* (singular *ghazwa*), Muslims were able to defeat other Arab tribes. Raiding expeditions were a common nomadic Arab practice in which a stronger tribe would carry out a sudden attack on a weaker tribe, defeating it and taking people and goods as booty. Raiding expeditions carried out by Muslims during Prophet Muhammad's time (primarily 620–632) resulted in consolidating major parts of western Arabia under the banner of Islam. The desire for expanding such raiding expeditions continued under the rule of the first caliphs (632–660), when pitched battles between Muslims and the Byzantine Empire resulted in significant gains for Muslims in Syria, Mesopotamia (Iraq), and Egypt. By the time of the Umayyad dynasty (661–750), Islam controlled the region from Spain to northern India as well as significant territories in central Asia. Muslims usually refer to the invasion of other territories as an act of religious duty for the purpose of expanding the territory of Islam, *Fatah*, and not as an invasion.
[2]For a comprehensive coverage of Muhammad's life and mission, see F. E. Peters, *Muhammed and the Origins of Islam* (Albany: State University of New York Press, 1994); Tom Holland, *In the Shadow of the Sword* (London: Little, Brown, 2012). Patricia Crone, *Meccan Trade and the Rise of Islam* (Piscataway, NJ: Gorgias, 2004). Also see W. Montgomery Watt, *Muhammed at Mecca* (Oxford: Clarendon, 1953) and *Muhammed at Medina* (Oxford: Clarendon, 1956), an older comprehensive account, some of whose findings have been disputed recently.

Under the first caliph (successor) of the prophet, Abu Baker (632–634), the Arabian Peninsula was unified under the banner of Islam after waging several jihad (holy wars) against those who refused to accept the new religion or lapsed from the faith. Many Arabs thought they would have the option of abandoning Islam after the death of its prophet and founder; however, the punishment for apostasy in Islam is death.

Less than a decade after the death of Prophet Muhammad, Arab armies, inspired by Islamic teaching, marched through the Persian and eastern Roman empires, taking over major territories. By 638, under the second caliph, Umar (634–644), Islam expanded into Syria and Mesopotamia (Iraq). Muslim armies took over Jerusalem in 640, and in 642 Islam entered Egypt. Alexandria was besieged for two years, and its famous library was burned to the ground. In 642 parts of Persia (Iran) came under Islamic domination. Umar was murdered by a Persian slave in 644, and Othman, a son-in-law of Prophet Muhammad, was chosen as the third caliph; he is known for codifying the Qur'an and burning other copies that did not match the one in use in his time. During his caliphate (644–656), the Islamic armies reached Carthage (Tunisia) in 647, and by 651 the rest of Persia was incorporated as a province in the caliphate. Othman was murdered in 656, and his death ushered in a bloody internal power struggle over who had the right to lead the Islamic empire. Ali, another son-in-law of Prophet Muhammad, was declared the fourth caliph (656–661).

For the previous three decades the followers of Ali had been creating tension in the community, wanting Ali, instead of the preceding three caliphs, to succeed his father-in-law, the Prophet. They insisted that leadership should be entrusted to a member of the Prophet's family. The followers of Ali were later called the Shi'ite (meaning "the partisan" or "followers of Ali"). The majority of Muslims maintained that leadership in Islam should be open to anyone in the community and that the leader should be chosen based on the consensus of the community. This mainstream Islamic branch was later called Sunni (referring to those who follow the principles of the Prophet). This disagreement over leadership led to the first and most significant division in Islam, which continues today, between the Sunni and the Shi'ite.

The fourth caliph, Ali, was assassinated in 661, and the nephew of the previous caliph Othman and his great general, Mu'awiya, assumed power. The Shi'ites, from their side, appointed Ali's son Hasan as the new caliph, but he was also assassinated. Their third attempt to appoint a caliph also failed with the assassination of Hussain, Ali's second son and Hasan's brother. These events started a hostile and sometimes bloody history between the Shi'ites and the Sunnis that remains a source of conflict to this day.

THE UMAYYAD EMPIRE (CALIPHATE): 661–750

Mu'awiya became the first of fourteen caliphs of the Umayyad caliphate (661–750), which lasted for almost a century with Damascus, Syria, as its capital. The expansion of Islam continued to the east in the Indus Valley region (India/Pakistan). By 715, the Islamic armies captured the entire Silk Road, covering all of central Asia and extending the message of Islam to western China. The Islamic expansion continued to the west through Morocco, where by 711 the Islamic army crossed the narrow band of water at the entrance of the Mediterranean into Gibraltar (Gibel Tarek) the mountain of Tarek, named after the military chief who commanded the Muslim troops into Europe. Within a decade, most of Spain was under Islamic rule, and Muslim armies crossed the Pyrenees and marched into what is today France. The Islamic armies were stopped by the Christian armies of Charles Martel in 732 between Tours and Poitiers. By 750, Islam dominated over a massive geographical territory that extended from Spain to western China. Two-thirds of the Byzantine Empire was under Islam's rule.[3]

The Umayyad dynasty was marked by massive conquest and expansion. The new rulers were able to manage and control this vast empire by benefiting from the expertise of skilled Christians and Jews who were entrusted with managing the day-to-day administrative responsibilities. One example of this arrangement is Mansur Ibn Sarjun, the former controller of the Byzantine governor, who continued to serve in the same position under the Muslim caliph. His grandson, John of Damascus, the great Christian apologist of the eighth century, grew up in the caliph palace and debated Muslim scholars in the presence of the caliph.

Significant Islamic structures were constructed during the Umayyad dynasty. In 691, the Dome of the Rock was built over the site of the Jewish temple in Jerusalem in the area known as the Temple Mount. It is

---

[3]See Kenneth Cragg and R. Marston Speight, *The House of Islam*, 3rd ed. (Belmont, CA: Wadsworth, 1988).

considered the third holiest site in Islam after the Ka'ba in Mecca and the Grand Mosque in Medina. In 710, the Church of John the Baptist in Damascus was converted into the Great Mosque of Damascus (also known as the Umayyad Mosque), which is considered the fourth holiest site in Islam. The establishment of the Dome of the Rock in Jerusalem over the holiest site in Judaism and the Umayyad Mosque in Damascus over one of the most historical churches in Christianity signifies how Islam surpassed previous revealed religions, Judaism and Christianity. The pattern of converting significant church buildings into mosques continued, as occurred with Hagia Sophia in the fifteenth century.[4]

Living in Dar al-Islam. The massive geographical territory, extending from India to Spain, controlled by Muslim rulers was called Dar al-Islam ("the house of Islam"). According to the Islamic religiopolitical system, Islamic principles and laws should govern the house of Islam, at least theoretically. Muslims and non-Muslims who lived in the house of Islam both had to adhere to religious, social, and political laws and regulations. Non-Muslims were allowed to live and practice their religions within the framework of the Islamic sociopolitical system of governance. In the early period of the dynasty, Muslim rulers were not prepared to manage the administrative infrastructure of such massive and sophisticated territories. They employed a shrewd tactic whereby an Islamic Arab commander was appointed to govern a particular territory while continuing to benefit from the expertise of the local administrators to manage the country's social and economic systems. For the average person nothing significant had changed except paying jizya, the poll tax, in exchange for maintaining their religious status. However, such measures started to change gradually when the power and authority of the Islamic state was firmly established.

The protected people: Dhimmis. Christians and Jews, who formed the majority inhabitants across the new Islamic empire, were given the status of protected people, or *dhimmis*.[5] According to this arrangement, they

---

[4]For a detailed history of Islamic expansion, see Marshall G. S. Hodgson, *The Venture of Islam: Conscience and History in a World of Civilization*, vol. 1, *The Classical Age of Islam* (Chicago: University of Chicago Press, 1974).

[5]Based on the Arab Bedouin tradition, if a tribe is defeated by a stronger tribe or becomes significantly weaker, it usually seeks a protection status to avoid complete annihilation. It is a way of survival under humiliating conditions. Christians and Jews who did not accept the message of Islam came under the status of protection. The name used to describe the protected people is

were given the choice to remain Christians or Jews, provided that they paid the poll tax. Christians and Jews were considered "People of the Book," since they possessed revealed scriptures. Such a privilege was not given to any other religious groups (besides Hindus; see below); the choice was either to accept Islam or to face the penalty of death. During the Umayyad dynasty, Christians and Jews did not convert to Islam in large numbers. By remaining under the protected status of *dhimmis*, they generated significant revenues for the empire through paying taxes.[6]

On one hand, the *dhimmi* status protected the People of the Book from being annihilated and gave them the opportunity to practice their religion. On the other hand, it created a context where they became second-class citizens in their own land, paying a tax to survive. Meanwhile, the protected status provided the most practical solution for the Islamic state to deal with millions of Christians and Jews. It enabled the Muslims to avoid the impossible task of either converting, killing, or expelling such a massive number of people from the territories under their control. Hindus, while considered pagans, were also given the status of protected people, since there was no way of fighting millions of them in India. The conditions governing protected people often involved humiliating provisions based on the Qur'anic instructions, "Fight those who believe not in Allah and nor the Last Day, nor hold that forbidden which has been forbidden by Allah and his messenger, nor acknowledge the religion of Truth from among the People of the Book until they pay the jizya with willing submission and feel themselves subdued [humiliated]" (9:29, see also 9:5, 14).[7]

---

dhimmi. Therefore, Jews and Christians, who had a special status as the People of the Book, became also *dhimmis* in need of protection from the stronger Islamic state. In a sense, they became vulnerable as a weaker group since they did not embrace the religion of the state that was in power.

[6]For detailed coverage of the status of non-Muslims under Islam, see Bat Ye'or, *The Dhimmi: Jews and Christians Under Islam* (London: Associated University Presses, 1985).

[7]The hadith (sayings of the Prophet) further explain the rules governing extorting jizya from non-Muslims. "If they refuse to accept Islam, demand from them the Jizya. If they agree to pay, accept it from them and hold off your hands. If they refuse to pay the tax, seek Allah's help and fight them" (Sahih Muslim 19:4924). "Our Prophet, the Messenger of our Lord, has ordered us to fight you till you worship Allah Alone or give Jizya; and our Prophet has informed us that our Lord says: 'Whoever amongst us is killed, shall go to Paradise to lead such a luxurious life as he has never seen, and whoever amongst us remain alive, shall become your master'" (Sahih Bukhari 53:386). This hadith was used during the reign of Umar, the second caliph, who sent Muslim armies to conquer Persia, Syria, and Palestine. Bukhari also recounts an incident that might suggest an amount of jizya equivalent to half of the total earnings. However, there is no consistent records of the amount of jizya required of non-Muslims. "When Allah's Messenger had conquered Khaibar (a Jewish settlement in western Arabia), he wanted to expel the Jews from it as its land became the property of

It is one thing for there to be some guiding principles in the Qur'an on how Christians and Jews should be treated under Islamic rule, but it is quite another task to govern a majority-Christian population in their own land. Considering the unprecedented circumstances, a covenant or pact was supposedly made in 717 between the Umayyad caliph Umar II (682–720) and the *Ahl-al-Kitab* ("People of the Book"), the Christians and the Jews who lived in the Islamic empire. According to this document, the Christians of Syria came to caliph Umar II demanding restrictions on their religious and social lives in lieu of gaining protection over their lives, a request that the caliph granted. The irony of this was that Christians, who formed the majority, were the ones who requested to be granted a protected status, *dhimmi*, in their own land, and actually requested restrictions over their social, religious, and political lives.

It is not clear whether the Christians and the Jews indeed proposed such restrictions on themselves, as the document portrays the situation. Regardless, according to the covenant of Umar II, Christians were permitted to keep their existing places of worship but were prohibited from building new ones. Several measures were taken to restrict Christianity in public, such as prohibitions on displaying crosses in public, parading during Easter or Christmas, and the use of church bells. On the social level, Christians and Jews were not allowed to ride horses, to serve in the military, or to carry weapons, and they were expected to wear certain clothes to distinguish themselves from Muslims. Christian men were not allowed to marry Muslim women; however, Muslim men were allowed to marry Christian women, though their children were expected to be raised Muslim.[8] The document explains the overall expectations and arrangements for non-Muslims in the Islamic state. It is clear from history that not every measure in this document was strictly applied; however, the document was often referred to in times of tension to remind the People of the Book of their status and obligations toward the Islamic state. As the Islamic state started to gain power, the relationship between Muslims and

---

Allah, His Apostle, and the Muslims. Allah's Messenger intended to expel the Jews, but they requested him to let them stay there on the condition that they would do the labor and get half of the fruits. Allah's Messenger told them, 'We will let you stay on that condition, as long as we wish.' So, they kept on living there until Umar forced them [out]" (Sahih Bukhari 14:19).

[8]Sobhy Al-Saleh, *Sharh al-Shorut al-Umria* [*Explanation of Umar's decree*] *as authored by Sheik Shams al-Dhin Abdullah Mohammed bin abi-Baker al-Jawzia (691–701)* (Damascus: Damascus University Press, 1961).

non-Muslims was clearly defined. On the one hand, Christians were not compelled to embrace Islam, though they were encouraged to do so. On the other hand, they were strictly prohibited from evangelizing Muslims, a practice that continues to the modern day in majority-Muslim countries. While Christians are welcome to embrace Islam, Muslims continue to be restricted from converting to other religions; the penalty for apostasy is death.

At the beginning of the Umayyad dynasty (660s), the Arabs lived in camps outside urban cities and had limited contact with the natives. Such measures prevented the natives from direct interactions with their new rulers and avoided revolts against the Arabs, who were very few compared to the indigenous population. By the end of the Umayyad dynasty (750s), the Arab rulers started to gain strength from the fact that many indigenous people were converting to Islam. By the time the Abbasid dynasty was established in 750, most urban cities were fully controlled by Muslim rulers.

Despite the restrictions imposed on non-Muslims, Christian communities managed to survive and even to grow in certain parts of the Islamic empire under the Umayyad dynasty. Christians in Egypt and Syria, for example, had experienced lengthy periods of persecutions, first under the Romans and then under the Byzantine Empire. The Islamic rule over their lands was another form of foreign intervention. In Egypt, Syria, and Mesopotamia, monasteries played a significant role in keeping the Christian faith alive for centuries. Christians were able to escape to the desert and keep a low profile away from major urban centers of political upheaval.

The Arabization of the caliphate. By the beginning of the eighth century, the process of Arabization was fully in place along with the process of Islamization. As the Arab rulers became more confident in managing state affairs, they required administrators to use the Arabic language in running state businesses and political systems. The majority indigenous people spoke all kinds of other languages—Greek, Berber, Syriac, and more. It became clear that Arabic was the language of the day, and if they were to succeed in the political and economic sectors of the empire, they had to learn the official language of the state. Many non-Muslims saw the advantages of learning Arabic to continue serving in their posts. The process of Arabization that started in the eighth century under the Umayyad dynasty continued through the Abbasid dynasty and resulted in establishing an

Islamic empire that was shaped by the Arabic language and culture. This created a climate in which, by the eleventh century, many of the native languages spoken across the region, such as Coptic, Greek, and Syriac, started to disappear. In the case of Egypt, the Coptic language survived as the language of church liturgy. The Coptic language ceased to exist as a day-to-day language of the people by the twelfth century apart from remote villages in Upper Egypt. Unlike the Egyptian Copts, Syriac Christians were able to keep the Syriac language as a spoken language in northern Iraq and parts of Syria up until today. The Berbers of North Africa (Tunisia, Algeria, and Morocco) were able to keep their indigenous Amazeric language up until today as well (40 to 50 percent of North Africans, although majority Muslims, consider themselves as Amazeric or Berber, not Arabs).

The process of Arabization had different impacts on other parts of the Muslim world. In the case of Persia and parts of India (Pakistan), the Persian and Urdu languages survived, but the alphabet used in both languages is Arabic. It is interesting to note that only one-third of contemporary Muslims speak Arabic; however, every Muslim is required to use Arabic in prayers and in reading the Qur'an. Such a firm stand makes Arabic a powerful unifying force across the globe among contemporary Muslim populations in spite of the fact that the classical Arabic of the Qur'an differs from the various contemporary dialectics of Arabic.

The Abbasid Caliphate (750–1258)

In 750 the Umayyad dynasty came to an end when the Abbasid toppled their power and relocated the capital of the Islamic caliphate from Damascus to Baghdad. The Umayyad continued to rule only in Spain until 1031. The Abbasid came to power by clinging to their right to rule through their birthright, being descendants of the Prophet's family.[9] They also gained the backing of the majority Shi'ite Muslims in Persia and Iraq. The Abbasid dynasty chose a strategic location to build its new capital, which they named Baghdad (meaning "splendor"), where the great rivers Tigris and Euphrates join. The new capital came to represent the most magnificent and splendorous era in the history of Islam. Baghdad became one of the most significant metropolises in the ancient world, presiding over

---

[9] The name *Abbasid* is derived from the youngest uncle of Muhammad, Abbas ibn Abdul-Muttalib.

the largest Islamic empire in history. Soon the new capital, built in 762, became one of the most influential centers of governing, arts, and sciences. The Abbasid benefited from the Persian expertise in governing, creating a sophisticated and advanced political system. The position of vizier (or cabinet minister) was introduced, wherein the sultan would delegate many governing responsibilities to his ministers.

The golden era of Islam. The early Abbasid caliphs fostered an era of great intellectual achievements, ushering in the golden era of Islamic civilization during the eighth and ninth centuries. Contrary to the Umayyad rulers, who enforced the supremacy of Arab culture, the Abbasid fostered a multicultural society where Christians and Jews were entrusted with the massive task of gathering and translating knowledge in every field from Greek, Latin, Persian, and other languages into Arabic. Their work was instrumental in connecting the Hellenistic world with Arabic culture. Muslim and non-Muslim scholars worked together in the advancement of science, medicine, philosophy, and education. Arts and literature flourished. Islamic art in the form of calligraphy and other styles of writing developed.[10]

The Abbasid success is a credit to their open-mindedness, which incorporated knowledge gained from ancient Roman, Greek, Egyptian, Persian, Indian, and Chinese civilizations. Astronomy, medicine, and mathematics also flourished at the time, including the mathematician al-Khawrizmi, the father of algebra (*al-jabr* means "to restore broken parts" in Arabic). He is also credited with introducing the Arabic numerical system in mathematics, which replaced the Roman numerical system. The term *algorism* is derived from his name. Persian scientist Ibn Sina (a.k.a. Avicenna) is known for his collection of a vast number of medical treatises, documented in his encyclopedia, *The Canon of Medicine*, a work that influenced European scientists during the Renaissance. Great discoveries in anatomy were also made in this time period. Ibn al-Haytham developed one of the earliest scientific methods of determining the reliability of scientific theory based on experiments. Jabir in Hayyan influenced great

---

[10]Calligraphy of Qur'anic verses became a way of praising God without picturing God, communicating the message of the Qur'an in an artistic format. Art in Islam symbolizes the indirect and abstract. Since Muslims believe that the Qur'an was inspired in the Arabic language, using the Arabic script provides for developing a variety of ornamental forms. Therefore, calligraphy is the most highly regarded and most fundamental element of Islamic art.

figures such as Roger Bacon and Isaac Newton in their study of chemistry. Al-Battani improved the precision of the measurement of the earth's axis, a methodology that was incorporated in the Copernican heliocentric model. At the center of this intellectual hub was the House of Wisdom, founded by Abbasid caliph Harun al-Rashid (786–809) and culminating with al-Ma'mun (813–833). The House of Wisdom hosted the greatest library at the time. It was a key institution in the translation movement and a major intellectual center from the ninth to the thirteenth centuries. Many a great scholar came to study at this excellent research and intellectual institute.

Baghdad also witnessed the development of the first Islamic schools of law. The five major schools of Islamic law are the Hanafi (the largest), the Shafi'i, the Maliki, the Hanbali (the most conservative), and the Ja'fari. Muslim judges and lawyers are trained in these schools to become experts in interpreting and applying the Islamic law, *shari'a*.

The well-known work of fiction *One Thousand and One Nights* (*Arabian Nights*) was initially developed during the Abbasid era, with further additions during the tenth and fourteenth centuries. This fairy-tale fiction depicts the lavish lifestyle of a well-known figure, Harun al-Rashid. A notable feature of this literature is its creativity in incorporating the cultures of Persia, India, the Middle East, and North Africa in one masterpiece of literature, a great early example of the interconnectedness of world civilizations. Various characters from the epic have become cultural icons in Western culture, such as Aladdin, Ali Baba, and Sinbad.[11]

As the empire embraced and encouraged contributions made by scholars and intellectuals, who took an active role in governing, education, and the economy, a new look for the Islamic empire started to emerge. The traditional Bedouin and mercantile culture of the Arabs gave way to an intricate cosmopolitan culture. The most notable feature of this era was the embrace of other cultures, religious traditions, and ethnicities as part and parcel of the Islamic community rather than excluding them from the day-to-day life of the empire. Islamic law, shari'a, was hardly implemented; otherwise, many non-Muslims would have had limited opportunities to contribute to the advancement of society. This was the

---

[11]Cragg and Speight, *House of Islam*, 29-32. For details on the culture of the early Islamic caliphate, see Hodgson, *Classical Age of Islam*.

golden era of Muslim civilization, to which Muslims in later times looked for inspiration.[12]

On the political level, the Abbasids began a new era of developing peaceful coexistence with other empires. One of the most significant caliphs of the Abbasid dynasty, Harun al-Rashid (763–809), is credited with being a shrewd diplomat. He negotiated peace treaties with the Byzantine empress Irene and the French king Charlemagne. He guaranteed both states peaceful relationships with his powerful Islamic empire. Irene and Charlemagne were able to protect their smaller empires through means of coexistence and peace treaties with what became the most powerful empire on the planet. By the end of the first millennium, Islam was firmly established across the Middle East, central Asia, North Africa, and Spain. Later, the expansion of Islam into Southeast Asia and sub-Saharan Africa was achieved primarily through trade. Europe and Asia Minor, the only remaining Christian territories, were less privileged socially and economically.[13]

Christian contributions to the empire. As in the first century of Islam, the church was able to survive and even to thrive during the second and third centuries of Islam (eighth and ninth centuries). Christians living in Dar al-Islam were able to flourish despite new restrictions imposed on them. At the same time, Europe was under many threats. Northern European pagan tribes often raided the newly developed Christian empire under the leadership of Charlemagne. Muslims in North Africa, also referred to as Saracens, frequently attacked Europe from the south. They took over Sicily while constantly raiding southern France and Italy. In 846 the Saracens raided the papal seat in Rome, plundering St. Peter's Basilica. Meanwhile, Christians living in areas such as Mesopotamia (Iraq) were able to expand the Christian faith beyond their territories. The well-known patriarch of the Assyrian Church of the East, Timothy (780–823), supervised over eighty districts (bishoprics) extending from Iraq to China. A list of churches in Uzbekistan, Tajikistan, Kazakhstan, and Turkestan, in central Asia, as well as Tibet, India, Arabia, Yemen, and western China serves as a strong testament of the far-reaching ministries of his bishopric.

---

[12]Bernard Lewis, *The Arab in History*, 3rd ed. (London: Hutchinson's University Library, 1956).
[13]William Muir, *The Caliphate, Its Rise, Decline and Fall*, rev. T. H. Weir (Edinburgh: J. Grant, 1915).

The international Silk Road provided significant access to merchants and educators, who exchanged goods and ideas from as far as China to Alexandria and Rome. It also paved the way for the message of the gospel to be heard across central Asia and China. By the seventh century, the gospel had reached what is now western China. The ancient cities of Tunhuang and Turfan had established Christian communities at the end of the seventh century. Discoveries made in the twentieth century revealed that Syriac, Armenian, Turkish, Mongol, and Chinese Christian communities lived in both cities. A significant discovery made in 1908 revealed caved-in monasteries near Tunhuang that hosted Buddhist and Christian manuscripts.[14] It is interesting to note that the Syriac church, under the leadership of Timothy (not to mention several other larger Christian communities under Islam), provided supervision to churches and Christian communities much larger in number than all Christian communities in all of Europe during the eighth century. England, for example, had only two bishoprics at that time: York and Canterbury.[15]

During the golden era of Islam, while the political structure was primarily Islamic, the cultural and religious landscape was still predominantly Christian. Christians and Jews were instrumental in the advancement of the Islamic empire through their roles in administration, science, and cultural and intellectual enterprises. Timothy lived during the golden era of Islam and was well connected with the Muslim caliph in Baghdad. He was able to navigate the political and governmental terrain with great wisdom while establishing respectable relations with Muslims, Buddhists, Taoists, and other religious groups across Asia. The Eastern church during this period was able to communicate the message of the gospel in a variety of languages and cultures. Instead of holding to its Syriac language and heritage, a truly biblical language that was spoken by Jesus and his disciples, it reached people in Persian, Turkish, Hindi, and Chinese. That was taking place in a context where, ironically, the Latin church in the West insisted on using Latin as a holy language for over ten centuries. The Eastern monks even collaborated with Buddhist monks in translating ancient manuscripts on Buddhist wisdom, which gave Christianity access to China for years to come. Some of these documents,

---

[14]Muir, *Caliphate*, 311-22.
[15]Philip Jenkins, *The Lost History of Christianity: The Thousand-Year Golden Age of the Church in the Middle East, Africa and Asia* (New York: HarperCollins, 2008), 10-16.

particularly the wisdom manuscripts, were instrumental in the spread of Buddhism to Japan because Japanese monks residing in China were influenced by them.[16]

Christians in Syria, Persia, and Mesopotamia (Iraq) were able to continue to survive and even to thrive during the Abbasid dynasty from the eighth to the tenth centuries, and Persian and Syriac Christians were entrusted with key political positions in the Islamic state. To the contrary, North African Christianity declined at an alarming rate, and by the twelfth century only small numbers of indigenous Christians continued to survive in remote villages. Constant divisions in the North African church, in addition to the fact that the Bible was not translated into indigenous languages, contributed to the rapid decline. In general, Christians who had the financial means to pay the taxes as well as useful skills that aided them in finding a means for living were able to survive. Often, their skills and wealth (real or perceived) brought trouble for them. They were targets for sporadic attacks and violence, which resulted in either weakening their status or empowering them to become more resilient.[17]

The golden era of the Islamic empire came to an end a century later. It became extremely difficult for the caliphs to rule over a vast empire extending from India to Spain. Realizing the apparent threats from within as well as from outside the empire, the caliphs recruited powerful cavaliers or slaves as their loyalists and protectors. These cavaliers/slaves were Christian boys abducted from their families across the empire and were trained in special camps to become fighters for the caliph. The trauma of their forced seizure from their families contributed to their savagery and fearlessness.[18] The empire's inability to control their brutality and power made them dangerous to the empire itself. Accordingly, these private armies of slaves became very influential, and they turned into competing warlords who were able to use their power to control the empire. For the next five centuries or so, various parts of the Islamic empire were ruled by this dynasty of slaves known as Mamelukes. By the ninth century, local provinces started to assert their independence, and the empire began to devolve into decentralized states, with the caliph as

---

[16]Jenkins, *Lost History of Christianity*, 91-95.
[17]See Bat Ye'or, *The Decline of Eastern Christianity Under Islam: From Jihad to Dhimmitude* (London: Associated University Presses, 1996).
[18]Such practices continued in later Islamic empires as the Ottomans expanded them.

symbolic figurehead. The caliph no longer had viable political power but only an honorary status. The Islamic community, however, continued to enjoy the power of a unified religion that was governed by Islamic laws and principles.[19]

Sufism. The extraordinarily lavish lifestyle of the Abbasid dynasty led to the emergence of an Islamic spiritual movement called Sufism.[20] Sufis emphasize a mystical-ascetic form of Islam by focusing on the spiritual dimensions of the religion rather than its political power and laws. They strive to reach a direct experience of God that is lacking in orthodox Islam, emphasizing the use of emotions in worship. The most characteristic form of Sufi worship is called *dhikr* ("remembrance"), wherein worshipers (dervishes) repeat the name of God hundreds of times while dancing in circles, recalling the Qur'anic verses "remember God much" (33:41) and to "remember God in the morning and evening" (76:25). The movement attracted a large number of followers through the centuries from both Sunni and Shi'ite Muslims.

The movement started in places such as Kufah and Basrah in Mesopotamia (Iraq) and Egypt, where Christian asceticism originated and was highly practiced. Several key Sufi figures lived in these regions and were influenced by Christian monasticism. One well-known Sufi figure, Rabi'ah al-Adawiyah of Basrah (713–801), lived an ascetic life, emphasizing the possibility of experiencing God's love in contrast to the common Islamic belief that God is remote and distant from the human realms of emotions and feelings. Her famous phrase is, "O God, if I worship you in fear of Hell, burn me in Hell and if I worship you in hope of Paradise, exclude me from Paradise; but if I worship you for your own sake, withhold not from me your everlasting beauty."[21] Rabi'ah became one of the most influential female leaders in Islam, and her idea of loving God for who he is and her ascetic lifestyle have influenced Muslims through the centuries.

Other Sufi figures, such as Bayazid Bistami (804–874), promoted the absolute union with and hence total annihilation in God (*fanaa* in Arabic).

---

[19]Amira K. Bennison, *The Great Caliphs: The Golden Age of the Abbasid Empire* (New Haven, CT: Yale University Press, 2010).

[20]Sufism (Arabic *tasawwuf*) is derived from the word *suf* in Arabic, which means "wool." Adherents to Sufism used to wear wool as a sign of contentment and poverty in contrast to wearing silk, which was considered a more luxurious cloth.

[21]Margaret Smith, *Rabi'a the Mystic and Her Fellow Saints in Islam* (Cambridge: Cambridge University Press, 2010), 252.

Husayn Mansur al-Hallaj (858–922), the most extreme Sufi leader, claimed that he was the Truth, Al-Haqq, which is one of the ninety-nine names of God mentioned in the Qur'an. In contrast with Bayazid, who preached the annihilation of the mystic in God, al-Hallaj claimed total identification of the lover with the beloved. In his famous ecstatic words:

> I am He whom I love, and He whom I love is I
> We are two spirits dwelling in one body.
> If you see me, you see Him.
> And if you see Him, you see us both.[22]

Such claims alarmed the *ulama*, the religious leaders, who saw in his claims a Christian heresy, as he used the word *hulul* in Arabic, which means "indwelling" or "incarnation." Al-Hallaj was crucified by the Abbasids as a Muslim heretic in 922. Sufis and other Muslims saw similarities between al-Hallaj and Jesus, since both were crucified while extending forgiveness to their executioners. Al-Hallaj, however, did not pray for God to forgive them because "they know not what they do," but because he thought they rightly condemned him to death in defense of God's religion. Commenting on Al-Hallaj's legacy, contemporary Shi'ite Muslim scholar Mahmoud Ayoub states, "Al-Hallaj lives on in the piety and imagination of many Muslims as the martyr who was killed for the sin of intoxication with the wine of the love of God by the sword of the *Sharia* of God."[23]

One of the great Sufi leaders and scholars, al-Gazali (1058–1111), sought to reconcile Sunni orthodox Islam with Sufi mysticism. He is referred to as the Thomas Aquinas of Muslim theology, and his theological work influences Islamic theology through today. He moderated Sufi mysticism by stressing a return to the Qur'an and the hadith as the only legitimate sources of reflection. His major work, *The Revival of Religious Sciences*, emphasizes a balance between religious interpretation and religious experience. Sufism attempts to provide an experiential dimension of relating to God in worship, while its emphasis on loving God addresses a significant void in mainline Islam. It is a desperate cry of reaching out to God.

Sufis played a significant role in preserving Islamic learning and spirituality after the fall of Baghdad to the Mongols in the thirteenth century.

---

[22] Al-Husayn b. Mansour al-Hallaj, *Kitab al-tawasin*, quoted in Annemarie Schimmel, *Mystical Dimensions of Islam* (Chapel Hill: University of North Carolina Press, 2000), 66.
[23] Mahmoud M. Ayoub, *Islam: Faith and History* (Oxford: One World, 2005), 145.

They are also credited with spreading Islam into Africa and Asia in later centuries. In modern times, Sufism is often associated with folk Islamic practices. Overall, Sufi beliefs and practices are considered unorthodox by the majority of Sunni Muslims, and Sufism is prohibited in countries such as Saudi Arabia, where a strict form of Sunni Islam is practiced. The Sufi belief in reaching intimacy with God and the practice of dancing while worshiping are considered blasphemous according to orthodox Islam.[24] Many contemporary politicians encourage Sufism since it has no interest in politics.

Early Christian Perceptions of Islam

Early Christians had different views of Islam. Majority Christians who came under the early Islamic empires never imagined that the Islamic rule over their territories would last for a long time. They saw the Arab invasion as another episode of foreign domination that would eventually come to an end like previous regimes. Nations across the Middle East endured Persian, Greeks, Roman, and Byzantine dominance over their lands for various periods of times. Ironically, the Arabs were never involved in any takeover of territories in the region, and they never presented any military challenge; their seizure of territories in the Middle East was thought of as a temporary occurrence. The Arabs' military power, however, was supported by uncompromising religious beliefs and a sociopolitical system that guaranteed an enduring religious and military control over these vast territories for centuries to come.

On the theological and religious level, many Christians perceived Islam as a Christian heresy since Islam denies basic Christian beliefs in the Trinity and the divinity of Christ. Others perceived the unprecedented dominance of Islam over their land as God's punishment for the sins of Christians and the division of the church at the time. Some Christians were attracted to the absolute monotheism of Islam; for them it presented an uncompromising alternative to the endless theological debates at the time. Many were frustrated with decades of religious disputes, and they thought that Islam might present a simpler alternative for belief in and worship of God.

---

[24]For a contemporary survey of Sufism, see Alexander Knysh, *Islamic Mysticism: A Short History* (Leiden: Brill Academic, 2000).

Overall, Christians across the Islamic empire found themselves in a context where they had to defend their faith against Islamic criticism of their beliefs while dealing with the powerful sociopolitical structure of the state. Christians attempting to explain their faith had to do so with caution, as any perceived attempt to convert a Muslim to Christianity would have serious reprisals for the Christian community.

One early Christian leader who attempted to defend and clarify Christian beliefs against Islamic criticism was John of Damascus (675–749), who was also the bishop of the city.[25] In his famous work, *Discussion Between a Christian and a Saracen*, he defends a host of Christian beliefs including the Trinity against the Islamic claim that Christians associate other beings with God.[26] He refers to Islam as a Christian heresy while referring to Muslims as *Sarakenoi* or Ishmaelites. He argues that the Saracens were influenced by pseudo-Christian writings and beliefs that were circulating during the seventh century. John of Damascus's open criticism of Islam reflected the semitolerant atmosphere of the early Islamic era, where an opportunity for dialogue between Christians and Muslims was allowed during the Umayyad dynasty.

A century later, in 781, Timothy, the bishop of Baghdad, the capital of the Islamic empire at that time, presented similar arguments in response to the Abbasid caliph Al-Mahdi. The caliph questioned Christian belief in the divinity of Christ and the reasoning for his crucifixion, arguing that God could not marry and have a son, that Jesus never claimed to be God, and that God could not die on a cross. He also questioned Christian belief in the Trinity. In response to the caliph's questions, Timothy argued that the concepts of Word and Spirit are used in the Qur'an in reference to God, adding that they represent the second and third *uqnum*, "hypostases," of the Trinity (*uqnum* is the Syriac word for "person," and it is used in Arabic only in reference to the persons in the Trinity). Timothy then went on to argue that God's Word and Spirit must be eternal, since God could never have been without a Word and Spirit. Timothy's answer to the caliph was

---

[25] John's grandfather Mansour ibn Sargon was the controller of the Byzantine government and continued to hold a high administrative position under the Umayyad caliph in Damascus. John was acquainted with the life in the caliph's courts and was a friend of the caliph's son Yazid.

[26] Muslims were also referred to as Saracens. See Frederic H. Chase Jr., ed., *Joannes of Damascus: Writings* (Washington, DC: Catholic University of America Press, 1970).

documented in Syriac and translated into Arabic a century later. It has also been translated into other languages in recent times.

Many Christian apologists drew comparisons between the ethical lifestyle in Islam and that of Christianity, emphasizing differences in upholding the sanctity of marriage, equality between men and women, and a host of other social and ethical trends and practices.

Other notable Christian apologists during the Abbasid dynasty were Abd-al-Masih al-Kindi, Ammar al-Basri, and Hunayn ibn Ishaq, all of whom lived in Mesopotamia (Iraq) during the ninth century and wrote extensively explaining and defending Christian beliefs. Some of the arguments made by Christians in defending their faith were polemical and harsh, while others were nonjudgmental. While such endeavors limited antagonism between the two communities, they did not convince Muslims to follow the Christian faith.

Early Islamic Perceptions of Christianity

Faced with Christian criticism of Islam, early Muslim apologists tried to defend their faith as well. Muslims in general were discouraged from getting involved in religious discussions with Christians based on the assumption that Christianity was a corrupt religion that might distort the truth presented in Islam. Some of the leading Muslim apologists' arguments are elaborated in *Refutation of the Christians* (*Radd Anasara*) by Al-Jahiz (776–868) of Baghdad, and *The Book of Discernment* (*Kitab al-Fisal*) by Ibn Hazim (994–1064) of Spain. The basic argument presented by these Muslim polemicists and others is that although Christians received the Gospel as a revealed Scripture through the prophethood of Jesus, at an unspecified point in history they altered their Scripture, and therefore Christianity became a corrupted religion. That Christians ended up with four Gospels and that none of them resembles the Qur'an became the starting point in these arguments. They pointed out that Christians altered their Scripture by adding the concepts of the divinity of Christ and the Trinity, which were not included in the original Gospel. The Qur'an affirms that God inspired the Bible and that it is protected by God's provision while instructing Prophet Muhammad to consult those who have been reading the Bible if he is in doubt about any revelation to him. "If you were in doubt as to what we have revealed unto you, then ask those who have been reading the

Book before you" (10:94). Muslim apologists emphasized other Qur'anic texts that give the impression that the People of the Book have altered their Scriptures.[27]

Overall, the refutation of Christianity was based on the supposed corruptibility of the Scripture in addition to the fact that Christians did not recognize the prophethood of Muhammad, which according to Islam is foretold in the original Torah and Gospel. The Qur'an asserts that Muhammad was the messenger and the prophet "whom they will find written in the Torah and the Gospel which they have" (7:157). Since the Qur'an makes such an argument, Muslim apologists tried to find biblical texts that supported that claim. Starting from the eighth century, Muslims asserted that three biblical passages foretold the coming of Muhammad. They argued that Deuteronomy 18:18, in which God promises the Israelites that "he will rise up from their brothers a prophet like Moses," was actually about the coming of Muhammad. Isaiah 21:7, which speaks of the "rider on a camel," was also interpreted as a prophecy about the coming of Muhammad, while Jesus' words in John 14:26 about the promise of the Paraclete or Comforter (which are understood by Christians to refer to the coming of the Holy Spirit) were also said to be a prophecy about the coming of Muhammad.[28] The Qur'an states, "One time Jesus, son of Mary, said 'O Banu Israel, I am a messenger of God to you confirming what I have of the Torah and announcing a messenger coming after me whose name is *ahmad*'" (61:6). In the context of refuting Christian belief in the divinity of Christ, surah 5:15 reminds the People of the Book, "O People of the Book! There has come to you our messenger [Muhammad],

---

[27] For passages that affirm the inspiration and protection of Christian Scripture, see "It is He who send down to you in Truth the Book confirming what went before you in the Torah and the *Injil* [Gospel]" (3:3); and "To you We send the Scripture in Truth, confirming the Scripture that came before it and guarding it" (5:48; see also 6:91, 154; 53:70). Many Muslim polemicists based their arguments that the People of the Book have altered their Scriptures on Qur'anic verses such as: "Of the Jews some *alter* the words from their sets" (4:46; see also 5:13). Although the Jews are accused of such alteration, the concept might also apply to the People of the Book in general. Other surahs indicate, "One of them is a group who twist their tongues in the Book, that you think it from the Book, though it is not from the Book" (3:78); "Woe to those who write the Book with their hands; they say, 'this is from God,' to buy a small gain. Woe to them for what they have written" (2:79).

[28] As early as 781, Timothy, the bishop of Baghdad, was challenged by the Abbasid caliph to explain whether the Bible was referring to Prophet Muhammad in the previously mentioned three verses. His answer was that Deut 18:18 refers to Jesus as it was understood by the early church (Acts 7:37), while Is 21:7 refers to the fall of Babylon by Cyrus. Jesus' words in Jn 14:26 about the coming of the Paraclete refer to the Holy Spirit.

revealing to you much that you used to hide in the Book [the Bible] and passing over much. There has come to you from Allah a light and perspicuous Book [the Qur'an]." The invitation here is for Christians to believe in the apostleship of Muhammad, who brought the final revealed Scripture, the Qur'an.[29]

Muslims were confident that they possessed the true and final religion; however, the presence of a large Christian community within the Islamic empire at the time presented challenges to the cohesiveness of society. Meanwhile, the various works of Christian apologists challenged many Islamic beliefs and assumptions. Unlike Christians, who used all sorts of reasoning and sometimes Greek philosophy to explain and defend their faith through the centuries, Muslim apologists were protected under Islam's military and political power. However, the strong Hellenistic culture across the Middle East prompted logical and even some sort of philosophical responses. As noted above, by the late eighth century, the House of Wisdom in Baghdad hosted a large library and center for intellectuals. A large collection of Greek manuscripts on various topics was translated into Arabic by Christians. This development encouraged Muslim scholars to consider Greek philosophy in their understanding and interpretation of Islam.

The use of Hellenistic thought by early Muslim theologians led to the development of *Elm al-Kalam* ("the science of speech"), or Islamic theology. Among the early advocates of Islamic rational theology were the Mu'tazala sect (who differ from Sunni Muslims in their emphasis on human free will in contrast to the absolute belief in God's predestination). Among the leading Muslim philosophers (*falasifa* in Arabic) of the time were Abu-Yusuf ibn-Ishaq al-Kindi, Abu-Baker ibn Zakaria al-Razi (a physician and philosopher), and Abu-Naser al-Farabi, whose work on neo-Platonic philosophy, ethics, and political philosophy influenced the next generation of Muslim philosophers such as Ibn Sina. These early practitioners of *Elm al-Kalam* were content with a limited use of Greek philosophical and scientific ideas, and although they hold an important place in the general history of philosophy, they had little influence on the Islamic world of their time.

---

[29]William Montgomery Watt, *Muslim-Christian Encounters: Perceptions and Misperceptions* (New York: Routledge, 1991), 59-73.

One significant challenge for Muslims during the eighth and ninth centuries centered on the lack of a reliable and cohesive Islamic historical record. Various historical events and references to persons such as Noah, Abraham, Moses, David, and Jesus (all regarded as prophets in Islam), among a host of other historical figures, are mentioned without any indication of how they relate to one another in time.[30] This difficulty reflected the limited historical understanding in Arab culture. Before 600, the Arabs had minimal historical records, with limited understanding of historical development in general. In response to these challenges, Muslim historians tried to reconstruct cohesive and acceptable historical records. Two outstanding figures of the ninth-century Abbasid dynasty were Jarrir ibn Yazid al-Tabari (838–923), the author of *History of the Prophets and Kings* (also known for his major work on interpreting the Qur'an, *Tafasir al-Tabari*), and Al-Husayn ibn Ali al-Masudi (896–956), who was the first to combine history and scientific geography in a large-scale work, *The Meadows of Gold and Mines of Gems: A World History*. Their historical works and others reflected greater awareness of the various historical events and developments before, during, and after the formative period of Islam in Arabia. However, some of the dates and events mentioned in their work are not accurate.

These early Christian perceptions of Islam and Muslim perceptions of Christianity influenced encounters and relations between the two communities through the centuries.

The Impact of Islam on World Christianity at the Close of the First Millennium

By the eighth century, over two-thirds of the world's Christian inhabitants were under Islamic rule. There are several reasons why the Muslim armies had such an easy victory over the eastern and southern regions of the Mediterranean. One of the leading reasons was the division and weakness of the Eastern church. In comparison to the life of the church in the first three centuries, when unity was one of the most significant marks of the church, the church of later centuries was characterized by divisions and fighting over doctrinal issues. The person and work of Christ, the core

---

[30] According to surah 3:31-37, Mary the mother of Jesus is said to be the daughter of Imran. This gives the impression that Mary and Miriam the sister of Moses and Aaron are the same person.

belief of the Christian faith, which was supposed to unite the church, became the very issue that separated it. The church was given the freedom to flourish and to minister in relative peace after Constantine, but that freedom was harmed by divisions and rivalry for power, which eventually resulted in weakening the church and its witness to the world.

For three centuries before Islam, churches in the East were excommunicating one another over theological disagreements. The Byzantine church of Constantinople even persecuted other Christians and imposed heavy taxes over the Christians in places such as Egypt and Syria. Centuries of fighting over Christian doctrines, combined with endless competitions for power, undermined the internal strength of the Christian communities across the Eastern church. It would be an exaggeration to say that some of these persecuted Christians welcomed the Muslim invaders or considered the Arabs to be liberators.[31] However, Christians' internal divisions, lack of unity, and weariness made it all the more possible for the Arabs to conquer their lands with relative ease.

In contrast to the many divisions and theological disputes that characterized Christianity between the fourth and seventh centuries, Islam provided a simple and yet an absolute statement of faith, "There is no God but God, and Muhammad is the messenger of God." Declaring and believing in such a simple statement of faith was all that it took to identify and render one a Muslim, one who submits to God and God's will in every sphere of life. By the time of the Abbasid dynasty, many saw great advantages in converting to Islam. Among the leading factors that attracted Christians to convert to Islam were powerful political positions and status as well as avoiding the heavy taxation imposed on non-Muslims.

Intensifying divisions between the eastern and western Roman Empire. Islamic domination over the Eastern church accelerated the division already begun between the Western and Eastern forms of Christianity. Constantine's era ushered in a break from Rome, the traditional capital of the empire, which also gave it its name. Starting from the fourth century, Constantinople replaced Rome as the seat of power in the empire. In contrast to the dominant use of Latin on the western side of the empire, Greek was

---

[31] Several historical documents indicate that it took the Arabs over two years to invade the fortified city of Alexandria, Egypt, while invading Upper Egypt took much longer time due to the significant resistance of indigenous Christians. See Alfred J. Butler, *The Arab Conquest of Egypt* (Oxford: Clarendon, 1902).

the dominant language of theology, culture, and social and political life on the eastern side of the empire. Justinian (482–565) was the last emperor to use Latin as an official language and the last emperor to rule over a unified Roman Empire. By 620, the official language of Constantinople and the eastern side of the empire was Greek, and the emperor no longer needed the connection with Rome. On the ecclesiastical level, the bishop of Constantinople was called the "ecumenical patriarch," an indication of his extended role and authority over other bishops and patriarchs across the empire. The use of such title evoked the anger of other patriarchs, especially the bishop of Rome, who by this point had witnessed the decline of not only his city's political significance but also Rome's ecclesiastical status, a concern that Constantinople ignored.

Rome always looked to Constantinople for political legitimacy and ecclesiastical approval. Roman bishops had to be ratified by the emperor in Constantinople. Before the tenth century, Rome did not make any significant contribution to theological discussions. The bishops of Rome never participated in any ecumenical councils; they always sent representatives to speak on their behalf. The lack of interest from Roman bishops spoke to a much deeper issue; it was their way of resisting the authority of Constantinople. Complicating this tension further was the way in which Constantinople carried out ecclesiastical decisions. Those who disagreed with the imperial court were often punished by torture or imprisonment or were sent into exile. In 653, the imperial troops from Constantinople marched through Rome, taking the bishop of Rome as a prisoner to Constantinople, where he stood for trial. Such cruel behavior by Constantinople created tensions among the churches across the empire, and this incident in particular had a lasting impact on Rome-Constantinople relations.

By the end of the seventh century, communication between the two cities declined drastically, and Rome was looking for its independence from Constantinople. At this time the Muslims marched through the Byzantine Empire, capturing every single region except the territories around Constantinople. By the 800s, the eastern Roman Empire was reduced to small parts of Asia Minor (Turkey) and Greece. The Islamic threat to the eastern and western sides of the empire was very real. In the light of this context, Pope Leo III crowned the powerful king of the Franks, Charlemagne, as Imperator Romanorum. Rome was able to finally establish its own ecclesiastical identity and to claim its own political power, manifested in the office of the emperor. Although Charlemagne never used the title "emperor"—he always referred to himself as the king of the Franks—this was the first step toward an independent European Christianity centered on Rome and separated from Byzantine Christianity, which dominated for almost five centuries.

The spread of Islam during the seventh and eighth centuries resulted in enhancing the position of Rome and making it the most viable Christian center in the world. At the same time, Constantinople's position weakened and started to fade. The rapid victories of the Muslim armies took the eastern empire completely by surprise. The Arab conquerors credited their sweeping victory to their obedience to God's calling to spread the new faith. Meanwhile, many Christians who witnessed the drastic decline of the Byzantine Empire at the hands of Muslims interpreted this unprecedented defeat and humiliation as God's punishment for their unfaithfulness and disobedience.

Differences between the Eastern and Western churches further intensified because of linguistic barriers. While Greek was the dominant language of theology in the east, Latin was the church's language in the west. Oftentimes theological terminology was misunderstood and distorted when translated from one language to the other. Church governing became another source of division between the East and the West. While the Eastern church adopted a patriarchal form of church leadership, where several patriarchs shared the responsibilities of leadership, the Western church opted for a papal form of leadership entrusted to the bishop of Rome, later known as the pope, who became the only head of the church. Even if the will had existed to bridge the gap between the East-West, Greek-Latin, and patriarchal-papal differences within Christianity, the strain in politics, military affairs, and communications now exercised by dominant Islam made the chance of resolution virtually impossible.

Although Muslims were relatively tolerant toward their Christian subjects, communication between the eastern and western Mediterranean became increasingly difficult. Gone were the days when church leaders were able to travel across the empire in relative ease and gather freely to discuss their theological differences. New restrictions on travel, trade, and communication were imposed by the new Islamic state. Under such restrictions, Christianity lost its main theological and educational hubs in

Alexandria, Antioch, and Carthage, which were not replaced by any flourishing theological centers for centuries to come.[32] From that point forward, the Eastern and Western churches walked different paths.

European Christendom. The rise of Islam created a new political, cultural, and ecclesiastical context for the church and Christians. By the eighth century, the majority of the world's Christians were under the rule of the Islamic empire and were treated as protected people, *dhimmis*. While they were able to survive under the new laws imposed on them, they were nonetheless restricted in many ways. The power and status of the Byzantine Empire were completely blown away. Against the backdrop of these new realities, a new model of Christendom began to emerge in Europe.

The massive expansion of Islam had a lasting and significant impact on the development of Western Christianity. With the slow fade of Byzantine Christendom, the Mediterranean form of Eastern Christianity started to weaken, and a Western European Christianity emerged on the scene. In 732, Charles Martel, the commander of the Frankish armies, was able to stop the Islamic avalanche that swept through the Persian and Byzantine empires. This remarkable event had an enduring impact on the future development of European Christianity. Martel defeated the Islamic armies crossing from Spain to France at Poitiers, emerging as the savior of Europe while securing his position as the political leader of France. Meanwhile, Martel was a strong supporter of the ecclesiastical order in Rome. He built strong ties with the popes and supported missionary activities to Christianize the Germanic tribes to the north. His military success and proven leadership won him the support of Rome.

In 768, Charles Martel's grandson, Charlemagne (or Charles the Great), became the new king of the Franks. He succeeded in expanding the power of France against the Saxons to the north and the east (Germany). He was able to suppress the Saxons, who had been harassing the Franks by carrying out raids on their towns and farms for decades. He even integrated them under his rule and forced them to undergo Christian baptism or face execution. In 782 he ordered the beheading of forty-five hundred Saxons who resisted forced conversion. Capital punishment was also

---

[32]Aziz S. Atiya, *A History of Eastern Christianity* (Notre Dame, IN: Notre Dame University Press, 1967), 24.

enforced for other non-Christian practices or forms of worship. Such savage measures resulted in severe casualties among the Saxons under Charlemagne and raised serious concerns about what kind of Christianity was imposed and practiced under his regime. This was the first full-scale form of enforced Christianization, using military force to compel people to become Christians.

Charlemagne also suppressed the Lombards of northern Italy and turned over several major cities to the possession of the pope in Rome. His power extended to the Avars (Austria), and he incorporated their land into his kingdom. At the height of his power Charlemagne ruled over most of modern France, Belgium, Germany, Austria, and the Balkans. Rome saw in Charlemagne a great potential for achieving its long-term goal of becoming the center of the Christian world. Accordingly, in an unprecedented move, Pope Leo III crowned Charlemagne as Imperator Romanorum (holy Roman emperor) on Christmas Eve of the year 800. This remarkable political move by the church in Rome ushered in the beginning of European Christendom, a model of Christendom that dominated Europe for the following nine hundred years. For the next nine centuries, European politics and social and cultural life would be identified with Christianity. The notion of church-state collaboration that started with Constantine was now bestowed on European Christianity.

Like in the Byzantine model of Christendom, European Christendom was associated with Christianity, but not necessarily with the ethos and the message of the gospel. It is interesting to note that the European model of Christendom, which started with the coronation of the king of the Franks at the close of the eighth century, was also ended by the French in the eighteenth century. The French Revolution in 1789 was instrumental in curbing the influence of the European Christendom model, and in 1806 Napoleon abolished the title "holy Roman emperor" altogether. However, Christendom models and practices have survived in several European contexts up until today.[33]

On the political level, the Franks dominated western Europe from the sixth to the tenth centuries. The Catholic faith became the most unifying force in Europe after the collapse of Roman rule in the West. Europe was fragmented and descended into political and social chaos by the end of

---

[33]Judith Herran, *The Formation of Christendom* (Princeton, NJ: Princeton University Press, 1987).

the sixth century. The most influential factor that linked European tribes such as the Franks, Goths, Vandals, Lombards, and Saxons around the year 800 was the Catholic faith. In contrast to the urban world of the Mediterranean, where people entered the Christian faith as individuals and families breaking from their previous religions, tribal solidarity and identity resulted in mass conversion to Christianity in Europe. Once kings and nobles were converted to Christianity, the whole tribe subsequently adopted the new faith. Some kings converted to Christianity simply because they were married to Christian wives, such as King Ethelbert of Kent, King Edwin of Northumbria (both in modern England), and King Mieszko of Poland. Marriages among royal families were based on establishing political alliances between different tribes that guaranteed a level of coexistence and mutual interest. Converting to Christianity gave several kings a great legacy to join the ranks of the Roman imperial life.[34]

On the ecclesiastical level, the church provided a network of moral and spiritual support. Monasteries served as educational and administrative centers and were supported financially by endowments from the nobility and upper class. Abbots and abbesses possessed greater spiritual power than bishops, with abbeys serving as centers of learning and cultural life. From the seventh to the tenth centuries, monks and nuns who devoted their lives to educating the people carried out the true Christianization of Europe. While many initially joined Christianity as part of a mass conversion, the monastery's mission helped them to live the Christian faith. The use of Latin as the language of theology, liturgy, and sacraments across Europe provided another tool for unifying churches and people. While other languages and dialects were used for preaching and evangelization, Latin became the proper language of education and was used in every aspect of the life of the Western church.

The unified Europe that was achieved by Charlemagne did not last for long. Shortly after Charlemagne's death, the empire dissolved into smaller and fragmented kingdoms and dukedoms, each trying to establish its own territorial power and identity.

The ninth and tenth centuries witnessed new expansions of Christianity to eastern and northern Europe. To the east, the Slavs and Bulgars were

---

[34]Mark A. Noll, *Turning Points: Decisive Moments in the History of Christianity* (Grand Rapids, MI: Baker Books, 1997), 38-52.

integrated into the family of Orthodox churches of the eastern Roman Empire. Some of their kings and nobles became Christians, and most of their people followed them. Missionaries were also sent to Russia during the ninth century. The conversion of King Vladimir in 988 brought the Russian state into the Orthodox family of churches. Later, he married Anna, the Byzantine emperor's sister, a move that created powerful political alliances with his kingdom. The Christianization of Russia that started in the ninth century progressed quickly, especially among the aristocrats and in major towns and cities. Christian missionaries to the Slavs and Russians helped by introducing a new alphabet for the Slavic and Russian languages based on Greek letters.[35] Byzantine art, architecture, and music were also dominant features of these Eastern European churches. One of the most significant contributions made by the Eastern European church, as in the case of the Bulgarian church, was the translation of Scripture and other Christian writings from Greek into Slavonic, the language used by most eastern Slavs.

To the north, the seafaring Vikings (Scandinavians) were sporadically attacking the inhabitants of the coastal lines from Scotland to the Mediterranean, raiding towns and monasteries, burning churches and taking monks as slaves. The Viking raiders indirectly introduced Christianity to their people; Christians taken captive and brought to Scandinavia as slaves soon introduced the Christian faith to the Vikings, who by the ninth century became Christians and abandoned their savage lifestyle. By the close of the first millennium, Christianity was the dominant religion all over Europe from Iceland to Russia.

At the end of the first millennium, a common civilization established on the principles of the Christian faith was emerging in Europe. A host of local cultures, political systems, and languages were incorporated under one ecclesiastical structure, led by clergy, monks, and nuns who used Latin in liturgy and theology. At the center of this ecclesiastical structure was the pope, who was able to claim both a religious and political authority over most of Europe. By the tenth century, the term *Christendom* was introduced by the Anglo-Saxons to describe this new amalgamating cultural force that was now dominating the European landscape. European

---

[35] J. M. Hussey, *The Orthodox Church in the Byzantine Empire* (Oxford: Clarendon, 1986); Timothy Ware, *The Orthodox Church* (New York: Penguin, 1993).

Christendom would shape the sociopolitical and cultural life in Europe for the next nine centuries.

Outside Christian Europe, the Islamic caliphate was controlling most of the Eastern world, extending from Spain to China. For the next millennium, the history of European Christianity would be shaped and defined by relations and encounters with the Islamic empire, dominating the largest landscape across the globe.

Conclusion

The advent of Islam in the seventh century presented significant challenges for Christianity around the Mediterranean. The Arab forces toppled the Persian Empire and shook the Byzantine Empire to its core. The Islamic caliphates that dominated over two-thirds of the world's Christian inhabitants introduced new sociopolitical arrangements wherein Christians, who were the majority population, became protected people in their own lands. Christians living in the Islamic caliphates, however, played noteworthy roles in the administrative structure and the advancement of society in various Islamic empires, especially during the golden era of Islam.

From the eighth century onward, the history of Christianity was linked to that of Islam. The new monotheistic religion that originated in Arabia during the seventh century challenged the core theological beliefs of Christianity and its very existence for centuries to come. The Islamic domination over two-thirds of the eastern Roman Empire by the eighth century further weakened the power of Byzantium and prompted southern Europe to use every measure, including military force, to stop the advancement of Muslim invaders. Rome in turn emerged as the most important center of the church's life in Europe, while the Franks arose as the political power that unified European Christendom. New territories in eastern and northern Europe were Christianized, and by the close of the millennium, Europe had become mostly a Christian continent.

3

CHRISTIANITY AND ISLAM DURING THE MIDDLE AGES (1000–1500)

THE ISLAMIC DOMINATION that extended from western China to Spain by the eighth century had a far-ranging impact on the world for centuries. A process of Islamization and sometimes Arabization was set in motion. As two-thirds of the world's Christian population fell under the new Islamic religious and political structures, Middle Eastern and North African Christians embraced the reality of living under Islam, a reality that continued for thirteen centuries and up to today. Most Christians did not convert to Islam and continued to form the majority of the population in areas under Islamic rule until the twelfth century. As cycles of toleration and persecution were set in motion by Muslim rulers, some indigenous Christians converted to Islam either because of direct pressure or the subtle stress of financial incentives and tax advantages. During the seventh century AD (the first century of Islam), Christians and Jews were not forced to convert to Islam simply because of their large numbers, as such a policy was more financially beneficial for the Islamic empire. By remaining under the status of protected people, Christians and Jews generated significant revenue for the empire by paying taxes. In later centuries, however, some became weary of paying such heavy taxes and did convert to Islam.

Outside Dar al-Islam ("the house of Islam"), the only Christian territories left were Europe and the remaining territories of the former

Byzantine Empire (mainly parts of modern Turkey and Greece). These areas, however, were much smaller in number than those under Islamic rule, less organized, fragmented, and weak. It is not surprising, then, that military power and forced Christianization were used in Europe during the eighth and ninth centuries as a desperate measure to secure whatever was left of what was considered Christian territory. For the next six centuries or so, Europe had to deal with the powerful Islamic empire that was now surrounding its borders.

A cluster of noteworthy historical developments during this period worked to affect the relations between Christianity and Islam right up until the modern era. Tensions leading to the Crusades and their aftermath had significant ramifications for Muslims' perceptions of Christians. Meanwhile, the Mongol invasion of central Asia and the Middle East reshaped the Islamic empire. Despite sporadic periods of tension, intellectual and spiritual encounters between the followers of the two religions presented better alternatives to hostility. At the close of the fifteenth century, as the Byzantine Empire collapsed and the Spanish Reconquista pushed Muslims out of western Europe, these major historical events had a significant impact on the development of Christianity and Islam.

THE TRAGEDY OF THE CRUSADES

The Middle Eastern context leading to the Crusades. As noted earlier, the powerful Abbasid dynasty started to disintegrate by the close of the ninth century, leading to the loss of effective power over much of the Muslim territories by the first half of the tenth century. Meanwhile, a series of smaller independent caliphates started to emerge. One of the dynasties that replaced the Abbasid was the Fatimid.[1] The Fatimid rule (921–1171), which extended from Morocco to Syria, was mostly tolerant to Christians. In 972 Caliph Al-Mu'izz moved the capital from Tunisia to Cairo. The caliph's broadmindedness and administrative skills created an atmosphere of tolerance, resulting in significant economic and social progress during

---

[1] The name is derived from Fatima the daughter of Prophet Muhammad, as the Fatimid claimed to be her descendants. The Fatimid were Shia'at Muslims from North Africa, primarily from Tunisia and Algeria. Caliph Al-Muizz conquered Egypt in 969 and established Cairo as the capital of the Fatimid caliphate. At its height, the caliphate included all of North Africa, Egypt, and the Levant (mainly Syria and Palestine) along with the Hijaz (western part of modern Saudi Arabia), northern Sudan, and Sicily. It continued in power until 1171, when it was replaced in Egypt by the Saladin and the Sunni Ayyubids empire.

his rule. He appointed Christians and Jews as administrators in his government and ordered the rebuilding of churches and monasteries that were destroyed during the Abbasid rule. Al-Mu'izz encouraged open debates in his court between Christians, Jews, and Muslims. Under his rule, the governor of Syria was a Coptic Christian from Egypt, Quzman ibn-Nima.[2] Al-Mu'izz's son and successor, Al-Aziz (976–996), maintained his father's legacy of religious tolerance.[3] The first Islamic university, Al-Azhar, was built during his time.[4]

Unfortunately, the ascent to power of the next caliph, Al-Hakim, ended this tolerant and progressive era.[5] His reign (996–1021) was one of the most irreparably damaging periods in the history of Christian-Muslim relations. Besides his bizarre policies of ordering people to work at night, preventing women from leaving their homes, and slaughtering all dogs, he ordered all Christians to wear only black garments along with five-pound wooden crosses on their necks to distinguish them from the rest of society. He tortured and executed his Christian and Jewish administrators and ordered the destruction of churches and monasteries across the region. In 1009 he destroyed the Church of the Holy Sepulcher in Jerusalem and prevented Christians from entering Jerusalem, a practice that continued for four decades and ultimately ignited the Crusades. Finally, he proclaimed his own divinity and declared himself a god, a move that led to his probable assassination.[6] While later Fatimid rulers were tolerant and accommodating, the insanity of one ruler created unnecessary tension between Christians and Muslims in the region.

Parallel to the ascendency of the Fatimid dynasty over North Africa, Egypt, and the Levant, another significant development was taking place in

---

[2]Aziz Suryal Atiya, *A History of Eastern Christianity* (London: Taylor & Francis, 1968), 87-88.
[3]According to Coptic tradition, Al-Aziz accepted Christianity and was baptized. He had to abdicate his rule as the sultan of the Fatimid empire and withdrew from society. He ended up living in a monastery for the rest of his life.
[4]Al-Azhar University is the oldest university in the world, and its original building in the old city of Cairo, Egypt, is still in use today. The concept of the university professorship chair originated in Al-Azhar and was adopted in European universities later on.
[5]Al-Hakim bi Amr Allāh (Arabic: الحاكم بأمر الله). His name means "Ruler by God's Command." Such a title gave him ultimate power to dictate. This title is commonly used today in Arabic as a rhetorical expression of arbitrary and dictatorial leadership.
[6]In the final years of his reign, Al-Hakim displayed a growing inclination toward withdrawal from society. In 1021, at the age of thirty-six, he left for a night journey to the Mokattam Hill outside Cairo and never returned. A search found only his donkey and bloodstained garments, which suggested that he was either assassinated by his opponents or had committed suicide.

Asia Minor (Turkey). The central Asian Seljuk Turks, who had accepted Islam, started an aggressive expansion to the west. Their target was the Byzantine Empire. Their first course of action was to take the kingdom of Armenia in 1064, forcing survivors to relocate the Armenian state to Cilicia (southwestern Turkey and northwestern Syria). In 1071, the Turks won a significant victory over the Byzantines at the Battle of Manzikert, giving them control over most of Asia Minor. The campaign of destruction continued through the eleventh century, resulting in the raiding and sacking of many cities and the massacre of hundreds of thousands of Christians. As agricultural fields were destroyed, a significant famine descended over major parts of Asia Minor, forcing the depopulation of several provinces.[7]

The European context leading to the Crusades. At the beginning of the second millennium, western Europe was divided into fragmented small kingdoms characterized by constant feudal conflicts. A variety of languages and cultures existed side by side in Europe. The only cohesive entity that brought this diversified continent together was the Roman Catholic Church. The papal office was entrusted with significant power that further advanced the unification of the church and the state under one authority, and the pope provided both a spiritual and temporal rule from Rome. The tension between the Latin West and the Greek East continued in spite of the fact that their territories were under direct threat from the powerful Islamic empire that surrounded their lands. The ongoing tension reached a new level in 1054, when each church excommunicated the other. In 1070 the new, powerful Islamic dynasty that emerged from the Seljuk Turks was able to seize Jerusalem from the Fatimid rulers of Egypt as well as make significant advances into the territories of the weak Byzantine Empire. The Turks then started persecuting Christians while preventing Christian pilgrims from visiting the Holy Land, an act that was interpreted in the eleventh century as preventing Christians from fulfilling the sacramental right of visiting the very land where Christ lived and was crucified. For European Christians, Jerusalem was considered the center of the world, a Holy Land that was consecrated by the very blood of Christ.

Reports of the persecutions of Christian pilgrims and the desecration of holy places by Muslims soon made their way to Europe. Meanwhile,

---

[7]Speros Vryonis, *The Decline of Medieval Hellenism in Asia Minor* (Berkeley: University of California Press, 1971), 157-72.

Byzantine emperor Alexius I pleaded for help against the crushing forces of the Muslim Turks. Ironically, he sought help from the rival Roman power that had excommunicated his ecumenical patriarch four decades earlier. In 1095, at the conclusion of the Council of Clermont in southern France, Pope Urban II issued the first appeal for a Crusade. His speech to thousands of French audiences set in motion one of the most disastrous moves in the history of Christian-Muslim relations.

In his speech Urban II described Muslims as aggressors who had destroyed churches and desecrated holy places. He twisted Jesus' words in Matthew 10:28, "Whoever does not take up their cross and follow me is not worthy of me," to mean fighting for Christ by carrying the sign of the cross. Those who committed to join the holy war would be wearing the sign of the cross as a shield, hence the word *Crusade* (literally meaning "marked by the cross"). He went on to list the spiritual and material gains that one might accrue by heeding such a call. The Crusade would be a "holy war," he said, assuring that participating in a Crusade would count as great penance for sin. He even assured his audience that they would be granted a place in heaven for fulfilling such a high calling. The pope also held out the prospect of materialistic rewards for those more eager for land than salvation, urging them to seize the Holy Land and make it their own.

The pope, however, did not have any military strategy for how to carry out such a task. The most powerful European kings—Philip I of France, George IV of Germany, and William II of England—who might have had the capability of accomplishing such a task, were all under papal sentences of excommunication at the time of Urban II's appeal. The response by the crowd at Clermont, "Deus vult!" ("God wills it!"), was immediately echoed across Europe. A mob of disorderly groups of peasants and townspeople was instantly formed in different cities in Germany and France and started toward the East. As they made their way along the Rhine and Danube, they raided and looted fields and destroyed crops, attacking Jewish communities and fighting against Christians who opposed them. Large numbers perished on the way due to hunger and fighting with locals who were defending their lands and properties. Those who made it to Constantinople had the support of the Byzantine Empire and later headed to Jerusalem. As they crossed through Asia Minor, they were met by powerful Muslim armies, who exterminated the majority of them outside Nicaea. Any survivors were sold into slavery.

The Crusades (1095–1291). Pope Urban II followed his historic speech by sending letters to nobles and knights across Europe, asking them to join the holy war. The response was unprecedented. Thousands of knights and nobles joined forces in the military operations, many at their own expense. Some even sold properties to finance their expedition. Many hoped that they would get significant rewards in return, whether wealth or land to rule. Most Crusaders, however, considered themselves to be pilgrim warriors and their mission to be a spiritual endeavor. Thus, the first organized Crusade departed to the East in the summer of 1096. The Crusaders gathered in Constantinople, where they received support from Byzantium. However, their presence there was met with mixed feelings. On one hand, they were welcomed as the needed liberators from the aggressions of the Turks, who were about to take over all of Asia Minor. On the other hand, they were feared for the possibility that they would take over the weak Byzantine Empire itself. As noted above, Emperor Alexius had appealed to the Latin West for military assistance to fight the Turks, but he had never envisioned anything along the lines of such massive Crusades. The Byzantines were not happy to see thousands of Latin warriors at the gates of their capital. Alexius was able to reach a deal with the Crusaders wherein their leaders made an oath to recognize the Byzantine rights to the land they captured in return for supplies and military support. Having made their promise, the Crusaders started off in 1097, marching toward Jerusalem. The Crusaders were able to capture the city of Nicaea in 1097 and restored western Anatolia to Byzantium.

After a dangerous and costly journey through Asia Minor and Syria, the Crusaders were eventually able to capture the city of Antioch. Jerusalem was captured in the summer of 1099. The Crusaders celebrated their victory by slaughtering thousands of Muslim and Jewish men, women, and children. Ignoring their promise to Emperor Alexius, they established the Latin kingdom of Jerusalem a year later, in 1100, with Baldwin of Flanders as its king. In a separate move, Baldwin was able to secure for the Latin kingdom other territories at the eastern end of Asia Minor. He was able to capture most of Cilicia and the strategic city of Edessa. Castles were built to defend strategic locations along the Mediterranean, and new monasteries constructed to accommodate monks who came to take residency in Syria and Palestine. Latin liturgical rites were introduced into churches, and Latin bishops were appointed in major cities. In the case of Antioch,

Orthodox bishops were banned from ministering to their people. The Crusaders even opened the door for western immigration to the region.[8]

Western control over Syria did not last long. When Emperor Alexius learned that the Latins had ignored their promise to give him control over the land they captured, he sent several military forces to Cilicia and Antioch, but none of his attempts at recapturing the cities succeeded. The more serious threat came from the Muslim Turks, who managed to recapture the city of Edessa in 1144. News of the fall of Edessa reached Pope Eugenius III, who immediately issued a call for another Crusade. The Second Crusade (1147–1149) was launched to recover Edessa, under the joint command of King Louis VII of France and Conrad III, the holy Roman emperor. Their troops suffered serious casualties as they crossed through Asia Minor, and by the time they arrived in Syria and Palestine, they were unable to contribute anything to defend the Latin kingdom there. Four decades later, the powerful Muslim leader Saladin led the combined forces of Egypt and Syria against the Crusaders and was able to recapture Jerusalem in 1187 along with most of Syria and Palestine.[9]

The news of this defeat ushered in the Third Crusade (1189–1192) under the leadership of Emperor Frederick Barbarossa, Philip II of France, and Richard I ("the Lionheart") of England. The drowning of Emperor Barbarossa in Asia Minor and Philip's early retreat left King Richard fighting Saladin alone. He succeeded in capturing some coastal cities; however, Jerusalem remained under the control of Saladin. A truce was reached whereby Christian pilgrims were permitted to go to Jerusalem. The furious fighting between Saladin and King Richard of England resulted in one of the bloodiest battles of the Crusades, with heavy casualities on both sides.[10]

---

[8]For extended coverage of the Crusades, see Jonathan Riley-Smith, *The Oxford Illustrated History of the Crusades* (New York: Oxford University Press, 2001); also Steven Runciman, *A History of the Crusades*, vol. 1, *The First Crusade and the Foundations of the Kingdom of Jerusalem* (Cambridge: Cambridge University Press, 1987).

[9]For more details on the Second Crusade, see Steven Runciman, *A History of the Crusades*, vol. 2, *The Kingdom of Jerusalem and the Frankish East, 1100–1187* (New York: Cambridge University Press, 1987); also Jonathan Phillips, *The Second Crusade: Extending the Frontiers of Christendom* (New Haven, CT: Yale University Press, 2008).

[10]For full coverage of the Third Crusade, see Steven Runciman, *A History of the Crusades*, vol. 3, *The Kingdom of Acre and the Later Crusades* (New York: Cambridge University Press, 1987); also James Reston Jr., *The Warriors of God: Richard the Lionheart and Saladin in the Third Crusade* (Garden City, NY: Anchor Books, 2002).

A Fourth Crusade (1202–1204) was called for by Pope Innocent III, to which only the French responded. They in turn sought the help of the Venetians, who had the ships and supplies to carry out this new undertaking. The interest of the Venetians was not simply the capture of Jerusalem; they also sought the capture of the Byzantine Empire itself. Due to several complicated historical factors, the Fourth Crusade ended up being a Crusade to capture the rival Christian empire rather than one liberating the Holy Land. This goal was achieved in 1204 by capturing Constantinople and creating a unified Christian empire with a Flemish noble as emperor and a Venetian priest as its patriarch. The Latin empire of Constantinople was formed, and a forced political and religious unification of East and West was achieved. Such unification lasted for only five decades, as in 1261 the Muslim Turks gained control over parts of Constantinople. The outcome of this tragedy was an intensified hatred between the Byzantine and Latin Christians.[11]

The scandal of the Fourth Crusade technically put an end to any organized attempts to liberate the Holy Land; however, an interesting development took place thereafter. A group of children started their own Crusade, drawn to the noble task of recapturing the Holy Land. Although they were advised by King Philip Augustus of France not to carry out such a mission, they went on to Marseilles, where they were offered free passage to Palestine on ships that were originally headed to Egypt and Tunisia. It is reported that around twenty thousand children participated in what was called the Children's Crusade. Many of them drowned on the way, and the rest were sold as slaves. Such an undertaking by young people reflected the fascination with a grandiose mission of liberating the Christian holy sites that captured the mind and hearts of people in early medieval Europe.

The story of the Crusades beyond this point is primarily that of disastrous losses and total failure. Other attempts were made between 1219 and 1270 to achieve the lost dream of recapturing the Holy Land. Innocent III organized a Fifth Crusade that attempted to reach Jerusalem through Egypt. Although he was able to capture the city of Damietta in northern Egypt in 1219 for a short period of time, he never made it to Jerusalem. In 1229, the Roman emperor negotiated a treaty with Sultan Al-Kamil of

---

[11]See Jonathan Phillips, *The Fourth Crusade and the Sack of Constantinople* (New York: Penguin Books, 2005).

Egypt that placed Jerusalem under Christian jurisdiction; however, that treaty was nullified in 1244. In 1248–1250, King Louis IX of France made another attempt to recapture Jerusalem through Egypt. His entire army was taken captive by Muslims, who executed most of his soldiers but kept him and his nobles alive. He was freed after paying a hefty ransom. His final attempt in 1270 to recapture the Holy Land also ended with failure, and he died later that year near Tunis. In 1250 a powerful Muslim dynasty, the Mamelukes (meaning "slaves"), took control over Egypt, and in 1291 they forced the remaining Europeans out of the Holy Land.

For the next two centuries or so, the spirit of the Crusades continued in Europe, primarily in fighting against groups or individuals whom the Catholic Church identified as heretics. It also led to the recapture of territories previously taken by Muslims. The Arabs who conquered Sicily in the ninth century were driven out in the eleventh century, and a long process of recapturing and integrating parts of the Iberian Peninsula resulted in the expulsion of Muslim rulers from Spain in 1492.[12]

Consequences of the Crusades. There are several consequences as well as lessons to be learned from the adventures of the Crusades, which had a lasting impact on Eastern Christianity as well as Christian-Muslim relations in general.

1. A new concept of just war. The Crusades were an unprecedented event in the history of Christianity. The idea of using force to accomplish political or religious gains was not new; unfortunately, since the time of Emperor Constantine in the fourth century, several rulers resolved to use force to achieve their goals in Eastern and Western Christendom. But the idea of a Crusade gave a whole new theological meaning to the use of armed forces that made it justifiable for the church to undertake warfare as part of its mission on earth. It is one thing to see emperors or kings waging wars against a real or imaginary threat to their territories, but it is a completely different enterprise to see the authority of the church represented in the pope calling and supporting warfare in the name of Christ.

Pope Gregory VII (1073–1085) paved the way by introducing a significant change in Christian attitudes toward just war. Previously, soldiers fighting for even a just cause were required to do penance for the deaths

---

[12]Riley-Smith, *Oxford Illustrated History*; Jonathan Riley-Smith, *The Crusades: A Short History* (New Haven, CT: Yale University Press, 1987).

they caused. Gregory argued that it was not sinful for soldiers to participate in a just war in order to promote right order in society and to restrain evil. On the contrary, this was a meritorious act, and therefore no penance was required. A decade later, when Pope Urban II called for the Crusades, the concept of just war had already been established in the minds of many people across Europe.[13] While many Christians might argue that they have the right to defend themselves against violent aggression, the concept of carrying out warfare under the banner of the cross has no backing in the life of Christ or the teaching of the New Testament.[14] Furthermore, defending the state is a political enterprise and not an ecclesiastical responsibility. This unprecedented model, however, was the direct result of fusing religious and political powers under the authority of the pope, with no distinction between his spiritual role as the head of the church and his political role as the guardian of Christendom. The process of merging the spiritual responsibilities of the church with the secular affairs of the state started with Pope Leo IX (1049–1054) and was continued by Pope Gregory VII, who gave Pope Urban II a new conceptual framework according to which he perceived his responsibility as defending Christendom both spiritually and politically. The call for the Crusade was issued at an official church council (the Council of Clermont in southern France in 1095). Ecclesiastical responsibilities became entangled with political endeavors.[15]

2. *Religious pilgrimages and holy wars.* The Crusades were associated with a significant surge in religious feeling in Western Europe. Religious fervor was frequently expressed by undertaking religious pilgrimages.

---

[13]St. Augustine of Hippo (354–450) was the first Christian theologian to develop a comprehensive theological argument for a just war. According to Augustine, there were certain criteria that needed to be met in order for a just war to be conducted. Such criteria covered the ethical obligation to restrain evil and to establish justice in society. Augustine's doctrine of just war was further modified by other theologians, e.g., Thomas Aquinas, and was adopted by several politicians and military leaders. In his famous work *The City of God*, Augustine argues, "They who have waged war in obedience to the divine command, or in conformity with His laws, have represented in their persons the public justice or the wisdom of government, and in this capacity, have put to death wicked men; such persons have by no means violated the commandment, 'Thou shalt not kill'" (14.28). See Augustine, *The City of God*, trans. M. Dodds, in *Nicene and Post-Nicene Fathers*, first series, vol. 2, ed. Philip Schaff and Henry Wace (repr., Peabody, MA: Hendrickson, 1994).

[14]Constantine was the first to use the sign of the cross on a battlefield, and his actions gave the impression that it was acceptable to use the sign of the cross on the shields of soldiers.

[15]William J. La Due, JCD, *The Chair of Saint Peter: A History of the Papacy* (Maryknoll, NY: Orbis Books, 1999).

While many opted to visit local shrines such as St. Paul and St. Peter's tombs in Rome or the shrine of Santiago (St. James) in northwest Spain, the supreme pilgrimage was that to Jerusalem in the Holy Land. Thousands of Europeans made their way every year to the Holy Land prior to the Crusades. Harassment and persecution of Christian pilgrims to the Holy Land by Muslim Turks was not tolerated.

The tension around the Holy Land should be viewed in a larger context. Several decades before the Crusades, in 997, Muslims had caused significant damage to the shrine of Santiago in Spain. These attacks ignited unpleasant religious tension between Christians and Muslims. In response, a band of Frankish knights and their supporters went from France to Spain in 1018 to help the Christians against the Muslims in the early stages of the Spanish Reconquista, a pattern that continued through the eleventh and twelfth centuries. Also, decades before the Turks took control of Jerusalem, Fatimid ruler Al-Hakim prevented Christian pilgrims from entering Jerusalem and demolished the Church of the Holy Sepulcher. Reports of the destruction of cities and the massacre of Christians in Byzantine Asia Minor caused shockwaves across Europe. European frustration with continuous episodes of violence and aggression reached a tipping point, but the concept of a holy war that was manifested in the Crusades had actually been developing within Europe several decades before it resulted in any organized campaign of heading to the Holy Land. The overall questions of why and how the Crusades took place must be viewed through the lenses of economic, social, religious, and political systems of medieval Europe.[16] Many analysts argued that the first two or three Crusades were defensive wars carried out to rescue beleaguered Christians who were being massacred in the thousands.

3. Christians' perception of Muslims. The earlier Christian perception of Islam was reinforced in the aftermath of the Crusades and continued to dominate in Europe during the Middle Ages. The harassment of European pilgrims to the Holy Land and continued raids into Europe by Muslims from North Africa aggravated European Christians, resulting in the tragedy of the Crusades. At the same time, as more territories were lost to the Muslims in Asia Minor, Byzantine Christianity started to crumble

---

[16]Thomas F. Madden, *The New Concise History of the Crusades*, Critical Issues in World and International History (Lanham, MD: Rowman & Littlefield, 2005). See also R. W. Southern, *The Making of the Middle Ages* (New Haven, CT: Yale University Press, 1959).

altogether, adding fuel to the fire of religious feelings against Muslims. The Crusades period is one of the lowest points in Christian-Muslim relations. Apart from a few European missionaries who sought to extend God's love and acceptance to Muslims, such as Francis of Assisi, Ramon Lull, and others, Europeans at the time were frustrated with the repeated violent attacks and associated Islam with hostilities.

One of the most debated issues in the aftermath of the Crusades revolved around its effectiveness in responding to Islamic threats. Decades before the Crusades, Europe was threatened by Muslims raiding its territories from every direction while pilgrims to the Holy Land were attacked and sometimes massacred. The Crusades, however, did not fully achieve their political or religious goals. They resulted in strengthening the power of Islam rather than restricting aggression. Having control over the Holy Land for intermittent periods of time heightened enmity between Muslims and Christians and created a deep rift that lasted for centuries. Earlier, Muslims had perceived Christians as People of the Book whose faith, though a corruption of the true religion, was still regarded with respect. The Crusades came as a response to provoked acts of aggression that needed to be restrained, but this mandate was reduced to freeing the Holy Land, which once was a Christian territory, for only a short period of time while intensifying hostilities with Muslims. Despite attempts to create western kingdoms in the East, no western state gained any significant benefit from the Crusades. To the contrary, the Crusades resulted in significant loss of lives and distracted European rulers from attending to their internal responsibilities at home. Meanwhile, the Crusades, which were supposed to support the Byzantine Empire in its struggles against the advancement of Islamic armies, ended up destroying the power of the empire itself. Two centuries later, Muslim Turks were able to take over Constantinople and capture all of Asia Minor (Turkey).

4. *Muslims' perception of Christians.* The Crusades presented the first serious challenge to the consistency and power of the Islamic *ummah* ("community"). As a result, Muslims perceived Western Christians as aggressors who dared to challenge the supremacy of the ummah, which had been powerful and triumphant since its inception in the seventh century. Thus, defeat was unthinkable. The Muslim military champion against the Crusaders, Saladin (1138–1193), reinforced the concept of jihad ("holy war") against the Christians at the time. Although the Muslims emerged

victorious from the Crusades, they have used the Crusades to speak of Christian aggression against Islam and Muslims through the centuries and up to today.[17] Muslims usually do not recognize the initial cause of the Crusades: the massacre of Christians and the destruction of churches.

5. *The rapid decline of Eastern Christianity.* Arguably the most disastrous consequence of the Crusades was the rapid decline of Eastern Christianity due to significant periods of persecutions by Muslim rulers. Middle Eastern Christians living in Dar al-Islam paid the ultimate sacrifice for Western military exploits as they endured intense times of persecutions set in motion by their Muslim rulers in the thirteenth and fourteenth centuries. The repeated military attacks (every few decades) of the Crusades, which lasted for almost two centuries, intensified hostilities between Christians and Muslims. Muslim rulers feared that the Middle Eastern Christians, who by the twelfth century still maintained majority status and outnumbered the Muslim population, might collaborate with Western Christians, turn against their Muslim rulers, and expel them out of the land, as in the case of Sicily and Spain. The Fatimid rule over the Middle East, which had been somewhat tolerant toward Christians, became weary of fighting Europeans in the Crusades, turned against local Christians, and started persecuting them.

The stories of destruction and persecution are dreadful. When the Turks recaptured the city of Edessa from the Crusaders in the 1140s, they massacred or enslaved virtually the whole population of about forty-seven thousand people. Thousands were massacred in urban centers such as Antioch, Jerusalem, and Aleppo. Churches, monasteries, and valuable Christian manuscripts were destroyed in places such as Ephesus.[18] What accelerated the crumbling of Christianity in Asia Minor was the destruction of all major urban centers where the leadership of the church was located. Soon after, small villages and towns had no support to survive and were absorbed by Muslim Turks who were active in Islamizing the countryside.

Since Egypt had been the main target of the later Crusades, Egyptian Christians took the brunt of the new intolerance. When the Mameluke

---

[17]William Montgomery Watt, *Muslim-Christian Encounters: Perceptions and Misperceptions* (New York: Routledge, 1991), 74-88.

[18]Vryonis, *Decline of Medieval Hellenism*, 157-72. See also Bat Ye'or, *The Decline of Eastern Christianity Under Islam: From Jihad to Dhimmitude* (London: Associated University Press, 1996), 342-48.

rulers established their dynasty in Egypt in 1250, they started a new campaign of persecuting Christians in Egypt and the Levant.[19] Persecution was not new to Egyptian Christians; they had endured several episodes of severe and brutal persecutions by the Romans, the Byzantine, and the Arabs. The persecution of Egyptian Christians by the Mamelukes, however, was the most destructive of all. The Mamelukes came to power primarily to repel the Crusaders, and many of their leaders became intolerant of Christians. General Baybars, one of the most celebrated Mameluke generals, was responsible for massacring thousands of Christians in Syria and Asia Minor in fighting the Crusaders in the 1260s.

CHRISTIANITY AND ISLAM UNDER THE MONGOLS

As if the destruction resulting from the aftermath of the Crusades was not enough, the thirteenth and fourteenth centuries witnessed one of the most disastrous times for both Christians and Muslims under the Mongols. The Mongols (from Mongolia), also known as Tatars, came to power in the early thirteenth century. After consolidating power through marriages from various tribes of Mongolia, Genghis Khan ("Great Khan") emerged on the world scene as the new warrior, sacking city after city in central Asia, destroying infrastructure and massacring inhabitants. The Mongols marched through central Asia to Anatolia, Georgia, and Armenia, pushing their way to Russia to the north and the Middle East to the south. They were able to annex the whole region from China to Russia as well as northern India and parts of the Middle East.

While the Mongols were nomadic and practiced traditional shamanistic rites, they were familiar with both Christianity and Islam. Christianity was well established among the Keriats, Ongguds, and Uyghurs of central Asia through the mission activities of the Syriac church of the East. Some of the wives and daughters of the Mongolian Khans were Christians, and many who worked in their courts were also Christians. Christian monks and priests were instrumental in helping the Mongols to use Uyghur letters to

---

[19]The word *mameluke* means "owned" or "slaved" in Arabic. The Mameluke were not slaves in the literal meaning; they were cavalrymen recruited as young boys from around the Black Sea and the Caspian Sea to fight the Crusaders. While they formed the machine of jihad that ultimately destroyed the Crusaders, they overthrew the dynasty of Saladin, who used them to fight the Crusaders and established their own rule over Egypt, Palestine, and Syria in 1250. They became the savior of the Islamic empire by defeating the Mongols.

write their language, which at the time had no alphabet or written format. Mongols also appointed Christians as administrators in some of the regions they conquered to benefit from their expertise. Muslims and Buddhists were also present in the courts of the Khans, as reported by Franciscans who were sent by the Catholic Church in an attempt to halt the devastating avalanche of the Mongols. Mongol tradition called for all people to believe in one supreme reality known as the Eternal Heaven without specifying any particular creed or practice. Accordingly, all religious traditions were respected without any distinction.[20]

Christian and Muslim pleas for peace. Despite this religious tolerance, the unstoppable force of the Mongols created significant fear in both Christian Europe and the Islamic empire, an apprehension that resulted in the sending of ambassadors on behalf of both the pope and the Islamic caliph to the courts of the Great Khan in order to negotiate peace treaties. The Christian ambassadors were primarily Franciscans who traveled halfway around the world from Europe to the Mongolian capital, Karakorum, to convey Pope Innocent IV's message to the Great Khan.[21] In their first encounter, under the leadership of John of Plano Carpini (1180–1252), they delivered a message from the pope explaining the Christian faith and their commission in advancing the apostolic mission of the church, even inviting the Great Khan to accept Christian baptism. The pope also called on the Mongols to put an end to their assault on the nations or otherwise face the wrath of God.

The Great Khan's response was that he was in fact appointed by God to implement God's law all over the world based on the Mongols' divine laws. His famous statement was, "I am the punishment of God. . . . If you had not committed great sins, God would not have sent a punishment like me upon you." He even charged the pope and the political leaders of Europe to submit to the Mongolian throne and serve the Great Khan in order to avoid the looming destruction of their cities and the annihilation of their people. This was made all the more concrete by the Franciscan reports of the presence of several European slaves, who had been taken captive from Russia and eastern Europe, serving at the courts of the Great Khan.[22]

---

[20]David Morgan, *The Mongols* (Oxford: Basil Blackwell, 1986).
[21]Travel between Europe and China was common practice for centuries. The famous Italian traveler Marco Polo made the same trip during the thirteenth century as well.
[22]Laurence E. Brown, *The Eclipse of Christianity in Asia: From the Time of Mohammed till the Fourteenth Century* (Cambridge: Cambridge University Press, 1933).

During the second Franciscan envoy to Karakorum, under the leadership of William of Ruburck in 1253, the Great Khan called for an interfaith debate wherein he invited Franciscans along with Syriac Christians, Muslims, and Buddhist monks to present their faith. The debate covered the nature of God and the created world, among many other issues. The debate did not result in convincing the Great Khan that any of these religious traditions were better than his own shamanistic beliefs. However, a spirit of tolerance and respect among the world's religious traditions was prevalent at the courts of the Great Khan.[23]

The Mongol expansion into Europe and the Islamic caliphate. The Christian and Muslim pleas for peace treaties did not last long, and the Mongol armies were once again on the move to conquer new territories. Starting in 1236, the Mongols decided to conquer as much of Europe as they could, and by 1240 they had control over Russia and Ukraine, seizing Romania, Bulgaria, and Hungary over the next few years. The Mongols also tried to capture Poland and Germany, but their defeat in the Middle East distracted them from achieving that goal. In the end, the Mongols' Golden Horde ruled over a vast swath of eastern Europe, and rumors of their approach terrified western Europe, but they went no further west than Hungary.

The Mongol expansion into Europe had several negative effects. The populations of entire regions that resisted them were almost wiped out, while vast agricultural landscapes were destroyed. This violent warfare spread panic even among Europeans not directly affected by the Mongol onslaught, sending refugees fleeing westward. One of the most disastrous consequences of the Mongol invasion of central Asia and eastern Europe was the spread of a deadly disease that resulted in wiping out approximately one-third of Europe's population in the 1300s in what is known as the Black Death. On a positive note, as the Mongols established their political power on a vast territory extending from China to central Europe, they were able to force peaceful coexistence among these territories, allowing for trade between Europe and China along the Silk Road. Travelers such as Marco Polo and Christian missionaries like the Franciscans took advantage of the secured trade routes across the ancient world. The

---

[23]Samuel Huge Moffett, *A History of Christianity in Asia*, vol. 1, *Beginning to 1500*, 2nd rev. ed. (Maryknoll, NY: Orbis, 1998).

Mongols' invasion of eastern Europe also forced the unification of Russia, which managed to defeat and expel the Mongols in 1480.

In 1256, the Mongol forces under the command of Hulagu decided to conquer the seat of the Islamic caliphate in Baghdad. Persia (Iran) was overrun by the Mongols, and in 1258 they seized Baghdad, demanding complete surrender. When their demands were not met, they completely destroyed the city of Baghdad and annihilated the majority of its inhabitants; an estimated eight hundred thousand were massacred. The Abbasid caliph was tortured to death, and his death ended the Abbasid caliphate itself. The massive destruction of Baghdad, which had been a hub of learning, arts, and social and political life for five centuries, brought an end to one of the great eras in Islamic history. The Mongol armies continued their assault on the Middle East, marching toward Egypt. They were finally stopped in 1260 at the famous Battle of Ayn Jalut, by the Sea of Tiberias in Palestine, by the newly established Mameluke dynasty of Egypt. This decisive battle put an end to the power of the Mongols. The Mongols were forced to retreat to Asia and never made it to western Europe.[24]

By the beginning of the fourteenth century, it became clear that Mongol leaders were unable to provide political leadership to the large geographical territories under their control. Constant infighting among the ruling elite resulted in significant economic losses. The Mongols were nomadic people and lacked knowledge and experience in the agricultural enterprise, the backbone of the economy at the time. Millions of acres of agricultural lands across Asia were devastated by destructive wars, and major urban cities lay in ruin. The population had suffered a catastrophic decline due to a combination of mass murder, famine, and forced immigration.

As the Mongol power started to disintegrate, another destructive force emerged in Southeast Asia. It was the army of the warrior Timur Lang (1336–1405), known to Europe as Tamerlane. Following the Mongols' practice, he went on a campaign of terror, plundering cities and massacring inhabitants from China to the Middle East. He was well-known for exterminating the whole population of any city that resisted him, mounting the skulls of his fatalities in a huge pyramid. He defeated the Mamelukes, destroying Aleppo, Damascus, Baghdad, and major urban centers in Persia.

---

[24]Vernon O. Egger, *A History of the Muslim World Since 1260: The Making of a Global Community* (Upper Saddle River, NJ: Pearson, 2008), 5-13. See also Ye'or, *Decline of Eastern Christianity*, 349-59.

Although his goal was to reestablish the power and authority of the Mongols, the motive for such needless bloodshed and destruction across Asia and the Middle East was not clear. During the fourteenth century, Timur Lang emerged as the most powerful Muslim leader from central Asia (Uzbekistan), paving the way for the establishment of the Turkish/Ottoman Empire a century later. Once again, Christians paid a heavy price, being targeted and violently massacred across the Middle East and central Asia. He boasted of "washing the sword of Islam in the blood of the infidels." Most Christian communities in central Asia were completely vanquished by the time of his grandson in the later part of the fifteenth century.[25]

The fourteenth century probably was one of the most devastating times in human history, adding to the religious tensions that were already mounting at the time. As most of Asia was bearing the aftermath of the Mongols' destruction, inhabitants across the ancient world were also seriously affected by the plague of the fourteenth century. The plague (or Black Death) resulted in the death of thousands of people across the ancient world. A few decades earlier, Europe and the Middle East had endured one of the most devastating natural disasters in the Middle Ages, a period of severe cold weather known as the Little Ice Age, which destroyed agricultural products and interrupted trade across the ancient world.[26]

The Impact of the Mongol Invasion on Christianity and Islam

Although the Mongol dynasty did not last for more than two centuries, its impact on Christianity and Islam in the Middle Ages was extremely significant. The combination of the Mongol destructive wars and the plague "transformed the political and social order the way a tornado scrambles anything in its path" across the Muslim world.[27] The Mongol conquests inflicted catastrophic damage on major urban centers across Asia and Europe such as Kiev, Merv, Bukhara, Samarkand, and Baghdad, along with many other cities that were hubs of civilization. During this period, hundreds of thousands of people were massacred across the ancient world.

---

[25]Egger, *History of the Muslim World Since 1260*, 27-30. See also Ye'or, *Decline of Eastern Christianity*, 349-59.
[26]Stuart J. Borsch, *The Black Death in Egypt and England* (Austin: University of Texas Press, 2005).
[27]Vernon O. Egger, *A History of the Muslim World to 1750: The Making of a Civilization*, 2nd ed. (New York: Routledge, 2018), 311.

The massive destruction of the Mongols also resulted in forcing tens of thousands of peasants, craftsmen, intellectuals, and merchants to flee territories under the Mongols to safer regions. This massive migration inadvertently boosted the fortunes of the Mamelukes (Egypt), the Ottomans (Turkey), and the Delhi Empire (India), territories that were not controlled by the Mongols. The Islamic empire experienced its most devastating wave of violence from outside forces during the thirteenth and fourteenth centuries. The Crusades of the previous centuries were nothing compared to the suffering and destruction caused by the Mongols.

Intensified tensions. The encounter with the Mongols also affected Christian-Muslim relations within Dar al-Islam, resulting in intensified tension between Christians and Muslims in the region. Both Christians and Muslims across Asia and the Middle East suffered from the Mongols; meanwhile, they sought the Mongols' support against each other. The Islamic caliphate in Baghdad, for example, pleaded for European help against the Mongols, which was flatly rejected. In another interaction, the Christian patriarch of Baghdad was commissioned by the Mongols to seek European help against the Mamelukes of Egypt. The fragmented relations between Christians and Muslims, following from the Crusades of the previous two centuries, were shattered in the aftermath of the Mongol invasion, resulting in complete mistrust. Consequently, the thirteenth and fourteenth centuries witnessed brutal persecution of Christians across the Middle East, a significant historical turning point that drastically reduced their numbers and influence for centuries to come.

The Mongols' destruction of Baghdad in 1258 and alleged Christian support of the Mongols ignited the fury of the Mamelukes. In 1260, General Baybars had been able to stop the Mongol forces from reaching Egypt. In the following years, he started persecuting Christians in Egypt and its surroundings. The persecution of Christians in Egypt was due to the fact that the Mamelukes were fighting two major powers right at the doorsteps of Egypt: Western Crusaders and Eastern Mongols. As a result, Egyptian Christians endured one of the most vicious and unbearable persecutions in history between the 1290s and 1350s.[28]

---

[28]Ye'or, *Decline of Eastern Christianity*, 359-60; also Amin Maalouf, *The Crusades Through Arab Eyes* (New York: Schocken, 1989).

By the thirteenth century, Egyptian Christians held an influential status among the *dhimmis* (Christians and Jews) living in Dar al-Islam. The fact that Egyptian Christians were wealthy and had great status in a predominantly Muslim society, as many of them held strategic governmental and administrative positions, did not sit well with the Mamelukes. The Mamelukes issued several decrees, from forcing Christians and Jews to wear distinctive clothing (blue for Christians, yellow for Jews) all the way to dismissing them from their financial and administrative positions. Such measures by officials enticed the masses to further harass Christians and Jews, looting and plundering their properties and businesses. Muslim historian Al-Maqrizi documented the destruction of churches and monasteries across the land, even in Upper Egypt, where Christians still held majority status. He emphasizes, "In all the provinces of Egypt, both north and south, no church remained that had not been razed; on many of those sites, mosques were constructed." The destruction further intensified with the killing and kidnapping of Christians and the destruction of their businesses.[29] The immediate result of these harsh measures and brutal persecution was the conversion of thousands of Christians to Islam.[30]

General Baybars (1223–1277) extended his jihad war even to the south, attacking Nubia and Ethiopia, two African Christian kingdoms closely associated with the Egyptian church.[31] Ironically, both kingdoms had never been involved in the Mongol-Mameluke encounters and were far away from the Middle Eastern–European encounters. While Ethiopia has been able to remain a basin for African Christianity until today, major parts of the country were Islamized (what is today Somalia, Eretria, and Djibouti). Nubia, once a hub of Christian culture, was virtually

---

[29]Donald P. Little, "Coptic Conversion to Islam Under the Bahri Mamelukes, 692–755/1293–1354," *Bulletin of the School of Oriental and African Studies* 39 (1976): 568. For Al-Maqrizi's fifteenth-century account of earlier persecutions in Egypt, see B. Evetts, ed., *The Churches and Monasteries of Egypt and Some Neighboring Countries* (Oxford: Clarendon, 1895), 328-40. For a detailed history of Christian persecution in Egypt, see B. Evetts, ed., *History of the Patriarchs of the Coptic Church of Alexandria* (Turnhout: Brepols, 1904).

[30]Little, "Coptic Conversion to Islam." See also Hugh Kennedy, "Egypt as a Province in the Islamic Caliphate," in *The Cambridge History of Egypt*, ed. Karl F. Petry (New York: Cambridge University Press, 1998), 1:62-85; Jill Kamil, *Christianity in the Land of the Pharaohs* (New York: Routledge, 2002).

[31]Baybars was the fourth sultan of Egypt under the Mameluke dynasty. He is nicknamed the "father of conquests" due to his role in defeating the Crusaders under King Louis IX of France. He also led the Egyptian forces in defeating the Mongol army at the battle of Ain Jalut in 1260, which marked the first substantial defeat of the Mongols, a turning point in history.

Islamized in a few decades and was transformed into an Islamic state by the fourteenth century.[32]

Christians living in a super Islamic state. The Mongols ended up adopting Islam, forsaking their shamanistic traditions. This striking transition resulted in creating a Mongol hegemony that marked the beginning of another powerful Islamic dynasty. Other religious traditions, primarily Christianity and Buddhism, found themselves under the control of a super Islamic state that extended from China to the Middle East. The destruction of urban centers across central Asia by the Mongols and heavy Islamization of the region by the later Muslim Mongols put an end to any future missionary activities from the Middle East to Asia. By the beginning of the fifteenth century, the Christian presence in central Asia was completely wiped out, and the Syriac church of the East, which over the course of a millennium had extended its mission and ministry across Asia from Mesopotamia to China, lost its influence across the whole region.[33]

Once the Mongol rulers converted to Islam, conditions for the Christians in the Levant (Mesopotamia [Iraq], Syria, and Lebanon) as well as Persia (Iran) drastically deteriorated. Churches and monasteries in major centers such as Aleppo, Tabriz, Mosul, and Baghdad were destroyed; tens of thousands of Christians were massacred or taken into slavery. Monks and priests were imprisoned and tortured. Even the patriarch of the Syriac church of the East, who at one point was supported by the Mongols, was attacked and tortured. Christianity in most of Persia as well as southern and central Mesopotamia almost vanished by the fourteenth century. The majority of Syriac Christians fled to the mountains in northern Iraq. From that time forward, the presence of Christianity in the Levant was confined to a small number of Christians in northern Iraq, parts of Syria, and Lebanon, a remnant that continued to exist until modern times.[34]

The unprecedented persecution of Middle Eastern Christians during the thirteenth and fourteenth centuries resulted in the reduction of their

---

[32]P. L. Shinnie, *Medieval Nubia* (Khartoum, Sudan: Sudan Antiquities Service, 1954); Paul Bowers, "Nubian Christianity: The Neglected Heritage," *Africa Journal of Evangelical Theology* 4, no. 1 (1985): 3-23; K. Koschorke, F. Ludwig, and M. Delgado, *History of Christianity in Asia, Africa and Latin America, 1450–1990* (Grand Rapids, MI: Eerdmans, 2007), 3.

[33]Moffett, *History of Christianity in Asia*, 1:424.

[34]Brown, *Eclipse of Christianity in Asia*, 147-55.

numbers to a minority status by the end of the fourteenth century. Christians had endured significant persecution under the Romans during the first three centuries AD; however, the persecution they endured under the Mamelukes was the most devastating. From that time onward, Middle Eastern Christians ceased to form the majority status in the land where Christianity began.

The Mongol-Mameluke encounter of the thirteenth century had a dreadful impact on other, smaller nations that were directly or indirectly involved with the Mongols. The Armenians, who supported the Mongols in their invasion of Syria, were later destroyed by the Mameluke forces that were able to defeat both the Mongols and the Crusaders. In 1303, the Armenian kingdom, the first Christian nation, was destroyed by the Mamelukes. Its historical churches were demolished, Christians were massacred, and its leadership were killed or tortured. Most of its inhabitants went into the diaspora. By the end of the fourteenth century, the forces of Timur Lang destroyed neighboring Georgia, demolishing churches and massacring Christians. By the fifteenth century, the Christian presence in central and western Asia crumbled.[35] As Philip Jenkins observes, "We can see the fourteenth century as marking the decisive collapse of Christianity in the Middle East, across Asia, and in much of Africa."[36]

In 1368, the powerful Chinese Ming dynasty put an end to the Mongolian presence in their land, forcing the Mongols out of China. A crackdown on "foreign" religious activities that were associated with the Mongols meant destroying any Christian or Islamic presence in China. The Eastern Syriac church, along with the smaller Catholic missions of the Franciscans, simply vanished from China. It would take another two centuries before any Christian missionaries arrived in China, this time not via the Silk Road across Asia but by sea from around Africa. The passage of the Silk Road for trade and travel was now completely under the Islamic rule, and Europeans had to find an alternative route around Africa in order to reach into India and China. The famous trade along

---

[35] Dickran Kouymijian, "Armenia from the Fall of Cilician Kingdom (1375) to the Forced Emigration Under Shah Abbas (1604)," in *The Armenian People from Ancient to Modern Times*, ed. Richard Hovannisian (New York: St. Martin's, 1997), 2:1-50. See also Angus Stewart, *The Armenian Kingdom and the Mamelukes* (Leiden: Brill, 2002); Razmik Panossian, *The Armenians* (New York: Columbia University Press, 2006).

[36] Philip Jenkins, *The Lost History of Christianity: The Thousand-Year Golden Age of the Church in the Middle East, Africa and Asia* (New York: HarperCollins, 2008), 98.

the Silk Road was diverted permanently northward into Russia and southward into Iran and India.

Alternative Paths: Spiritual and Intellectual

While the Crusades were taking place, spiritual and intellectual renewal was emerging in Europe. This renewal had a significant impact on the social and economic development of the continent for the centuries that followed. The period between the eleventh and thirteenth centuries, known as the high Middle Ages, witnessed significant social changes in Europe. The development of cities and towns provided great opportunities for advancement in trade and commerce. Venice and Genoa in Italy became instrumental in the exchange of goods and trading with the Muslim world. Urban centers such as Paris influenced the advancement of arts and education. The building of Notre Dame de Paris in 1163 prompted a new era in cathedral building that spread across Europe. The impressive cathedrals that still stand as an enduring monument today were an expression of a new social and religious transformation, an expression of the Christian faith in the form of art and magnificent architecture.

This era of renewal began in monasteries. Early attempts to reform the church resulted in the establishment of several religious movements, often stemming from monasteries. In 910 a monastery was founded at Cluny, France, in order to foster a stricter observance of the Benedictine monastic life. This monastery became so significant in reforming religious life that by the eleventh century it had over two hundred daughter monasteries across the continent. From 1122–1156 Peter the Venerable (1092–1156) was the administrator of one of the most influential monastic movements, with ten thousand monks serving in six hundred monasteries across Europe. He and Robert of Ketton took on the challenge of translating the Qur'an into Latin with the purpose of facilitating understanding of Islam and Muslims. He wrote extensively on explaining Islam to Europeans while refuting false beliefs. His work inspired later generations of European scholars to write about Islam during the following two centuries.

Also by the eleventh century, new movements calling for religious reform started to emerge. Among the most common features of these movements was the practice of popular preaching and penitential practices that called for devotion to spiritual life. At the heart of these movements was often a call to abandon individual wealth and to adopt a life of poverty and chastity. Although the church banned any new orders, the papacy eventually sanctioned some and allowed them to flourish. Two of the most significant orders that received recognition by the church in the thirteenth century were the Franciscans and the Dominicans.

The Dominicans and the Franciscans. The founder of the Dominican order, Dominic Guzman (1170–1221), a well-educated Spaniard, spent a decade in southern France, where he was instructed in preaching and church doctrines. He spent most of his life preaching and debating with heretics, primarily Cathar and Waldensian, who were considered a great threat to the church at the time. The Dominican order emphasized learning, preaching, and a life of poverty. Major theologians such as Albert the Great and Thomas Aquinas were attracted to this order. The papacy benefited from their expertise in theology and debating. Unfortunately, their theological expertise and debating skills were used to suppress heretics in what became one of the most notorious aspects of medieval Europe—the Inquisition. Under the auspices of maintaining the church's unity and providing social order, the Inquisition resulted in the torture and execution of thousands of people at the hands of local authorities who were receiving orders from the church. The worst cases of the Inquisition took place in Spain and France. Apart from the Inquisition, the Dominicans were influential in their peaceful approach to convert Muslims through preaching as an alternative to the military force of the Crusades. They were active in preaching beyond the cities of western Europe, especially in Muslim lands.

The horrors of the Inquisition were countered by the mission and service of the Franciscans, who valued preaching, service, and mission over theological debates and fighting heretics. The founder of the order, Francis of Assisi (1182–1226), a wealthy Italian merchant, gave away all his wealth to the poor and lived a simple life of chastity. The Franciscans dedicated their lives to preaching and ministering to the sick and the poor, often moving from one place to another, not restricting themselves to living in monasteries. They traveled barefoot, sleeping wherever they could find shelter for the night. They were easily recognized by the brown robes they adopted as a Franciscan uniform. The order grew significantly in number, in spite of the fact that their leadership was not based in ordained clergy, or maybe *because* it was not, to the extent that their mission reached across Europe, North Africa, central Asia, and even to China by 1219.[37]

One of the most significant contributions made by Francis of Assisi and the Franciscan order was their attitude toward Muslims. While the Crusades were in their final stages trying to recapture Jerusalem, Francis had a different vision of how to deal with Muslims. His mission was one of tolerance and acceptance. He believed that Muslims could be won over by extending God's love through acts of service and ministry. In 1212 he set off for Syria as a missionary, intending to preach to Muslims there, but his trip faced many challenges and he never made it to Syria. A year later he attempted another trip to North Africa through Spain, but once again the trip was never realized. In 1219, while King Louis IX of France was fighting in northern Egypt, Francis was preaching a gospel of peace to the Egyptian sultan al-Kamil. Despite linguistic and cultural barriers, the sultan welcomed Francis to his court and extended hospitality. The sultan did not convert, as Francis had been hoping, but Francis's attitude toward Muslims was different from that of the Crusaders, one of tolerance and acceptance. While Francis did not convert any Muslims to Christianity, his example paved the way for others to catch this new vision. A wealthy Spaniard from the Island of Majorca, Ramon Lull, was ready to take the challenge.

Ramon Lull. Ramon Lull (1232–1315) became one of the most well-known Christians to reach out to Muslims in the Middle Ages. Lull's personal conversion and visions played a significant role in his commitment to reach out to Muslims. He was convinced that God was directing him to evangelize the nomadic Muslims, the Saracens—the most hated and feared enemies of Christendom at that time. He wrote, "I see many Knights going to the Holy Land beyond the seas and thinking that they can acquire it by force of arms, but in the end, all are destroyed before they attain that which they think to have. Whence it seems to me that the conquest of the Holy Land ought . . . to be attempted . . . by love and prayers, and the pouring out of tears and blood."[38]

---

[37]For details on the spiritual and intellectual renewal in Europe between 1000 and 1450, see Southern, *Making of the Middle Ages*; Joseph H. Lynch, *The Medieval Church: A Brief History* (New York: Longman, 1992).

[38]Quoted in Samuel M. Zwemer, *Raymond Lull: First Missionary to the Moslems* (New York: Funk & Wagnalls, 1902), 52-53.

Lull spent nine years studying the Arabic language before starting his mission to the Muslims of North Africa. His missionary strategy included apologetic, educational, and evangelistic ministries. In 1276 he opened a monastery in Majorca to train monks in mission to Muslims. The curriculum included courses in Arabic, Greek, and Hebrew and in the "geography of missions." While his idea of establishing mission training centers in Europe for the purpose of reaching out to Muslims was met with complete disapproval in Rome, he was successful in influencing the Council of Vienna (1311) to decide to have Arabic taught in European universities. His goal was to educate Christians on how to communicate efficiently with Muslims. His approach to evangelizing Muslims in Tunis and Bugaia, east of Algiers, was primarily through debates. He often used an offensive approach in debating Muslim leaders in both cities, which resulted in his imprisonment and expulsion. He was stoned to death in Algeria on June 30, 1315.[39] Lull's confrontational method of preaching to Muslims may not have been the best approach, yet his conception of missions as an alternative to the violence of the Crusades and his advocacy of a comprehensive model that included linguistic study and translation pointed in the direction that future missionaries would adopt.

Intellectual encounters. While the monastic orders along with their preaching and service ministries played a key role in Christian relations with Muslims during the high Middle Ages, intellectual encounters dominated the late Middle Ages, the fourteenth and fifteenth centuries. Out of the economic growth and urbanization of Europe, new interests as well as new professions started to emerge, and with them came the need for education. This led to the rise of great universities across Europe. The model of medieval universities that started in Italy flourished across the continent. The Sorbonne of Paris and the University of Toulouse were established in France in the thirteenth century; Oxford (twelfth century) and Cambridge (thirteenth century) in England; and the University of Heidelberg in Germany in the fourteenth century, to mention just a few. Education that started in monasteries and cathedrals gradually moved to larger universities. An educational system based on the study of liberal arts, grammar, and logic, among many other disciplines, provided the

---

[39]Ruth A. Tucker, *From Jerusalem to Irian Jaya: A Biographical History of Christian Missions*, 2nd ed. (Grand Rapids, MI: Zondervan, 2004), 56-60.

basis for the study of law, medicine, and theology (with theology being the queen of sciences).

Those who specialized in a discipline of study became known as scholastics, and their collective work was known as scholasticism. Scholasticism had its beginning in monastic and cathedral learning but reached its peak at schools such as the University of Paris, which was the center of medieval intellectual life. While the study of law depended on Latin texts from ancient Roman resources such as Justinian's *Codex*, the study of medicine depended primarily on Latin translations of Arabic texts, which were by far the most advanced during that time. The famous work of Persian scholar Ibn Sina (980–1037; known as Avicenna), the *Canon of Medicine*, provided instructions for a range of new medical procedures and detailed drawings of medical instruments. Avicenna's philosophical treatises, which combined Aristotelianism and neo-Platonism, had great influence on early scholasticism as well as on later Muslim thinkers. Another major source of medieval medical and philosophical work came from Ibn Rushd (1126–1198; known as Averroes), a great philosopher, physician, and lawyer from Cordoba, Spain, who considered Aristotle the supreme expositor of truth and whose extensive commentaries on Aristotle's works gave him universal recognition as "the Commentator."

Aristotle's work, translated into Latin from Arabic, was instrumental in shaping the intellectual movement of the thirteenth and fourteenth centuries in general and the development of theological works in particular. Theological work in the era of scholasticism sought to demonstrate the harmony of faith and reason. Many great theologians, such as Anselm of Canterbury, Peter Abelard, and Thomas Aquinas, were all influenced by Aristotelian philosophy. Their main interest was in relating faith and reason, explaining the Christian faith using logical and philosophical categories. Anselm (1033–1109), for example, gave priority to faith over reason, his famous phrase being "faith seeking understanding." Aquinas (1225–1274), to the contrary, argued that the knowledge of God could be attained through both reason and revelation.[40] Aquinas is considered the

---

[40]The knowledge of God, according to Aquinas, is necessary for salvation; he argues, however, that a simple person contemplating God's mighty work in nature might arrive at the same conclusion. Aquinas, like Aristotle, based his epistemological theory (i.e., the theory of knowledge) on the use of senses, which means that our knowledge of the world and reality comes to us through our senses, though it is possible to gain indirect knowledge through analogical reasoning. Aquinas, however, emphasized the validity of revelation as the ultimate source of knowing the metaphysical

most influential theologian in medieval times; his renowned *Summa Theologiae* is one of the most significant theological writings in history. It consists of twenty-one volumes that cover more than six hundred topics in more than three thousand articles.[41]

The fascination of scholastic theologians with Aristotelian philosophy did not deter them from pointing out their disagreements with Aristotle's thinking. This pattern was previously adopted by Islamic theologians and philosophers such as Al-Ghazali (1058–1111), who concludes in *The Destruction of Philosophy* that rational philosophical thinking and religious revelation might not be compatible. What is fascinating about the late Middle Ages intellectual exchange between East and West is that European works such as the philosophies of Plato and Aristotle, which originated in Greece during the fourth and third centuries BC, were introduced back to Europe through Arabic translations. Great works that were previously translated from Greek into Arabic during the eighth and ninth centuries by the Christians and Jews living in Egypt, Persia, and Mesopotamia (Iraq) made their way back to Europe in the thirteenth and fourteenth centuries.

This is a reminder that civilizations are usually built on collaborative efforts, when people of different cultures and religious backgrounds are given the opportunity to thrive and to contribute to the advancement of society. The intellectual movement that contributed to the establishment of modern Europe in the centuries to come and had its roots in the Greek and Roman cultures made its way back to Europe through Arabic translations.

Diverging Intellectual Roads in the European and the Muslim World

By the fourteenth century, Europe and the Muslim world were on entirely different paths. The contrasting trajectories of Europe and the Muslim world in terms of their approach to intellectual endeavors are significant for understanding later development for both religious communities. Both cultures had access to the Greco-Roman civilization along with its

---

or supernatural realm. According to Aquinas, that we cannot use analogical reasoning or senses to prove the Trinity, for example, does not mean that it is an untrue or irrational belief; it is simply a supranational reality that requires revelation and the assistance of divine grace.

[41]For more details on the European intellectual movement and the influence of scholasticism, see Steven Ozment, *The Age of Reform 1250–1500: An Intellectual and Religious History of Late Mediaeval and Reformation Europe* (New Haven, CT: Yale University Press, 1980).

philosophical and scientific endeavors. They enjoyed the same opportunities to access vast areas of human knowledge. However, Europe and the Muslim world embarked on different trajectories that eventually determined their future cultural outlooks.

As early as the tenth century, western Europe was able to defend its borders against outside invasions and subsequently enjoyed a period of economic growth that resulted in political centralization and social and cultural advancement. Although the Crusades were costly for Europeans and did not achieve their goals, they were instrumental in creating a cultural milieu of self-searching and reflection. By the fourteenth century, there was a productive atmosphere around intellectual life in Europe, wherein scholars were given the opportunity to excel in their fields of knowledge. European scientists and philosophers benefited from the exchange of ideas and constructive criticism from colleagues belonging to other communities of scholars. The establishment of the university system in Europe enhanced scholarly works in a highly organized and autonomous academic structure.

Tendency toward conservatism. To the contrary, the Muslim world was not able to overcome the effects of the Crusades or the Mongol assault. It is ironic that in both cases the Muslim world emerged victorious militarily. The Crusaders were defeated and were pushed back to Europe, while the Mongols, albeit causing significant damage, were eventually included in Dar al-Islam, and their power was incorporated to form a super Islamic state. The Muslim world, however, entered a period of decline when it came to the advancement of science, technology, the arts, and intellectual and philosophical work. In contrast to Islamic philosopher Averroes (1126–1198), who concludes that points of conflict in the Qur'an disappear when the Qur'an is interpreted allegorically (he even claims that all religion is an allegorical way of expressing philosophical ideas and truth), fourteenth-century Muslim religious scholars shut the door for any speculative thought in religious matters.[42] While in previous times creativity in Islamic interpretation was encouraged in major learning centers such as Cairo, Damascus, and Baghdad, by the fourteenth century, philosophical speculation, or *ijtihad*, as it is known in Arabic, had practically ceased, and the door for innovation in religious interpretation had been closed. The

---

[42]Ibn Rushed (Averroes), *On the Harmony of Religion and Philosophy*, trans. George Hourani (Beirut: American University of Beirut Press, 1961).

word for "heresy" in Arabic, *bid'a*, is derived from the word *ibd'a*, "innovation." Faced with various threats from the outside world, beginning with the Crusades and ending with the Mongols, the Muslim world tried to protect itself by clinging to conservative interpretations of Islamic tradition. Muslim religious scholars became increasingly intolerant of any speculative thought. A growing tendency toward Islamic intellectual conservatism was about to start.

This new religious conservatism is expressed in the writings of Ibn Taymiya (1262–1327). He was born in the city of Harran (located at the modern border of Syria and Turkey), but when the Mongols invaded the region, he was forced to relocate in Damascus, where he lived under the Mamelukes. His studies focused on the Qur'an, the hadith (sayings of the prophet), Islamic jurisprudence, and Sufi metaphysics. He became increasingly critical of speculative and philosophical works that could be applied to interpreting the Qur'anic text. He also criticized the traditional Sufi practices of visiting the shrines of imams. His main contribution to Islamic law and jurisprudence was his interpretation of shari'a (Islamic law). He severely criticized previous jurists for not applying and abiding by Islamic law. For Ibn Taymiya, there were only two sources of legislation: the Qur'an and the Sunna (the example of the Prophet). He was convinced that scholars of the Islamic law had an obligation to interpret the will of God as it applied to contemporary society, and any society for that matter, provided that all such decisions were firmly grounded in the two major sources of the law: the Qur'an and the Sunna. He allowed for analogical reasoning but did not encourage Muslim scholars to take that route.

Ibn Taymiya's conservative ideas and uncompromising dedication to the strict interpretation of Islamic law put him in constant conflict with intellectuals and officials. It was his way of defending Islam against any perceived threats from the outside world as well as an expression of his own frustration with the sudden social changes he endured in being forced to relocate in Damascus. He led an opposition group against the Mongol occupation of his adopted city of Damascus, and even when the Mongol leaders adopted Islam, he continued to oppose them. He wrote extensively on the duty of Muslims to oppose rulers who professed to be Muslims and performed Islamic rites but failed to apply the shari'a.[43] Ibn

---

[43] Egger, *History of the Muslim World Since 1260*, 46-50.

Taymiya's conservative interpretation of Islamic law has inspired conservative Islamic movements in later centuries up until today, from the conservative Wahhabi movement in Arabia to the Muslim Brotherhood in Egypt. He is often quoted by Islamic militant groups around the world today. His stance of opposing Muslim rulers who do not adhere to shari'a inspires modern-day traditionalist Muslim groups that attempt to topple and assassinate moderate Muslim leaders.

Contrasting social and intellectual endeavors. For the most part in the thirteenth and fourteenth centuries, scholars in Europe as well as in the Muslim world were under the scrutiny of political and religious authorities. The church in Europe prosecuted, tortured, and harassed scholars and scientists whose opinions did not conform to what the church thought of as the right way of thinking. In the Muslim world, majority scholars were attached to the ruling elites, and their opinions had to conform to religious authorities, otherwise they were condemned. However, a transition took place in Europe during the Renaissance era that paved the way for the modern age, when scholars were able to express their findings through various channels away from the scrutiny of church authority. In later centuries, modernity allowed for the freedom of expression, intellectual thinking, and criticism.

During the same period, the Muslim world entered a period of intellectual decline and conservatism, suppressing any speculative thinking. Intellectual decline in the Muslim world was primarily due to sociopolitical conservatism, expressed in the traditional systems adopted by various Islamic regimes that ruled over most Islamic territories—from the Almoravids of North Africa to the Mamelukes of Egypt and the Levant, as well as the Seljuk Turks in Asia Minor (Turkey) and the Mongols and their alliances in central Asia. These regimes came to power through military campaigns and lacked intellectual and cultural sophistication. They had no interest in pursuing advancement in science and technology; their ultimate goal was defending their territories militarily. Muslim intellectuals and scholars suffered, and their contributions to society were restricted. Under these conservative structures, minorities were suppressed; the People of the Book, the Christians and the Jews who were previously instrumental in the administration of the state and who contributed significantly to the advancement of science, medicine, and technology, were either annihilated or silenced. They were perceived as infidels. These prevailing models of sociopolitical conservatism were mainly concerned with defending the Muslim community against outside threats. Inadvertently, they curbed the role of non-Muslims in the Islamic state, resulting in significant decline in the cultural and intellectual life of the community at large.

During the late Middle Ages, several developments in Europe resulted in drastic changes in the church and society in general. As described above, in the era of the Renaissance, academic studies in universities along with the revival of arts and the building of great cathedrals ushered in a social transformation in Europe. While preaching and mission activities, such as those of the Dominicans and the Franciscans, were influencing people throughout Europe and around the world, and intellectuals and theologians were contributing to what would become modern Europe, the Western church itself was going through its worst time. It was a period of decline and fragmentation. The devastating effects of the plague and the disintegration of traditional social institutions had a significant impact on Western society. Religion remained a dominant factor in almost all aspects of life; however, a growing dissatisfaction with the church resulted in increasing secularism.

The papacy, which enjoyed dominant and integrated power in the high Middle Ages (eleventh and twelfth centuries), started to decline and disintegrate in the late Middle Ages. Schism and ecclesiastical corruption in Rome dominated much of the fourteenth century. People started to question the validity of many religious practices such as indulgences and the emphasis on pilgrimages.[44] The fourteenth century also witnessed a decline in monastic life due to misbehavior, laziness, and financial mismanagement. On top of all that, the horror of the Inquisition as a result of any alleged heresy created fear among people and resentment against the authority of the church. The lack of interest in the church's life was evident to the extent that the Fourth Lateran Council of 1215 made it mandatory for every Christian to go to confession and take Communion at least once a year. For many Christians, the church of the late Middle Ages bore little resemblance to the community of believers described in the New Testament. Many voices started calling for reforming the church's beliefs and structure,

---

[44] An indulgence was the remission of temporal punishment of sin made possible by drawing on the surplus merits of the saints. During the late Middle Ages, one could purchase such a remission of sin.

a cry that would grow louder and louder in the following two centuries across Europe, resulting in significant transformation in the religious and the sociopolitical life of the continent.

The Collapse of the Byzantine Empire

The ongoing tension between the churches of the East and the West reached its peak in 1054, when the two churches formally split. Theological differences seemed to be the main reason for the split.[45] However, political and personal disagreements also contributed to the schism. During the high days of the Byzantine Empire (fifth and sixth centuries), the bishop of Constantinople was made "the ecumenical patriarch," a title that angered other bishops, including the bishop of Rome, at the time. Now the tide had changed, and the ecumenical patriarch of Byzantium was presiding over a much smaller church, while the majority of Eastern churches came under Islam. Meanwhile, the bishop of Rome was declared the pope over a much larger church and territories in western Europe.

This situation obviously frustrated the churches in the East, which were dealing with the devastating consequences of centuries living under various Islamic regimes and constant upheaval. Unsurprisingly, churches in the East promoted the view that all bishops are equal, and the bishop of Rome was no different. When it came to theology, the view of the Byzantine church was that the bishop of Rome was not an ecclesiastical monarch who had the right to add words to creeds or to make unilateral decisions concerning the church's beliefs and practices. The two churches ended up excommunicating each other.

The events that preceded the First Crusade could have mended the broken relations. The Eastern and Western churches' cooperative efforts to encounter the increasing threats of the Turks, and their common goal of protecting their territories, could have resulted in restored unity. The Crusaders, however, repeatedly violated their promises to Byzantium and in 1204 even destroyed Constantinople and vandalized the church of Hagia Sophia. The Byzantine Empire was under constant threat of Muslim invasions, and the Greek church of the East was unable to negotiate from a

---

[45]The *filioque* (the affirmation that the Holy Spirit was sent not only from the Father but also from the Son), which was added to the Nicene Creed in the West; clerical celibacy (the Eastern church allowed priests to marry, while the Western church did not); liturgical differences; and the sort of bread to be used in Communion all were serious theological issues at the time.

position of strength with the Western church. Several attempts to reconcile the two churches failed; many of these attempts were based on concessions from the Greeks due to their vulnerable and weak position.

Between the eleventh and the fifteenth centuries, Asia Minor (Turkey) suffered the most devastating destruction of church institutions and a significant decline in Christian population. The Seljuk Turks were able to push their way into the region through constant raids and aggressive wars. The destruction of churches and monasteries as well as the massacre of Christians resulted in reducing the number of Christians in Asia Minor from twelve million in the early Byzantine era (fifth century) to a mere five million by the thirteenth century. In 1085, for example, the Turks destroyed the ancient churches of Antioch when they captured the city, a pattern that continued all over Asia Minor with the destruction of the celebrated church of St. Basil of Caesarea and the legendary shrine of St. Nicolas (the original place of St. Nicolas of Myra, or Santa Claus).[46] In the 1140s the city of Edessa, which was a hub of Christian learning and administration, was destroyed, and all its Christian inhabitants were either massacred or taken into slavery. Precious biblical manuscripts were burned and destroyed in Ephesus and Edessa.[47]

Such atrocities were further aggravated by the repeated Crusades from Europe. The Turks were primarily targeting the Byzantine Empire, and they differentiated in their treatment of the Greeks and other Christians such as the Syrians and Armenians, whom they spared from complete destruction and massacre. They knew that the Byzantines had persecuted other Christians, and by sparing the persecuted ones they aimed at gaining their support against Byzantium. European Crusaders received the worst treatment of all as they were perceived as intruders who had no business interfering in the affairs of the region; accordingly, they were not spared massacre whenever the opportunity arose. These catastrophic treatments of Christians in Asia Minor were accompanied by forced conversion to Islam, which expedited the process of annihilating the Christian communities of Asia Minor in the following centuries.

The cycle of violence intensified in the thirteenth and fourteenth centuries, when many historical churches completely disappeared along with

---

[46] Antioch was one of the very first churches in Christian history (see Acts 13).
[47] Vryonis, *Decline of Medieval Hellenism*, 157-72.

their congregations. This included many churches on the western coast of Asia Minor such as Ephesus, Colossae, Smyrna, and others that were established by the apostle Paul and others in the first century. The majority of Christians in Ephesus, for example, were massacred, and the remaining became slaves or were imprisoned, including the priests and monks. Islamic traveler ibn Battuta reported when visiting Ephesus in 1330 that the great cathedral, which he described as one of the most beautiful in the world, had turned into the great mosque of the city. By the end of the fifteenth century, the number of bishoprics in Anatolia went from 373 to only three.[48] The Islamization of Asia Minor was almost complete even before the collapse of Constantinople.

The Byzantine Empire came to an end when a group of Turkish invaders from central Asia moved to Anatolia in Asia Minor and established a new kingdom called the Ottomans.[49] In the 1350s the Ottomans advanced in eastern Europe, west of the Bosphor, securing new territories in the Balkans. In 1389 they defeated the Serbs in Kosovo and were able to incorporate Bulgaria, Macedonia, and Serbia under their control. Most of Greece came under the rule of the Ottoman sultan as well. The Ottomans started recruiting large numbers of Christians into their army, giving them special privileges, a tactic that secured a strong army while reducing the number of Christians in the Balkans.[50] In 1453 the final siege of Constantinople under the leadership of Mehmed II was achieved. Thousands of people were massacred, including the priests who were celebrating the last mass at Hagia Sophia. The last Byzantine emperor was tortured and killed. The city was renamed Istanbul (its current name), and the church of Hagia Sophia, one of the first Christian cathedrals, was turned into a mosque along with hundreds of other churches in the city.[51] The fall of Constantinople brought about the end of the Byzantine Empire; from that time forward the Byzantine church

---

[48]Vryonis, *Decline of Medieval Hellenism*, 170.
[49]In 1300 a Turkish warrior named Othman emerged in Anatolia and established the new kingdom that was named after him.
[50]The Ottoman Turks followed the Mamelukes in recruiting (kidnapping) young boys from their Christian families in eastern Europe and training them as cavalrymen. As in the case of the Mamelukes, the trauma experienced by these young boys due to their forced seizure from their families attributed to their savagery and fearlessness. These new slave soldiers or cavalrymen under the Ottomans were called Janissaries and would be the Mamelukes' final adversaries.
[51]Roger Crowley, *The Holy War for Constantinople and the Clash of Islam and the West* (New York: Hachette Books, 2006). See also Steven Runciman, *The Fall of Constantinople 1453* (New York: Cambridge University Press, 1990).

joined the rest of the Eastern churches in living under Dar al-Islam. The only remaining Orthodox churches outside Dar al-Islam were those of Russia and very small remnants of eastern Europe along with smaller parts of Greece, since most of eastern Europe came under the Ottoman rule.

The tragedy of the Byzantine collapse was another example of the costs of the church's disunity and fragmentation. It was a déjà vu of what happened when Islam took over the Middle East. Seven centuries later, the remaining territories of the Byzantine Empire faced the power of Islam weak and fragmented. Instead of supporting and empowering each other, the churches of the East and the West spent their energy fighting each other.[52] Their strategies to encounter the Seljuk Turks further accelerated the advancement of the Islamic empire under the rule of the Ottomans.

A year before Constantinople fell to the Muslim Turks, Italy and central Europe faced serious military threat from the Ottomans, promoting Pope Nicolas V to unite European Christendom against the Islamic threat. When his attempts failed, he granted Portugal the right to subdue Muslims and other pagans in the papal bull *Dum Diversas* (1452). Several decades later, Pope Alexander VI awarded Portugal and Spain colonial rights over the newly discovered land in the Americas for the purpose of Christianizing these new territories. It was a preemptive move to encounter the power of Islam in the East.

THE SPANISH RECONQUISTA

One of the most significant historical developments in the Muslim-Christian encounters of the Middle Ages was the reconquest of Spain. The Islamic rule of Spain, which lasted for seven centuries, came to an end by the late fifteenth century. The Muslims were able to conquer the Iberian Peninsula in 711 with only seven thousand soldiers due to the division and weakness of its rulers. From the eighth to the tenth centuries, Spain lived under several Islamic dynasties, but by the eleventh century the power of the Islamic rule over Spain started to disintegrate. The collapse of Muslim rule gave an opportunity to the Christian princes in northwestern Spain to declare independent territories and to extend full control over them. The first major success was the recapturing of Toledo in 1085, which is considered to be the beginning of the reconquest.

---

[52]Koschorke, Ludwig, and Delgado, *History of Christianity*, 13, 283.

Muslims in Toledo were not harmed or forced to convert; however, this event alarmed other Muslim rulers in Spain as to what might happen later. They looked for assistance from the powerful Islamic state in North Africa, based in Tunisia, known as Almoravids (Al-Murabidun in Arabic, which means "the resistant"). The Almoravids were very conservative Islamic rulers who did not appreciate the relaxed lifestyle of Muslim rulers of Spain. Instead of supporting the Muslim rulers of Spain who asked for help, the Almoravids ended up taking power from the Spanish Muslim rulers. The fighting between the Almoravids and the Spanish kings, who were also supported by French nobles and knights, continued through the twelfth century, resulting in the collapse of the Almoravids, who were replaced by another group called Almohads (Al-Muwahhidun in Arabic, which means "those who believe in the oneness of God"). During the twelfth and thirteenth centuries, fighting over Spain resulted in reducing the number of Muslims in Al-Andalus, as it is known by Muslims. With the disappearance of the Almohads, the Reconquista of Spain was accelerated when Cordova (the capital) was captured in 1236 and Seville in 1248. The marriage of King Ferdinand of Aragon and Queen Isabella of Castile, formerly antagonistic kingdoms, in 1469 created the first centralized political power that was able to incorporate its armies, finance, and nobles into one. In 1492 they were able to complete the reconquest of Spain by recapturing the kingdom of Grenada. This victory resulted in the expulsion of Muslims from the Iberian Peninsula, along with many Spanish Jews, who later made their home in what is today Morocco.[53]

Islamic rule over Spain resulted in introducing the Arabic culture and language to major Spanish cities, where many Christians and Jews were fluent in both Latin and Arabic. The Spanish Christians and Jews were also instrumental in the work of translations from Arabic to Latin along with their counterparts in Egypt, Syria, Mesopotamia, and Persia. Al-Andalus was one of the least strict Islamic communities; there Islamic rules and regulations were virtually not enforced. On the cultural level, Al-Andalus marked the high point of Islamic art, poetry, philosophy, science, and

---

[53]For a detailed study of the Spanish Reconquista, see Joseph F. O'Callaghan, *Reconquest and Crusade in Medieval Spain* (Philadelphia: University of Pennsylvania Press, 2003). O'Callaghan makes the argument that Spanish Reconquista was a form of a Crusade that received the support of several popes who accorded Christian warriors willing to participate in the peninsular war against Muslims the same status and benefits offered to Crusaders who fought in the Holy Land.

medicine. While Christians, Muslims, and Jews lived side by side in major cities and contributed to the cultural complexity of Al-Andalus, the majority in the countryside remained Christians during the time of Muslim rule. Overall, Spain was one of the most tolerant and culturally vibrant communities in medieval Europe.

Conclusion

Christian-Muslim encounters between the eleventh and fifteenth centuries were generally intense and destructive. Major events during this period had an impact on the sociopolitical developments of Europe and the Muslim world for centuries to come. The Islamic empire dominated larger geographical territories that extended across Asia, the Middle East, and North Africa. The Abbasid dynasty that ruled out of Baghdad, epitomizing the height of Islamic civilization (the golden era of Islam), gave way to other Islamic empires such as the Fatimid, who ruled over North Africa and parts of the Middle East; the Mamelukes, who ruled over the Middle East; and the Ottoman Turks, who formed the last dominant Islamic empire until the twentieth century. Christians formed the majority population in Dar al-Islam until the twelfth century and were instrumental in the advancement of the social, political, and economic life of the various Islamic empires.

European Christendom was confined to smaller geographical territories, and its main concern was defending its territories against the powerful Islamic empire. A cluster of noteworthy events contributed to significant social and political changes during that time. The Crusades, which lasted over two centuries, did not achieve their political or religious goals of securing the Holy Land; to the contrary, Europe endured significant losses both in personnel and financial resources, while the Islamic empire emerged victorious militarily in the aftermath of the Crusades. The Mongol invasion caused tremendous destruction to the Islamic empire; however, the Mongols ended up adopting Islam, forming a super Islamic state that extended from China to Europe, including parts of the Middle East. The Christian communities living in Dar al-Islam endured their worst time during the fourteenth century and were completely wiped out in central Asia and Asia Minor (Turkey), while they were reduced to a minority group across the Middle East. By the middle of the fifteenth century, the Byzantine Christian empire had collapsed. Christian-Muslim encounters during the Middle Ages stand as a clear reminder that violence often begets further violence, while nothing is gained from mistrust and intolerance.

The era also included noteworthy spiritual and intellectual encounters, in which Christian missionaries from Europe tried to reach out to Muslims through dialogue rather than fighting. Christians and Jews continued to play important roles in fostering intellectual accomplishments in science, medicine, arts, and works of translation within the Islamic empire, contributing to the golden era of Islam during the Abbasid dynasty. However, their role, as well as their numbers, was curbed by the fourteenth and fifteenth centuries. While Europe had endured significant losses during the same period, it was able to emerge more powerful economically, socially, and politically. A period of self-searching and intellectual progress enabled Europe to embark on social and economic transformation; at the heart of such transformation was the Renaissance. The Muslim world, on the other hand, while emerging militarily victorious, was not able to maintain steady growth economically. Social development was stagnant; the door for critical thinking and progressive intellectual accomplishments was shut due to increased religious conservatism. The role of Christians and Jews, who were instrumental in the social, economic, and political developments of previous Islamic empires, was restricted, while their numbers started to dwindle. The Islamic empire had lost its heart, its capital dynamo and powerhouse. From that point on, Europe and the Islamic empire took different paths in terms of social, economic, and political development.

4

CHRISTIANITY AND ISLAM IN THE AGE OF DISCOVERY (1500–1750)

BOTH CHRISTIANITY AND ISLAM saw significant territorial expansion during the era from 1500 to 1750, setting the framework for what later became globalized Christianity and globalized Islam. However, sociopolitically and culturally, each community had quite different experiences during that time span. While European Christianity went through a significant time of religious and social transformation, resulting in substantial changes, the Muslim world entered an era of religious conservatism that led to social stagnation. The territorial expansion of Christianity through colonization in the Americas and parts of Asia was remarkable, but the quality of the Christian faith in these territories suffered due to massive and sometimes coercive Christianization. Islamic territorial expansion into eastern Europe, Africa, and Asia was also remarkable; however, such expansion was not supported by substantial sociocultural transformation, which resulted in rapid sociopolitical decline.

It is worth observing that both Christianity and Islam expanded during this period as a result of a combination of coercive and voluntary acceptance of the faith. The age of discovery, colonization, and the Reformation all had significant impacts for the future development of Christianity, similar to the effect of Islamic dynasties—the Ottomans (Middle East,

North Africa, and eastern Europe), the Safavid (Persia) and the Mughal (India)—on the future development of Islamic nations.

THE AGE OF DISCOVERY (1450 TO 1640)

For seven centuries (eighth–fifteenth centuries), Europeans were interested in securing trade routes to the Far East instead of paying high prices to Muslim traders who controlled most of the trade routes across Africa and Asia. The Muslims' capture of Byzantium in 1453 posed a military threat in the eastern Mediterranean and necessitated new trade routes to the Far East. Muslim invaders approached Venice in northern Italy and captured Otranto in southern Italy during the 1480s. Moreover, Muslim naval forces frequently attacked the British Isles up until the end of the fifteenth century. The Spanish Reconquista of the Iberian Peninsula by the end of the fifteenth century did not really put an end to the Islamic power in the western Mediterranean; the Moroccans defeated the Portuguese in the Battle of the Three Kings in 1578. In the East, the Ottomans advanced into the Balkans, capturing significant territories and reaching into central Europe. It was not until 1683 that the second Ottoman retreat from the siege of Vienna limited the Muslim presence in Europe to what is today Turkey and the Balkans.

For these reasons, European merchants hoped to find a way of bypassing the Muslim-controlled territories and connecting to India and China, where significant resources would enhance the capitalistic economy that had started to flourish in Europe. Advances in naval technology as well as new awareness of the geographical landscape of the planet made such ambition a reality. By the end of the fifteenth century, two possibilities were contemplated. The first option was to sail south along the coast of Africa and then east to India. The second entailed greater risk into the unknown—to sail west across the open Atlantic Ocean, hoping to reach India by navigating uncharted water.

Taking the greater risk in crossing the Atlantic, Spanish ships under the command of Christopher Columbus reached the shores of the Caribbean in 1492. They thought they had reached the eastern shores of India, and thus the natives of the newly discovered America were called Indians. The Caribbean Islands did not offer the spices or the gold that explorers were looking for, but they promised to deliver much richer land and greater future for the Spanish kingdom. In the following years, several explorers' expeditions to the New World landed the Spanish in what is today South America.

The Spanish exploration of South America was generally ruthless, as they had superior military technology to that of the natives. However, the most devastating weapon against the natives was the diseases that Europeans brought to their lands. Millions of Native Americans perished by simply encountering European colonials. The same year that Spanish sailors reached the shores of the New World, 1492, back in Europe Ferdinand and Isabella were able to expel the Muslims from the Iberian Peninsula, putting the kingdom of Spain under a unified monarchial power. The huge assets gained from the exploration of the New World gave the Spanish monarchs enormous financial resources to secure stability for the empire for the next hundred years.

The Spanish adventures, however, were not confined to the New World; they benefited from the experiences of the Portuguese in reaching out to the Far East and were able to secure a territory for the Spanish monarchy in Southeast Asia. The territories were named after King Philip II of Spain (1527-1598) and thus were called the Philippines. The Spanish colonization of the Philippines, started in 1521, culminated with formally organizing the Philippines as a Spanish colony in 1565. This colonization continued for three centuries, until 1898.

In 1498 the small kingdom of Portugal surprised other, wealthier European kingdoms when a force under Vasco de Gama sailed around the southern tip of Africa and successfully reached the western shores of India. They soon destroyed the power of Muslim shipping in the Indian Ocean along the eastern cost of Africa, establishing bases along the eastern coast of Africa and the western coast of India. They then sailed eastward to China and Japan. As a result, the Portuguese monarchy and the explorers who supported the expeditions to the East made staggering profits that also secured a stable future for the Portuguese Empire. Following the Spanish lead in discovering South America, the Portuguese were able to secure a large territory in South America by colonizing Brazil.

Colonialism and the Spread of Christianity

The age of discovery marked the beginning of European colonialism, which continued until the twentieth century. As naval technology advanced and as Europeans started to realize that there was a much larger world with significant resources at their disposal, they naturally attempted to colonize these foreign lands. The territories of South America were considered part of the kingdoms of Spain and Portugal, and native populations were often forced to submit to European governing systems. Their civilizations, indigenous beliefs, and patterns of life were either destroyed or suppressed. This pattern of colonization did not work in Asia. The Portuguese came to realize that it was impossible to colonize the vast territories of India, China, and Japan, and they settled for establishing trade relationships with these nations rather than colonizing them. However, it was necessary to secure several coastal cities and posts around Africa and Asia in order to ensure trade routes. Fortified military posts provided refilling stations for Portuguese ships and secured the sea lanes for trade. The ultimate goal of the European powers was to exploit the colonies for their profit at home. Unfortunately, the wealth gained for the royal treasury ushered in a cycle of inflation in Europe that added to the misery of European peasants.

European colonialism was accompanied by the spread of Christianity not only to the New World but also to Africa and Asia. Missionaries such as Francis Xavier (1506–1552), Di Nobili (1577–1656), and Mateo Ricci (1552–1610) were instrumental in spreading the Christian faith by adapting to the cultures of India, China, and Japan. In Latin America, priests often accompanied the Spanish and Portuguese expeditions of conquest and sought to convert the native populations to Christianity. Some conversions were voluntary; others were coerced. The European colonizers perceived the natives as savage and uncivilized, and therefore they had to be Christianized. Spain was just recovering from fighting the Muslims in the Iberian Peninsula, and they treated the natives of the newly discovered territories as infidels who had to be converted. Oftentimes, natives were rushed into accepting Christian baptism without any basic understanding of the Christian faith. They were ordered to confess that they believed in only one God and in Jesus Christ as the redeemer as well as being instructed on reciting the Lord's Prayer and the Hail Mary. Sometimes even these conditions were not enforced.

In some cases, when the natives perceived that their gods had been defeated by the Christian God, they rushed into baptism in order to gain the support of the superior god. In other cases, when missionaries faced resistance from the natives, they sought some type of compromising approach where the native gods and goddesses were incorporated into Christianity and were given certain status as saints, syncretizing Christianity with native religions, a practice that is still in existence in many parts of the world where Catholic missions performed the task of Christianizing the native inhabitants. For several centuries, natives were not given sufficient access to education and were not trusted to provide leadership for the church on their own land. Instead, they had to settle for lesser positions and were not consulted on major decisions. It was not until the twentieth century that natives were given leadership positions or were even allowed to govern their own church business.

Religious arrangements in the New World followed the patterns common in Europe at the time. The pope gave power to the Spanish and Portuguese rulers to act as the broker of political and religious affairs. The monarchies were given a royal patronage over the church, which gave them power to appoint bishops and other high-ranking ecclesiastical officials as well as to administer church finances. Many priests and bishops were political appointees who had no concern for the plight of the natives. Such a system paved the way for the entanglement of religion and politics in the following decades, particularly in South America.

While some missionaries and priests were caught in the political agenda of the colonies, others were faithful servants who preached the gospel and taught the natives basic farming techniques. They established schools and hospitals and ultimately contributed to the overall well-being of the natives. Many of the Dominican, Franciscan, and Jesuit missionaries spoke openly against the colonizers' abuse and exploitation, defending the basic rights of the natives. Oftentimes missionaries would side with the natives against their own political and ecclesiastical orders that oppressed the natives. Contrary to common practices of other missionaries and to their surprise, missionary Pedro Claver (1581–1654), for example, considered slaves to be brothers and sisters who ought to be treated with dignity and respect. Often when a ship arrived with thousands of slaves on board, he would provide food, shelter, and medical treatment. He befriended the slaves, lived among them, and preached the gospel to them.[1] Historically, the Catholic Church in South America displays two faces of Christianity: one that is concerned with the poor and the oppressed, and another that is highly political and exploitative of the natives. In the nineteenth and twentieth centuries, when Latin American countries demanded their independence from Spain and Portugal, many Christian missionaries supported the natives against the colonizers.

By the beginning of the seventeenth century, the power of the Spanish and Portuguese monarchies started to decline. Although the colonies

---

[1] Justo L. Gonzalez, *The Story of Christianity* (New York: HarperCollins, 2010), 1:462-64.

controlled by the Spanish and the Portuguese provided tremendous assets for the Iberian Peninsula, the monarchial system maintained outdated methods of governing wherein nobles and church authorities were given absolute power to rule. State finance and diplomacy were handled by incompetent nobles who had no experience in governing. Such policies contributed to the rapid deterioration of their empires both abroad and at home.

During the seventeenth century, the Dutch and the British emerged as the new colonial powers. With their well-equipped navy and aggressive merchants, the Dutch claimed a colonial empire that included parts of the East Indies in the Caribbean, small colonies in Africa, and the southern parts of India as well as Indonesia. For most of the seventeenth century, the Netherlands was the example of wealth and power in Europe. However, superiority was seized from them by the British, who for the next three centuries were able to control colonies in every corner of the globe. Meanwhile, the British and the French were able to secure their control over North America (the US and Canada). Overall, the age of discovery presented an era of significant change in Europe and had serious impact on the rest of the world as well as the rapid spread of Christianity, resulting in a global religion.

The age of discovery ushered in the expansion of European power internationally. In the following centuries, European power continued to dominate the world, politically, economically, and to some extent culturally.

Meanwhile, the age of discovery facilitated for European missionaries an opportunity to spread the Christian faith around the globe. The natives of the New World were Christianized, oftentimes by force; others in Asia and Africa were also Christianized through preaching and social services. However, from the sixteenth to the nineteenth centuries there were minimal efforts to evangelize Muslims. Europeans were surprised to find a large number of Muslim communities in Asia and Africa and were ambivalent about how to relate to them. Ultimately, they perceived Muslims as a threat and fought against them.

While the Catholic Church was focused on combating the Reformation in Europe during the sixteenth century, the age of discovery presented the largest expansion of the Catholic Church globally, a reality that shapes the Catholic presence in the world in the twenty-first century.

The age of discovery ushered in an era of enormous wealth and political stability for European powers while unleashing unprecedented misery for the natives who were exploited by the Europeans. Some native groups were annihilated, while others were subjected to harsh treatment and slavery while their civilizations, indigenous beliefs, and patterns of life were either destroyed or suppressed.

THE REFORMATION AS A TRANSFORMATIONAL MOVEMENT IN EUROPE

By the beginning of the sixteenth century, the church provided a broad scope of social, political, and cultural cohesiveness in Europe. The quality of papal leadership, however, suffered from divisions and rivalry to the extent that some Christian theologians and scholars thought of replacing the papal seat with a council of bishops. Clergy likewise were accused of corruption and mismanagement of church affairs. With the advent of scholarly education and the establishment of universities centuries earlier, much of the church's power, structural system, and theology came under fire. Many scholars, scientists, and theologians started to challenge the church's absolute power over every sphere of life. Attempts to reform the church and recapture the spirit and simplicity of the early church came from many directions: monks, popular preachers, Renaissance humanists, and others. Many were condemned as heretics and paid with their lives, while others survived. Their call for reformation was finally heard across Europe, and by the sixteenth century waves of reformation changed the social and religious landscape in major parts of the continent.

As early as the fourteenth century, several early Reformers such as John Wycliffe (1320-1384), Jan Hus (1373-1415), and William Tyndale (1495-1536) challenged the church's authority and called for the reformation of its practices. They criticized a host of religious beliefs and practices such as the cult of saints and the excessive focus on pilgrimages, which they asserted to be unbiblical. They translated the Bible into the common language of the people, providing a significant tool for the masses to find for themselves the basic tenets of the Christian faith without the church's corruption and elaborate rituals. They paved the way for the Reformation of the sixteenth century.

The Protestant Reformation of the sixteenth century is one of the most significant and complex movements in European history. Attempts at reforming the church finally picked up momentum, and the economic and social climate in Europe provided a setting for a fresh start. On the economic front, capitalism ushered in a new era of unlimited potential profit in agriculture and trade, in contrast to local and undeveloped medieval economic life. Merchants in Italy and Germany were reinvesting their profits and found out that managing their investments produced greater wealth than simple forms of trade. International commerce further developed, and payment with money instead of the exchange of goods became a common practice.[2] Aristocrats gained significant profits from their land, while peasants were left to struggle with new cycles of poverty.

Eventually, capitalism created a new social stratum of wealthy bourgeoisie who were able to challenge the typical social order of knights, nobles, and clergy. They were competing for power with nobility and knights and did not have much respect for the authority of the clergy. Meanwhile, capitalism empowered European rulers to weaken the power of the church over the people and thereby enhance their own authority, gaining financial resources necessary to develop stronger centralized governments. Such social changes were also inspired by the Renaissance ideas of freedom of thought and equality among people, and earlier calls for democratic systems.[3]

On the intellectual front, a group of educated scholars known as humanists (not to be confused with the modern humanistic movement) promoted studying classical antiquity, or what is known today as the liberal arts, the literature that shaped previous civilizations and contributed to the development of humanity. Most humanists tended to place humans at the center of the universe or made humans the measure of all things, therefore coining the term *humanism*. Many, however, were aware of the limitations of the human mind, recognizing the effect of the sinful nature on humanity.[4]

Reformers such as Martin Luther (Germany), John Calvin (Geneva), Ulrich Zwingli (Zurich), John Knox (Scotland), and others emerged in sixteenth-century Europe, not in any organized or coordinated efforts. They simply started questioning ecclesiastical teachings and practices that they found unacceptable and incompatible with biblical teaching. Their vocal calls for change often put them in conflict with the church authorities of their day. Some were supported by local governments and were able to avoid execution, such as Martin Luther. Others had to escape to other

---

[2]The concept of trade and the use of money in trade were not new. Money had been used extensively since the Roman Empire. However, money rather than barter became common practice and started to gain dominance in capitalistic Europe of the sixteenth century.
[3]Lewis Spitz, *The Renaissance and Reformation Movement* (St. Louis: Concordia, 1971), 2:265-72.
[4]Spitz, *Renaissance and Reformation Movement*, 303-23.

countries, such as John Calvin, who left France and settled in Switzerland. Still others were captured and executed, such as John Penry of Wales.

Martin Luther (1483–1546) is perhaps the best-known Reformer, such that his name is usually attached to the Reformation movement. As he started studying and interpreting the biblical text in its original languages, he came to the conclusion that salvation was not based on human merit but God's grace, against the common belief that humans could contribute to their own salvation.[5] Based on his conviction that the Bible, not medieval theology, ought to be the standard for Christian belief and practice, Luther composed ninety-seven theses critical to scholastic theology as the basis for debate and posted them in 1517. These theses did not create any interest among the people beyond the university circle. Later that year, he composed another ninety-five theses, directed more precisely at the practice of selling indulgences. Based on his previous experience, he circulated fewer copies. On October 31, 1517, he posted one of those copies at the door of the Castle Church in Wittenberg. This was actually a very common practice, since the church's door was used like a bulletin board to post announcements or invitations for academic debates at the university. He called for a debate over his ninety-five theses, but no one showed up. Previously Luther had asked several bishops to intervene in order to stop the practice of selling indulgences, and when his attempts failed, he sent them copies of his theses arguing for an end to such unbiblical practice.

Many church leaders and educated Christians knew that the sale of indulgences was not based in the teaching of the Bible. Ordinary Christians, however, were confused about indulgences' effectiveness. Those who sold indulgences often gave people the impression that buying the indulgences would result in the removal of their sins, and without indulgences they would suffer severe punishment in purgatory. Some actually believed that through indulgences they could acquire salvation and the remission of their sins as well as remission of sins for their deceased loved ones. The issue was much more complicated due to the level of corruption that

---

[5]Luther came to see God's righteousness as not a punishment but a gift from God—a gift that, when accepted in faith, results in redemption. This realization led to a complete transformation in Luther's theology. God offered salvation to sinners while they were still sinners. This also meant that God was not angry but rather loving and forgiving. The cornerstone of Luther's theology was that justification by God's grace alone, received only in faith through Christ's atoning work, was the only means for salvation. See *The Magnificent*, trans. A. T. W. Steinhaeuser, in *Works of Martin Luther* (Philadelphia: Muhlenberg, 1943), 3:142-45.

dominated church leadership at the time. In 1510, Pope Julius II announced an indulgence to pay for the construction of St. Peter's cathedral in Rome. Meanwhile, Luther's local German archbishop, Albert of Brandenburg, needed significant amounts of money to pay his own debt accumulated from offering hefty bribes in order to attain his position overseeing several posts in his territory. The following pope, Leo X, made Albert of Brandenburg the high commissioner of the sale of indulgences in his territories, provided that they could share the profit.[6]

Much to Luther's surprise, humanists published copies of his theses in several European cities. Humanists were more than happy to use Luther's arguments for their own interest in advancing a new atmosphere of learning, debate, and free thinking away from the control of the church. Some humanists were not even religious or did not care about the content of Luther's theses; they simply saw an opportunity to attack the absolute power of the church. Meanwhile, newly developed printing techniques invented by Johannes Gutenberg made it possible to print large quantities of materials and distribute them widely. Interest in Luther's ideas started to spread not only in Germany but also across Europe. Contrary to the low-key academic debate that Luther sought to ignite in Wittenberg, his theses became well-known across the continent, and people were interested in debating his ideas.

This development prompted Albert of Brandenburg to contact Rome, demanding action against Luther. Rome's reaction was tactful, and the pope tried to control Luther without creating larger problems. Luther was called to Heidelberg to appear before the Augustinian council. As an Augustinian monk, he was expected to submit to his superiors, but as a professor he was given the chance to debate his ideas. Luther made it clear that he would not recant unless convinced on biblical basis. Luther went through several trials; the most notable was in the city of Worms, where he was convicted of heresy and was eventually excommunicated in 1521. His excommunication meant exclusion from the church as well as the loss of all his civil rights. Luther, however, was supported by the German authorities, including King Frederick, who secured a place for him in Wartburg Castle, where Luther continued to direct the Reformation movement until his death in 1546.[7]

---

[6]Lewis Spitz, *The Protestant Reformation, 1517–1559* (New York: Harper & Row, 1985), 89-95.
[7]Hans J. Hillerbrand, *The Reformation: A Narrative History Related by Contemporary Observers and Participants* (New York: Harper & Row, 1964), 54, 379-82.

John Calvin (1509–1564), one of the most influential Reformers of the sixteenth century, is often called "the theologian" for his great contribution to developing the theological structure that shaped the Reformation. His famous *Institutes of the Christian Religion*, an organized explanation of the doctrines and basic principles of Reformation theology, gave the reformation its theological and structural cohesiveness. Calvin's *Institutes* was clear, organized and easy to read, and provided an intellectual tool that was well received across Europe.[8] Contrary to many Protestant writings at the time that were polemical in nature, defending Reformation theology or attacking Catholic theology, Calvin sought to explain the basic principles of Reformed theology rather than getting into heated debates.[9] Like other Reformers, Calvin used original sources such as biblical languages and church fathers' writings to interpret the Scriptures. Calvin, however, did not have any theological training and was not ordained as a monk or a priest. Calvin, like Luther, had no intention of starting a movement; in fact, he was shy and avoided being at the center of debates. However, his writings led to accusations against him, forcing him to flee from France to Switzerland, where he ended up living in Geneva. From there he played a significant role in shaping not only Geneva's Reformed ecclesiastical structure but also its political systems according to Reformed theology.[10]

Transforming European Christianity

The Reformation movement that swept across Europe during the sixteenth century contributed to theological and organizational transformation in European Christianity as well as Europe's social and political structure, ushering in the modern age.

Ecclesiastical reformation. At the heart of the Reformation was a renewed emphasis on the centrality of Scripture, *sola Scriptura*, as the basis of the Christian life and practice, and an emphasis on faith alone, *sola fidei*, as the foundation for human salvation. Reformers constantly argued that their ideas were not innovative but rather a return to the teachings and practices of the early church. The absence of Eastern theology from world

---

[8]John Calvin, *Institutes of the Christian Religion*, ed. John T. McNeill, 2 vols. (Philadelphia: Westminster, 1960).
[9]Williston Walker, *John Calvin: The Organizer of Reformed Protestantism, 1509-1564* (New York: Schocken Books, 1969), 203-325.
[10]For more details, see William Monter, *Calvin's Geneva* (New York: Wiley, 1967).

Christianity due to the dominance of Islam in the Middle East had negatively affected European Christianity. The Reformation was an attempt to bring back Christianity to its eastern/Mediterranean roots and biblical foundation. The Reformation transformed institutionalized Christianity, which had been corrupted in its leadership along with a host of beliefs and practices such as the selling of indulgences. The Reformation eventually was a break from the power and authority of the Catholic Church. The church's response to the challenges of such an unstoppable movement came in the form of a national church council. The Council of Trent (1545–1563) tried to clarify Catholic doctrines while defending the practices and behavior of church leadership that were also under fire, attempting to emphasize both right teaching and right practice. The council was significant in granting new life and energy to the Catholic Church against sweeping change across Europe.[11]

Social transformation. The ideas introduced by the Reformers started to fan social agitation across Europe and debates among intellectuals. This produced a powerful disorienting effect throughout the continent, where thousands of people were cut off from institutions and patterns of life that they had been accustomed to for centuries. For some, this experience felt liberating; others, however, were troubled and anxious about such a sudden shift. Many responded to this sweeping change by clinging to familiar traditions, among them Roman Catholicism. Others opted to adopt one of the various Protestant traditions. The most significant outcome of the Reformation was the freedom to challenge the status quo. Once the Reformers established the precedent that revolt against the power of the church was possible, it seemed that any other change could happen, whether political, social, or religious. One of the remarkable social

---

[11]The Council of Trent reaffirmed the traditional beliefs and practices of the Catholic Church, including the ecclesiastical structure of the church; clerical celibacy; the seven sacraments; the doctrine of transubstantiation (the belief that during the Mass the consecrated bread and wine truly become the body and blood of Christ); the veneration of relics, icons, and saints (especially the blessed Virgin Mary); the necessity of both faith and good works for salvation; the existence of purgatory; and the issuance (but not sale) of indulgences. In other words, all the Reformers' objections and concerns were strictly rejected. The council, however, emphasized the need for educating parish priests in order to better serve their congregations while equipping them with the necessary tools to respond to the new challenges presented by the Reformers. The establishment of seminaries for the purpose of training priests and new religious orders such as the Jesuits was at the heart of what came to be known as the Counter-Reformation movement, which maintained all traditional practices and Catholic doctrines.

outcomes was the use of Reformation slogans in the 1525 Peasants' Revolt. Peasant revolts were common in Europe, but what was different about the 1525 revolt was that their leaders were aware of Luther's theology, and they used Scripture as the basis for demanding changes in contrast to appealing to common laws, as had been the case in previous revolts.

Freedom of thought. The Reformation is credited with facilitating a new atmosphere of intellectual debate and freedom of thought. While universities in Europe provided a place for research and intellectual endeavors, the Reformation took such freedom of expression to a new level. Based on Reformed theology, the Reformers argued that all people were created equal and had the same right to express themselves, giving birth to the ideology of the modern age. In the following centuries, freedom, equality, and logical thinking dominated across Europe. The concept of equality as introduced by the Reformers led to significant change in the social context of Europe and gave people the necessary permission to apply the same concept in the political arena. While the Reformation's calls for eliminating the differences between clergy and laity were primarily theological, the concept of equality had a far-ranging impact in terms of accelerating the development of modern democratic political systems.

In northern Europe, where intellectual freedom was guaranteed by the Reformation model of social and political structure, intellectual achievements and scientific research flourished, while in southern Europe, where the Catholic Church scrutinized every new idea, scientific exploration suffered and was suppressed. A case in point would be the way the church treated one of the great scientists in history, Galileo. Italian physicist, mathematician, and philosopher Galileo Galilei (1564–1642), who played a significant role in the scientific revolution, was tried by the Inquisition and put under house arrest for the rest of his life. His achievements included the creation of an advanced telescope system and consequent advanced astronomical observations. He refined and further advanced Copernicus's heliocentric theory (of a sun-centered cosmos), which was condemned by the authority of the church and considered heretical. From a scientific point of view, Galileo remains the father of modern observational astronomy and modern physics.

Political transformation. The Reformation also caused significant political ripples across Europe, providing an opportunity for local kings to gain control over their territories and to break from a centralized

European governing system represented by the pope and the emperor, who followed Rome's orders. Several attempts by Holy Roman Emperor Charles V (1500–1558) to crush the movement failed. Local political authorities saw a great opportunity in supporting the Reformation movement where a break with Catholicism would strengthen their own political authority. This was certainly the case in England, where King Henry VIII (1509–1547) supported the establishment of the Anglican Church as the national Church of England. The establishment of the Anglican Church secured his control over both the church and the people.

In France, political authorities were able to maintain ties with Catholicism while eroding its political power over the country. Francis I (1515–1547) succeeded in creating a strong nationalistic feeling and a centralized bureaucratic system that enhanced France's position relative to other countries. In Germany, Lutheranism became the dominant form of religious and social life, rejecting the power of the Catholic Church altogether. In Switzerland and the Netherlands, Calvinism provided not only a reformation of the church but an alternative political system for their territories. Reformed theology became the dominant theology of the church in northern Europe and influenced the social and political systems in the Scandinavian countries.

The Reformation had minimal impact on Eastern Orthodoxy. Correspondence between the ecumenical patriarch of Constantinople, Jeremiah II, and the Lutherans took place between 1573 and 1581. The patriarch was interested in learning about this new reformation movement, and in response a group of Lutheran scholars from Tübingen presented him with a Greek translation of the Lutheran Augsburg Confession in 1573. While such a move created an amicable dialogue between the Protestant and the Orthodox churches at the time, the Reformation had no influence on Orthodoxy. The influence of the Reformation on Orthodoxy came in later centuries, indirectly through the establishment of various Protestant churches in countries where the Orthodox Church was dominant.

During the seventeenth century, Russia started to undergo significant social transformation and gain political power. Under Peter the Great (1689–1725), Muscovy became known as Russia. The military modernization and expansion of the fifteenth and sixteenth centuries enabled Russia to push its territories in central Asia into the Black Sea. The use of modern agricultural techniques also enabled the Russians to increase agricultural production, the backbone of the economy at the time. In 1783, Catherine the Great annexed Crimea, which was under the control of the Tatars, into Russia.[12]

Overall, the age of discovery enhanced the power of Europe internally while allowing its major kingdoms to expand into new territories globally. Meanwhile, the Reformation presented a significant transformation in European religious, social, and political life, leading into the modern age as a new political structure known as the nation-state emerged by the 1780s. At the same time, the Islamic Ottoman Empire was expanding its territories inside Europe.

Islamic Dynasties and Expansion During the Age of Discovery

At the end of the fourteenth century, relations between Europe and the Islamic territories, led by the Ottoman Empire, were characterized by political and economic tension as well as territorial rivalries. Encounters that took place during the fifteenth and sixteenth centuries have had significant implications for relations between the two religious communities up until the present day. During the age of discovery and the Reformation era, Europe was transformed economically, politically, religiously, and culturally. In contrast, the Muslim world was experiencing rapid decline starting from the fifteenth century. In the Muslim world, opportunities to challenge traditional social and religious beliefs and structures were limited. Islamic empires maintained military power and trade as their only viable means of expansion.

Muslim societies survived the destructive era of the Mongols (1260–1405) and emerged more powerful militarily than before. By the beginning of the fourteenth century, the majority population from Morocco to northern India were Muslims; nonetheless, significant numbers of Christians, Jews, and adherents to other religions were still living in these territories. From the fifteenth century onward, Islam expanded into Africa as well as central and Southeast Asia, mainly through trade. However, Islamic expansion into Europe faced many challenges, and by the seventeenth century the Ottoman Empire had lost its dominance over eastern Europe as its political power started to decline. In western Europe, the Spanish Reconquista of the Iberian Peninsula in 1492 put an end to Islamic rule.

---

[12]Michael Khodarkovsky, *Russia's Steppe Frontier: The Making of a Colonial Empire, 1500–1800* (Indianapolis: Indiana University Press, 2002).

By the eighteenth century, Islamic territories in Asia and Africa started to experience significant political and economic decline due to internal as well as external challenges. The European domination over strategic ports and trade routes in Asia and Africa presented significant challenges to the political power of these territories while weakening their economy and trade. Meanwhile, internally, many of these communities grew more conservative in their social and cultural settings, eliminating the active participation of other religious traditions in the sociopolitical and economic sectors, resulting in furthering the social and economic decline. During this period, and in spite of the twin cataclysms of the Mongols' devastation at the eastern end of the empire and the Spanish Reconquista at the western end of the empire, three Islamic dynasties emerged to control the vast territories of the Muslim world. The Ottomans dominated over the whole Middle East, North Africa, and parts of eastern Europe, while the Safavids ruled in Iran, and the Mughal ruled India.

THE OTTOMAN EMPIRE

In 1453, the Ottomans took Constantinople, the city that had represented the seat and power of Eastern Christianity since the fourth century. Although its significance and influence had declined since the Islamic invasion of Asia Minor (Turkey) centuries before, the fall of Constantinople to the Muslims posed a significant psychological blow to Eastern and Western Christians. For centuries, Constantinople had been the center of Christian urban life and cultural heritage. No other city in Europe at the time matched the significance or the wealth of Constantinople. Although its population had dwindled through the centuries due to the constant attacks by Seljuk Turks, the city served as a shield for Europe against Turkish armies. The city's name was changed to its current name, Istanbul, and it became the new capital of the Ottoman Empire, securing imperial control over the trade routes from east to west as well as the water routes from the Black Sea to the Mediterranean.

The expansion of the Ottoman Empire. Six years later, in 1459, the Ottoman armies marched through the Balkans, capturing Serbia and establishing an Islamic state in eastern Europe. Many Christian Serbs were massacred by the Ottomans, leading to tension between Christians and Muslims in the Balkans that still marks the relationship between the two communities. A century later, by the 1560s, major parts of eastern Europe including Hungary, Romania, and parts of southern Russia fell under

Ottoman control. Rhodes, Crete, and Cyprus were taken between the 1570s and 1660s. Vienna was captured for two years in 1529 to secure full control over the Hungarian empire.

The expansion of the Ottoman Empire continued to the south and around the Mediterranean. Several battles with the Safavid Sufi order of Iran limited their control over the region, and in the 1470s Mesopotamia (Iraq) was incorporated into the Ottoman Empire. By the early sixteenth century, Syria, Palestine, and Egypt were captured by the Ottomans, putting an end to the Mameluke dynasty in the region. The expansion of the Ottomans continued in the sixteenth century to include all of North Africa, the eastern parts of Arabia including Mecca and Medina, and parts of Iran. By the end of the sixteenth century, the Ottoman Empire was ruling over a territory that extended from Morocco to Iran as well as significant parts of eastern Europe.[13]

One of the Ottomans' major achievements was military power and geographical expansion. The use of cannons and gunpowder made such military superiority a possibility, and the empire's expansion was achieved through bloody wars. Infighting across the region, from Iraq to Egypt to North Africa, resulted in the Ottomans massacring thousands of Muslims. Thousands of Christians were also massacred, particularly in Europe. Rivalry among the ruling sultans was very common, wherein a son would depose his father or kill his siblings to secure his place as sultan. Sultan Selim I (1512–1520) for example, deposed his father and killed all his brothers. The ascendency of a sultan to the throne was achieved after a bloody war between the sons of the former sultan, in which each candidate gathered an army and fought each other until one emerged triumphant. Many Ottoman sultans were involved in wars against other Muslims. While such wars could not be legitimized as jihad against infidels, other reasons, including the labeling of other Muslims as heretics, were used to justify such actions. Meanwhile, the Ottoman sultans reinstated the title of caliph (the Prophet's successor), which was added to the sultan's title in order to gain legitimacy and to secure a strong leadership position among the vast number of Muslim communities under their rule.[14]

---

[13]Colin Imber, *The Ottoman Empire, 1330–1650: The Structure of Power* (New York: Palgrave Macmillan, 2002).

[14]Rhoades Murphy, *Ottoman Warfare 1500–1700* (New Brunswick, NJ: Rutgers University Press, 1999).

The Ottomans ruled over large territories with diverse cultural and ethnic groups. Dealing with the business, trade, social, and religious diversity of the sixteenth and seventeenth centuries necessitated augmenting Islamic religious laws, shari'a, with other local judicial laws and administrative systems. Accordingly, a comprehensive judicial system called *qanoun* was developed, allowing for a creative synthesis between Islamic laws and local customs.[15] The Ottomans also established a comprehensive administrative system called *waqf* ("religious endowment") that controlled Islamic religious institutions while managing the diverse religious groups within the empire. The system ensured governmental control over every religious establishment from mosques to religious schools as well as other social services.[16] The *waqf* system created by the Ottomans is still used in administering religious institutions in many Muslim countries today.

The religious administrative system also included a structure that governed non-Muslims, the millet system (the word *millet* means "sect" or "religious group" in Turkish). The various religious communities were allowed limited internal self-governance according to their own laws, such as family laws that governed marriage, divorce, and inheritance. Each group or millet was also directed by its own religious leader, who was responsible for civil as well as religious matters. The millet system included a host of laws that regulated the process of gaining permission to build churches or synagogues, which was usually granted by the sultan or his representative. Non-Muslims were not allowed to take any higher governmental positions or participate in the army; however, some exceptions were made, as many Christians and Jews held key positions in the court of the sultan, and their expertise was much needed.

The millet system guaranteed the continuation of the Islamic tradition according to which non-Muslims had to pay the poll tax, jizya. As in previous centuries, many non-Muslims across the empire were not able to pay the heavy taxes and had to convert to Islam. The Ottomans were aware of the distinctions and hostilities among religious groups and sometimes discreetly supported one against the other. The Ottomans, for example, supported the Orthodox against the Catholics (due to the long history of hostility between the Turks and Europeans). They also supported the Protestants against the

---

[15]The word *qanoun* means "law" in Arabic. It is derived from the Greek κανών (*kanōn*). The English word *canon* is also derived from the Greek.

[16]Norman Itzkowitz, *Ottoman Empire and Islamic Tradition* (New York: Alfred A. Knopf, 1972).

Catholics in Europe since Protestants eliminated the use of statues and pictures (icons) in worship, a change that was welcomed by the Muslim Turks.[17]

The decline of the Ottoman Empire. By the end of the sixteenth century, Istanbul had a population of over four hundred thousand, double that of London or Paris at the time, with a diverse population of Armenians, Arabs, Berbers, Greeks, Slavs, and Turks. The Ottoman Empire contained the largest multicultural and multifaith population on the planet. The opportunity was ripe for the empire to advance in science, technology, politics, and economy; however, the quality of social life was lacking. While non-Muslims had some key positions in the state, they were restricted socially and religiously. They had to pay heavy taxes, lived as second-class citizens, and were prohibited from joining the military. Meanwhile, Muslim religious leaders challenged every attempt toward religious or social reform. Education suffered, and freedom of speech was almost nonexistent.

The expansion of the Ottoman Empire was evident in its military power. Incorporating Syria and Egypt under the empire provided much-needed agricultural resources. While the Ottomans attempted to make some advances in science, medicine, and mathematics, the ulama's (Islamic religious leaders) control over the social life of the empire hindered progress. In the mid-seventeenth century, when Ottoman bureaucrats tried to introduce the printing press to aid their governmental bureaus, the ulama forced its removal, condemning the use of such technology as contrary to religious piety. It was considered *bida*, an Arabic word that refers to both innovation and heretical religious ideas. In contrast, the printing press facilitated the spread of the Reformation in Europe, leading to significant social and cultural changes across the continent.

By the mid-seventeenth century, it became obvious that the Ottomans were lacking in military techniques, social development, and education. Several attempts to reform the army had failed. Internal unrest and religious strife weakened the central government and accelerated the collapse of its power. As the new generation of sultans did not have the expertise or charisma to lead a large empire, several regions started to break up, claiming their semi-independence from the central government in Istanbul. Economic slumps and social unrest prompted the Ottomans to make an

---

[17]Roy R. Andersen, Robert F. Seibert, and Jon G. Wagner, *Politics and Change in the Middle East: Sources of Conflicts and Accommodation* (Englewood Cliffs, NJ: Prentice Hall, 1982).

irrational move and attack Vienna again in 1683. It seemed like a desperate move to assure the masses that the empire was still powerful and could expand. A coalition of European armies came to the rescue of the city, and the Ottoman army endured a humiliating defeat. Such a miscalculation resulted in further advancement by European armies when Hungary and other parts of the Balkans were taken from the Ottomans, while the Russians moved south to claim territories by the Black Sea.

Fighting between the Ottomans and Europeans continued through the mid-eighteenth century. Europe emerged more powerful militarily and more advanced sociopolitically. Europe's progress was a result of advancements in science and technology, both of which also required quality education and freedom of speech, among other features—which were deeply lacking in the Ottoman territories. While social and religious strife accelerated the disintegration of the sociopolitical structure of the Ottoman Empire, technological advancements in Europe led to an even more stark imbalance of power. As Vernon Egger writes, "Although Western and Eastern Europe developed in quite different ways during the eighteenth century, both regions pulled ahead of the Ottomans in military and economic power by the mid-eighteenth century. The stage was set for a series of catastrophic setbacks for the Ottomans beginning in the second half of eighteenth century."[18]

The Safavid Dynasty of Persia

To the east of the Ottoman Empire, a rival Islamic empire emerged in Persia (Iran). During the fourteenth and fifteenth centuries, an influential Islamic group rose to power in Persia under the leadership of Shi'ite spiritual leader Shayk Safi al-Din (1252–1334). The Safavid movement (named after its founder) emerged on the scene as a rival to the power of the Ottomans. The movement was credited with the transformation of Persian society from Sunni Islam into Shi'ism in a few decades. While the Shi'ite sect of Islam had originated in neighboring Iraq during the seventh century, the Safavids forced Iranian Sunni Muslims to accept Shi'ism instead, making it the state religion.[19]

---

[18] Vernon O. Egger, *A History of the Muslim World to 1750: The Making of a Civilization*, 2nd ed. (New York: Routledge, 2018), 374. See Halil Inalcik, Suraiya Faroqhi, Bruce McGowan, Donald Quataert, and Sevket Pamuk, *An Economic and Social History of the Ottoman Empire*, 2 vols. (Cambridge: Cambridge University Press, 1994).

[19] As noted earlier, Shi'ites believe that the religious and political leader, known as the imam, should be from the Prophet's family or its successors. That is why Shi'ites supported Ali, the Prophet's son-in-law, as the leader of the Islamic community and were called "the partisan" or "the followers

By the sixteenth century, Persia became a Shi'ite empire, a reality that continues to characterize the religious life of Iran. Safavid Persia became a well-established empire during the sixteenth and seventeenth centuries, with a population of six million inhabitants; however, it was much smaller than the neighboring Ottoman Empire, which boasted more than quadruple the number of inhabitants, and the Mughal Empire of India, which had ten times the number of the population of Iran. Despite its small population and smaller demographic territory, the empire was able to stand against these two rival empires that surrounded its borders on each side.[20]

The cultural and religious diversity of the Ottoman and Mughal Empires had no parallel in Safavid Persia. Under the Safavids, Zoroastrians (followers of the indigenous religion of Persia) and Jews suffered the most. Nearly all surviving Zoroastrians had to flee to India, while many Jews were forced to convert to Islam. Christians were able to survive; however, they endured several episodes of persecution. Since the majority of Christians lived in the northwest territories of Persia, many of them were massacred during the wars between the Safavids and the Ottomans. Armenia became the battlefield of many of these wars, and its Christian population suffered heavily.[21]

The Safavid Empire started to decline by the late seventeenth century. Persia, however, maintained its independence from the powerful Ottoman Empire and was never incorporated into its territories. The influence of the Persian culture that had dominated central Asia started to fade and was replaced by the Turkish culture, which was on the rise due to the influence of the Ottoman Turks.

THE MUGHAL DYNASTY OF INDIA

The Arabs introduced Islam to India around 711, the same year Islam came to Spain in the West. The Arabs conquered the area known as Sind in the

---

of Ali" (the Arabic word *Shi'i*). The Sunnis, to the contrary, believe that leadership in the Islamic community can be derived from anyone, not necessarily the Prophet's family. One of the core differences between Sunni Islam and Shi'ism revolves around the role of the Mahdi, the expected imam. The Mahdi is expected to appear sometime in history in order to combat the power of evil and establish a just society. Throughout the history of Islam, the role of the expected Mahdi took on different interpretations and expectations. Some Muslim scholars even attributed the role of the Mahdi to Jesus. Shi'ite Muslims believe that the Mahdi is the hidden Twelver imam who will appear sometime on the world stage to assume such an anticipated political and social role.

[20]Charles Melville, ed., *Safavid Persia: The History and Politics of an Islamic Society* (New York: I. B. Tauris, 1996), 32-35.

[21]Gene Garthwaite, *The Persians* (Malden, MA: Blackwell, 2005), 95-102.

Indus River Valley (Pakistan), and in the following centuries Islam expanded in that region. By the year 1000, as the Abbasid caliphate started to decline, the Arabs recruited and trained slaves (mainly Turks) from central Asia to control the territories under their rule in India. The Turks assumed control over the area, and their rulers were intolerant of other religious traditions, causing significant damage to the indigenous religious cultures of India. Mahmoud of Ghazna, for example, earned the title "the idol smasher" for damaging several Hindu temples, while Ala al-Din was called "the world burner" for his role in burning Buddhist temples. The constant raids and destruction of Buddhist monasteries and temples wiped out Buddhism in India by the twelfth century. Such waves of destruction were only stopped by the coming of the Mongols in the thirteenth century, when Muslim presence in India was confined to smaller territories and their influence over the subcontinent started to fade.[22]

The following centuries witnessed a significant blending of Islamic and Hindu cultures. The climax of such peaceful coexistence took place during the Islamic Mughal dynasty, which ruled over India from 1526 to 1700. The greatest of the Mughal rulers was Akbar the Great (1556–1605), who established a strong and stable state, allowing his three successors—Jahangir (1605–1627), Shah Jahan (1628–1658), and Aurangzeb (1658–1707)—to keep expanding the Mughal realm. The Mughal were well-known for their tolerance of Indian cultures and religious traditions, allowing different religions to coexist peacefully without upholding Islam as a superior religion. Unlike the Ottomans or the Safavids of Iran, the Mughals did not impose Islam as the state religion, and they avoided the development of elaborate bureaucratic structure that regulated the religious life of the masses. India experienced a flourishing of the arts with the fusion of Persian and Hindu styles. The famous Taj Mahal, built by Shah Jahan for his wife, reflects the thriving arts and culture of that era. The subcontinent of India, apart from what is today Pakistan and Bangladesh, was never fully Islamized, considering the large size of its population. The majority still followed Hinduism and other Asian religious traditions.

The later Mughals started persecuting Hindus, banning music and the arts. Such conservative measures resulted in the decline of their dynasty,

---

[22]Richard M. Eaton, *The Rise of Islam and the Bengal Frontier, 1204–1760* (Berkeley: University of California Press, 1993).

which was taken over by the British in the eighteenth century.[23] The three Islamic empires—the Ottomans, the Safavids of Persia, and the Mughal of India—came to an end during the eighteenth and nineteenth centuries.

CENTRAL ASIA

Central Asia, what is today the countries of Kazakhstan, Uzbekistan, Turkmenistan, Kyrgyzstan, and Tajikistan, formed the main trade routes for Eurasian caravans through the centuries. While this massive geographical territory facilitated trade between China and the Mediterranean, its location at the intersection of several large empires resulted in its being a peripheral region with no significant political power. The region was constantly controlled or influenced by other powers until modern times. Before the advent of Islam, central Asian people adopted the cultures and religions of Asia, primarily Hindu and Buddhist traditions. Many were also influenced by the Persian culture at the western end of their territories. From the seventh to the twelfth centuries, several urban cities along the Silk Road adopted Christianity. As the Arabs started their trade business with China, by the eighth century, many central Asian cities along the Silk Road were introduced to Islam through Arab and Persian merchants. During the Mongol dynasty, most of the Christian population was massacred.

The Mongols' control over central Asia in the fourteenth century accelerated the Islamization of the region. By the sixteenth and seventeenth centuries, several Islamic states were established across the region, supported by the Turks, who were originally from central Asia and had been converted to Islam over the centuries. The Turks' control over the Ottoman Empire further accelerated the Islamization of central Asia. Many, however, syncretized their Asian traditional religious beliefs with that of Islam. During the sixteenth and seventeenth centuries, central Asia witnessed a momentous economic decline, and with it came significant social deterioration. Furthermore, when Europeans were able to avoid the traditional Silk Road that connected China with the Mediterranean in favor of using the sea routes around Africa and Asia, many central Asian cities that once boasted economic and cultural prosperity faded into obscurity by the close of the eighteenth century.[24]

---

[23]Susan Bayly, *Saints, Goddesses and Kings: Muslims and Christians in South Indian Society 1700-1900* (Cambridge: Cambridge University Press, 1989).
[24]S. A. M. Adshead, *Central Asia in World History* (New York: St. Martin's, 1993).

From the sixteenth to the eighteenth century, major parts of central Asia came under the influence or control of Russia. After decades of fighting the Mongols in central Asia, China annexed what is today Xinjiang province in 1759. The province, which is located in northwestern China bordering Tajikistan, has one of the largest Muslim communities in China today.[25]

Southeast Asia

Southeast Asia encompasses a large territory that includes the Malayo-Polynesian territories, Indonesia, and the Philippines. Islam was introduced to Southeast Asia by Muslim merchants from Persia, Oman, and India. The intensification of the spice trade during the fifteenth and sixteenth centuries resulted in a commercial surge in the Indian Ocean. Centuries before that, Muslim merchants had full control over trade in the Indian Ocean and were able to establish several posts in Indonesia, Malaysia, and the Philippines. Some Muslim merchants ended up becoming political rulers over these territories, intermarrying with locals and establishing themselves as members of the social strata of those societies.

In the sixteenth century, the Portuguese started their expeditions by establishing a strategic port in the cape of the southern tip of Africa while annexing parts of the western coast of India, establishing a base in Goa, and controlling the province of Kerala in 1510. The Portuguese reached Melaka, Indonesia, in 1511, establishing a port to control the spice trade in the Indian Ocean. They also secured the strategic port of Hormuz in the Persian Gulf. When the Portuguese arrived in Southeast Asia, Islam was firmly established in the region. Their strategy of fighting the Muslims while sacking and destroying well-established cities did not serve their goals well, and by the mid-sixteenth century Portuguese attempts to control the trade routes in the region collapsed. It became obvious that the Portuguese navy could not support dominance over such a large and well-developed area. Anti-Portuguese sentiment in various Indonesian islands resulted in further cooperation between the Muslim and Hindu rulers to push the Portuguese from their territories. Such alliances resulted in further Islamization of the Indonesian islands, where the adoption of Islam became an ideological and nationalistic symbol of resistance. Portuguese efforts to expel Muslims from Indonesia had the opposite effect. Islam spread rapidly from the

---

[25]S. Frederick Starr, ed., *Xinjiang: China's Muslim Borderland* (Armonk, NY: M. E. Sharpe, 2004).

coastal cities into inland territories, where many indigenous Indonesians sympathized with the cause of persecuted Muslims and adopted Islam themselves. Today Indonesia is the largest Muslim nation in Asia.

As Portugal was cutting back its expedition in Southeast Asia, Spain started its own adventures in the region. The Spanish navy was able to control the Philippines in 1565, naming the archipelago after King Philip II of Spain. The Spanish were shocked to find a large number of Muslim inhabitants. Like the Portuguese, the Spanish called the indigenous Filipino Muslims *Moros* or *Moors* (the name is derived from Morocco, describing North African Muslims, with whom Portugal and Spain fought brutal wars). The Spanish expedition to the Philippines took place during the height of fierce clashes between the Ottomans and Spain for control over the Maghrib (Morocco, in North Africa). As a result, the Spanish expedition in the archipelago of the Philippines turned into a mission of Catholicizing the area. In 1571, the Muslim sultanate of Manila was destroyed, and a Spanish settlement was established instead. The Christianization of the Philippines was underway as several Spanish expeditions were sent in the following decades. The Philippines is the largest Christian nation in Asia today. The only remaining substantial Muslim community in the Philippines continued to live in the region of Mindanao.[26]

By the beginning of the seventeenth century, after gaining independence from Spain, the Dutch navy proved to be powerful enough to establish a global trade network. The Dutch marines became the main supplier of sea transport in the North Atlantic. They reached Indonesia in 1596 in an attempt to take part in the lucrative spice trade. In 1602, the United East India Company was established. The company possessed the power to execute political and economic treaties, build fortresses, and wage war in the vast area of the Indian Ocean. In 1619, the company chose Jakarta (the current capital of Indonesia) as its headquarters, and the city became a hub for business and trade. While the main focus of the United East India Company was to control the spice trade, they also allowed some Christian missionaries to operate in the region. The following decades witnessed some bloody encounters between the United East India Company and the natives. The Dutch, however, had managed to control the various Indonesian islands due

---

[26] Anthony Reid, *Southeast Asia in the Age of Commerce, 1450–1680*, 2 vols. (New Haven, CT: Yale University Press, 1993).

to rivalries among local rulers. During the first two decades of the seventeenth century, the Dutch monopoly over trade in Indonesia was seriously challenged by the British, who were operating in the region at the same time through the English East India Company. However, the British focused their trade in India, China, and the Malay islands.[27]

From the mid-sixteenth to the mid-seventeenth century, both Christianity and Islam gained notable presence in Southeast Asia. Catholic missions to the Philippines, parts of Indonesia, and the Malay islands resulted in introducing Christianity for the first time to the region. Meanwhile, the Islamization of the region surged. The Portuguese's brutal treatment of the already established Muslim communities in the region resulted in a significant increase in the number of Muslims, especially in Indonesia. Islam provided a symbol of resistance and made significant gains in the interiors. At the same time, several local Muslim rulers forced the Islamization of large communities in order to defend their territories against Western powers. With the Christianization and Islamization of the region, Hinduism suffered great losses, and the Hindu community was restricted to the island of Bali as well as some surrounding smaller islands.[28]

AFRICA

The Sahara (meaning "desert" in Arabic), the largest and most extreme desert on earth, posed a formidable barrier to the Arab conquest of the seventh and eighth centuries. Until the ninth century, the expansion of Islam in Africa was mainly confined to the Mediterranean coastal plain of North Africa and northern parts of Egypt. The Arabs were stopped in southern Egypt from entering the kingdom of Nubia (southern Egypt and northern Sudan) and were not able to make any advances into Africa through the Nile. Starting from the ninth century, Islamic expansion in Africa happened primarily through trade around the eastern and western coastal shores of the continent. Commercial activities in the Sahara were extremely dangerous, and only a few people were able to venture through the vast desert terrain and shifting sand dunes. Merchants therefore

---

[27]K. N. Chaudhuri, *Trade and Civilization in the Indian Ocean from the Rise of Islam to 1750* (Cambridge: Cambridge University Press, 1990).

[28]Anthony Reid, "Islamization and Christianization in Southeast Asia: The Critical Phase, 1550–1650," in *Southeast Asia in the Early Modern Era: Trade, Power, and Belief*, ed. Anthony Reid (Ithaca, NY: Cornell University Press, 1993), 138-51.

preferred to use the coastal routes in western and eastern Africa, where trade had flourished for centuries before Islam. Starting from the ninth century, Islam was introduced to sub-Saharan Africa primarily through trade.

West Africa. The main item of trade in West Africa was gold, and it is estimated that the region provided over two-thirds of the gold circulated around the Mediterranean (both in Islamic territories and Europe) during the Middle Ages. Arab merchants saw the possibility for significant profit in expanding their trade in West Africa, and while gold was the major commodity, other valuable items such as salt, cocoa, and spices were also part of the trade business. Most of these items needed laborers, and Arab merchants saw an opportunity to work in the slave trade as well, a lucrative trade that provided the labor needed in the fields of Africa as well as in other territories under their control. Arab merchants were involved in the slave trade for centuries before the Europeans, and they continued to play a key role until the nineteenth century. Recent research suggests that between 1530 and 1780, there were around a million slaves traded by the Arabs, and many of them were white Christians from Europe.[29]

One example of early Islam in West Africa was the kingdom of Mali. The first known Muslim king of Mali was Mansa Musa (1307–1336), who made a pilgrimage (hajj) to Mecca with a visit to Cairo en route. He distributed a significant amount of gold to Muslim leaders in both places as an expression of the wealth of his country. One well-known place for Islamic learning and culture was the city of Timbuktu in Mali. Islam expanded from Mali to neighboring Ghana as well as south to northern Nigeria. However, visitors to the West African region in the fifteenth century reported that Islam did not have deep roots in the society, while traditional animistic culture and African religious traditions were dominant. The majority of the population in sub-Saharan Africa were not practicing Muslims.[30] To the west and south of Mali, other Islamic communities started to form in what is today Gambia and Senegal.

A cluster of scattered groups of people known as the Hausa were the main inhabitants of the Sahara. They connected the trade routes between Mediterranean coastal cities such as Tripoli (Libya), Oran and Algiers (Algeria), and

---

[29]Robert C. Davis, *Christian Slaves, Muslim Masters: White Slavery in the Mediterranean, the Barbary Coast and Italy, 1500–1800* (New York: Palgrave Macmillan, 2003), 23.
[30]Nehemiah Levtzion and Ronald Lee Pouwels, eds., *The History of Islam in Africa* (Athens: Ohio University Press, 2000).

Tangier (Morocco) with the inland desert and remote areas. In the sixteenth century, Muslims existed in areas around Lake Chad and were connected through caravan routes with Tripoli in the north. As early as the fourteenth century, various groups of Hausa embraced Islam. One well-known Islamic kingdom in the Hausa territories (northern Nigeria) was the kingdom of Bornou (which is currently a province in northeast Nigeria under the name Borno). Bornou strictly enforced Islamic customs and traditions, which characterized the territory up to today. From the fifteenth century to the seventeenth century, Islam was introduced to other regions in West Africa, in what is today Niger, Guinea, and Gambia. By 1750, the Fulani had full control over large territories in West Africa through jihad wars.[31]

In the fifteenth century, Portuguese expeditions in West Africa interrupted traditional trade routes between the Magrib (North Africa) and West Africa territories. The Portuguese established ports on the coasts of West Africa while sailing inland along the Senegal and Niger Rivers, reaching to the sources of gold, cocoa, and other goods. Such a move, combined with continued internal clashes in these Islamic territories, resulted in significant economic losses as well as political and social decline.[32] The Portuguese were not interested in converting the Muslims they encountered in West Africa. It was not before the late sixteenth century that Catholic missions were established by the Spanish in sub-Saharan Africa. A rare occurrence when the Portuguese established a Christian base in central Africa took place after the Portuguese sailed into the Congo River in 1491, where a couple of local chiefs accepted baptism. A decade later, the Catholic Church was established in Kongo, and what is today Angola, under King Afonso in 1506. Afonso was instrumental in introducing Christianity in the region. He used his grasp of learning Portuguese and Latin to ask the kings of Portugal and popes to send missionaries to his African kingdom.

Soon afterwards, the Portuguese became quite involved in the lucrative slave trade. Prior to the sixteenth century, slavery was one of the main trades that thrived in the region, and thousands of slaves supplied the demands in the Mediterranean basin while others mined the fields of salt, gold, and copper in the area. With the Portuguese control of the coasts of

---

[31]Roland Oliver and Anthony Atmore, eds., *The African Middle Ages, 1400-1800* (Cambridge: Cambridge University Press, 1981).
[32]J. F. A. Ajaye and Michael Crowder, eds., *History of West Africa*, 2nd ed, vol. 1 (New York: Columbia University Press, 1976).

West Africa, they also controlled both the gold and slave trades, establishing several trading posts along the Atlantic Ocean from Senegal to Angola. By the sixteenth century, the Dutch, British, Danish, and French were all involved in the slave trade, which had extended across the Atlantic to supply the working force for the New World. It is estimated that by 1750 more than seventy thousand slaves were sent across the Atlantic annually.[33] Many Africans who were recruited to work in Latin and South America also introduced Islam to the Caribbean islands and South America.

East Africa. The introduction of Islam to East Africa started as early as the eighth century. The Arabs had a long history of trading with Ethiopia (the Abyssinian kingdom; the name is mentioned in the Qur'an several times). However, the Arabs did not invade the Horn of Africa or Ethiopia during the early period of Islam. After the collapse of Nubia (northern Sudan), in the fourteenth century, Christianity was almost wiped out of Nubia, while Islam extended into western and eastern Sudan. (Nubia became a Christian kingdom in the sixth century and boasted a long Christian history and culture until the Mamelukes of Egypt invaded their territories in the fourteenth century and forced the Islamization of the kingdom.) Several nomadic groups who claimed Arab descent controlled significant parts of Sudan, ruling from cities such as Dar Fur and Wadi. The natives were often subjected to the Islamic system of governing, established by rulers who claimed the title *amir al-mu'minin* ("prince of the believers" or caliph) and had little awareness of Islamic religious traditions. These territories were not politically or socially advanced, and their main trade was in slavery. Slaves were brought from what is today central Africa, Chad, and Cameroon to supply slaves to Ottoman Egypt and beyond.

Islam also expanded into the Swahili coast of the Horn of Africa through trade and made its way inland, spreading at the expense of traditional African religions in what is today Somalia, Eritrea, and eastern parts of Kenya. Mogadishu, the current capital of Somalia, was established as an Islamic city-state in the tenth century. Other cities, such as Mombasa, Kenya, and Kilwa, Tanzania, were also established as Islamic city-states along the east coast of Africa. In the sixteenth century, Muslims from Somalia under the leadership of Ahmad ibn-Ibrahim al-Ghazi unsuccessfully attempted to

---

[33] J. E. Inikori, ed., *Forced Immigration: The Impact of the Export of Slave Trade on African Societies* (New York: Africana, 1982).

convert Ethiopia to Islam. Ethiopia pleaded for Portuguese support against the Islamic invasion and has been able to keep its Christian territories primarily inland up until today. However, the Ethiopian territories from the east were constantly reduced due to the creation of Islamic territories in what became Somalia, Eretria, and Djibouti. By the sixteenth century, Mogadishu, Somalia, Mombasa, Kenya, and Dar al-Salam, Tanzania, became hubs of Islamic trade in East Africa.

The Portuguese involvement in Ethiopia was not an isolated event. The Portuguese under Vasco da Gama and others raided many of the coastal cities in East Africa on their way to India. Clashes between the Portuguese and these smaller Muslim city-states accelerated in the sixteenth century, resulting in significant damage to their power and trade. Da Gama was surprised to find Muslim merchants controlling such large territories in the Indian Ocean. Despite the ethnic difference between the Muslims in the Magrib and those of East Africa, he still called them *Moors* or *Moros*. The Ottomans, who were able to capture Egypt and Syria from the Mamelukes earlier in the century, were also interested in securing trading posts along the Red Sea. The Ottomans and the Portuguese often competed for control of cities along the East African coast. By the end of the sixteenth century, as the Portuguese were suffering several setbacks due to their violent attacks on cities across the Indian Ocean, they tried to establish a fortified garrison in the region. In 1593 they sacked Mombasa and established a Portuguese colony. A century later, Omanis became powerful enough to establish their own power in the Indian Ocean. Their fleet was able to force the Portuguese out of East Africa. The Omanis captured Mombasa and Zanzibar and incorporated parts of the East African coast into their empire.[34] Such encounters between Europe and the Muslim world had significant ramifications for Christian-Muslim relationships in the following centuries.

Christian-Muslim Encounters During the Age of Discovery

During the age of discovery, as several European powers aimed at securing trading posts around the coasts of Africa and Asia, they were surprised to find well-established Muslim communities in many parts of the two

---

[34]Michael N. Pearson, *Port Cities and Intruders: The Swahili Coast, India, and Portugal in the Early Modern Era* (Baltimore: Johns Hopkins University Press, 1998).

continents. They were ambivalent about how to relate to Muslims in these vast territories. Given the presence of Ottoman threats at home, along with the hostile history of encounters in previous centuries, the Portuguese and Spanish resolved to fight Muslims and destroy their trading posts across the coastal ports of Africa and Asia. Such practices resulted in intensifying hostility between Europeans and the Muslim communities. The brutal treatment of the already established Muslim communities in those regions resulted in a significant surge in the number of Muslims. Islam provided a symbol of resistance and made substantial gains in the interior. At the same time, several local Muslim rulers forced the Islamization of large communities to defend their territories against Western powers.

While the Reformers were occupied with socioreligious changes taking place on the continent, the Ottomans were expanding their empire into Europe during the sixteenth and seventeenth centuries, generating a tremendous amount of anxiety amid Europeans. The question of how Europe should respond to the military campaigns of the Turks in eastern Europe became increasingly paramount. Luther, for instance, initially did not speak on the topic. But as the Turks advanced up the Danube River basin toward Vienna, and the more he heard about the pope appealing for a Crusade against the Turks, the more he found himself compelled to address the issue. Luther believed that the responsibility of the earthly kingdom, or the secular realm, was to combat threats against its territory and inhabitants. While he supported the concept of a just war in defending Europe, he warned against religious Crusade. He also believed that Christians were facing much deeper issues than physical warfare, and he called for prayer and repentance in combating such threats.

About the time of the second siege of Vienna, Luther viewed the Turkish advancement as an apocalyptic threat, arguing that while the Turks would be successful for a time, their days were numbered. Until then, Christians needed to be aware of and informed about Islam. He was concerned about the fact that many Christians living in the Ottoman Empire eventually became Muslims. He even spent some energy in writing about and inquiring into the theology and culture of Islam for the purpose of equipping Christians on how to respond to its claims. Some of his work was practical and pastoral; his later work was polemical and apologetic. Throughout it all, he remained committed to making as much information as possible on Islam available. This culminated in his involvement in the publication of a Latin translation of the Qur'an in 1543, a work that was included in the first collection of texts relating to Islam ever to be printed.[35]

Conclusion

The age of discovery facilitated European expansion around the globe through various naval expeditions and colonization. This era ushered in enormous wealth and political stability for Europeans while unleashing unprecedented misery for natives, who were exploited by the Europeans. Christian missionary activities resulted in the spread of Christianity to North and South America. The natives of the New World were Christianized, oftentimes by force, while others in Asia and Africa were Christianized through preaching and social services. However, minimal attempts were made to reach out to Muslims during this period.

The Reformation resulted in significant religious as well as social and political transformation in several European societies. It ushered in the beginning of a break from the power and authority of the Catholic Church, reforming its theology, worship, and structural system. The Reformation also facilitated a new atmosphere of intellectual debate and freedom of thought, establishing the foundation for the modern age. One of the significant outcomes of the Reformation was that it enabled people to challenge the sociopolitical status quo, which resulted in further political reforms in the following centuries.

Contrary to Europe's economic gains and political stability during the age of discovery, along with its religious and cultural transformation during the Reformation era, the Muslim world witnessed rapid economic, social, and political decline. The three major Islamic empires at the time—the Ottomans, who ruled over the Middle East, North Africa, and eastern Europe; the Safavids of Iran; and the Mughal of India—either collapsed or weakened significantly by the late eighteenth century. While the Islamic territories doubled in size globally during that period, many suffered from deep economic and political decline due to the increased inclination toward religious conservatism. Muslim communities along the coasts of Asia and Africa were challenged by various European powers, while internal conflicts and lack of social reform resulted in an economic and political downturn.

---

[35] Adam S. Francisco, *Martin Luther and Islam: A Study in Sixteenth-Century Polemics and Apologetics* (Leiden: Brill, 2007).

5

CHRISTIANITY AND ISLAM IN THE MODERN AGE (1750-1910)

Between 1750 and 1910, global Christianity expanded substantially, while Western Christianity in Europe and North America experienced cultural and social changes that created a sharp cultural gap between the West and the rest of the world, including Muslim societies. In the era of modernization, some core Christian beliefs were challenged, leading to an era of secularization where religion was pushed to the periphery in many Western societies. This span of time also saw important advancements in science and technology in the West that were lacking in other parts of the world. Freedom of speech and debate of ideas further challenged the power of the church and even the state in Western societies.

The sociocultural differences between the West and Muslim societies resulted in misunderstanding, frustration, and sometimes hostility. Many outside the Western world were not able to distinguish between Christianity, as a seemingly Western religion, and Westernization, modernization, and secularization. Western culture wove all these threads together, sending mixed messages to the rest of the world. While the modernization and secularization of the West was going full force during the eighteenth and nineteenth centuries, there were also meaningful spiritual revivals in Western Christianity, resulting in one of the most remarkable mission movements in the history of Christianity. Thousands of Europeans and

North Americans extended the faith to areas where Christianity had never been before. Western Christianity was able to balance the seeming contradiction of modernization and secularization alongside religious revivalism and a momentous mission movement. Meanwhile, Muslim societies embarked on their own cultural and sociopolitical developments that were influenced by a combination of conservative and modernized religious and sociopolitical structures. Western Christian societies and the Muslim societies were on different trajectories, laying the foundation for current sociopolitical and cultural outlooks.

The Modern Age

The modern age, which started in the 1750s, saw conscious human efforts to break from religious and social traditions, substantially transforming politics, economics, science, technology, medicine, industry, and culture.[1] Some historians consider the Enlightenment era (1720–1780) to be an early modern period. The enormous shift in European social, political, and intellectual outlook during the modern era did not start in a vacuum. A series of religious conflicts, commonly referred to as the Thirty Years' War (1618–1648), devastated Europe in the early seventeenth century. These religious wars led to questioning the validity of religious disputes and a rejection of religion as the dominant cultural force in society.

Western civilization made a gradual shift to modernity as rational thinking and scientific development reached a momentous apex in the 1790s.[2] The rise of university education, the influence of the classical ideas of the Renaissance, and the Reformation's influence on religion and society all contributed to the creation of the modern age. By the beginning of the nineteenth century, developments in science and technologies spearheaded the Industrial Revolution. Other significant political events, such as the French and the American Revolutions with their emphasis on freedom, justice, and equality for all, contributed to the creation of democratic societies. There was a reciprocal relationship between modernity and

---

[1] The term *modern* was used for the first time in 1585 to describe the beginning of a new era, the European Renaissance (1420–1630). The Renaissance that started in Italy is considered an important transitional era between medieval Europe and the modern age.

[2] In the premodern era, people's understanding of reality, self, and the world around them was primarily expressed through a faith in some form of deity, a single God or many gods. Premodern cultures were governed by traditions that were considered to be sacred. Such traditions usually directed the social life and moral behavior of people.

Christianity, particularly in its Reformed tradition. Reformed Christianity provided a suitable atmosphere for modernity to flourish, while modernity shaped the outlook of Reformed Christianity in the following centuries.

The ideologies of modern philosophers such as René Descartes, John Locke, and Immanuel Kant, along with vital contributions made by modern science, resulted in a powerful intellectual movement, the Enlightenment, which set the stage for modernity. The movement started and was firmly established in western and central Europe by the mid-eighteenth century. The influence of modernity did not affect southern and eastern Europe until the late nineteenth and early twentieth century. The movement flourished where Protestantism was influential in western Europe, since many of its principles resonated with the heart of the Reformation as a call for a change, including challenging religious authority itself.

Enlightenment thinkers affirmed the centrality of rational thinking as key to understanding reality and explaining the world. Kant, for example, criticized ritual practices in the church, superstition, and ecclesiastical hierarchy, asserting that these practices were illogical and unnecessary efforts for worshiping God. He argued that people could adhere to moral values through reasonable and conscientious decisions.[3] Kant's criticism of religious organizations and practices was an attempt to construct a reasonable form of Christianity compatible with rational thinking. The Enlightenment also emphasized the autonomy of the human being, which gave people the capability to discern what was right and wrong morally, with no need for religious principles or sacred scriptures to guide their moral behavior. Human reason was considered capable of discovering and following universal natural laws, which would safeguard against lawlessness.

Based on the Enlightenment's optimistic belief in progress, modernity gave the impression that humanity was progressing not only on the scientific and intellectual levels but also socially and politically. The assumption was that a well-defined democratic system, where all citizens could freely participate in governing themselves, could be achieved. This would eventually lead to a new level of productivity, which in turn would lead to better living conditions for all. Improving social conditions accompanied

---

[3]Immanuel Kant, *Religion Within the Limits of Reason Alone* (1793), IV.1.1. Kant's phrase "dare to know" has shaped the thrust of modernity, in which people are called to examine for themselves every phenomenon rationally and objectively, away from the influence of cultural or religious traditions.

by quality education would also contribute to an improvement in human behavior. The political philosophy of the Enlightenment emphasized the basic rights of all and contributed to the formation of the standards of human rights, including freedom of thought, conscience, and religion. The ideals of modernity were believed to be universal and applicable to all social contexts and cultures.

The utopian world of the Enlightenment, which shaped the culture of modernity in the West during the eighteenth and the nineteenth centuries, came crashing down in 1914 with the start of World War I, and any hope for such a utopian world was completely shattered during World War II. The optimistic views of modernity were replaced by intellectual and cultural gloom in the twentieth century as humanity faced the devastating destruction and the significant loss of life in two world wars. Achievements in science and technology, as well as various political systems, did not result in changing people's moral behaviors.

The Impact of Modernity on Christianity and the West

The ideas of modern thinkers and progress made in scientific research reshaped social, economic, and political life in the West. An emphasis on education resulted in large numbers of people attending universities, gaining access to new ideas as well as opportunities for work. Industrialization and urbanization resulted in creating an individualistic culture wherein people were free to make their own choices away from traditional expectations.

Natural sciences. Development in social and natural sciences as well as philosophical ideals had significant ramifications for Western society in general and Christianity in particular. Many basic Christian beliefs, related to God, the origin and nature of humanity, and the place of the church in society, were challenged. Discoveries made in the natural sciences, for example, challenged the concept of an orderly universe governed by unchanging systems that were established and governed by God. The implication of Albert Einstein's (1879–1950) theory of relativity (1905), that space and time are relative to each other and to the observer, led people to consider religious relativity, the idea that truth is also relative. Charles Darwin's (1809–1882) proposal that plants and animals, including human beings, had evolved from one form of existence to another based on a process of natural selection seemed to contradict the basic belief in creation by God, challenging the biblical affirmation that humans are created in the image of God and therefore are set apart from the rest of the animals. While nineteenth-century criticism of biblical truth, such as questioning the authenticity of the Bible or the divinity of Christ, has been addressed today, some of these ideas still dominate within Western culture.

Modern philosophy. The modern philosophical ideas that arose in the nineteenth century had significant implications for Christianity and the sociopolitical development of Europe. Kant's arguments a century earlier, that reason could not fully comprehend God or metaphysical realities, were replaced by stronger arguments emphasizing that reason should be above any religious claims and that reason alone should be the basis for understanding reality. Later philosophers called for the abandonment of religion altogether. Ludwig Feuerbach (1804–1872), for example, argued that belief in God was simply a projection of human ideals. He contended that people used concepts such as God's mercy, love, and justice simply to describe the moral standards they strived for. Friedrich Nietzsche (1844–1900), well-known for his claim that "God is dead," ridiculed Christians for believing in God and the well-being of all people; for Nietzsche, such ideals were for the weak. Instead, he spoke of the *Ubermensch*, or "superman," the strong human who is capable of dominating over others. Nietzsche commended war and control as the best way forward for mature humanity rather than love and equality. Nietzsche's ideas contributed to the Nazi ideology in Germany that rose to power a few years later along with its consequent horrors.

Among the most prominent and disconcerting philosophical ideas of the nineteenth century were those of Karl Marx (1818–1883), whose work inspired communist revolutions in Russia and China in the twentieth century. Marx rejected religion in its entirety; his famous phrase, "Religion is the opiate of the masses," set the stage for his materialistic ideologies, emphasizing that reality is matter and there is nothing beyond that. For Marx, religion was the main reason for human misery, since people put their trust in a God who ultimately did not exist. Marx argued that human progress could be achieved through a communist society wherein social and economic forces were grounded on material reality. Nineteenth-century philosophy led to diminishing the role of religion within the social fabric of the West, while some of its ideals had disastrous sociopolitical consequences in Europe and the rest of the world.

The progress made in science and the ideologies of modern thinkers had significant ramifications for Western Christianity, its theology, and its institutions. While the reformation challenged the institutionalized structure of the Roman Catholic Church, its theology, and its ways of worship, modernity challenged the basic beliefs of Christianity. Early responses to the Enlightenment critique of Christianity took the form of accommodation. John Locke's *Reasonableness of Christianity* (1695), for example, suggested that the beliefs of Christianity were rational enough to withstand criticism. Later thinkers of the eighteenth century argued that the reasonableness of Christianity was derived from reason, not from revelation, affirming the ability of reason to judge revelation. Liberalism was inspired by the ideal that the human mind is capable of explaining every phenomenon that exists. It was equally motivated by the concept of progress. The ideal that history was progressing resulted in the belief that Western culture had become the most advanced and civilized society.

The liberal theology movement that dominated the European and North American landscape in the nineteenth and early twentieth centuries tried to bridge the gap between Christian faith and modernity. In accommodating the modern culture of rationalism, liberalism abandoned some Christian beliefs (i.e., belief in original sin, miracles, and supernatural beings such as angels and demons) while reconstructing or reinterpreting some other beliefs (the divinity of Christ, the search for the historical Jesus). Liberalism reached its apex in the early twentieth century (the era of the world wars) and continued to influence Western theology all through the twentieth century. It is interesting to note that some contemporary Muslim scholars used the arguments of liberal theology to refute Christian beliefs. They referred to liberal theology's skeptical views of the authenticity of the biblical text and the divinity of Christ as proof that Christians had finally come to agree on what Muslims had argued through the centuries, namely that Christ is not divine, and the Bible has been corrupted.

SIGNIFICANT CHRISTIAN MOVEMENTS DURING THE AGE OF MODERNITY

Excessive reliance on reason during the age of modernity resulted in questioning the absolute confidence in rationalism as a way of interpreting the Christian faith. A significant Christian movement rooted in German pietism and English Puritanism referred to as the First Great Awakening was born in the context of the eighteenth century.

Christian revival movements. The revival movement was characterized by its fiery preaching and passionate responses from audiences. Revivalism was based on the conviction that faith must be rooted in a personal relationship with God, often reflected in a life-changing conversion experience. In response to rationalism, the revival movement affirmed that being truly Christian meant trusting the heart and not only the head, relying on biblical revelation rather than human reason. Under the leadership of John Wesley (1703–1791), George Whitefield (1714–1770), and Jonathan Edwards (1703–1758), the First Great Awakening swept across Great Britain and Britain's colonies in North America between the 1730s and the 1770s. The movement's emphasis on experiencing God in a personal way had remarkable effects on a large segment of American society at the time.

Some historians credited the revival movement in Britain with saving the country from a bloody revolution like that of France, which occurred at the close of the eighteenth century. Religious transformation through preaching and repentance led to creating a relatively stable society in Great Britain, both socially and politically. One notable contribution of the First Great Awakening in the British colonies of New England was that it paved the way for independence from Britain. Revivalism communicated a message of independence from religious authorities; the later generation who grew up in a climate of religious independence started to apply those very same principles to political independence. The mindset was that if a break from the authority of the church could be achieved, a similar break from the authority of the monarchy might be as well. Such attitudes were fully articulated in the words of the United States' Declaration of Independence in 1776.

A Second Great Awakening took place in the last decade of the eighteenth century and flourished in the early years of the nineteenth century across the United States. The movement centered on camp meetings, where people would gather for a week or so to listen to passionate preachers and enjoy a lengthy time of worship and fellowship, resulting in religious and social transformation as people committed themselves to renewed ways of living.

A Third Great Awakening took place in the nineteenth century as several evangelist preachers such as Charles Finney (1792–1875), Dwight L.

Moody (1837–1899), Charles Spurgeon (1834–1892), and others were instrumental in continuing the revival movement across the United States and England.[4] A later development in the movement focused on attending to the social needs of the people along with preaching the gospel message. William Booth (1829–1912) and Catherine Booth (1829–1890) were instrumental in establishing the well-known Christian organization the Salvation Army.

The revival movement presented a valuable alternative to the rationalism of modernization and liberal theology. While large numbers of Europeans and North Americans dismissed the authority of the church and questioned the validity of religion altogether, many others affirmed anew their faith and commitment to living a Christian life of sacrifice and service. It is important to clarify the difference between Christian and Islamic revivalism. In Christianity, revivalism refers to a religious experience of a renewed and committed life, upholding higher moral standards based on deeper understanding of biblical teaching. Islamic revivalism generally refers to committed adherence to religious law, shari'a, being established through Islamic sociopolitical structure.

The Great Century of Christian Mission. While the Enlightenment ideologies were taking hold of Western Christianity, a mission movement that started in the 1790s and continued through the twentieth century was also reshaping Christianity globally. Christian missionaries were active in spreading the gospel message all through previous centuries; however, the nineteenth century is usually referred to as the "Great Century of Christian Mission" because large numbers of missionaries were sent out from the West to every continent.[5] The eighteenth-century revival movement that began in England and the eastern United States influenced a new generation of church leaders and ordinary Christians to commit their lives to spreading the gospel message worldwide. They were motivated by a sense of urgency to evangelize the whole world.

---

[4]Other key leaders, such as Jeremiah Lanphier, who led thousands of people in prayer meetings in New York City, were instrumental in influencing the revival movement. It is reported that in 1858 10,000 businessmen (out of 80,000) used to gather daily for prayer in New York City. There were also several prayer meetings sponsored by the Young Men's Christian Association (YMCA). Nowadays the organization is primarily a secular social organization.

[5]Kenneth Scott Latourette introduced the term in *A History of the Expansion of Christianity*, vol. 4, *The Great Century: In Europe and the United States of America, A.D. 1800–A.D. 1914* (Grand Rapids, MI: Zondervan, 1941), 1-8.

Both Catholic and Protestant missions were sustained by well-organized missionary societies that were able to support such an unprecedented scale of mission ministry. In spite of the fact that after the French Revolution the state eliminated financial support to missionaries, France continued to be the main hub for Catholic missions. By the 1870s more than sixty thousand Catholic missionaries were serving across the globe, and most of them were Catholic nuns serving in hospitals and educational institutions. Protestant churches also founded numerous mission organizations that supported Western missionaries to reach out to millions of people on every continent. Many nineteenth-century missionaries were convinced that "the white man's burden" included preaching the gospel to the "heathen" as well as introducing Western civilization, which was considered superior to other cultures.[6] Thousands of churches were established, the Bible was translated into hundreds of local languages, and numerous hospitals and schools were built, serving millions of people across the globe. By the nineteenth century, three hundred years had passed since the Portuguese and the Spanish introduced Christianity to South America, where various Catholic missions were active in the Christianization of the continent. By the nineteenth century, Protestantism had been introduced to South America through various Protestant missions; however, the vast majority of Latin America remained Roman Catholic.

It is also worth mentioning that a large number of single and married women participated in mission work during the nineteenth century. The contribution made by women was remarkable. In 1890, the American Baptist Missionary Union listed thirty-four women's societies supporting 926 women in mission. Combining those who were single and those who were married, women totaled over 60 percent of the American missionary force.[7]

While several mission organizations were active globally, very few had interest in doing mission among Muslims. Centuries of conflict and misunderstanding between the Muslim world and the West contributed to such hesitation. It is challenging to preach Christianity to Muslims for a

---

[6]Rudyard Kipling first introduced the phrase "the white man's burden" in his poem "Recessional" for the diamond jubilee celebration of Queen Victoria's reign (1837–1901). Later, Kipling wrote "The White Man's Burden" to address the American colonization of the Philippines.

[7]J. N. Murdock, "Women's Work in the Foreign Field," in *Report of the Centenary Conference on the Protestant Missions in the World, Held in Exeter Hall (June 9th–19th), London, 1888*, ed. James Johnson (London: James Nisbet, 1888), 160-68.

number of reasons. Islamic theology criticizes outright basic Christian beliefs in the divinity of Christ, the Trinity, and the trustworthiness of the Bible, among a host of other religious affirmations. Muslims' perception of Christianity is often negative from the start, requiring significant effort on the part of missionaries to change. Add to this the presence of close family and community ties in Eastern/Muslim societies, which makes it hard for Muslims to abandon their religion and culture. As a result, Western mission to Muslims had been limited. However, interest in mission in Muslim lands grew during the eighteenth and nineteenth centuries as various Catholic and Protestant missions provided medical and educational services. Yet many of these Christian organizations ended up redirecting their efforts to convert the Christians living in these Muslim countries to either Catholicism or Protestantism since very few Muslims responded to their efforts.

The Great Century of Christian Mission led to noteworthy expansion of the faith around the globe, where Christians could be found in every continent for the first time in history. It is estimated that by 1910 there were 612 million Christians worldwide, or around 35 percent of the total population of the world.[8]

The Impact of Modernity on the Rest of the World

Outside Europe and North America, the philosophical and scientific ideas of the Enlightenment and modernity had limited influence on sociocultural development around the globe during the eighteenth and nineteeth centuries. Such ideas were introduced to the rest of the world through Western forms of education in the twentieth century. The implications of this cultural disparity were tremendous. While the West experienced social and cultural changes, the rest of the world, including all Muslim societies, lived in what was perceived to be a premodern culture. Religious authority and institutions were not challenged by philosophical or scientific criticism, as was the case in the West. Social transformation in the form of industrialization and urbanization did not occur on a large scale before the twentieth century, and most of the world population enjoyed traditional structures of craftsmanship and family businesses.

---

[8]Todd M. Johnson and Kenneth R. Ross, eds., *Atlas of Global Christianity* (Edinburgh: Edinburgh University Press, 2009), 9.

Concepts of freedom, equality, and progress were gradually introduced by the twentieth century as well, yet questioning or challenging the validity of religion and the authority of the state was limited or unthinkable. Such cultural disparity resulted in misunderstanding, frustration, and sometimes conflicts between the West (which was perceived as predominantly Christian) and the rest of the world, including Muslim societies. The reaction to modernization and Western secularization took different forms starting from the early twentieth century. While some embraced Western modernization as a way forward, others struggled with and rejected such abrupt social and cultural changes, resulting in confusion and even attacks on Western ideas, including an attack on Christianity itself as part of Western thought and culture. Muslim societies struggled with the concept of secularization, which Islam considered unacceptable.

Muslim Encounters with the West During the Eighteenth and Nineteenth Centuries

As noted in chapter four, the three major dynasties that ruled over the world of Islam by the beginning of the eighteenth century were the Ottoman Empire (the Middle East, North Africa, and parts of eastern Europe), the Safavid dynasty of Persia (Iran), and the Mughal dynasty in the subcontinent of India. By the beginning of the eighteenth century, as Europe was expanding its power around the globe, the Muslim world started to experience significant losses both politically and territorially.

The Ottoman Empire. By 1800, the decline of the Ottoman Empire was well underway and only accelerated over the next hundred years. For centuries, Ottoman rulers thought they were more powerful than the West and therefore dismissed Western models of governing and were reluctant to adopt Western modernization. By the eighteenth century, however, such attitudes started to change as it became obvious that the West possessed more advanced military and agricultural techniques. The so-called tulip period (1718–1730) saw changes in terms of seeking out and adopting Western methods of agriculture.[9] Luxurious, French-style palaces were built, and the elite were pursuing education in Western universities, creating a new intellectual atmosphere among the Ottomans.

---

[9]The name of the movement was derived from the Ottoman interest in importing tulips for their gardens.

Later in the century, Ottoman caliph Selim II (1789–1807) attempted to reform the military and judicial systems. While he made some progress, religious authorities pushed back against his attempts. Selim II faced threats even from his own government officials, some of whom opposed his policies as anti-Islamic. While some Western-style institutional structures were adopted in the Ottoman Empire, no genuine changes occurred in the social fabric of society. For most of the nineteenth century, the Ottoman Empire had to defend itself against European powers that were competing to control the Middle East and North Africa. The collapse of the Ottoman Empire by the beginning of the twentieth century resulted in a massive bloodbath and much destruction to the region.[10]

Egypt. One of the most significant encounters between Europe and the Ottoman Empire occurred in 1798 when the French navy, under the leadership of Napoleon, managed to take over Egypt, the most strategically important country in the Middle East. Napoleon's invasion of Egypt destroyed the Mameluke power that had ruled Egypt for over three centuries under loose Ottoman control. In securing his presence in Egypt, Napoleon invaded Palestine and Syria, though the Ottoman forces halted his advancement while the British navy attacked the French fleet in Alexandria. Facing significant revolts from inside Egypt, Napoleon ended his mission and withdrew from Egypt in 1801.

The brief French presence in Egypt was remarkable. On one hand, it gave advance warning to the Ottomans of what was coming in the following decades—increased European interest in Middle Eastern affairs. It also became obvious that European military power, techniques, and organizational skills were superior to those of the Ottomans and their allies. On the other hand, the short-lived expedition of the French in Egypt restored to Egypt its long and prominent history going back to the Pharaonic era. The discovery of the Rosetta Stone in Damietta as well as other significant archaeological discoveries linked Pharaonic Egypt with its Hellenistic history and civilization, which predated Islam.

On the political level, the French invasion of Egypt resulted in Egypt's semi-independence from the Ottomans under the leadership of Muhammad Ali (1805–1849). Realizing the need for significant reform in

---

[10]Carter Findley, *Bureaucratic Reform in the Ottoman Empire: The Sublime Porte 1789–1922* (Princeton, NJ: Princeton University Press, 1980).

Egypt, Muhammad Ali started modernizing the army and building a new infrastructure in the country. In previous centuries, any attempts for social reform were met with resistance from religious authorities, preventing any major social or political reform. However, under the leadership of Muhammad Ali, Egypt achieved reasonable military, industrial, and agricultural reforms. In the 1830s Muhammad Ali challenged the Ottomans by annexing Syria and invading Anatolia. However, the British put a stop to his military ambitions in the 1840s, and the Egyptian armies were forced out of Syria.[11] In 1882, the British forces took control of Egypt to protect their interest in the Suez Canal, which shortened the distance between England and India by over four thousand miles. While British Prime Minister William Gladstone assured the British that England had no intention of occupying Egypt and that its mandate was to protect the financial interest of Britain, British troops did not leave Egypt until 1956.[12]

Lebanon, Syria, and Iraq. Similar patterns of European colonization of the Middle East followed in Lebanon, Syria, and Iraq. Inspired by Western movements of independence, the Maronite Christians who formed the majority of the Lebanese declared Lebanon a republic in 1858. For centuries under Ottoman rule, the Druze (a sect of Islam), Sunni Muslims, and the majority Maronite Christians endured periodic times of tension related to their religious identity. According to the new political reforms in the Ottoman Empire, all non-Muslims theoretically enjoyed protection as well as rights similar to those of the Muslim majority. However, declaring a Christian republic in the land of Islam did not sit well with the Ottomans. A large-scale religious clash ensued wherein thousands of Maronite Christians were massacred by the Turks. In 1860, the French landed troops in Lebanon under the pretext of helping the Ottomans calm the situation. The republic of Lebanon was confined to the mountainous region, where a Maronite Christian was appointed as the general governor, while the Ottomans maintained a presence in the coastal area of the country. A few years later, the Ottomans were pushed completely out of Lebanon as the French took military and political control of the country. By the beginning of the twentieth century, Syria and Lebanon were under French control, while Iraq, Iran, and Palestine were under British control.[13]

---

[11]P. J. Vatikiotis, *The History of Egypt from Mohammed Ali to Mubarak*, 4th ed. (Baltimore: Johns Hopkins University Press, 1991), 49-69.
[12]Vatikiotis, *History of Egypt*, 169-88.
[13]William Harris, *Lebanon: A History 600-2011* (Oxford: Oxford University Press, 2014), 235-65.

North Africa. The French interest in North Africa (Tunisia, Algeria, and Morocco) became obvious during the period of the Napoleonic wars (1800–1815). Many European bankers and merchants were involved in various trade businesses in North Africa. When many of these trade agreements were disregarded by both sides, tensions started to rise. In 1830 the French seized the port of Algiers after one of these disputes. In the following decades there were significant conflicts between the French troops and the Algerian resistance movement. The situation escalated to a full occupation of Algeria in 1834. Some analysts think the ultimate reason behind this costly occupation was King Charles X of France's own political agenda. Charles X came under severe criticism from his bourgeoisie, who were demanding governmental reform. The occupation of Algeria was a way of distracting the French at home while seeking opportunities to expand the French economy.

In 1881, in a move to curb Italy's interest in taking over Tunisia, France declared Tunisia a French protectorate. By 1911, Morocco came under French and Spanish control. Italy hoped to join the elite club of European nations that possessed land overseas. However, the choices on the southern Mediterranean coast of North Africa were limited; the only country left was Libya. In 1911, Italy invaded Libya and annexed the country with the hope that it would provide an opportunity for Italians who were seeking to immigrate to a new land. More than half a million Italians had immigrated each year of the first decade of the twentieth century. The result of these European annexations was that by 1912 the Ottoman Empire had lost its grip on all of North Africa and the Middle East.[14]

By the end of the nineteenth century, it was obvious that the Ottomans were losing territory everywhere. However, the losses had actually started more than a century earlier. After a high point in the sixteenth century, the Ottomans' failure to keep pace with social and military advancement in Europe proved disastrous. The Russians defeated the Ottomans in a war that lasted from 1768 to 1772. The humiliating treaty of 1774 gave Russia access to the Black Sea and other political privileges over the Ottomans. In the following century, the Ottoman Empire was regarded as the "sick man of Europe." While Russia was aiming at destroying the Ottomans and

---

[14]Philip C. Naylor, *North Africa: A History from Antiquity to Present* (Austin: University of Texas Press, 2015), 245–79.

seizing portions of their empire to the south of Russia, western European powers were willing to defend the Ottoman Empire to curb Russian ambition in the region since the Ottomans were no longer a military threat to Europe.

Greece. In 1821 Greece gained independence from the Ottomans. Independence was achieved after bloody wars in which thousands of Christians and Muslims died. The agreement reached between Greece, backed by European powers, and the Ottomans resulted in exchanging thousands of Muslims and Christians between the two countries. Christians living in what is today Turkey were sent to Greece, while Muslims living in Greece were sent to Turkey. In 1783 Russia annexed Crimea, forcing its majority Tatar inhabitants to flee to Ottoman territories. The Crimean War of 1853–1856 between Western powers and Russia halted Russian expansionist ambitions in Europe (similar to the 2012 annexation of Crimea and the recent tension between Russia and Western Europe). Subsequently, Russia annexed additional territories around the northern coast of the Black Sea. For most of the nineteenth and early twentieth centuries, European powers were competing to secure trade routes and control over world resources. The British, for example, cooperated with the Ottomans against the French, while the British and the French cooperated with the Iranians against the Russians.[15]

The Balkans. The Ottoman losses in the Balkans provide important background for understanding the conflict in the region that erupted in the late twentieth century. During the 1870s, Russia endorsed the principle of pan-Slavism, with the goal of promoting the cultural unity of the Slavic people as well as securing its own political power in the Balkans. The Serbs were passionate about the concept, which ignited the dream of resurrecting their medieval empire. The weak Ottoman administrative system in the Balkans led to significant uprisings in the region due to heavy taxation and lack of resources. The frustration with the Ottomans spilled over into attacks against Muslims. For the next decade or so, clashes between Christians and Muslims in Serbia and Bosnia resulted in intervention from European powers to prevent the Ottoman army from killing Christians in the region.

Meanwhile, similar tensions were taking place in Bulgaria, where nationalists inspired by pan-Slavic ideology started killing Muslims. Again,

---

[15]John Baddeley, *The Russian Conquest of Caucasus* (Richmond, UK: Curzon, 1999).

the Ottoman intervention to save Muslims resulted in the deaths of thousands of Christians and Muslims. The situation was aggravated by European intervention when more than a quarter million Muslims were massacred in what European newspapers described as the "Bulgarian horrors." As a result, Russia forced the Ottoman sultan to sign a treaty in 1878 to halt any intervention in the Balkans. The treaty alarmed western Europe as to Russia's motivation to curb the Ottoman Empire. Another treaty between Russia, Britain, Germany, and Austria was signed in Berlin in 1878, which resulted in granting Bulgaria, Romania, Serbia, and Montenegro independence from the Ottomans while giving Austria administrative responsibilities over Bosnia and Herzegovina. According to this treaty, the Ottomans lost all their territories in eastern Europe. The treaty also resulted in a new cycle of tension between Christians and Muslims in the Balkans as well as other territories in the Ottoman Empire.[16]

The Ottomans' hostility toward the British and the French became increasingly evident as they continued restraining Ottoman territories by the early twentieth century. Meanwhile, Germany was developing its own military power and naval forces, which alarmed both France and Britain. The Ottomans seized the opportunity and looked to Germany for help. Germany became the only European investor in the Ottoman Empire. A new political relationship between the German chancellor, Kaiser Wilhelm II (1888–1918), and the Ottoman sultan, Abdulhamit, was cemented. Internally, however, the sultan was losing grip over his power. The continued losses of Ottoman territories, combined with financial crises and accelerated unrest within the empire, prompted a military group called the Young Turks to seize power in a coup in 1908. The Young Turks, who came from the military cadet, formed the Committee of Union and Progress, which took full control over the fragile Ottoman Empire a year later. The group desired to modernize the empire in line with European models; however, their relationship with western Europe turned into one of continuous frustration and hostility as Europe implemented full control over the territories that formerly comprised the Ottoman Empire.[17]

Persia (Iran). The collapse of the Safavid dynasty of Persia (Iran) in 1722 at the hands of the Afghans gave Russia the chance to expand its

---

[16]Justin McCarthy, *The Ottoman Turks: An Introductory History to 1923* (London: Longman, 1997).
[17]Donald Quataert, *The Ottoman Empire, 1700–1922* (Cambridge: Cambridge University Press, 2000).

territory in central Asia, extending its borders to the Caspian Sea. The Qajar dynasty (1779–1925), which came to power fifty years after the fall of the Safavid Empire, was able to secure the current borders of modern Iran in 1795, establishing Tehran as its capital. By the 1850s, two major European powers, England and Russia, pulled Iran into the arena of Western political conflicts. The Russian annexation of Georgia and other territories in central Asia alarmed the British, who offered their help to Iran against the Russian threat. The second half of the nineteenth century saw much intrigue between the British, Russian, and French as they entered into various agreements related to their roles in Iran, while the shah of Iran attempted to play off one power against the other to maintain the sovereignty of his nation. Overall, while Iran was not immune to the reach of European commercial interests during the eighteenth and nineteenth centuries, it did not experience full-scale military control from the West until 1907, when Russia and Britain reached an agreement to divide Iranian territories among them. The Anglo-Russian Convention of 1907 was reached to counter the increasing German threat in the region. Britain was willing to cooperate with Russia against Germany since Russia presented less of a threat than Germany at that time. However, in 1917 Britain took full control of Iran in response to the Russian Revolution.[18]

The Russian interest in securing territories in central Asia for economic gains frequently provoked British reactions in an attempt to halt the Russian advance. Nevertheless, Russia was able to annex several territories in central Asia in the later part of the nineteenth century—what is today Kyrgyzstan, Kazakhstan, Turkmenistan, and Uzbekistan. The majority of the inhabitants of these territories were Muslims. Later on, these territories were incorporated into the Soviet Union. The Russian move to exercise power over Afghanistan in the 1870s resulted in a full takeover by the British in order to protect their presence in India.[19]

Iranian society maintained a Shi'ite Muslim majority for centuries. Traditionally, the Shi'ites opposed any secular form of government based on their belief that the betrayal of Ali (the son-in-law of Prophet Muhammad and the legitimate leader of Islam according to Shi'ism) gave rise to a series of illegitimate rulers. Shi'ites believe that the clergy have a

---

[18]Ann K. S. Lambton, *Qajar Persia* (Austin: University of Texas Press, 1987).
[19]Edward Allworth, ed., *Central Asia: 120 Years of Russian Rule* (Durham, NC: Duke University Press, 1989).

responsibility to ensure that the country is run according to Islamic principles, aligning any secular laws with Islamic ones. The Shi'ite political system requires the creation of a specialized hierarchy of religious authority that controls the state, the current political system of Iran. This political arrangement differs from the Sunni system, which does not require the involvement of religious authorities in politics. Although during the Qajar dynasty in Iran there were several bloody conflicts internally, the religious leaders of Iran grew stronger. They controlled a significant portion of the land and demanded the implementation of Islamic rules in social life and the judicial system. Therefore, the Qajar shahs were limited in their abilities to enact any social reform in Iran.[20] At the same time, the divide between Shi'ite Iran and the Sunni Ottomans increased the divide between the two sects, resulting in further tension in the region.

Asia. The collapse of the Mughal dynasty in south Asia created a vacuum of power that was swiftly filled by European ambition in the region. Due to several trade agreements and wars, the British East India Company had control over one-third of the subcontinent of India in 1850, while the rest of the subcontinent was indirectly controlled by the British through the collaboration of various smaller states whose leaders were willing to accept British rule. The territories under British control included vast numbers of Muslims in India as well as what is today Pakistan and Bangladesh. British rule over India brought significant social and political changes while establishing a British-style administrative and judicial system.

Many Muslim leaders reacted against these changes; some considered the territories under the British rule an area of Dar al-Harb ("abode of war"), which ought to be fought against, in contrast to Dar al-Islam ("the house of Islam"). Others called for the application of shari'a law or an independent Islamic state in which other religious traditions could be restricted—a dream that came true a century later when Pakistan was created as an Islamic state. However, such calls were met at the time with flat rejection from the British rulers, and revolts ensued, resulting in causalities among Muslims, Hindus, and Sikhs, who were often fighting the British as well as clashing with one another.[21]

---

[20]Hamid Algar, *Religion and State in Iran, 1785–1906: The Role of the Ulama in the Qajar Period* (Berkeley: University of California Press, 1980).
[21]Peter Hardy, *The Muslims of British India* (London: Cambridge University Press, 1972).

By the beginning of the nineteenth century, the British East India Company extended its trade business as well as its military control to China and from there to Southeast Asia. According to the Treaty of London in 1824, the Dutch had full control over what is today Indonesia after several wars, and the British extended their control over the Malay Peninsula, including what is today Malaysia and Singapore. Britain was able to reach an agreement with the king of Siam (Thailand) to annex a substantial segment of his country that was primarily Muslim-ruled territories and incorporated them under the British protectorate of Malaysia. The Malay Muslim sultans found themselves in a situation where they had to deal with both the British and their Chinese clients, both of whom were controlling trade and businesses in their land. While European trading companies profited massively from their trade business, their presence throughout vast Asian territories eventually weakened the economies of these Asian regions.[22]

By the close of the nineteenth century, the United States was keen to expand its power in Southeast Asia. The American interest in claiming the Indonesian territory of Aceh was met with swift action by the Dutch, who were able to gain full control over Aceh as well as every other island in the archipelago including Irian Jaya or western New Guinea through several wars. America, however, saw a prime opportunity to grab the Philippines from Spain. Taking advantage of several revolts against the Spanish, the Americans portrayed themselves to the Filipinos as a liberator from "Spanish tyranny." To the Filipinos' shock, the Americans reached an agreement with Spain to purchase the islands instead. The most furious struggle against the American occupation of the Philippines took place in the Muslim territory of Mindanao, whose inhabitants violently resisted the American plan to be incorporated in a Christian Philippines.[23] This conflict still ravages the relationship between the current Filipino government and the province of Mindanao, which demands full independence. Overall, the Muslim domination over Southeast Asia was severely challenged by the European and the American powers that technically controlled the whole region.

---

[22]Peter G. Riddle, *Islam and the Malay-Indonesian World: Transmission and Responses* (Honolulu: Hawai'i University Press, 2001).

[23]Nicholas Tarling, ed., *The Cambridge History of Southeast Asia*, vol. 2 (Cambridge: Cambridge University Press, 1992).

Africa. By the early nineteenth century, demand for various African products needed for industrialization necessitated an approach to Africa different from exchanging goods for slaves. By 1862, trade in the delta of the Niger River became so valuable for Britain that it declared the port of Lagos a British colony. The British advanced to the interiors, claiming territories around the Niger River in what is today Nigeria while controlling the Gold Coast (Ghana). The move by the British fueled the French aspiration to establish a large African empire of its own. The last two decades of the nineteenth century saw the incorporation of most of the West African coast from Senegal to Mali along with Gabon under French colonial rule as well as controlling the inland region north of Lake Chad.

French and British ambitions in West Africa were met with many challenges, primarily from jihadi Muslims who had been operating in the region for decades.[24] The form of traditional Islam that was introduced to northern Nigeria during the fourteenth and fifteenth centuries continued to heavily influence the sociocultural life of the region through the eighteenth and nineteenth centuries. In 1804, Uthman dan Fodio, a Fulani traditionalist Muslim, established the Sokoto caliphate, enforcing jihad against infidels. The brutal implementation of enforced jihad resulted in the destruction of many villages and significant loss of life. These jihadi movements in northern Nigeria were so powerful that it took the British several decades to enter the Sokoto caliphate. During the nineteenth century, the heavy Islamization of the north was due in part to the fact that Christianity was making significant gains in southern Nigeria.

The British desire to control East Africa also came to fulfillment in the same time period as Zanzibar, Uganda, and East Africa (Kenya) were declared British protectorates, while Egypt and Sudan had been captured earlier. The French reacted by annexing parts of the Horn of Africa and French Somaliland (Djibouti), while Italy colonized Eretria as well as sharing Somalia with Britain. Germany took over Tanganyika (Tanzania) and German southwest Africa (Namibia). Belgium colonized the Congo, while Portugal maintained its territories in East and West Africa in what is today Angola and Mozambique. By 1920 all of Africa apart from Ethiopia and Liberia was under European control.[25]

---

[24]J. Spencer Trimingham, *A History of Islam in West Africa* (Oxford: Oxford University Press, 1962), 193-224.
[25]R. W. Beachey, *History of East Africa, 1592-1902* (London: I. B. Tauris, 1995), 167-89.

Religious Conservatism and Modernization in the Muslim World

In contrast to the intellectual-scientific development that resulted in significant social and political transformation in the West (Europe and North America) during the age of modernity, Muslim societies descended into a spiral of political and social decline. While several attempts at modernization in the Muslim territories during the modern age were tried, they never achieved their potential due to constant resistance from religious leaders, challenges from the masses, and widespread political and economic corruption. To understand the dynamics between the West and the Muslim world during the modern era, it is imperative to reflect on some sociopolitical movements that influenced the Muslim world during that time.

The Ottomans. During the *tanzimat* ("reorganization" in Turkish) period (1839–1876), the Ottomans attempted to modernize the military and build advanced infrastructure in the empire. They also set out to secularize the educational and judicial systems. The Ottomans opted for a secularized educational system not based on religious ideologies often adopted by religious schools or madrassas. It introduced secular laws in addition to religious laws (shari'a), applying the secular laws to non-Muslims. However, most of the ulama (religious leaders) were antagonistic to the new judicial and educational plans. While the new system created modernized secondary schools where subjects such as mathematics, the sciences, and liberal arts were taught, the ulama continued to control primary education and insisted on teaching the Qur'an and the hadith as required topics for proper education. Several governmental bureaucrats used the introduction of *tanzimate* for their own interests, attempting to centralize authority in their own hands and weaken the power of the sultan. Many Ottomans were not pleased with the *tanzimat* reform as they thought it substituted Islamic shari'a for a secular legal system.

In 1876, the Ottomans introduced a European-style national constitution to govern the empire, the first of its kind in the Muslim world. A year later, in 1877, an Ottoman parliament was formed, following the European model of governance. However, when criticism mounted to a real threat to Sultan Abdulhamit II's (1876–1909) grip on power, he seized the opportunity and canceled the constitution while dissolving the parliament. He clung to the familiar title of caliph, referring to himself as the successor of the Prophet, which resonated better with the Muslim masses than holding to the European-style constitution and Western parliamentary system. Modernization never came to fruition, and the empire continued with its traditional socioreligious structure. Helmuth von Moltke, a Prussian general appointed by the late Ottomans to modernize the army, expressed deep concern about how traditional religious views had influenced the empire's sociopolitical structure.[26] During the same period, bubonic plague raged unchecked throughout the Ottoman Empire well into the nineteenth century, two hundred years after the last major outbreak in Europe, because the ulama insisted it was not a matter of hygiene or quarantine but of God's will. The predominance of the ulama and the absence of a literate print culture of the kind that sparked the Reformation in Europe enabled the Muslim clergy to maintain their monopoly over culture for far longer than their European counterparts.

One of the most disturbing developments that took place during the *tanzimat* period came as a result of introducing a modernized legal system wherein non-Muslims, mainly Christians, were granted rights similar to those of Muslims. In light of how Muslims were treated by Europeans in the territories lost by the Ottoman Empire in eastern Europe, Ottoman Muslims could not come to terms with such a proposal, believing that such terms were in direct violation of shari'a. Muslims were furious with the way Europeans highlighted the massacre of Christians by Muslims while ignoring the massacre of Muslims by Christians. The loss of territory across the Ottoman Empire resulted in sending thousands of Muslim refugees to Anatolia, adding to the anger of Muslims who were ready for revenge. Armenian Christians suffered the most from these internal tensions.

Armenians enjoyed a special place in the Ottoman Empire, in which many held high-ranking governmental positions. Armenians were known for their skilled professions, which gave them a special social status; many were rich merchants, while others occupied professional jobs in finance and education. Their success and above-average wealth generated resentment among the Ottomans. Meanwhile, in the 1870s, when Russia defeated the Ottomans and carved out significant territories in the north, some Armenians aided Russia, whom the Ottomans considered their archenemy. Some Armenians went even further, demanding an independent Armenian state. Such demand angered the majority Muslims, who were still reeling from the

---

[26]Findley, *Bureaucratic Reform*.

significant losses of Ottoman territories in the Balkans to Christians in Europe. What seemed to be a promising future for the Armenians by the late nineteenth century ended up in horror. In 1894, when a group of Armenians defended themselves against Kurdish attacks in eastern Anatolia, the Ottomans responded by massacring thousands of Armenians in the territories. In the following two years, 1895–1896, when Armenians held peaceful demonstrations in Istanbul demanding equal treatment, the Ottomans responded by killing around three hundred thousand of them. The horror of these massacres was just a prelude of what was coming in the next two decades.[27]

Persia (Iran). In neighboring Persia (Iran), the Qajar shahs enacted a few reforms. They started by modernizing the military, building a new military academy and replacing the tribal warriors that formed much of its army. A few government officials and intellectuals called for educational and legislative reform; however, their aspirations were challenged by the ulama, and some were even assassinated. The Qajar shahs seemed unable to see the need for reform, resulting in economic and political stagnation, and Qajar Iran plunged into another cycle of religious unrest. After Russia defeated Iran in 1828 and the British in 1838, the economy collapsed, while the country was plagued with famine and disease. Then, in 1843, the Ottomans murdered five thousand Shi'ites in one day in the city of Karbala, Iraq (a holy site in Shi'ism). When Qajar Shah Muhammad (1834–1848) did not respond to the brutal killings carried out by Sunni Ottomans, the Shi'ites were left with a feeling of helpless outrage. Against the backdrop of such events, Shi'ites started reviving the idea of the return of the hidden imam, the one who would set the world on the right path of justice. The time was ripe in 1844, which corresponded to the year 1260 in the Islamic calendar, marking a millennium since the disappearance of the hidden imam in the year 260 according to the Shi'ite calendar. The world seemed like it was collapsing politically, socially, and economically, and thus it was time for a religious breakthrough.

In 1844, a young merchant from Shiraz, Iran, Sayyid Ali Muhammad, declared he was the *bab* ("door" or "gate" in Arabic), which meant, according to Shi'ism, that he would have a special access to the hidden imam. Later he announced that he was the hidden imam himself. He was

---

[27]Halil Inalick and Donald Quataert, eds., *An Economic and Social History of the Ottoman Empire, 1300–1914* (Cambridge: Cambridge University Press, 1994).

able to gather significant followers, calling for religious purification and a boycott of European trade. The royal family, wealthy Iranians, and clergy became weary of the movement; the hidden imam was arrested, tried for heresy, and executed in 1850. The followers of the hidden imam were severely persecuted and tortured, and thousands of them fled the country. The movement was revived through another figure, Baha'ullah, who fled to Iraq and announced that he was the hidden imam. He started a new sect called Baha'i, based on the universality of all religions and the brotherhood of all humanity. The sect was condemned as heretical by mainline Islam.[28]

The Iranian shah, Nasi al-Din (1848–1890), attempted a new program of reform. He structured the treasury based on a European-style model whereby he granted concessions to several European companies and individuals in order to build the necessary infrastructure. Some of these concessions resulted in technically selling the Iranian economy to Europeans. Many intellectuals and clergy members were alert to such developments and started several revolts during the second half of the nineteenth century, resulting in the cancellation of many of these concessions. The last and most significant of these revolts, known as the tobacco riot, had far-ranging implications for the future of Iran. Members of the clergy became extremely powerful and were able to mobilize the masses against the government in 1906, weakening the power and legitimacy of the Qajar dynasty. (The clergy were also responsible for toppling the Pahlavi dynasty in the 1979 Iranian Revolution.) While the Qajar dynasty limped along until 1925, its power was significantly weakened by the clergy and their supporters. In 1906, a new constitution was introduced, and a consultative assembly formed; however, no significant cultural reform came about.[29]

Arabia. One noteworthy conservative movement in Islam started during this period in al-Hejaz, western Arabia, what later became Saudi Arabia. A former Sufi teacher, Muhammed ibn Abdel Wahhab (1703–1792), under the influence of the strict Sunni Islamic Hanbali school of law, started one of the most influential Islamic conservative movements. He called for the purification of Islam from evil innovations, which he believed were responsible for the weaknesses of the Ottoman Empire. His

---

[28] Algar, *Religion and State.*
[29] Abbas Amanat, *Pivot of the Universe: Nasir al-Din Shah Qajar and the Iranian Monarchy, 1831–1896* (Berkeley: University of California Press, 1997).

extreme puritanical reforms called for opposing all forms of folk Islam and severely criticized Sufism and its spiritual orders. He denounced most Muslims as infidels or idolaters who had to be fought against. With the support of a local ruler, Ibn Saud, who was converted to the movement, the Wahhabi started demolishing Islamic shrines in the Hejaz and killing thousands of those who resisted them. The Ottomans saw a political danger in the increased influence of the movement and sent an Egyptian army in 1811 and 1818-1820 that suppressed the movement and pushed it to the interior of Arabia. However, the movement resurfaced in the beginning of the twentieth century with the support of the house of Saud and was able to integrate most of Arabia under its control. The movement laid the foundation for the conservative socioreligious and political structure of contemporary Saudi Arabia.[30]

West Africa. During the sixteenth and seventeenth centuries, various powerful jihadi groups started to flourish in the West African nations of Senegal and northern Nigeria. They called for the application of Islamic shari'a and for the purification of society from non-Islamic traditions that dominated the African landscape. They were alarmed by the way many Muslim rulers enslaved other Muslims in their territories while not adhering to Islamic laws and religious principles. Some of them were charismatic preachers such as Uthman dan Fodio (1754-1817), the founder of the Sokoto caliphate in northern Nigeria. He called on Muslims to follow Qur'anic prescriptions regarding food and modesty. He preached against a host of African customs such as divination and the use of magic, and even against dancing and music. Fodio had a great number of followers and was able to establish a strong Islamic state, of which he appointed himself caliph. Others, such as Seku Ahmadu of Nigeria (1773-1845) and Al-Hajj Umar Tal of Senegal (1797-1864), were powerful jihadis who called for strict application of Islamic laws, established mosques and Islamic schools in their respective territories, and subjected non-Muslims to harsh treatment.

Sudan. By the end of the nineteenth century, Egypt extended its rule over Sudan, while the British controlled both Egypt and Sudan. Concerned with the modernization that was taking place in Egypt as well as Egyptian ambition in Sudan, a new political/religious leader under the

---

[30] Alexei Vassiliev, *The History of Saudi Arabia* (London: Saqi Books, 2000).

title Mahdi emerged as the political savior of Sudan. The figure of the Mahdi (meaning "the guided one") has a religious meaning similar to that of the expected hidden imam. The Mahdi is believed to appear on the world scene in order to establish justice in society and to rule according to shari'a. The Sudanese Mahdi appeared during a time of upheaval and later appointed his own caliph in an open display of disapproval of the current Ottoman sultan as being an unfit caliph. The ideology of the Sudanese Mahdi found support across the Muslim world; however, his disparagement of the Ottomans led to the movement being crushed by the British in the 1890s.[31]

The effects of intellectual retreat across the Muslim world were profound. The various Islamic movements of the eighteenth and nineteenth centuries appeared during a time of social, political, and cultural upheaval. Their leaders provided the necessary charisma needed to mobilize the masses against political chaos while promising a better political and social future. These movements adopted a restitutionist outlook, portraying their mandate as restoring the original purity of Islam with the ultimate goal of solving the socioreligious problems of their societies. Such trends continued and even mushroomed in the twentieth century. But in contrast to the role played by the Reformation in Europe and modernity's contribution to social transformation in the West, these movements did not contribute to noteworthy changes in Islamic societies.

Islamic Reformers During the Modern Age

Several Islamic reformers emerged during the late nineteenth century inspired by the ideologies of Western modernization and alarmed by the military and political superiority of the West. Two centuries earlier, Muslims had lost control over trading routes around Africa and Asia as European naval technologies surpassed that of the Muslims, who had controlled the trade routes for centuries. It became obvious that Western societies had superior technologies, advanced administrative and political structures, and superior military power. Islamic reformers or modernists acknowledged Western achievements with varying degrees of emulation or criticism, while aiming at overcoming the perceived impasses regarding cultural development in Islamic societies. Their goal was to help Muslim

---

[31]Mervyn Hiskett, *The Course of Islam in Africa* (Edinburgh: Edinburgh University Press, 1994).

nations to be on the same level as Western nations in order to halt European domination over their land and culture.

At the time of the French invasion of Egypt in 1798, there were just twenty schools in Cairo, compared to seventy-five at the turn of the fifteenth century. Al-Azhar, the oldest Islamic university in the world, was suspicious of science, despised philosophy, and had not produced an original thought for centuries. Confronted by such appalling realities, Islamic reformers sought to follow the path that gave Europe its power: science and rationality, economic and administrative reforms. They argued that rational thinking, scientific research, and democratic systems were compatible with the "original" message of Islam, not the corrupted Islam of their time (as they saw it). Their methodology was to rediscover the pristine Islam of the Prophet and the first generation of Muslims, which in their view was in harmony with modernization. They viewed modern political concepts through early Islamic lenses: the Prophet commanded shura, or consultation among Muslims on the affairs of the community, and this was elementary democracy. They asserted that the first caliphs obtained their legitimacy from the *bay'a*, a pledge of allegiance from the members of the community, another element of democratic structure. They even argued that the Qur'an and the hadith should be interpreted with the public interests, or *maslaha*, in view over the literal interpretation of religious texts.

The late nineteenth-century reformers acknowledged that Islam had lost its footing in the world due to a lack of modern understanding of science, rational thinking, and administrative structure. They argued that "original" Islam contained the necessary means for modernization, and what was needed was reasserting these original Islamic values as well as reinterpreting Islam so that it fit in the modern world. These reformers emerged during the height of attempted institutional changes, and they envisioned an Islamic society where innovations in science, reinterpretation of Islamic laws, and a new political structure would transform Muslim societies the way Europe was transformed centuries earlier. They used the Arabic word *nahda*, which means "renaissance" or "revival," in order to describe their vision of modernizing Islamic societies.

One of the great Islamic reformers, Jamal al-Din al-Afghani (1838–1897), argued that Islam needed a Martin Luther to dispel the thickets of superstition from Muslim minds. He lived during the time when the

British put an end to the Islamic Mughal dynasty in India in 1857. He condemned Europe's colonial aggression and opposed its political domination over Muslim lands. However, he pointed out the necessity of acquiring Western forms of science and technologies in order to combat the power of the West. He emphasized the importance of education and the need for religious and political reform, and he was the first reformer to argue for reinterpreting Islamic laws and doctrines in a way that suited the modern time rather than holding on to traditional views. One of the most notable contributions made by al-Afghani was his vision of pan-Islamism, which influenced Islamic nationalists in the twentieth century. Al-Afghani emphasized the compatibility of Islam with science and reason, the unity of the ummah (community) against local and ethnic loyalties, and the need for a unified leadership modeled on the piety of early caliphs.

One of the most influential reformers of the late nineteenth century, Muhammad Abdu (1849–1905), was the grand mufti of Egypt and the head or sheikh of Al-Azhar University. Abdu sought to reverse the inertia of Egypt's religious and cultural norms by introducing European modernization while remaining committed to the Qur'an as the source of governmental and legislative legitimacy. He aimed at an alternative Islamic modernity from that disseminated by the West. Abdu's main goal was to reform Al-Azhar, the foremost Sunni university, which had authoritative intellectual and religious influence on the rest of the Muslim world. He was met with much resistance from the religious leaders and ulama and was not entirely successful. However, he was a catalyst for legislative and educational reforms in Egypt and other Islamic nations. His argument that rational and revealed knowledge could coexist resulted in later reformation at Al-Azhar as well as the introduction of the semisecularized educational system in Egypt and other Arab countries. Abdu encouraged studying Western science, as sanctioned by Islam, on the basis that Islamic medieval knowledge facilitated the transfer of classical science to Europe, affirming that the Muslim world played a major role in the development of science and technology in modern Europe.[32]

Christian and Muslim reformers both appealed to religious texts (the Bible and the Qur'an, respectively) in their attempts to reform religion and

---

[32]Scott Morrison, "Abduh, Muḥammad," in *The Oxford Encyclopedia of Islam and Politics* (New York: Oxford University Press, 2014), 1:9–14.

society. However, their plea to listen to religious texts led to different outcomes that eventually shaped the cultural norms and ethos of their societies. While religious reformation in Europe opened the door for further separation of religion from other spheres of life, resulting in the secularization of culture, Islamic reformists cautioned against any attempts toward secularization. As much as the Muslim reformists noted that European advancements in science and technology resulted in better life conditions, they did not endorse Western secularization. The thrust of Islamic reform was to restore the legitimacy of Islam, making Islam along with its doctrines, law, education, and culture relevant to the modern state, thus resisting the secularism of modernity.

European and Islamic attempts at modernization went through different processes. Europe went through centuries of gradual and challenging social and cultural transformation. A long tradition of quality education led to the debate of ideas, freedom of speech, democratic systems, even religious wars. Europe's modernization could not have been easily diffused into societies that had not undergone fundamental social and economic transformation. Traditional cultural norms developed over centuries are not easily replaced by hurried imitation, which is enormously disturbing and disorienting. This was the case in various parts of the world during the late nineteenth and early twentieth century, including Muslim societies. The call for modernization in Islamic context was often filtered through and expressed in particularly Islamic or Islamicate symbols and motifs. The power of Islam as a source of public values had waxed and waned many times; it intensified in the eighteenth and nineteenth centuries, receded in the early twentieth century, and resurged after the mid-twentieth century. European colonizers along with their ideas of modernization appeared in the midst of an ongoing process that they greatly affected but did not completely transform.

Conclusion

The modern age transformed the social and cultural life of the West (Europe and North America). The role of religion (Christianity) was marginalized, and the Christian faith endured severe criticism, creating predominantly secularized societies. Christianity, however, witnessed a significant revival movement as Western missionaries extended the faith to millions of people in every continent during the Great Century of

Mission, creating a globalized faith. Christianity was able to keep intertwined these seemingly contradictory threads of modernization and secularization alongside religious revival and mission endeavors.

Meanwhile, advancement in technology and military superiority accompanied by advanced organizational structures enabled the West to exercise political and cultural dominance globally through various forms of colonization. Western culture, politics, and economics resulted in disrupting the sociopolitical and cultural structures of every territory that came under Western domination. Attempts to curb Western domination failed, and several reactionary movements tried to protect their cultural, political, and economic sovereignty with varying degrees of success.

While the modern age resulted in many advancements in Europe and North America, the Muslim world witnessed a period of sociopolitical stagnation, resulting in losing its grip on various geographical territories. Several attempts toward modernization were attempted but never came to fruition due to constant resistance from religious leaders, challenges from the masses, and widespread political and economic corruption. Intellectual retreat resulted in social and cultural inertia as well. The West was viewed with deep ambivalence; it was despised as predatory and morally corrupt, while its cultural, technological, and military accomplishments became a source of both admiration and fear. The Islamic consolation that they were spiritually superior to materialistic Europe was diminished by European control of every Muslim territory by the beginning of the twentieth century. The different trajectories of sociopolitical development in the West versus in Muslim societies during the eighteenth and nineteenth centuries served as the backdrop for twentieth-century encounters, which continue to shape our world today.

PART TWO
RELIGION AND POLITICS

As the number of both Muslims and Christians continues to grow globally, it is expected that they will influence political systems around the world. In theory, Christianity and Islam have different views on the role of religion in politics. However, they have used religious rhetoric, beliefs, and symbols to influence political decisions. While Christianity generally endorses the separation of religion and state, Islam affirms *deen wa dawlah* (religion and state) as an inseparable realm. This is not to suggest that religion and politics have been entirely separated in Christianity; surveying various contemporary models suggests some connection between the church and the state even in secularized Western cultures. Christian ethos continues to influence the social fabric of the West, including the drive for democratic systems and the standards of human rights. Majority-Muslim societies affirm the role of Islamic religious principles in guiding the economic and political life of society, since there is no separation between religion and state in Islam. While some measures of secularization have been implemented in various Muslim countries, the notion of a secularized society is not fully embraced. To the contrary, various types of political Islamism adopted by the second half of the twentieth century point to a trajectory of continued religious influence on political structures in many Muslim nations.

The previous survey of the long history of interaction between Christians and Muslims globally serves as the background to understanding current political contexts and structures. A comprehensive evaluation of the sociopolitical developments in Islamic communities provides a wide-ranging understanding of the current state of Muslim nations globally along with the status of Christians living in these territories. Also, surveying the status of Muslims in the West suggests future patterns of interaction as Muslims continue to influence sociopolitical and cultural norms in the West.

6

HISTORICAL DEVELOPMENTS AND POLITICAL INTERACTIONS (1910–2020)

VARIOUS CULTURAL DEVELOPMENTS in the West and Muslim societies resulted in a mix of secularism, religious conservatism, semisecular political systems, capitalism, socialism, and liberal democracies across the globe. These polarizing structures and contradicting cultural norms often contributed to conflicts and misunderstanding, coloring the interaction between the two communities during the twentieth century. The aftermath of world wars during the first half of the twentieth century resulted in the collapse of most European empires as well as the last Islamic caliphate (the Ottomans). Within the secularized culture of the West, the influence of religion on society and politics was restricted. Various Islamic societies took different paths in reaction to Western modernization, secularization, and political democracy, resulting in the existence of the current semisecular political systems as well as political Islamism. Contrary to the Western model of secularization, Muslim societies opted for broadly upholding the role of religion in the sociopolitical structure of their nations since there is no separation between religion and politics in Islam.

A WORLD AT WAR

The deterioration of the last Islamic empire, the Ottomans, resulted in widespread tension in the Balkans as none of the former Ottoman territories were satisfied with their borders, demanding territories from each other and threatening to use force to achieve their goals. Russia and Austria, the main brokers in the Balkans, were entangled in the conflict. Serbia aspired to take Austrian territories where a majority of Slavs lived, creating an enemy in Austria. Meanwhile, Russia seized the opportunity to support the Serbs in their claims, aiming at controlling territories between the Black Sea and the Aegean Sea while halting Austrian ambitions in the region. By 1914, international conflicts in many parts of the world as well as domestic tensions in Europe were running high. Several international alliances were formed in anticipation of a conflict of such great magnitude.

The spark that ignited World War I might not seem enough to have resulted in such wide-scale conflict. In June 1914, a young Serb nationalist assassinated the Austrian heir to the throne in Sarajevo, the capital of the former Ottoman province of Bosnia-Herzegovina. Austria responded by threatening to take over Serbia. The threat resulted in Russia mobilizing its troops to the Balkans in anticipation of the Austrian takeover. The alliances that were formed a few years before were set into motion. The alliance of Austria-Hungary supported by Germany (Central Powers) was facing Russia, which was supported by the British and the French (the Allies).[1]

On July 28, 1914, World War I started in response to the Russian mobilization of its troops in the Balkans while Austro-Hungarians declared war against the kingdom of Serbia. Germany's advancement through Belgium and Luxembourg, toward France, resulted in Britain declaring war against Germany. What started as a European battle escalated into a world conflict. Thousands of people under the protectorate of European powers were deployed to fight a war that they had no understanding of their involvement in. France recruited and deployed three hundred African subjects to fight in the French army, and in April 1915 they were victims of the first gas attack by Germany. Britain sent more than one million Indians to Europe and the Middle East, where most of them perished. Many countries in the Muslim world were caught in the war since various Ottoman territories in the Balkans were involved in the conflict and their geopolitical disputes had ignited the war. Some tried to maintain a neutral position, while others sought to seize the opportunity for their own gains. While World War I was primarily a European

---

[1] Later on, several countries joined the Allies: Italy, Portugal, Belgium, Montenegro, Serbia, Romania, Greece, Japan, and others. The US joined the Allies when it was attacked militarily and threatened by Germany.

conflict, Muslim nations were major players and Muslim territories were dragged into the conflict, in which thousands of their inhabitants perished.

For the first three months of the war, the Ottomans maintained a neutral position; however, it became almost impossible not to be involved. While the Ottomans did not favor Austria or Hungary, since Hungary had been annexed from previous Ottoman territories in Europe, Germany had supported the Ottomans for the previous two decades. The Ottomans were alarmed by the British and the French moves in taking more lands from their territories in the Middle East and North Africa. Russia also became another threat to the Ottomans by annexing significant territories in the northern region of the Black Sea. As the Germans were defeating the Russians, driving them back into the Russian interiors, the Ottomans thought it was an opportune time to regain sovereignty over some of their lost territories in the region by supporting the Germans. The Young Turks, who ruled the Ottoman Empire at the time—or what was left of it—called the sultan to initiate a jihad, hoping to unite the Turkic population from the Balkans to China. They even presented the sultan as the Islamic caliph who might unite all Muslims under the banner of Islam. From January 1915 to January 1916, the Ottomans, with the support of the Germans, were able to keep the British away from their territories. However, the tide shifted, and the British-led Indian army defeated the Ottomans in several battles in Iraq. The Ottomans' fight against the Russians went horribly awry when thousands of Ottoman troops vanished.[2]

Meanwhile, other Muslim leaders sought to use the opportunity for their own gains. The Ottoman governor of the Hijaz (western Arabia), Sharif Hussein, offered his support to the British, ignoring the Ottoman sultan's call to join forces in jihad against the British, with hope to become the ruler of the Arab lands taken from the Ottoman Empire. Hussein sent his troops to fight the Ottomans, which was an added gain for the British, who used the Arabs to fight the Ottomans for them. By 1918, the Ottoman Empire collapsed as it was fighting multiple battles with a weakened army and limited resources.

During the first two years of the war, the Turkic Muslims across central Asia ignored the Ottoman call for jihad against the British, French, and Russians; instead, they supported the Russians, which was a great relief for

---

[2]Ross F. Collins, ed., *World War I: Primary Documents on Events from 1914 to 1919* (Westport, CT: Greenwood, 2008).

Russia since most of the central Asian territories were under Russian control. While central Asian territories were not directly involved in the war, as the war dragged on, Russia requested the deployment of thousands of central Asian nomads to fight in the war. Such calls resulted in revolts against Russia from the Kazakh and Kyrgyz nomads, who also started killing Russian settlers in the region. The uprisings, however, were crushed, and thousands of central Asian inhabitants were killed, while many fled to Xinjiang, a province in western China today.

The Russians also met some resistance from the Tatars, who still had a significant presence in Crimea; Russian reprisals, however, reduced their influence and power in Crimea. By the time the war ended, central Asian territories were cemented in the Soviet Federation. Meanwhile, many Chechen and Tatar Muslims supported the Russian Bolshevik Revolution of 1917. The new Russian government supported the Muslims in their aspiration for a pan-Islamic movement against Western imperialism, claiming that Islam and Marxism had the same goals and aspiration. Later, many Muslims in central Asia adopted Marxism and were integrated in the sociopolitical system of the Soviet Union.

Despite Russia's early victory in 1916, dissatisfaction with the Russian handling of the war resulted in the collapse of the government in March 1917 and the removal of the ruling tsar dynasty. The following month, the Bolshevik Revolution, led by Vladimir Lenin, formed the new Marxist government. While Germany supported the Russian Revolution, Russia's own allies, Britain and France, did not acknowledge the new communist regime and were not willing to negotiate further agreements with Russia. Such a move resulted in Russia conceding territories won or promised during the war in subsequent agreements. On November 4, 1918, the Austro-Hungarian Empire agreed to a cease-fire. Germany's later defeat in the war while facing its own revolution resulted in Germany's agreement to a cease-fire on November 11, 1918, the final event that ended the war, with victory going to the Allies.[3]

Political Consequences of the War

The war resulted in the collapse of the German Empire, the Russian Empire, the Austro-Hungarian Empire, and the Ottoman Empire. New national

---

[3]The date is still observed as Remembrance Day in the West.

borders were drawn, with several new states being created. Several agreements were negotiated after the war in an attempt to settle conflicts between world powers. Some of the agreements were implemented, while others were not. The League of Nations was established with the hope of preventing future large-scale wars. As the Allies, the winners of the war, imposed their own terms in some of these agreements, a sense of humiliation and defeat (particularly in Germany and Russia) eventually led to World War II.[4]

As the Ottoman Empire was breaking up, the same circumstances that led to the Armenian massacres two decades earlier were reactivated during the war. At the beginning of the war, the Ottomans carried out systematic killings of Armenians. Fearing for their lives, some Armenians sought the help of Russia, which was against the Ottomans. As the Young Turks were fighting against the Russians, the British, and the French, in order to save whatever was left of the empire, they used the Armenians' call for help from Russia to issue the infamous law of deportation, which authorized the deportation of Armenians from Anatolia to Syria. Accordingly, between 1915 and 1918 hundreds of thousands of Armenians were marched to death in the Syrian desert, while thousands were killed by the Ottoman army. While the exact number of Armenians massacred is hard to determine, most scholars estimate between 1.5 and 2 million.[5]

The policy of extermination and ethnic cleansing of Christians in the Ottoman Empire during World War I included the massacre of thousands of Assyrians and Greeks. Thousands of Assyrians living in what is today northern Iraq were forced to relocate and were killed by Turks, Kurds, and Chechens between 1914 and 1920. Unlike as was the case for Armenians, there were no orders to deport Assyrians. Local Kurdish tribal leaders and Ottoman military officials often initiated the rounding up of men in small villages, killing them while taking their properties and selling women into slavery. The killing of Assyrians was also taking place in Iran and Anatolia at the same time. An estimated quarter of a million Assyrians vanished by 1920.[6] While several countries today recognize the extermination of the Armenians, Assyrians, and Ottoman Greeks as genocide, the Turkish

---

[4]H. P. Willmott, *World War I* (New York: Dorling Kindersley, 2003), 10-15, 307.
[5]Taner Akcam, *The Young Turks' Crime Against Humanity: The Armenian Genocide and Ethnic Cleansing in the Ottoman Empire* (Princeton, NJ: Princeton University Press, 2012), 20-25.
[6]Joseph Yacoub, *Year of the Sword: The Assyrian Christian Genocide, a History* (London: Hurst, 2016).

government insists that they were simply victims of interethnic fighting during a time of war.[7]

The war led to disillusionment in the West about the concept of progress and human advancement, one of the basic tenets of the modern age. Meanwhile, the notion of the supremacy of Western civilization was challenged. More than seventy million military personnel were involved in the war, and over ten million of them were killed in addition to twenty million injured. Civilian casualties mounted to seven million killed, while another fifty million civilians suffered from injuries, famine, and disease. Advancement in military technology, sophisticated armed techniques, and trench warfare made this war one of the deadliest in human history. Chemical weapons, submarines, and aircraft were used for the first time in warfare. The aftermath of the war resulted in breaking up countries, ending empires, and starting revolutions in various regions. Since most of the economic powers of the world were involved in the war, the war had disastrous economic consequences, and famine and disease spread in many parts of the world.[8]

Several Islamic nations were directly involved in World War I. They were less involved in World War II, though the outcome of the war affected their economies and political alliances. The West's interest in controlling natural resources, primarily oil, resulted in its entanglement in the internal politics of several Islamic countries, primarily in the Middle East; this in turn resulted in conflicts and wars between the West and several Islamic nations.

By the 1920s, every Muslim territory around the globe was under one form or another of Western domination. By the 1950s, most Muslim territories had gained independence from the West while creating their own nation-states. Many were inspired by the Western model of governing, emulating modernized political structures; others, however, maintained traditional Islamic forms of governing. While the Middle East continued to be the epicenter of Islam, India was the home to the world's largest concentration of Muslims, and the number of Muslims in the

---

[7]Dominik J. Schaller and Jürgen Zimmerer, *Late Ottoman Genocides: The Dissolution of the Ottoman Empire and Young Turkish Population and Extermination Policies* (London: Routledge, 2012), 5-8.

[8]Alan J. P. Taylor, *The First World War and Its Aftermath, 1914-1919* (Oxford: Oxford University Press, 1998), 73-119.

Netherlands Indies (Indonesia) was rapidly growing. Islamic countries in Asia and Africa, which had been on the periphery of Dar al-Islam, were moving to the center, influencing the rise of a new pan-Islamism by the mid-twentieth century.

While a new sense of nationalism and significant modernization movements were taking place across the Muslim world during the first half of the century, the second half of the twentieth century witnessed significant retreat to conservative social structures and political Islamism. It is imperative to analyze the sociopolitical processes that resulted in establishing contemporary Muslim nations and their impact on international relations as well as on Christian-Muslim relationships globally. The following survey provides a comprehensive analysis of historical developments and political interactions globally, explaining the roots of our contemporary context in the twenty-first century.

The Middle East

Several agreements were made between the Allies (primarily Britain and France) and the political leaders under the control of the Ottoman Empire in the Middle East. Such agreements eventually contributed to the collapse of the Ottoman Empire while creating some of the current states in the Middle East. Some of these agreements caused much frustration and bitterness that is still present among Middle Eastern nations today.

According to the McMahan-Hussein correspondence (July 14, 1915, to January 30, 1916), Sharif Hussein, the governor of the Hejaz (western Arabia) under the Ottomans, agreed to initiate an Arab revolt against the Ottomans rather than answering the call for jihad that was initiated by the Ottoman sultan. In return, for entering the war on the Allied side, Hussein was promised large territories of the Ottoman Empire in the Middle East that would include western Arabia as well as what is today Syria, Iraq, and Jordan. Meanwhile, the British made a separate agreement with another Arab fighter from Arabia, Ibn Saud, who controlled the central and eastern parts of what is today Saudi Arabia. Upon the discovery of oil in the region, the agreement allowed for the creation of several smaller emirates in the Gulf area that would be outside Ibn Saud's control: Kuwait, Bahrain, Qatar, and the United Arab Emirates.

While these agreements with the Arabs were being made, France and England were negotiating their own agreements specifying their spheres of influence in the region. According to the Sykes-Picot Agreement (1915–1916), the French were given control over Lebanon and Syria. The British would assume control over what is today Jordan and Iraq. The Palestinian territory would be an international zone. When the terms of these agreements were revealed to Hussein by the Russians, the British managed to calm his fears by downplaying the document's significance. A year later, on November 2, 1917, the British foreign minister issued the well-known Balfour Declaration, conveying Britain's intention to create a homeland for the Jewish people in Palestine in support of the Jewish Zionist aspiration.[9] The cautiously articulated statement communicated by Lord Balfour was designed to elicit Jewish support for the Allies without alienating the Arabs. While the statement succeeded in the former part, it failed in the latter, creating more confusion and mistrust among the Arabs.

The Jewish aspiration for a homeland was growing during the last decades of the nineteenth century. Influenced by the European sense of nationalism, many European Jews were hoping to have their own homeland. Some had lived in Palestine, and others decided to move there for religious or personal reasons; however, there was no organized movement aimed at such a goal before the late nineteenth century. Being a minority in Europe, albeit a generally successful one, the Jews suffered from episodes of anti-Semitism and discrimination. Starting in the late nineteenth century, the World Zionist Organization had been financing and organizing the relocation of Jews to Palestine for two decades before the war. However, the Jews did not comprise more than 15 percent of the total population in Palestine, and they suffered from harsh treatment under the Ottomans similar to that of Palestinian Christians, who comprised around 40 percent of the population.

From the Ottoman Empire to Turkey. In 1920, the Allied forces met in Sèvres, a suburb of Paris, to determine the future of Anatolia, part of the

---

[9] "I have much pleasure in conveying to you on behalf of His Majesty's Government the following declaration of sympathy with Jewish Zionist aspiration, which has been submitted to and approved by the Cabinet:

'His majesty's Government view with favour the establishment in Palestine of a national home for the Jewish people, and will use their best endeavours to facilitate the achievement of this object, it being clearly understood that nothing shall be done which may prejudice the civil and religious rights of existing non-Jewish communities in Palestine or the rights and political status enjoyed by Jews in any country.'"

Available at "Origins and Evolution of the Palestine Problem: 1917–1947 (Part I)," United Nations, www.un.org/unispal/history2/origins-and-evolution-of-the-palestine-problem/part-i-1917-1947/.

current state of Turkey. The proposal was to divide Anatolia into smaller states. The straits and Istanbul were promised to Russia during the war. However, since Britain and France were not willing to negotiate further agreements with the new communist government of Russia, and the new Russian government refused to recognize war agreements, the area was placed under international control instead. The province of Smyrna (Izmir) in western Anatolia was given to the Ottoman Greeks, but the war of independence incorporated the region into Turkey. Two areas in eastern Anatolia were designated as possible territories for future states for the Armenians and the Kurds. However, such a plan was never realized as most Armenians were either killed or forced out of Anatolia as hundreds of thousands were annihilated by the Turks. The only group with substantial numbers that continued to exist in eastern Anatolia was the Kurds. Overall, the British and French policies in the region a century ago have had significant ramifications for current unresolved tension in the region, such as that between Turkey and the Kurds and the fighting over borders between Turkey, Syria, and Iraq.[10]

The Treaty of Sèvres, which was supposed to divide Anatolia into smaller states, was never implemented. Instead, a powerful military officer, Mustafa Kemal (1881–1938), emerged as the new military and nationalistic leader in Anatolia. He discredited the power of the sultan in Istanbul and formed a new government in Ankara (the current capital of Turkey) incorporating Anatolia under his leadership. He fought a furious war with the Greeks (1920–1922), in which thousands of Christians and Muslims were massacred in western Anatolia in the Greek-dominated province of Smyrna. The Armenian and Greek quarters in the city were demolished, including historical Christian sites, while thousands of Christians were forced to deport their historic homeland of Asia Minor.

The atrocities committed against civilians during this war led both sides to realize that the two peoples could not live together. Under the Treaty of Lausanne (1923), over one million Greek Orthodox Christians (many of whom spoke Turkish, not Greek) were deported to Greece, while four hundred thousand Muslims living in Greece (many of whom spoke Greek, not Turkish) were deported to Turkey. Thus, Turkey became almost exclusively a Muslim state, while Greece became an exclusively Christian nation.

---

[10]David Fromkin, *A Peace to End All Peace: The Fall of the Ottoman Empire and the Creation of the Modern Middle East*, 2nd ed. (New York: Owl Books, 2001).

Turkey secured full sovereignty over its current territories with the addition of the Greek region of Edirne and the Syrian province of Antioch. Meanwhile, Kemal agreed with Russia to divide Armenia between them, with Russia controlling the northern part (the current state of Armenia) and Turkey incorporating the southern section into its territory. Instead of being divided into smaller territories, Turkey under Kemal emerged more powerful, adding more territories that form the current state.

In November 1922 the sultanate was abolished, ending the Ottoman Empire while announcing the new Republic of Turkey in 1923, with Ankara as its capital. In March 1924, the caliphate was abolished, ending the long-standing Islamic state system that had started in the seventh century. Kemal blamed Islam for the backwardness of the Ottoman Empire and regarded it as the main obstacle toward progress. He declared Turkey a secular state and implemented significant measures to secularize it. He abolished the use of shari'a and replaced it with the Swiss civil code and the Italian penal system. He abolished Islamic schools, madrassas, and replaced them with a secular educational system. The Arabic alphabet was replaced by the Latin alphabet (currently used in the Turkish language), and Arabic or Persian words were purged. Kemal even replaced Friday (the Islamic day of prayer) with Sunday as the official day of rest. Women were granted full equal rights with men and were given the right to vote and to be elected to political office. While Kemal's unprecedented secularization of an Islamic society was welcomed in the West, his forced secularization did not gain the support of the majority of inhabitants of Turkey, especially those living in the remote areas of the country, where Islamic traditional ways of life continued to dominate. Kemal was awarded the title Ataturk ("the father of Turks") in 1934.[11]

Turkey became the first Muslim nation to fully adopt secularized social and political structures while implementing Western-style reform programs. The process of democratization in Turkey came about through the encouragement of opposition movements. However, Ataturk used a technique of allowing opposition parties to survive while suppressing them whenever they gained power. The 1950 elections resulted in the opposition party taking over the parliament. The election marked a turning point in Turkish politics as a change of government came about by popular vote.[12] After World War II,

---

[11]Eric J. Zurcher, *Turkey: A Modern History* (New York: I. B. Tauris, 2004).
[12]Feroz Ahmad, *The Turkish Experiment in Democracy, 1950–1975* (Boulder, CO: Westview, 1977).

Turkey became an ally of the West, especially the United States, which supported Turkey with military and economic aid with the goal of combating the power of the Soviet Union in the region. Turkey became a full member of the North Atlantic Treaty Organization (NATO) in 1952, which allows Turkey full military and economic support from NATO member countries.

Turkey's experiment with secularization points to the vital role of religion in politics in Muslim societies. The secularization that was adopted by civil servants, teachers, professors, and the military during the first half of the twentieth century was never shared by the rest of the population, who continued to uphold a strong commitment to Islamic religious values. While Turkey did not have an organized Islamic advocacy group like the Muslim Brotherhood at that time, most Turks, regardless of their religious orientation, thought of religious norms as the standard for social and political life. When the opposition group that was supported by the popular vote took power in 1950, they reversed some of the secularized measures implemented earlier by Ataturk. They brought back religious education to schools while allowing the call to prayers to be given in Arabic once again. They promoted religious radio programs and emphasized the role of religion in politics. However, their attempts to veil women, return the alphabet to Arabic, and enforce other radical measures to Islamize the country were faced with strong opposition from the secularists as well as the military.

The tension between secularists and Islamists continued to grow in the following decades, with significant hostility and violence that resulted in military coups in 1960 and 1971. A new party, the National Salvation Party, was formed in the 1970s with the goal of restoring Islamic law and practice in the country. However, the party was outlawed after another military coup in 1980. The Islamists emerged as another powerful group in the 1980s under the Welfare Party, which grew to become the largest party in the country in 1995. The party was able to control power in 1996 using Islamic rhetoric and running on a platform that opposed joining the European Union. A year later, in 1997, the military took over the country, banning the Islamic Welfare Party in 1998.

In 2001, Recep Tayyip Erdogan led a moderate faction of Islamists under the Justice and Development Party and won the 2002 election, becoming the new leader of Turkey. His proven leadership as the mayor of Istanbul won him the support of both Islamists and secularists. His program to combat poverty and injustice was well received. Once in power, his government started implementing Islamic laws and provisions. He succeeded in developing better relationships with Greece and the West, putting in place economic reforms that resulted in boosting the economy and tourism with the hope of joining the European Union. Tensions between Erdogan's government and the military intensified; however, military attempts to take over the country failed, and the military leaders were either suppressed or replaced. The Turkish experiment with secularization was never fully achieved, and the country is moving further toward Islamization.

One issue that continues to trouble Turkey is its significant Kurd community, which forms 18 percent of the total population. While the Kurds are calling for an independent state that would include a significant portion of the southeastern territories of Turkey (along with other territories in Iran, Iraq, and Syria), the Turkish government constantly rejects the legitimacy of such claims. Turkey's continuous conflict with the Kurds within its borders as well as within Syria has resulted in the deaths of tens of thousands of civilians.

At the beginning of the twentieth century, the Christian population in Asia Minor (Anatolia) accounted for 25 percent of the total population of sixteen million (i.e., four million Christians). The aftermath of the Armenian genocide, Greek massacres, population exchange between Greece and Turkey, and the emigration of Christians during the 1920s reduced the number of Christians to 7 percent by 1927 (1.5 million). This pattern continued through the twentieth century, and in 2020 there were only 320,000 Christians left in Turkey (less than 0.4 percent of the total population of 85 million Turks), most of them Armenian and Greek Orthodox. Christianity was the dominant faith in Asia Minor starting from the first century of Christianity, and the apostle Paul along with others established several churches in the region, to which the apostle John sent messages at the close of the first century (Rev 1). Asia Minor continued to be the hub of Byzantine Christianity from the fourth to the fifteenth centuries.

In January 2011, the Turkish newspaper *Milliet* (meaning "Religious sects") published a report indicating that some thirty-five thousand Muslim Turks are turning to Christianity every year due to the influence of social media. This is a significant number considering that Christians make up only 0.4 percent of the population. Many of the converts are descendants of Christians who converted to Islam during the 1920s to avoid being killed by the Turks. However, most converted Christians are not vocal about their faith given the restrictions on religious freedom in Turkey. Based on the *Milliet* report and others, there are more converted or reconverted Christians in Turkey than the official number of Christians.[13] While most of the population in Turkey adheres to Islam (over 90 percent), there are also atheists in the country (estimated at 3 percent).

From Persia to Iran. After World War I, as Russia and Britain agreed to evacuate their troops from Persia (Iran), Colonel Reza Khan emerged as the new military leader of the country. In 1925, Reza Khan convinced the Majlis (the Islamic parliament) to depose the incompetent Ahmad Shah, the last Qajar king, bringing an end to the Qajar dynasty in Persia. He called for the establishment of a republic, but the ulama (religious leaders) rejected the idea on the basis that a republic would compromise the establishment of an Islamic state based on shari'a. Accordingly, in December 1925 the monarchy was transferred to Reza Khan, who crowned himself Reza Shah Pahlavi in April 1926, reclaiming the ancient Persian title of emperor. Like Kemal Ataturk of Turkey, Reza Shah (1878–1941) wanted to build a strong modernized Persia (Iran). He modernized the army with the latest technologies while setting out to improve the country's infrastructure. His modernization program also included the secularization of the educational system. However, he could not curb the role of religious leaders, and as a compromise he enhanced the status of Qum, the religious seat of scholarly Shi'ism. On March 21, 1935, Reza Shah introduced the use of the term *Iran* instead of *Persia*.[14] He also introduced the use of the Arabic alphabet instead of Persian. In contrast to Turkey, Iran never went through a process of secularization; Islam remained at the center of its sociopolitical life.

As in many parts of the Middle East, oil politics played a significant role in the Iranian internal economy as well as its international relationships. After World War II, Iran tried to break the autonomous power of the Anglo-Iranian Oil Company, which provided less control and smaller royalties to Iran while benefiting Britain with over 90 percent of Iranian oil production. Iran's attempt to nationalize its own oil production was met with severe measures by Britain, which convinced the United States to impose

---

[13]*Milliet*, January 12, 2011.

[14]*Iran* is the historical name used by Iranians through the centuries. The change from Persia to Iran also applied to its citizens; the word *Iranians* was also used instead of *Persians*. However, in 1959, Reza Shah's son Muhammad Reza Pahlavi argued that *Persia* and *Iran* could be used interchangeably. See Ehsan Yarshater, "Persia or Iran, Persian or Farsi," *Iranian Studies* 22, no. 1 (1989): 62–65.

economic sanctions on Iran, claiming that such nationalization was the act of communist revolutionists within Iran. The United States acted swiftly, as it was alarmed at the possibility of a Soviet attempt to control Iran, which was a serious concern during the Cold War era. The sanctions destroyed the Iranian economy and forced Iran to negotiate a new treaty in 1952, when the United States became the major broker of its oil company instead of Britain.[15]

The rule of Muhammad Reza Shah (1941–1979) witnessed several upheavals as he tried to consolidate power in Iran. His modernization program was met with hostility and criticism from the ulama (religious leaders). His response was to curb their power through a land reform program that resulted in confiscating lands owned by religious leaders and Islamic institutions. The shah also took harsh measures against his critics, who were often arrested and tortured. However, his attempts to marginalize the religious leaders resulted in enhancing their position. In the 1970s, a charismatic preacher, Ayatollah Khomeini, started a campaign against the shah's policies and lavish lifestyle. He escaped execution in Iran and fled to Iraq and then France, where he continued to mobilize the masses through his powerful preaching from exile. The doubling of oil revenues after the 1973 Arab-Israeli war benefited Iran tremendously. The shah was able to carry out many of his desired economic and social reforms. However, inflation increased, and many in the middle class bore the brunt of the new economic gains. The shah was even accused of pocketing a significant sum of oil money for his personal use. By the 1970s, Iran was facing a complex situation in which people were dragged into a modernization process while the majority were still holding on to traditional Islamic values. The rapid social changes and economic instability resulted in the 1979 Iranian Revolution, when the shah was deposed and replaced by Ayatollah Khomeini, who declared Iran an Islamic republic. Once in power, Khomeini moved swiftly to eliminate those who resisted the Islamic revolution. Thousands of secular and moderate Muslims, military officers, and many Christians were executed or imprisoned during the first two years of the revolution.[16]

The Iranian Revolution of 1979 had far-reaching impacts not only on Iranian society and politics but also on the sociopolitical development of the whole Middle East. The Iranian Islamic revolution marked the first time in

---

[15]Elton Daniel, *The History of Iran* (Westport, CT: Greenwood, 2001).
[16]Nikki Keddie, *Modern Iran: Roots and Results of Revolution* (New Haven, CT: Yale University Press, 2006).

modern history where an Islamic religious leader became the head of the state. Shi'ite Muslims, who had been awaiting the coming of the hidden imam to restore justice in the world, made a socioreligious transition where such religious aspiration could be fulfilled, at least partially, through political and military revolution. The title given to Khomeini was Ayatollah (meaning "sign of God") Ruah Allah (meaning "the spirit of God"), indicating his supernatural nature, while the addition of the title imam resonated with the anticipation of the hidden imam. The rule of ulama in Iran created a new political framework where religion and state were fully fused into one entity.

The aftermath of the revolution resulted in several Americans being taken hostage in Iran for four hundred days, a move that empowered Muslims in Iran and around the world to believe that Islamic states under pious religious leaders could challenge the West along with its perceived immoral social life and injustices. The Iranian Revolution inspired the creation of another militant Shi'ite group, Hezbollah ("the party of God"), in Lebanon while enhancing the position of Shi'ite Muslims in neighboring Iraq, Syria, and Bahrain. Meanwhile, the influence of the Iranian Revolution also extended to Sunni Muslims, despite their religious differences with Shi'ites, who saw in the Iranian Revolution a victory for Islam and its aspiration for the establishment of an Islamic ummah (community) in the modern world context. The revolution offered a precedent for Muslims, who came to the conclusion that revolutionary measures were the most powerful answer to the troubles of the Muslim world.

Christians in Iran endured several episodes of persecution through the centuries. The latest wave came with the 1979 Islamic Revolution, resulting in reducing the number of Iranian Christians to fewer than three hundred, the majority of them from Armenian and Assyrian ethnic groups. Thousands of Iranian Christians were killed or tortured, or emigrated during the last three decades. However, several reliable reports indicate that the number of Christian converts is growing significantly in Iran. Open Doors puts the number at 450,000, while the *Christian Post* affirms one million converts following a report by the London-based Pars Institute. These converts meet in house churches and endure significant persecution that varies from death threats and torture to long prison sentences for their faith.[17] There is also a growing trend of conversion to Christianity among

---

[17] *The Christian Post*, March 3, 2016; Open Doors USA, February 15, 2016.

Iranians in the West, where many vibrant Persian churches are being established in Europe, North America, and Australia. The majority of the population of Iran, however, is Muslim (97 percent).

From Mesopotamia to Iraq. After World War I, the ancient territories of Mesopotamia were renamed Iraq. The borders of Iraq that were drawn in 1920 by the Treaty of Sèvres included three distinct territories: (1) a northern territory of majority Sunni Kurds (who spoke Kurdish, not Arabic) as well as Assyrian Christians (their history goes back to the Assyrian kingdom, and they mainly spoke Syriac, not Arabic), with Mosel (ancient Nineveh) being the main urban center of the northern region; (2) a central territory dominated by Sunni Arabs with few Christians from Assyrian and Chaldean descents and a substantial Jewish community, with Baghdad being the main urban city; and (3) the southern territory, mainly Shi'ite Muslims who migrated from Arabia a century earlier and settled around the Shi'ite religious sites of Karbala and Najaf, fleeing the harsh treatment of the Wahabis, who considered Shi'ism a heretical sect. These territories came under British mandate according to the Treaty of Sèvres, while their ethnic and religious compositions were a perfect storm for tension and disputes, a description that characterizes the history of Iraq up until today.

To fulfill their promise to the sharif of Hejaz, who supported the Arab revolt against the Ottomans, the British installed his son Faisal as the king of Syria. However, Faisal was expelled from Syria by a major revolt that was supported by the French. Alternatively, Faisal was crowned the king of Iraq in 1921, while his brother Abdullah became the emir of the newly created kingdom of Transjordan (Jordan). Faisal was able to rule (1921-1933) over these diversified territories, albeit crushing some revolts from the central territories around Baghdad, while managing constant conflicts between the Kurds and the Arabs as well as hostility between Sunnis and Shi'ites. His son King Faisal II also ruled Iraq (1935-1958), with the support of the British. However, in July 1958 a bloody revolution put an end to the monarchy. From 1958 until 2003, Iraq was ruled by generals who came to power through bloody coups.[18]

---

[18]The 1958 revolution was led by General Abdul Karem Qasim, who put an end to the monarchy, executing the king, the prime minister, and many elites. The reign of Qasim was filled with violence as various political groups fought each other in bloody battles. Qasim's turbulent five-year rule came to an end in a 1963 coup led by General Abdel Salam Aref, one of the generals who led the 1958 revolution and was later purged from governing. Aref executed Qasim along with others in the ruling government. Aref's death in a helicopter accident two years later, in 1966, brought to

The last dictator to rule over Iraq before the American invasion of 2003, Saddam Hussein, turned the country into a draconian police state in which thousands of people were tortured, massacred, or imprisoned. The difficulty in having any stable government in Iraq has been complicated by the pressure exercised by the various religious and ethnic groups competing for power. Although Sunni Muslims form less than 30 percent of the population, they have ruled the country since the installation of King Faisal by the British. While current Iraqi governments since the American invasion have been predominantly Shi'ites, Sunnis and Shi'ites clashing with each other in bloody battles dominated the era between 2005 and 2014, while antigovernment protests resulted in constant political chaos until the modern day.

During the last two decades, Iraq entered three major battles that destroyed its economy and resulted in the social and political collapse of the country. Conflicts over territories around the Persian Gulf resulted in a ten-year war (1980–1990) between Iraq and Iran, which claimed the lives of more than a quarter of a million military personnel and civilians. The Iraqi invasion of Kuwait (1990–1991) and its aftermath resulted in thousands of casualties, while subsequent economic sanctions resulted in the starvation of one million children and the death of hundreds of thousands. The American invasion of Iraq in 2003 (based on unfounded claims that Iraq possessed weapons of mass destruction) resulted in the final blow of its economy and a total collapse of its political structure. Sunni and Shi'ite Islamic militants fought each other in bloody clashes between 2005 and 2014, followed by the takeover of the Islamic State (ISIS) of northern Iraq between 2014 and 2017, resulting in two hundred thousand civilian casualties. Due to such substantial internal conflicts, most of the economic resources and infrastructure of the country were debilitated.

The Kurds, who form 17 percent of the population, create another constant political challenge for Iraq. While the Treaty of Sèvres in 1920 called for the establishment of an independent Kurdistan, this plan was never carried out. The Kurds are scattered in four different countries—Iraq, Iran, Syria, and Turkey—and as of 2020 they numbered over 35 million. The

---

power his brother Abdel Rahman Aref, who had been the prime minister. Two years later Aref was ousted by another coup, led by General Ahmed Hassan Al-Baker, who executed Aref and other generals. Al-Baker brought along his cousin Saddam Hussein, who rose to the second-highest position in power and became the president of Iraq when Al-Baker died in 1979. Hussein ruled Iraq until he was ousted by the American invasion of Iraq in March 2003. See William L. Cleveland, *A History of the Modern Middle East*, 3rd ed. (Boulder, CO: Westview, 2004).

largest number of Kurds are in southern Turkey, with an estimated 16 million (18 percent of the Turkish population), 9 million in Iran (10 percent of the total population), 8 million in Iraq (18 percent of the population), and 2 million in Syria (11 percent of the population). After the American invasion, the Kurds of Iraq were given autonomous rule over the northern territories—a situation that Turkey continues to observe anxiously, as Turkey has the largest number of Kurds and the most vocal group, which is actively demanding the creation of an independent state. The twenty-first-century fighting in Iraq and Syria fed the Kurds' aspiration to establish an independent state for the Kurds in both countries. However, Turkey is taking every measure to prevent the Kurds from creating an independent state within its southern borders.[19]

By the beginning of the twentieth century, Christians in Iraq, primarily Assyrians, formed 35 percent (1.7 million) of the total population of 5 million. After the Ottoman massacres of the Christians in the 1920s, Christians were reduced to 12 percent in 1947, while their number reached 8 percent (1.8 million out of a total population of 23 million) in 2003. The American invasion and the Islamic State's attacks on Christian villages and towns in northern Iraq between 2014 and 2017 resulted in the deaths of thousands of Christians, while many others were forced to leave. Several historic churches and monasteries that dated back to the early centuries of Christianity were destroyed. A report released in March 2016 by the Assyrian Archdiocese of Erbil (northern Iraq) put the number of Christians in Iraq at 275,000 (less than 0.6 percent of the total population of 43 million). The Assyrian church in Persia and Mesopotamia, which was instrumental in introducing Christianity to the rest of Asia in the early centuries of Christianity, is being wiped out in the twenty-first century. It is also interesting to note that the current seat of the Assyrian Orthodox patriarch is in Chicago, not Assyria (northern Iraq). However, several reports indicate that thousands of Kurds are turning to Christianity in northern Iraq.[20]

Jordan. Transjordan (Jordan) was created by the British mandate over Palestine with the hope of serving two main purposes. The ultimate purpose was to create a place for Palestinians who wished to move east of the Jordan River in order to facilitate the creation of the state of Israel on the west side

---

[19]Cleveland, *History of the Modern Middle East.*
[20]Eliza Griswold, "Is This the End of Christianity in the Middle East?," *New York Times Magazine*, July 22, 2015.

of the Jordan River. While thousands of Palestinians were forced to relocate after the 1948 Arab-Israeli war, many did not consider such a move a viable option. Meanwhile, the creation of the new state allowed Britain to fulfill its promise to the Sharif of Hejaz, who supported the revolt of the Arabs against the Ottomans. Accordingly, his son Abdullah was appointed the emir of the new kingdom. Abdullah ruled (1921–1951) with the support of the British. The total population of the new kingdom in 1920 was fewer than 200,000 inhabitants. His grandson Hussein ruled (1952–1999) over Jordan during a significant time of transition. The kingdom welcomed millions of refugees from all surrounding countries, with over 2 million Palestinians and over 1 million Iraqis. King Abdullah II (1999–present) is ruling over a much larger population of 12 million, comprising 4 million Palestinians and over 1 million Syrian refugees.

Christians in Jordan, a community that has its roots in first-century Christianity, comprise 2 percent of the total population of 12 million, or 240,000, down from the 30 percent (225,000) in 1950 out of a total population of 750,000 at that time. Christians in Jordan did not face any systemic persecution like that experienced by Christians in Turkey, Iran, or Iraq; the significant decrease in their number is due to high emigration rates of Christians to the West as waves of conservative Islamism have intensified, accompanied by high immigration rates of Muslims into Jordan. While it is illegal for Muslims to convert to another religion in Jordan, an estimated 6,500 converted Muslims are secretly practicing Christianity.[21]

Syria. In contrast to Mesopotamia, which received a new name in the twentieth century (Iraq), Syria continued to enjoy its historical name, which dates to the third millennium BC. The capital of Syria, Damascus, is one of the oldest continuously inhabited cities in the world. The modern borders of Syria, however, were determined at the Treaty of Sèvres in 1920. In the same year, Faisal, the son of Sharif Hussein, who initiated the revolt against the Ottomans, was able to capture Damascus from the Ottomans and was declared the king of Syria and Palestine in March. However, the French mandate over Syria prevented the British from fulfilling their plan of installing an Arabian king over the territory. Instead, a local government was created under French control.

---

[21] Duane Alexander Miller and Patrick Johnston, "Believers in Christ from a Muslim Background: A Global Census," *Interdisciplinary Journal of Research on Religion* 11 (2015), article 1.

After gaining independence from France in 1946, Syria experienced several political upheavals, including several military coups. For most of the twentieth century, Syria as well as Iraq was governed by Baath parties, which promoted socialist ideologies. In 1958, Syria joined Egypt to form the United Arab Republic with the hope of expanding a unified Arab state to include other Middle Eastern countries. The United Arab Republic symbolized the drive for Arab self-determination. That unity, however, came to an end in 1963.[22] In 1970, an Alawite (a branch of Shi'ite Islam) general, Hafez Al-Assad, led another military coup and became president. His son Bashar Al-Assad became president in 2000. Like in Iraq, Syrian leaders ruled their country with a draconian police system, curbing the power of any revolts while imprisoning and torturing opposition groups.[23]

Syria has a diversified ethnic and religious society, including various Christian groups and Muslim sects. The majority of Muslims are Sunni; however, a minority branch of Shi'ite Islam, the Alawites, has been ruling the country since 1970. There used to be a significant number of Armenian and Assyrian Christians along with Kurds, Druze, and other ethnic groups. In 1900, Syrian Christians counted for 40 percent of the population (2 million); in 1950 there were 4 million Christians, representing 20 percent of the population; and in 2015 Christians were only 10 percent or 2.1 million of the total population of 21 million. The Syrian civil war (2011–2016), along with the formation of the Islamic State in Syria, displaced over 5 million Syrians, including large numbers of Muslims and Christians who fled the country. The civil war claimed the lives of over half a million Syrians as well. The number of Christians in Syria is facing significant decline since 2011 due to massive emigration and mass killing by militant Islamists.[24]

Lebanon. The French mandate over Syria facilitated the creation of the current state system as well as the current borders of Lebanon. The size of the country was quadrupled in 1920, a move that created tension between Syria and Lebanon, resulting in Syria's interference in Lebanese political affairs for most of the twentieth century. Lebanon is diverse in terms of

---

[22]Cleveland, *History of the Modern Middle East*.
[23]Michael Broning, "The Sturdy House That Assad Built," *Foreign Affairs*, March 7, 2011.
[24]Bethany Allen-Ebrahimi and Yochi Dreazen, "The Real War on Christianity," *Foreign Policy*, March 12, 2015. The article begins, "In the Middle East, the Islamic State is crucifying Christians and demolishing ancient churches. Why is this being met with silence from the halls of Congress to Sunday sermons?"

ethnic and religious groups. For most of the twentieth century, Lebanon was the only country in the Middle East with a majority-Christian population. In 1932, an agreement was reached to govern the country based on its religious demographics at the time. The president (the head of the state) would be chosen from the Maronite Christians, who formed 55 percent of the population at that time, while the speaker of the house would be chosen from Shi'ite Muslims, and the prime minister would be chosen from Sunni Muslims. The arrangement continued until the 1980s, when the Lebanese president was the only Christian head of a state in the Middle East. As the Muslim birth rate exceeded that of Christians by the late twentieth century, the Shi'ites became the largest group in the country. The 1975–1990 Lebanese Civil War resulted in a new governmental arrangement in which the prime minister became the head of the state instead of the president, who retained only ceremonial status.

The Lebanese Civil War epitomized the fragility of Middle Eastern political systems and the struggle for power of various religious and ethnic groups. While Lebanon did not engage in any wars with Israel, many Palestinians who fled to Lebanon after the 1948 and 1967 wars made Lebanon their home. The Palestine Liberation Organization chose to operate from Lebanon (after being pushed out of Jordan in 1970), attacking Israel from southern Lebanon, a move that initiated several Israeli attacks on Lebanon and full occupation in 1983, driving the Palestine Liberation Organization from Lebanon. Syria continued to interfere in Lebanese politics, positioning several military units in the country until 2007. The presence of a large number of Syrians and Palestinians, compounded with a significant increase in the Shi'ite and Sunni Muslim population, resulted in the Maronite Christians being outnumbered. Such significant demographic change in a short period of time created the perfect storm for a civil war that claimed thousands of lives and destroyed most of the infrastructure of the country. Christians were fighting Muslims, and Palestinians were fighting Lebanese, while Syrians were taking advantage of the situation.

In 2020, the number of Christians in Lebanon stood at 2.2 million (31 percent of the 7 million total population), while Shi'ite and Sunni Muslims equally comprised 32 percent each. The Druze (a sect that broke out of Islam) comprise 4 percent. While these diversified religious groups are coexisting together for now, any outside tensions might pull the country into unrest.[25] After 2010, Lebanon faced several economic crises, resulting in the collapse of its economy. One of the main challenges facing Lebanon is the increased tension between Israel and the militant group Hezbollah ("the party of God"), which is supported by Iran, resulting in several attacks from both sides.

The Arab Gulf states. In May 1908, a British company discovered oil in Iran, setting in motion waves of exploration and exploitation in the region. Early research for oil did not consider the Arabian Peninsula as a possible location for the black gold. That changed when oil was discovered in Bahrain in 1932 and in Dammam, Saudi Arabia, in 1938. Advancement in transportation methods (use of cars, then airplanes) by the 1920s created a significant need for oil. The demand for oil in almost every conceivable industry mushroomed in the following decades. Starting from the 1930s onwards, oil politics shaped the sociopolitical life of the Gulf states and the rest of the Middle East.

In January 1902 Ibn Saud, a military leader, took Riyadh (in central Arabia) from the Rashid tribe. In 1913, his forces captured parts of eastern Arabia from the Ottomans, consolidating vast territories of Arabia. In 1925 his forces conquered the Hejaz in western Arabia, putting an end to the rule of Sharif Hussein, the ruler of Hejaz who supported the British in the Arab revolt against the Ottomans. It became obvious that the British would support the Saud family since they were able to consolidate power in all of Arabia. In 1932, the kingdom of Saudi Arabia was proclaimed, with Ibn Saud as its first king. The Saud family adopted a strict form of Islam, as they were influenced by the conservative religious ideologies of the eighteenth-century Wahhabi movement.

In the following decades, conservative Islamism controlled the social and political life of Saudi Arabia, making it one of the most conservative Islamic states. Several historic sites (Christian and Islamic) were destroyed, while strict observance of religious practices and moral behavior was enforced through religious police (*mutauown*). Conservative Islam and its social system spread rapidly to other Middle Eastern countries through the thousands of workers and professionals who came to work in the rich oil kingdom starting in the 1970s. The Saudi conservative social and

---

[25]Latif Abul-Husn, *The Lebanese Conflict: Looking Inward* (Boulder, CO: Lynne Rienner, 1998); see also Kenneth Cragg, *The Arab Christian: A History in the Middle East* (Louisville: Westminster John Knox, 1991), 204-32.

religious model also extended to other Islamic nations in Asia and Africa, influencing their political systems while financing the building of mosques and Islamic institutions globally.[26]

Oil money transformed Saudi Arabia from one of the most impoverished countries in the world in the 1950s to one of the richest by the 1980s. Before the first collapse in petroleum prices in the mid-1980s, Saudi Arabia's revenue from petroleum income exceeded $100 billion annually. Social changes within the country, however, were very much lacking. By the beginning of the twenty-first century, as a new generation of Saudis gained access to Western education and social life, many started to challenge the country's conservative religious and social structure while demanding more democratic participation. Women were not allowed to drive prior to 2018, when a new law was enacted by the crown prince allowing women to drive. Women are still not allowed to travel without a male guardian's consent. Strict Islamic shari'a is fully implemented in Saudi Arabia. However, several measures aiming at modernizing the country, including abolishing the religious policing system and promoting religious dialogue, are being enacted. The country is building a massive infrastructure to attract tourism and economic development.

Upon the discovery of oil in the smaller Arabian Gulf states—Kuwait, Qatar, Bahrain, and the United Arab Emirates—the British kept full control over the region until 1968. Arab leaders thought there was a possibility for union between these smaller sheikhdoms of the Gulf; however, Bahrain and Qatar maintained their independent status, while the small seven emirates formed the United Arab Emirates in 1971. The United Arab Emirates is one of the richest countries in the world, and Dubai is a global hub for business, trade, tourism, and sports. The United Arab Emirates maintains open-door policies within a pluralistic society, allowing different ethnic and religious groups to live harmoniously. The Gulf states are vulnerable to attacks from Iran, while Saudi Arabia never agreed to define its borders with these smaller states. Despite waves of revolution and significant political and social changes across the Middle East since the 1950s, the Gulf states have been able to maintain traditional political systems where monarchies have absolute power. The oil revenue provided significant economic compensation

---

[26] Alexei Vassiliev, *The History of Saudi Arabia* (London: Saqi Books, 2000); also Said K. Aburish, *The House of Saud* (New York: St. Martin's, 1996).

for the masses, while the harsh police system would curb any possibility of revolt. Since the Gulf oil production amounts to over half of the world's oil production, the Gulf states receive full political and military support from the United States and Britain. Western powers have interest in keeping the status quo of these oil-rich countries despite their dismal record of human rights in order to secure a steady flow of oil.[27]

While the Arab Gulf states are majority Sunni Muslim, there is a substantial Shi'ite minority in each country. Bahrain is the only country with majority Shi'ites, at 70 percent, though it is governed by a Sunni minority. Kuwait is 24 percent Shi'ite, the United Arab Emirates 18 percent. Conflicts between the two Islamic sects are growing, especially because neighboring countries have a substantial Shi'ite majority (Iraq, 65 percent; Iran, 93 percent). Tension between Iran and other Arab Gulf states continues to present significant challenges for political stability in the region as well as having detrimental effects on the world economy since these countries along with Iraq have over 60 percent of the global oil reserve.

Egypt. Egypt was one of the first Muslim countries to modernize its political and social life. By the 1920s, Egypt enjoyed democratic parliamentary elections, and soon after women were given the right to vote and hold political office. Education through major universities also contributed to the transformation of society in general. The nationalist movement that started in the 1920s gained widespread popularity with the hope of establishing a modernized secular system. By the 1930s the nationalists adopted socialist ideologies, not Marxist, calling for an end to economic disparities in society. Many intellectuals supported the nationalist movement, which also demanded an end to British control over the country. The British (who occupied Egypt from 1882 to 1952) were able to suppress the movement, but the 1952 peaceful revolution put an end to the British exploitation of Egypt.

The Egyptian revolution of the mid-twentieth century, led by Gamal Abdel Nassir (1952–1970), had significant ramifications not only in Egypt but also for the rest of the Middle East and the Arabic-speaking countries. The revolution was peaceful and gained the support of the masses. It presented an unprecedented model of bloodless revolution to the rest of the world. Nassir's socialist, not Marxist, ideologies also gained momentum in implementing land reforms and embarking on a significant industrialization

---

[27] Abdul Kubbah, *OPEC: Past and Present* (Vienna: Retro Economic Research Center, 1974).

program. Nassir's ambitions were not confined to establishing a powerful, modernized Egypt; he was aiming at creating a pan-Arabism movement that would unify the like-minded and progressive Arab nations in one powerful state. Such ambitions cost Egypt economically—a failed unification in 1958 between Egypt and Syria to form the United Arab Republic—and militarily—fighting an independent war in Yemen in 1962 while entering war with Israel in 1967.[28]

The nationalistic movement in Egypt adopted a semisecular political model, a structure that continues to characterize Egyptian sociopolitical life until the present time. While Islamic principles are a vital component of the social fabric of the society, the political system itself separates religion from the state. This model, however, has been constantly challenged by traditionalist Islamists. In fact, Egypt is the birthplace of a highly organized and intellectual traditionalist Islamist movement, the Muslim Brotherhood.

In 1974, under Anwar Sadat (1970–1981), Egypt became the first Arab and Islamic nation to establish a peace treaty with Israel, normalizing political relations and economic cooperation. The move resulted in isolating Egypt from other Arab and Islamic countries that did not approve of Egypt's peace treaty with the "Zionist state."[29] Under Hosni Mubarak (1981–2011), Egypt continued its open-door economic (i.e., capitalistic) policies that started during Sadat's era. The economic gains benefited the wealthy, political elites, and the military, while the rest of the population descended into cycles of poverty and oppression. Regime corruption, economic injustice, police brutality, and human-rights abuses dominated Egypt in the second half of the twentieth century, resulting in the 2011 and 2013 revolutions.[30]

Egypt has a long history of civilization dating back before Christianity and Islam. Egyptians are aware that one of the oldest and most sophisticated civilizations, lasting for over five millennia, developed on their land. This was a civilization that featured innovations in agriculture, writing, mathematics, philosophy, arts, law, medicine, and engineering. Egypt was instrumental in influencing the Islamic intellectual enterprise globally through various religious publications and educating generations of Muslim scholars at the prestigious Al-Azhar University, the oldest Islamic university,

---

[28]P. J. Vatikiotis, *The Modern History of Egypt*, 4th ed. (New York: Praeger, 1969).
[29]Raymond Hinebusch Jr., *Egyptian Politics Under Sadat*, 2nd ed. (Boulder, CO: Lynne Rienner, 1988).
[30]Charles Tripp and Roger Owen, *Egypt Under Mubarak* (London: Routledge, 1989).

established in 995. During the twentieth century, Egypt became the epicenter of the social, cultural, and political life of the Muslim world while providing a significant leadership role in various political and Islamic organizations.

Egypt is also home to the largest Christian community in the Middle East. Egyptian Christians, the Copts (the name is derived from the Greek word for Egypt, *Aegyptus*), represented 12 percent (12 million) of the Egyptian population of 102 million in 2020. The Egyptian church has a long history, dating to the first century of Christianity, and was instrumental in spreading the Christian faith into Europe and Ethiopia. Its catechetical school of Alexandria was the first Christian educational institution, while Egypt introduced one of the most important spiritual Christian movements, monasticism. From 1980 to 2012 Egyptian Christians witnessed several episodes of sporadic persecution and intolerant policies, resulting in thousands of casualties and the destruction of many church buildings and Christian businesses. It is estimated that over one million Egyptians have turned to Christianity in the last twenty years. It is also estimated that over two million have embraced atheistic ideologies as they became disillusioned with the violent practices of militant jihadi movements in the region.[31]

AFRICA

North Africa. By the 1920s, France had full control over Morocco, Algeria, and Tunisia, while Italy occupied Libya.

Algeria. Large numbers of French people resettled in northern Algeria, while thousands of Algerians immigrated to France. Though the French living in Algeria were protected by the French military and had full citizenship and political rights, their Algerian counterparts struggled to integrate into French society, an ongoing reality for Algerians living in France. That France did not recognize the contribution made by Algerians who fought in the French army during World War I (170,000 Algerians were recruited and 25,000 were killed) generated cycles of resentment against the French in Algeria.

In 1945, at the end of World War II, violence broke out in Algeria as France again did not recognize the contribution made by Algerians who were forced to join the French army in the war. Sentiment against the French occupation of Algeria started to gain momentum, and it took different approaches, one secular and the other religious. Secularists wanted full integration in French

---

[31]*Al-Ahram*, January 15, 2017.

society; many of them had access to French education and were inspired by modernization's principles. Some secularists adopted Marxist ideologies advocating for the creation of a socialist society. The majority, however, wanted to maintain an Islamic religious identity in contrast to French occupation and culture. France considered Algeria its territory and was not willing to tolerate any call for independence. Between 1948 and 1962, when Algeria finally gained independence from France, more than one million Algerians were killed and entire villages were eradicated by the French. Meanwhile, one million Europeans out of ten million who had settled in Algeria fled to France by 1962. The Algerian struggle for independence was one of the most violent in the twentieth century. As some observers put it, "The French were willing to destroy Algeria in order to retain it."[32]

Algeria continued to suffer from political instability after independence. Several nationalist groups competed for power, resulting in thousands of casualties. The semisecular government of Houari Boumediene (1965–1978) introduced a socialist state system with one-party rule. Algeria was not able to make significant political or social changes in general; changes in women's status were minimal in comparison to neighboring Tunisia or Morocco. Meanwhile, Algeria was not able to maintain national unity. The 1960s advocacy for the Arabization of the country was met with resistance from the elite and educated, who were comfortable using French rather than Arabic. This Arabization also resulted in creating a major rift between the Berber people, who formed 40 percent of the population and were instrumental in the movement for independence, and other Algerians. Soon the Berbers were suppressed; their Amazeric language was restricted and their territories were prevented from developing economically. Algeria and Morocco continued to a have substantial number of indigenous Berbers (45 percent of the population in Morocco and 40 percent of Algeria as of 2000). Recently, the Algerian government recognized the rights of indigenous Berbers, granting them permission to use Amazeric instead of Arabic in education and social media.

In 1988 the Algerian government removed restrictions on the formation of Islamic parties after two decades of suppressing them. The government was responding to outside pressure to allow greater democratic participation in governing. Soon after, Islamists formed the Islamic Salvation

---

[32]Michael Brett, ed., *Northern Africa, Islam and Modernization* (London: Cass, 1973).

Front, which gained popularity by 1991 and was about to win majority seats in the parliament. In 1992, the military canceled the election and arrested the leaders of the Islamic party, banning the party altogether. This drastic move by the military resulted in a ten-year civil war that claimed 150,000 lives. Islamist extremists embarked on a campaign of killing secular Algerians and Europeans, including many Christians. Ethnic violence between Arabs and Berbers ensued, resulting in the massacre of the population of entire villages. At the end of the unprecedented civil war, it was not clear who was attacking whom and for what purpose. By 1997, Islamists lost the support of most Algerians, who were horrified by the mass killings and widespread destruction done by the extremists.[33]

The Algerian civil war resulted in economic collapse and social fragmentation that is still present in the country. Despite its significant oil and natural gas resources, Algeria struggles economically. After 2000, Algeria witnessed a significant surge in the number of Muslims turning to Christianity. It is estimated that over one million people, especially among the Berber (Qabil), have abandoned Islam. The extremists' massacre and terrorizing of civilians during the civil war left many Muslims puzzled about the religious mandate of jihad. Many Berbers were Christians up until the sixteenth century, when they were Islamized under the Ottoman rule of Algeria.[34]

Morocco. The French protectorate over Morocco kept in place the royal family that ruled during the Ottomans, appointing Muhammad V (1926–1961) the new king. The king was initially able to maintain a balance between pleasing the French and attaining the backing of the masses, who sought independence from the French. Affirming Islam as the religion of the state and governing according to Islamic principles were key in securing such a balance. Yet the Algerian war of independence was viewed with great interest in neighboring Morocco, where nationalists demanded full independence from France and the withdrawal of the Spanish from Morocco's northern territories. The nationalists' demands were met in 1956 after periods of unrest and violent encounters with the French and the Spanish.

The rule of King Hassan II (1961–1999) was characterized by ruthless suppression of dissent; the king survived two coups, in 1971 and 1972.

---

[33]Shireen T. Hunter, "The Algerian Crisis: Origins, Evolution and Lessons for the Maghreb and Europe," Center for European Policy Studies paper no. 63 (1996).
[34]David Garrison, *A Wind in the House of Islam*, 5th ed. (Monument, CO: WIG Take Resources, 2015).

While several social reforms were introduced, Morocco remained for the most part a traditionalist Islamic monarchy. The revolts of 2011 across the Middle East and North Africa forced the current king, Muhammad VI (1999–present), to allow for greater democratic participation. Such measures resulted in the rise of Islamist groups who currently control the parliament. The king is trying to maintain a balance between allowing for democratic measures, which has resulted in a surge of power for traditionalist Islamists while maintaining a modernized and semisecularized state.[35] New measures of freedom for indigenous Moroccan Christians were offered after 2014. It is estimated that over 250,000 Moroccans have turned to Christianity in the last three decades.[36]

Tunisia. Tunisia gained independence from France in 1956, the same year Morocco did. However, Tunisia's encounter with France was more peaceful than that of Algeria. Tunisia is by far the most secular state in North Africa. While Algeria and Morocco maintain strong connections to Islamic religious principles, Tunisia has featured secularist governments starting from the era of Habib Bourguiba (1956–1987) until the present. Just a few months after independence, the new secularist government seized religious endowments and absorbed the shari'a courts into the state judicial system. Polygamy was outlawed, and women were given rights of divorce and child custody. Bourguiba went as far as calling for abandoning the fast of Ramadan. His reasoning was that a modernized Tunisia needs the efforts of all citizens to be engaged in economic jihad to build the country. Therefore, people would be exempt from fasting just as warriors were entitled to be exempt from fasting. While his secularist ideology did not convince the ulama (religious leaders), who saw in Bourguiba an enemy of Islam, he won the support of many educated people and secularists in the country.

Bourguiba's secularist and authoritarian regime, however, was challenged by various Islamists, who called for mandatory veiling of women, restrictions on women's employment, and permission to practice polygamy, which is allowed under shari'a and considered a basic right for men. Bourguiba was suspicious of any religious groups trying to compete for governance. The regime crushed the Islamic tendency movement of the 1980s and discouraged the formation of religious parties. The Algerian experience with

---

[35]Brett, *Northern Africa, Islam and Modernization.*
[36]Garrison, *Wind in the House of Islam.*

Islamists in the 1990s made the Tunisians cautious about the rise of Islamist parties. While many Tunisians had hoped that a new era of political freedom was dawning, the only viable alternative was to support Islamists, which was rejected based on what took place in neighboring Algeria.[37]

Tunisia led the Arab revolt movement in 2011 against injustices, police brutality, and corruption that dominated the Arab world. Its revolution resulted in new democratic measures while curbing the power of Islamists, who tried to seize the opportunity to establish an Islamic state system. Though the Islamic party, Al-Nahda ("the renaissance"), is part of a coalition government today, Tunisia remains one of the most semisecular states in the region. Although it monitors closely the activities of indigenous Tunisian Christians, the Tunisian government allows limited freedom for the group, which is estimated to number around one hundred thousand.

Libya. The Italian occupation of Libya faced significant resistance from the Sanusis, a Sufi order that controlled eastern Libya, Cyrenaica (Cyrene) as it was known at the time. The Italians had to use harsh measures to quell the movement. For most of the first half of the twentieth century, Libya was controlled by traditional Muslim sheikhs (religious leaders). Before the discovery of oil, Libya was the least economically developed country in North Africa. Its predominantly nomadic society was characterized by tribal loyalties rather than national unity. After World War II, the Italians were pushed out of Libya and replaced with British and French troops. Italy maintained a small presence in western Libya, Tripolitania (what is today Tripoli). In 1947, Sayyed Idris was installed as the new king in Cyrenaica in the east; however, it took him three years to establish his rule over a unified Libya that included the eastern and western parts of the country, Cyrenaica and Tripolitania.[38]

As an impoverished country, Libya depended on leasing air bases to Britain and the United States to generate revenue. However, that changed after 1959, when large quantities of oil and natural gas were discovered in the Libyan Desert. Gamal Abdel Nassir's (1952–1970) pan-Arabism and his anti-imperialistic rhetoric inspired nationalists in Libya to demand that the government remove all foreign troops from the country. As a result, the British and Americans evacuated the Libyan bases in 1964. In

---

[37]Brett, *Northern Africa, Islam and Modernization.*
[38]E. E. Evans-Pritchard, *The Sanusi of Cyrenaica* (Oxford: Clarendon, 1949).

1969, Mouamr Qhadafi led a revolution that ended the monarchy and started a long rule of tyranny. Inspired by Nassir's pan-Arabism, Qhadafi embarked on several unplanned and failed unifications with Egypt, Syria, and Sudan. He supported violent political movements across the globe, from left-wing organizations in Japan to the Irish Republican Army. He wasted the wealth generated from oil on supporting terrorist groups in the Middle East and Africa.

The 2011 revolt in Libya, which resulted in military intervention by NATO to end the massacre of civilians by Qhadafi's forces, also put an end to his long rule (1969–2011), as Qhadafi and one of his sons were killed by the rebels. The country spiraled into a civil war that is still raging, with two governments competing for power. The two governments are based in the same two territories, Cyrene and Tripoli, that represented the competing powers a century ago, before the formation of a country called Libya. While Libya has no indigenous Christian population, thousands of Christian expatriates work in the country; the majority are Christians from Egypt. The infamous video of the beheading of twenty-two Egyptian Christians on the beach in Tripoli in 2014 became a symbol of ISIS atrocities against civilians in the region.[39]

Sub-Saharan Africa. By the beginning of the twentieth century, France controlled most of West Africa. Despite France's ideology of *mission civilisatrice* ("civilizing mission"), most African territories occupied by France were left with no proper education or access to social development. It was easier and cheaper for France to let traditional Muslim and African religious rulers control their territories under French occupation while France pocketed their natural resources. In the 1940s France introduced a political arrangement consisting of a West African federation of states, whereby France maintained its control over foreign policy, trade, and economics, allowing limited internal self-rule. As France continued its policies of forced labor and expressed racist attitudes toward Africans, demands for independence started to grow, resulting in the granting of full independence to all its West African territories in the 1960s. Most West African nations, such as Mali, Niger, Guinea, and Chad, are predominantly Muslim states, while Senegal, the Ivory Coast, and Ghana have considerable numbers of Christians. Muslims and Christians in these

[39]*Economist*, March 12, 2012.

West African nations have overall harmonious relations; however, sporadic tensions often result in mistrust and conflict.[40]

In 1960, Nigeria, Africa's most populous nation (210 million as of 2020), gained independence from England. Nigeria is religiously and ethnically divided into a predominantly Muslim north (47 percent) and a Christian south (49 percent). Hausa, Fulani, and Kanuri are the traditional ethnic groups of Nigeria's Muslim north, while Ibo and Yoruba are the Christian tribes. As the number of Christians started to grow by the mid-twentieth century, Nigeria witnessed several episodes of strained relations between Muslims and Christians. The 1966 killing of thousands of Ibo Christians by the Hausa and Fulani Muslims led to tension between the two communities. Subsequent events, such as forcing the implementation of shari'a in Nigerian courts by Islamic-led governments, terrified the Christians.[41] The political arrangement in Islamic northern Nigeria allows for local emirs to rule over Islamic territories with full implementation of Islamic laws and customs.[42] The terrorist group Boko Haram, which was formed in 2009, presents a significant challenge to the political and social stability of Nigeria. The group is responsible for destroying several villages, kidnapping schoolgirls, and killing Christians and Muslims who oppose them.

Kenya, Uganda, and Tanzania have a larger percentage of Christians (between 60 and 70 percent) as well as a substantial number of Muslims (15 to 30 percent). While the two religious communities enjoy relatively peaceful coexistence for the most part, the perceived Christianization or Islamization of these countries occasionally results in tension.

The most predominantly Muslim nation in the Horn of Africa is Somalia, with a 99.9 percent Muslim population. Somalia continued to be tormented by the terrorist group al-Shabab ("the youth"), which contributed to a total collapse of its economy and its sociopolitical structure. Ethiopia is the largest Christian nation in the Horn of Africa, with a population of 118 million as of 2020 (65 percent Christian and 33 percent Muslim). The Christian-Muslim ratios in these African nations,

---

[40]J. Spencer Trimingham, *A History of Islam in West Africa* (Oxford: Oxford University Press, 1962).
[41]In 1986, the Muslim Nigerian president Babangida changed Nigeria's observer status at the World Islamic Organization into full membership, a move that created concerns among the Christians that Nigeria was moving toward full Islamization.
[42]Stuarts Mews, ed., *Religion and Politics: A World Guide* (London: Longman Group, 1989).

while embodying a great mosaic of interreligious and cultural diversity, can also result in significant strain.[43]

Tensions between northern and southern Sudan resulted in creating two states in 2011. South Sudan (10 million) is predominantly Christian, with a substantial number of animists, while Sudan (45 million) is predominantly Muslim. Much of Sudan's recent history has been characterized by natural disasters and political turmoil. Several Islamist governments imposed strict Islamic laws, resulting in the persecution of Christians and moderate Muslims. Since 1985, a large number of Christians have been forced to leave the country, while some Christian villages were sacked and destroyed.[44]

Most of the southern African nations are majority Christian with some Muslims. By the 1960s, traditional African religions started to give way to Islam and Christianity. Africa witnessed the largest surge in the number of Christians in the twentieth century, an increase from 12 million (9.4 percent of the total population) in 1910 to 494 million (47.9 percent) in 2010.[45] Meanwhile, the number of Muslims in Africa increased from 40 million (32 percent of the total population) in 1910 to 417 million (40.5 percent of the total population) in 2010.[46] Sporadic tensions between Christian and Muslim communities occur, especially when evangelization results in converting Muslims to Christianity or imposing Islamic shari'a on Christians. Africa is home to large independent churches, which comprise over 10 percent of all Christians.[47]

Asia

India and Pakistan. Calls for independence from British rule in India gained momentum in the 1930s. While Gandhi's nonviolence and noncooperation movement was increasingly supported among Hindus, Muslims were weary of his ideologies. Although Gandhi wanted to lead an all-India

---

[43]Haggai Erlich, *Islam and Christianity in the Horn of Africa* (London: Lynne Rienner, 2010).
[44]Abdelwahab El-Affendi, *Turabi's Revolution: Islam and Power in Sudan* (London: Grey Seal, 1991).
[45]Todd M. Johnson and Kenneth R. Ross, eds., *Atlas of Global Christianity* (Edinburgh: Edinburgh University Press, 2009), 9.
[46]Johnson and Ross, *Atlas of Global Christianity*, 11.
[47]These churches tend to blend patterns of native African religious practices with Christian forms of worship and theology. Africa is also home to the largest Anglican community in the world, with over 120 million adherents. The Anglican Church is in significant decline in England and North America.

campaign against the British, he was most successful when employing Hindu symbols and rhetoric. Throughout the campaign of the 1930s, it became clear to the Muslims of India, who comprised a quarter of the population, that independence movements (there were several independence movements; however, Gandhi's movement in particular was able to mobilize millions of followers) were aiming at creating a Hindu political structure in which Muslims would have minimal participation. Accordingly, an Islamic organization called the Muslim League advocated for the creation of a Muslim India within India. The concept of an independent Islamic state within India had been first introduced by Sayyid Ahmad Khan (1817–1898). However, the mastermind behind the plan proposed in the 1930s was the well-educated Muhammed Iqbal (1877–1938), a graduate of Cambridge, lawyer, philosopher, and poet. A group of Cambridge students from the Punjab suggested the name *Pakistan* for the independent territory, which means "Land of the Pure" in Urdu.

While many Indians were hoping to create a modern democratic state where various religious and ethnic groups could live together, many Muslim leaders became obsessed with the concept of a separate Islamic territory against the fear of a predominantly Hindu state. Meanwhile, Muslims were scattered all over India, and it seemed unrealistic to create a state for Muslims only. Ideologically, a state for Muslims would not necessarily be an Islamic state. The early generation who worked on the creation of Pakistan, such as Iqbal and Muhammad Ali Jinnah (1876–1948), did not envision a strict Islamic state where shari'a would be applied. Jinnah, who lived most of his life in Britain, envisioned a secular state rather than a religious one.[48]

In 1946, as negotiations for India's independence started, the Muslim League of India demanded the creation of a self-governing Pakistan within an Indian federation, while the Islamic Congress of India called for a full independent state. When Britain gave full independence to India on August 15, 1947, two countries emerged: India and Pakistan. The new Muslim state was composed of two regions, East (current Bangladesh) and West Pakistan, which were separated by nine hundred miles of Indian territory. In the next few months millions of Hindus and Sikhs left Pakistan for India, while millions of Muslims left India for Pakistan. Over one

---

[48]Peter Hardy, *The Muslims of British India* (Cambridge: Cambridge University Press, 1972).

million were massacred in a bloody civil war in both countries. Several wars between India and Pakistan ensued in the following decades. The first war resulted in dividing Kashmir between the two countries.

Pakistan was formed as an Islamic state; however, perspectives varied on what constituted an Islamic state. As the secularist generation of Jinnah and Iqbal passed on by the late 1940s, new conservative voices called for the strict application of shari'a. Agreement on the Islamic meaning of democracy, freedom, and equality meant that Muslims should conduct their lives in accordance with the teaching of the Qur'an and Sunnah. For the next two decades, Pakistan could not agree on a constitution that explained the structure of an Islamic state. As riots and violence erupted between secularists and conservative Muslims, the army took control of the country and enforced martial law, a situation that characterizes most of the political history of the country. Several coups took place during the second half of the twentieth century. Tensions between East and West Pakistan over political power resulted in the creation of Bangladesh (East Pakistan) in 1971 with the help of the Indian army.[49]

The separation of East Pakistan (Bangladesh) and the defeat of Pakistan by India in the 1970s created a sense of humility while shattering the dream of establishing an Islamic state based on religion, which resulted in ethnic tension and rivalry. Furthermore, Indian Muslims who immigrated to Pakistan were dissatisfied with the way the country was heading. In a time of social and political upheavals, traditionalist Muslims attributed the disastrous situation to Pakistan's failure to establish a true Islamic state. Strife between various Islamic groups followed as Shi'ite Muslims were marginalized, while Ahmadiah Muslims were considered apostate and were persecuted and banned from the military and governmental positions.

Under the leadership of Zia ul-Haq, who came to power after a military coup in 1977, Pakistan witnessed further Islamization. Political parties were banned and a strict Islamic law nullifying all secular laws was declared. The Islamic banking system was also introduced. Pakistan witnessed a momentous surge in Islamic schools, madrassas; its religious certificate was declared equal to a university degree, while secular education was underfunded. The total number of Islamic schools increased from nine hundred in 1971 to thirty-three thousand in 1988. Practically, it

---

[49]Leonard Binder, *Religion and Politics in Pakistan* (Berkeley: University of California Press, 1961).

became impossible for the government to maintain oversight over such a large number of Islamic schools, and many became indoctrination centers for radical Islam. The strict Sunni Islamization of Pakistan should be viewed in light of the political challenges in countries surrounding Pakistan: the Iranian Revolution of 1979 created a powerful Shi'ite state to the west of Pakistan, while the Soviet invasion of Afghanistan was perceived as an attack on Islam itself.[50]

In the following years, thousands of Afghani refugees fled to Pakistan, where many of them were incorporated into the social fabric of the country. The Saudis poured millions of dollars into supporting the Islamic educational system as well as the Afghani Muslim mujahideen (those who carry out jihad wars) who were fighting the Russians. Strife between Sunni and Shi'ite Muslims accelerated in the 1980s due to the application of strict Sunni laws. In 1982, a "blasphemy law" was introduced, according to which desecrating the Qur'an or Prophet Muhammad is punishable by death or imprisonment for life, respectively. Since then, many Christians have been accused of violating the blasphemy law, while any attempts to change the law have resulted in the murder of high-ranking officials who dared to speak against it. Christians in Pakistan (fewer than 3 million) make up only 1.2 percent of the 230 million population. They live in deplorable conditions and endure severe persecution.

India is home to one of the largest Muslim communities in the world, with 170 million Muslims (14.2 percent of the total population of 1.4 billion), while Christians comprise only 2.3 percent of the population (27 million). Although Christianity is the third largest religion in India after Hinduism and Islam, Christians are sporadically persecuted for their faith by Hindus and Muslims. South Asia, or the subcontinent of India (India, Pakistan, and Bangladesh), is home to the largest Muslim population in the world, with over 480 million Muslims, comprising 40 percent of the global population of Muslims.

Afghanistan. Afghanistan is an Islamic state, with 99.7 percent Muslims out of its total population of 40 million.[51] Continuous unrest and tribal warfare dominated the political and social landscape of the country during the first half of the twentieth century. The Soviet invasion of Afghanistan

---

[50] Eqbal Ahmed, *Islam: Politics and State; The Pakistan Experience* (London: Zed Books, 1985).
[51] Its rugged mountainous terrain makes it difficult to traverse, which is why it became a safe haven for Al-Qaeda and other terrorist groups that operate from the country.

in 1979 resulted in a critical chain of events involving both Russia and the United States. During the 1980s, the United States supported the Afghani mujahideen against the Soviets. Meanwhile, the Soviet Union's occupation of Afghanistan was a factor in weakening the power of the Soviet Union itself, leading to its dissolution in 1991. Once the Russians left Afghanistan, radical Islamists controlled the country through the Taliban up until the American invasion of Afghanistan in 2001 in the aftermath of al-Qaeda's attack on the United States on September 11, 2001. The American invasion of Afghanistan continued until 2014. Afghanistan continued to spiral into violent tribal wars and radical Islamism, resulting in the total collapse of its economic, social, and political system.[52]

Southeast Asia. Indonesia. During the 1930s and 1940s, Islam did not present a viable unifying force in the context of the multiethnic culture of Indonesia. One of the key nationalists who emerged during that time was Sukarno (1901–1970). He established the Indonesian National Association, which became the strongest catalyst for the independence movement. He proposed changing the country's name from the Netherlands Indies to Indonesia and its capital's name from Batavia to Jakarta. He also proposed adopting the Malay dialect as the national language of Indonesia, known as *Bahasa Indonesia* ("the language of Indonesia"). The nationalists had a secular bent, desiring to uphold the multifaith fabric of Indonesian society, which also included Buddhism, Hinduism, and animistic religions. Indonesia retained a multifaith culture for several decades as Islam, while the main religion, did not dominate the sociopolitical structure or the cultural life of the country.

After the country became independent in 1945, various Islamic groups demanded that its political and social structure be based on Islamic principles. However, the secular nationalists, including Sukarno, were alarmed that such a move would alienate the large number of Christians, Hindus, and Buddhists as well as nominal Muslims. Instead, the political structure of Indonesia was founded on what is called Pancasila, or Five Principles: monotheism, nationalism, humanitarianism, social justice, and democracy. These principles make up the ideological foundation for Indonesia up until today.[53]

---

[52] Larry P. Goodson, *Afghanistan's Endless War: State Failure, Regional Politics and the Rise of the Taliban* (Seattle: University of Washington Press, 2001).

[53] Anthony Reid, *The Indonesian National Revolution* (Hawthorn, Australia: Longman, 1974).

For most of the second half of the twentieth century, the political structure of Indonesia was primarily secular, with a socialist orientation. Muslim groups were silenced during the rule of Sukarno (1945–1967) and Suharto (1967–1998). Suharto presided over an era of impressive economic growth and was credited with launching educational programs that raised the literacy rate from 40 percent to 90 percent. He restricted polygamy, increased women's freedom, and empowered civil courts while dismantling shari'a courts. He also restricted the formation of Islamic political parties. Such moves angered traditional Islamists, who saw in these measures a systemic war on Islam itself. By the turn of the century, several Islamic groups started to gain power in Indonesia, challenging its long-standing secular political system. Islamic extremist groups became violent, attacking tourists and Christians and bombing businesses. The most violent groups operated on the islands of Western Java and Ache.[54]

Indonesia is the largest Muslim country in the world, with a population of 270 million, which is 87 percent Muslim and 10 percent Christian. Tension between Christians and Muslim extremists has increased during the last two decades. The appointment of Basuki Purnama, a Christian, as the governor of Jakarta did not sit well with many Islamists. His running for reelection in 2016 resulted in massive riots and rallies from Muslim extremists, who accused him of insulting Islam, resulting in his imprisonment. Bias against non-Muslims, primarily Chinese, is evident in Indonesia (and Malaysia). Chinese control over business and the economy in Southeast Asia usually triggers riots and violent reactions from the natives.

Malaysia. In contrast to Indonesia, which maintained a multicultural and multifaith society, the Malay Peninsula (Malaysia) was predominantly Malay and Muslim. Although many Chinese and Indians poured into the peninsula to work for the rubber and tin industries in the 1930s and 1940s, forming almost half of the population, Malays demanded that citizenship be reserved only for Malays. Three years after the Malay Peninsula gained independence from Britain in 1957, a new constitution was drafted that made Islam the official religion of the state while affirming Islamic shari'a as the law of the state for family law and some criminal laws. According to the constitution, all Muslims must observe Islamic laws. In addition, the

---

[54]Robert W. Hefner, *Civil Islam: Muslims and Democratization in Indonesia* (Princeton, NJ: Princeton University Press, 2000).

constitution grants special status for Malays while defining an ethnic Malay as a Muslim who speaks Malay and observes Malay customs. Such provision automatically excludes all Malays who adhere to other religions or are ethnically not Malay. In 1963, the Malay Peninsula was renamed Malaysia. Considering its predominantly Chinese ethnicity and religiously diversified population, Singapore left the federation of Malaysia and became an independent state in 1965.[55]

A new wave of support for Malay identity and culture reinforced Islam as the state religion and Malay as the ethnicity of the country. Several radical Islamic groups emerged in the aftermath of riots in 1969 demanding the implementation of new measures to Islamize the country. One prominent group, called Dakwa (a Malay variant of *da'wa*, "calling," the Arabic word for "propagation"), demanded further Islamization of the country. In response to these growing pressures from Islamists, the Malaysian secular government established an Islamic university and Islamic banking system; however, the Malaysian governing system remained semisecular.[56]

The Philippines. The US occupation of the Philippines, which began in 1898, came to an end in 1946. After independence, Muslims in Mindanao demanded self-rule within a federated Philippines where shari'a could be implemented. The government in Manila perceived the Muslims' demand as a threat to the unity of the country, and it was rejected. The following decades witnessed several bloody civil wars in the region of Mindanao, where tens of thousands were killed. Several agreements were drafted, and a 1976 agreement granted a semi-independent state for the majority Muslims in the region within the Philippines. The Philippines is the largest Christian nation in Asia, with 92 percent Christians out of the 110 million total population, and home to the largest Asian Catholic population, with 65 million Catholics, while Muslims form 5 percent of the total population.[57]

Starting in the 1950s, several influential Muslim leaders in Southeast Asia—in Indonesia, Malaysia, and the Philippines—received their education at the prestigious Islamic Al-Azhar University in Cairo, Egypt. They became the powerful voices advocating for the Islamization of their countries.

---

[55] Robert Day McAmis, *Malay Muslims: The History and Challenge of Resurgence Islam in Southeast Asia* (Grand Rapids, MI: Eerdmans, 2002); also M. B. Hooker, ed., *Islam in Southeast Asia* (Leiden: Brill, 1983).
[56] Zainah Anwar, *Islamic Revivalism in Malaysia: Dakwah Among the Students* (Petaling Jaya, Malaysia: Penlanduk, 1987).
[57] P. Gowing, ed., *Understanding Islam and Muslims in the Philippines* (Quezon City: New Day, 1988).

Meanwhile, several Arabian Gulf states financed the establishment of Islamic centers and universities, facilitating the spread of Islam in the region. By the 1980s several radical Islamic groups emerged, such as Abu Sayyaf in the Philippines and Laskar in Indonesia, demanding stricter forms of Islam. They carried out several deadly attacks against foreigners and their governments.

Central Asia. The Bolshevik Revolution of 1917 created a new reality for the millions of Muslims living in what became the Soviet Union. Between 1924 and 1936, the Russian government created Soviet republics, drawing new borders, mixing several ethnic groups, and even giving new names to certain languages. The communist regime, while encouraging a sense of Russian nationalism among the various republics, curbed the role and power of religion altogether. Most mosques and Islamic schools across central Asia were closed. Many Muslims participated in secularized social life, while others practiced Islam in secret. The adoption of the Cyrillic alphabet put an end to the use of Arabic by the various Turkic, Tajik, Uzbek, and Persian groups living in central Asia. By the 1950s, those who did not assimilate to the new social structure of the Soviet Union were sent north to Siberia or displaced to other provinces. Various groups of Muslims, including the Chechen, suffered great losses during this period. After the breakup of the Soviet Union in 1991, Muslims in central Asian countries such as Kyrgyzstan, Uzbekistan, Tajikistan, and Turkmenistan started to assert their Islamic identity and culture.

In the 1930s, Muslims in the western Chinese province of Xinjiang accounted for 98 percent of the total population, with the Uyghurs (of Turkic ethnicity) representing 80 percent of the population. The Cultural Revolution (1966–1976) in China and the rule of Mao Zeitung resulted in diluting the demographic presence of the Turkic Muslims with the relocation of many Chinese Han to the province. According to a 1998 census, the settlement policy resulted in reducing the number of Muslims in Xinjiang to 60 percent of the total population. Tension between Uyghurs and other ethnic groups intensified during the second half of the twentieth century, while various radical Islamic groups in the province carried out deadly attacks on civilians and government institutions. The Cultural Revolution curbed the influence of Islam in the province, abolishing shari'a in the court system while restricting the power of Islamic institutions and mosques.[58]

---

[58]S. Frederick Starr, ed., *Xinjiang: China's Muslim Borderland* (Armonk, NY: M. E. Sharpe, 2004).

Muslims in China account for 25 million (1.8 percent) of the total population of 1.4 billion, while Christians in China account for 95 million (7 percent) of the total population. Christianity is growing steadily despite the persecution Christians endured during the Cultural Revolution and the various restrictions imposed on the church thereafter. The official number of Christians who belong to the government-approved Three Self Church is 5 percent of the population; however, the estimated number of Chinese Christians who belong to the underground house churches accounts for another 2 or even 5 percent of the population.[59]

The continent of Asia has the smallest percentage of Christians, while Christians sporadically face persecution in predominantly communist, Islamic, Hindu, and Buddhist countries. However, Christianity grew significantly during the twentieth century, at an estimated rate of 2.5 million people newly identified as Christians per year. Christians represent over 40 percent of the South Korean population, with several megachurches in the capital, Seoul. The number of Muslims is also growing in South Korea, with an estimated 150,000 or 0.03 percent of the total population. Christians in North Korea are not allowed to practice their faith publicly and are among the most persecuted Christians in the world. Japan has one of the smallest Christian communities in Asia, at less than 1 percent. The rise of Japanese nationalism, symbolized in the revival of Shinto practices, combined with the Japanese being on the opposite side of the United States and Britain in World War II resulted in the closure of many churches and the suppression of Christianity in general. There are also a very small number of Muslims in Japan, less than one hundred thousand, mainly foreigners working in the country.

Europe

Eastern Europe. The collapse of the Ottoman Empire in the 1920s, which encouraged the emergence of various nationalistic movements in the Balkans, along with the Bolshevik Revolution in Russia in 1917 had a dramatic impact on Eastern Orthodoxy in Europe. By the beginning of the nineteenth century, Russian Orthodoxy enjoyed a strong presence in society, and a sense of Russian nationalism was also expressed in a new commitment to religious traditions. Russian nationalism encouraged a

---

[59]Johnson and Ross, *Atlas of Global Christianity*, 140-41.

rejection of Western Protestantism and Catholicism, and in 1819 Russians reacted against Western influence on their country and expelled Jesuit missionaries who had entered Russia from neighboring Poland and Lithuania. Some even called for a stronger Russian nationalism based on Orthodox tradition.

Also, during the nineteenth century, monastic life started to flourish anew in the Russian Orthodox Church. Whereas in 1810 there were 452 monasteries in Russia, by 1914 there were 1,025.[60] The great novels of Fyodor Dostoevsky (1821–1881) and Leo Tolstoy (1828–1910) reflected the height of Russian Christian spirituality, exploring redemption through suffering and loving one's enemy. A few years later, in 1917, the Russian Orthodox Church suffered a disastrous blow when the Bolshevik Revolution led to the establishment of a communist regime under Vladimir Lenin.

Lenin abolished the Holy Synod, which had been responsible for leading the church, and restored the office of the patriarch.[61] The leadership of the church welcomed the move and thought that the new government supported freedom of religion. However, a year later, the Soviet Union confiscated all church buildings and lands, making them state property. In 1920, the teaching of religion was outlawed in schools, while thousands of bishops, priests, monks, and nuns were arrested. Some were executed, while the majority were imprisoned. Distribution of Bibles was banned, and all religious activities were considered antirevolutionary. In the following decades, Christians in Russia suffered severe persecution. Despite these hard times, some congregations survived, while others flourished in the underground church. The collapse of the Soviet Union in the 1990s resulted in restoring freedom of religion in Russia and other Eastern European countries where the practice of Christianity was formerly banned. Although decades of atheism and antireligious policies have eroded the Christian culture in Russia and eastern Europe, new waves of re-Christianization are bringing back millions of people to Christianity.

According to the national census conducted in 2012, there are 9.5 million Muslims in Russia, or 6.5 percent of the total population, with the province of Chechnya boasting the largest number of Muslims in the

---

[60]David B. Barrett, George T. Kurian, and Todd M. Johnson, eds., *World Christian Encyclopedia*, 2nd ed. (New York: Oxford University Press, 2001), 1:130.

[61]The Holy Synod had been established by Tsar Peter the Great to control the church while abolishing the office of the patriarch.

Russian Federation. Chechnya was Islamized between the sixteenth and the nineteenth centuries. Chechnyan Muslims are demanding an independent Islamic state apart from the Russian Federation, where social life and political structure could be governed by Islamic rules and principles. The Chechnyan separatist movement continues to present a political challenge to the Russian government, as they have carried out several deadly attacks on Russian civilians and government institutions.[62]

For centuries, Orthodox churches in eastern Europe were under the leadership of the patriarch of Constantinople (Istanbul), also known as the ecumenical patriarch. Once the Ottoman Empire collapsed, several nationalistic movements in the Balkans asserted their independence from the Islamic caliphate. Orthodox churches in the Balkans—Serbia, Bulgaria, Romania, Greece, and Albania—sought independence from the authority of both the ecumenical patriarch and Russia.[63] They formed self-governing national churches (autocephalous churches), each with its own patriarch, by the early nineteenth century, corresponding to movements of independence from the Ottoman Empire itself, ending the harsh treatment of Christians that had lasted for four centuries.[64]

After World War II, some of the Balkan states—Croatia, Bosnia-Herzegovina, Kosovo, Macedonia, Montenegro, Slovenia, and Serbia—formed the Republic of Yugoslavia. The collapse of the Soviet Union and communism created a political vacuum in the region. In 1991, Slovenia and Croatia seceded from Yugoslavia, provoking a war with Yugoslavia. The intervention of the European Union encouraged Bosnia-Herzegovina and Macedonia to announce their independence as well. A civil war ensued in the following years, based not only on nationalistic disparities but even more on religiously motivated encounters between Christians and Muslims, reviving memories of the sixteenth-century atrocities committed by the Ottomans in the region.

Complicating the matter further was the fact that each one of these territories had a significant number of both Christians and Muslims.

---

[62]Yaacov Ro'i, *Islam in the Soviet Union: From the Second World War to Gorbachev* (New York: Columbia University Press, 2000).

[63]The ecumenical patriarch of Constantinople was left with limited authority over smaller churches in Jordan and the Palestinian territories, the much smaller Greek Orthodox communities in Turkey, and some Greek islands, including Crete, as well as the Greek Orthodox archdiocese of America. Each one of these churches has a few thousand adherents.

[64]Timothy (Kallistos) Ware, *The Orthodox Church* (Baltimore: Penguin Books, 1964), 96-108, 130.

Bosnia-Herzegovina was 60 percent Christian and 40 percent Muslim, while Serbia had 16 percent Muslims. The massacre of Muslims in Bosnia-Herzegovina by national Serbs who wanted to form a unified country that included both Serbia and Bosnia-Herzegovina, claiming their historical right in the region, resulted in international interference in which the United States suppressed the Christian Serbs in support of the Muslim Bosnians. By the end of the war, 1.8 million people had been killed, most of them Christians. Meanwhile, atrocities committed by Christians against the Muslims galvanized the Muslim world, and thousands of jihadis rushed to aid the Muslims in the Balkans. Even with the current political arrangements in the Balkans, strife could erupt at any time.[65] However, relationships between Christians and Muslims and among the former Yugoslavian countries of the Balkans are improving significantly, and some of these countries are joining the EU.

Western Europe. A Christian continent for over ten centuries, Europe is experiencing one of the fastest rates of de-Christianization in modern times due to decades of secularization. The situation in Europe is very complex; as the current population is aging, while the birth rate is below average, Europe is on the verge of significant population decline. The rapid decline in the workforce is necessitating the recruitment of immigrants to prevent a deteriorating economy. Several reports suggest that Europe needs more immigrants to survive.[66] As waves of wanted and unwanted immigrants reach Europe year after year, the demographics of historically homogenous societies are changing to become increasingly more multicultural and multifaith. Many Europeans are struggling to cope with such sudden social changes, while new immigrants are not truly integrating into European societies. One challenge Europe is facing in the twenty-first century is the rapid increase in the number of Muslims who would like to see European society adhere to Islamic principles and laws. Social and political challenges continue as two divergent social and religious orientations are clashing with each other.

The exact number of Muslims in Europe is unknown, since religious affiliation is not required to be provided in any collecting of statistics in Europe. According to estimates by the Pew Forum conducted in 2016, Muslims numbered around 25.8 million (4.9 percent of the total

---

[65]Shireen T. Hunter, *Islam, Europe's Second Religion: The New Social, Cultural, and Political Landscape* (Westport, CT: Praeger, 2002).

[66]Ian Black, "Europe Should Accept 75 Million New Migrants," *Guardian*, July 28, 2000; Barbara Crossette, "Europe Stares at a Future Built by Immigrants," *New York Times*, January 2, 2000.

population).⁶⁷ Europe is seeing a notable surge in the number of Muslims, making Islam the second-largest religion after Christianity. During the last two decades, the number of Muslims in Western Europe has increased by over 60 percent. Muslims count for over 7 percent in France, over 5 percent in England, over 4 percent in Holland, Belgium, and Sweden, and over 3 percent in Germany. Muslims in Europe represent vast cultural and ethnic diversity. The majority of Muslims in Germany are from Turkey, while French Muslims are mostly from North Africa, primarily Algeria, and the majority of British Muslims are from India and Pakistan. Albania is the largest Muslim country in Europe, over 70 percent Muslim, while some Eastern European countries such as Kosovo, Bosnia, and Herzegovina boast a large percentage of Muslims.

The future of Islam in Europe is debatable. Some scholars predict that the number of Muslims will surge and in 2050 Islam will be the dominant religion in Europe due to higher birth rates and the significant flow of immigration from majority-Muslim countries. Others believe that the birth rates among Muslims will decrease in the next decades. According to projections by the Pew Research Center, by midcentury the number of Muslims in Europe is expected to reach 10.2 percent from today's 4.9 percent. The growth of Christianity is expected to slow. These projections are dependent on migration patterns that could be affected by geopolitical changes.⁶⁸

The reality that Islam is the second-largest religion in Europe presents new challenges both for Muslims who decide to live in Europe and European societies, which face pressure to accommodate the culture of their new citizens. One of the most significant difficulties facing Muslims in Europe is the Western perception of Islam, which is often rooted in fear. The view of Islam and Muslims in Europe is usually tainted by the long history of encounters between Europe and the Muslim world. At the same time, terrorism carried out by Muslim extremists around the globe as well as on European soil is fueling this sense of fear and confusion. However, the presence of largely peaceful, friendly, visible communities of Muslims across Europe is eliminating some of that fear and contributing to positive

---

[67] "Muslim Population by Country: The Future of the Global Muslim Population," Pew Research Center, January 27, 2016.
[68] Pew Research Center, "The Future of World Religions: Population Growth Projections, 2010–2050," April 2015.

perceptions toward Muslims and Islam. Attitudes toward Muslims vary: the current surge in the number of Muslim immigrants across the continent has resulted in enhancing negative attitudes, based on the fear that European culture and sociopolitical structures will be compromised. Others are embracing the presence of Muslims in their communities, believing that their participation will enrich European multiculturalism. Overall, the majority of Muslims in Europe are much younger and have more children than average Europeans, and many are trying to integrate with the larger society.[69]

One of the critical challenges facing Muslims in Europe is the issue of identity and assimilation. What does it mean to be Swedish, German, or French Muslim without losing one's Islamic identity? On one hand, Muslims appreciate many of the cultural norms of Europe, such as democracy, standards of human rights, and modernization. But, on the other hand, many struggle to reconcile the secularized structure of Europe with their basic understanding of what it means to be a practicing Muslim. The separation of church and state was settled in Europe more than a century ago, and religion was confined to the private life of the individual. To the contrary, Islam believes in a comprehensive socioreligious system in which the whole of life should be guided and governed by religious principles.

While not all Muslims in Europe demand the application of shari'a or insist on a separate educational system for their children, a significant number do indeed seek the implementation of Islamic laws and send their children to private Islamic schools if they can. Wearing Islamic dress in public is considered a basic right for Muslims, but at the same time it isolates them from the larger society. The focus on public presence and appearances often creates tension between Muslims and society. Muslim insistence on the freedom to publicly display religious symbols oftentimes leads to discomfort on the part of non-Muslims and occasionally results in the government taking legal measures to curb such practices. The constant demand for the establishment of Islamic banks, adherence to Islamic dietary rules, and so on might seem religiously obligatory for Muslims but does not help with their integration into a widely secularized society.

---

[69]Conrad Hackett, "5 Facts About the Muslim Population in Europe," Pew Research Center, January 15, 2015.

Considering that European societies have a long history of homogeneity, the integration of other cultures and ethnicities is often difficult. Incorporating a religiously conscious culture within a secularized society makes assimilation even more challenging. The European ethos of embracing multiculturalism allows for a certain degree of accommodation; however, Europe is growing less tolerant in embracing a cultural structure based on religious ethos, laws, and regulations that are different from its historical cultural norms. Earlier generations of European Muslims were more secularized and adopted modernist views, while new generations are more generally conservative, clinging to Islam as a way of expressing their identity.[70] Some observers think that such habits of cultural hibernation could change and that either future generations of Muslims will be able to better adapt to European cultural norms or their influence and number will eventually change the cultural norms in Europe to better suit an Islamic culture.

Muslims in Europe are politically active, many with the goal of creating a society that adheres to Islamic laws and social systems. While current Muslim politicians might not openly express such as their motivation, there are growing voices calling for such an ambitious goal. Debates on the application of shari'a took place in England and France during the first decade of the twenty-first century. The current mayors of London and Birmingham, England, are both Muslim, while Muslims hold several positions in city councils across Europe.[71]

The Americas

North America. While the United States and Canada are essentially secular societies, around 70 percent of the population in both countries claims some sort of Christian affiliation. A century of liberal theological ideologies and secularization debilitated the church and weakened its witness in Europe and North America, resulting in a post-Christian culture. Multicultural churches as well as immigrant congregations are reshaping the outlook of Christianity in North America in the twenty-first century. Three decades of "seeker-friendly" strategies might make the quality and the depth of the Christian faith in North America a serious concern,

---

[70]Yvonne Yazbeck Haddad, ed., *Muslims in the West: From Sojourners to Citizens* (Oxford: Oxford University Press, 2002).

[71]Jorgen Nielsen, *Towards a European Islam* (New York: St. Martin's 1999).

diluting the cost of discipleship associated with a mature form of Christianity. One of the main issues that faces the church and the Christians in North America, the United States in particular, is the role of religion in politics and global conflicts. Oftentimes the use of Christian language and symbols in politics creates confusion, igniting reactionary attitudes in other contexts around the world.

By the beginning of the twenty-first century, Islam became the second-most popular religion after Christianity in North America. An estimated ten million Muslims live in the United States, and another 2.5 million live in Canada. During the last two decades, the number of Muslims increased by 30 percent in the United States and 65 percent in Canada. Today there are over one thousand mosques and Islamic centers in North America, along with hundreds of Islamic schools and various Islamic organizations. While the recent increase in the number of Muslims in North America is due to Muslims emigrating from the Middle East and Asian countries, there is also a substantial community of African American Muslims in the southern United States. In contrast to Europe, Muslims often integrate well in the cultural mosaic of North American society.

Muslims in North America represent various branches of Islam, including Sunni, Shi'ite, Ahmadiah, and many others. In the 1930s, a former Baptist who converted to Islam, Elijah Muhammad, established the Nation of Islam in the United States. His successors, Louis Farrakhan and Wallace (Warith) Deen Muhammad, provided leadership for the organization. The Nation of Islam, however, is not considered a legitimate Islamic group by Sunni Muslims. In 1992, Wallace Deen Muhammed tried to bring the Nation of Islam into the mainstream Muslim community. He also started the American Muslim Mission, with the goal of spreading the message of Islam in North America.

The attitudes of Muslims living in North America, and in the West in general, have changed over the years. While traditionally Islam has portrayed territories such as Europe and North America as the "abode of war" (Dar al-Harb), nations that should be fought and brought into the abode of Islam (Dar al-Islam), a new generation of Muslims see their presence in these territories differently. In contrast to earlier ideas that Islam cannot be practiced in a foreign environment, or even that Muslims should not live permanently in non-Muslim societies, a new generation of Muslim immigrants are reinterpreting their function in Western societies. They view the West as part of Dar al-Islam, since Muslim communities are actively living and contributing to its transformation. This new sense of mission is supported by the Islamic tradition whereby Prophet Muhammad chose emigration (*hijra*) from Mecca to Medina for the purpose of establishing the first Muslim community. Accordingly, Muslims who choose emigration are inspired to engage Western societies, or any society for that matter, with the message and practice of Islam. This sense of a grander mission usually provides better opportunities for integration and assimilation in the framework of Islamic provisions that safeguard against secularization and westernization.

Several Islamic organizations, such as the Islamic Circle of North America, were formed with this goal in mind. The Islamic Circle of North America promotes the notion of America as the "abode of Islamic call or propagation" (Dar al-Dawa). Its primary objective is to help Muslims maintain their identification within the universal Islamic community (ummah) while propagating Islam freely in America, engaging society and government at all levels with the purpose of spreading the message of Islam. Other Islamic organizations, such as the Islamic Society of North America and the Muslim American Society, advocate for Muslims' social and religious rights while promoting the universality of the Muslim community and the integration of Muslims in the pluralistic society of North America.[72] Muslim integration in the North American society usually swings from the call for full participation within the limit of Islamic ethos to a cautious integration for fear of being tainted with the attitudes and practices of *kuffer*, or disbelief.

Various Islamic organizations, such as the American Muslim Council and the American Muslim Political Coordination Council, have worked to establish the role of the Muslim community in American political life. They encourage Muslims to register and vote in American elections, lobby on behalf of Muslim communities in the US Congress, organize fundraising events for potential political representatives, and present Muslim demands to various political groups. Muslims in North America are represented in various political bodies, including the Senate and the Congress of the United States as well as the Canadian parliament and cabinet.[73]

---

[72]Haddad, *Muslims in the West*, 169-84.
[73]Earle H. Waugh, Baha Abu-Laban, and Regula B. Qureshi, eds., *The Muslim Community in North America* (Edmonton AB University of Alberta Press, 1983).

North American society is grounded on multiculturalism, on the contributions made by those of various cultural heritages and ethnicities. Canada was the first country to institute an official policy of multiculturalism and is the only country to have a law recognizing the cultural diversity of its population. Muslims find it relatively easier to integrate into North American society compared to Europe. This is not to suggest that Muslims are fully tolerated in North America. Stereotypes about Muslims portrayed in social media play a significant role in ostracizing Muslims. Since many Muslims living in the West are newcomers, they often face social and cultural challenges in their attempt to integrate. Many feel powerless and marginalized by host communities even in countries that champion human rights and cultural pluralism. Meanwhile, the sudden changes in the demographic landscape of Europe and North America because of the significant influx of new immigrants are creating anxiety among those who lived in homogenous communities for most of their history. Western societies are facing significant challenges in accommodating new cultures and religious norms while maintaining their core cultural values and sociopolitical structure.

Latin America. In Latin America, most Christians belong to the Catholic Church. Brazil is the largest Catholic nation, with over 140 million Catholics, while Mexico is the second largest, with a population of 92 million Catholics. However, many Catholics are embracing Pentecostalism and evangelicalism. By 2010, the number of non-Catholic Christians reached over 20 percent of the total population of the continent.[74] Islam is also growing in Latin America. According to 2015 statistics, there are 3 million Muslims in Latin America, an increase of 25 percent.[75]

Conclusion

The world wars resulted in breaking up countries and ending empires, including the last Islamic empire, the Ottomans. Thousands of Christians and Muslims perished in religious wars that stemmed from political conflicts, particularly in the Middle East and eastern Europe. Ethnic cleansing resulted in thousands of casualties while displacing entire communities.

---

[74]David Stoll, *Is Latin America Turning Protestant?* (Berkeley: University of California Press, 1990).
[75]2016 International Religious Freedom Report.

At the beginning of the twentieth century, every Muslim land globally was under Western domination. Agreements reached between European powers and the discovery of oil in the Middle East resulted in establishing current state boundaries in several Muslim lands and even creating new states to control their resources. Political and territorial strife between these nations is being reenacted a century later and contributing to current unrest in many regions of the world.

By the mid-twentieth century, almost all Islamic countries gained independence from the West. While many Islamic states adopted and adapted various Western models of governing—semisecular, capitalistic, socialist, and Marxist—by the mid-twentieth century, the majority of Islamic nations opted for the Islamization of their political systems at the close of the century. Secularization as implemented in countries such as Turkey, Indonesia, and some Middle Eastern nations was not fully realized.

Interactions between Christians and Muslims are increasingly influencing political decisions and sociocultural dynamics globally. Over 120 countries worldwide are majority Christian, while Christians count for less than 10 percent in fifty countries that are majority Muslim, and even less than 1 percent in some Muslim and communist nations. The number of Christians has decreased significantly in Islamic countries during the twentieth century, a pattern that is characteristic of the history of these nations. Meanwhile, some Muslims are adopting Christianity, enduring various levels of persecution as a result. Migration from Muslim nations to the West is reshaping the cultural outlook of Western societies. Issues related to accommodation, integration, and mutual respect between Christians and Muslims are instrumental for world peace and future coexistence between the followers of the two major world religions.

7

RELIGION AND POLITICS IN CONTEMPORARY WORLD CONTEXTS

THE WEST

Modernization in the West led to the separation of church and state, a concept that is often credited to John Locke's (1632–1704) philosophical ideologies. Locke argued that the individual conscience should not be ruled by any religious or political authority. Locke's arguments for the liberty of human conscience and religious tolerance influenced the US Constitution. Scholars often distinguish between "friendly" and "hostile" separation of church and state.[1] The friendly model limits the intrusion of the church in matters of the state as well as the intrusion of the state in matters of the church, while maintaining a positive relationship between the two. By contrast, the hostile model curbs the role of religion in public and confines religious activities to the private sphere. The French Revolution is an example of a hostile model, while the American Constitution represents a friendly model. Meanwhile, the French (1905) and the Spanish (1931) models of separating the church and the state are considered the most extreme in the twentieth century, though today church-state relations in both countries are friendly.

---

[1] Hans Maier, *Totalitarianism and Political Religions*, trans. Jodi Bruhn (New York: Routledge, 2004), 109.

A variety of models exist today in the West in terms of how politics and religion relate to each other. Generally, there is wide latitude in terms of religious freedom and tolerance alongside highly secular political cultures. The concept of a state church still exists well into the twenty-first century, and some Western governments have financial ties with religious organizations. In England, for example, Christianity is a constitutionally established state religion; however, other faiths are tolerated. Since 1536, the British monarch is the supreme governor of the Church of England, and twenty-six bishops (Lords Spiritual) sit in the House of Lords, the upper house of government.

According to the Finnish constitution, the state administers the Evangelical Lutheran Church of Finland and the Finnish Orthodox Church, giving them a special status in Finnish legislation compared to other religious bodies. They are usually referred to as national churches or state churches. Recently the Finnish Freethinkers Association has criticized this arrangement and is demanding a total separation of church and state. In neighboring Sweden, the Lutheran Church is the state church, and until the 1870s Swedish citizens were not allowed to leave the national church unless they registered in an officially approved church. On January 1, 2000, the Church of Sweden officially separated from the state; however, the separation is still not complete. The church is still regulated by the government, while the members of the Swedish royal family must confess to an Evangelical Lutheran faith to maintain their rights to rule the country. It is safe to say there has been a change in relation between the church and state in Sweden rather than a separation.

The German constitution guarantees freedom of religion, but there is no complete separation of church and state in Germany. The state might collect taxes on behalf of recognized religious communities while a fee is charged for the service. The German government is neutral when it comes to religious beliefs and enforces a secularized system that governs all citizens. The French model of separation of church and state was formalized in 1905 by the *laïcité* law ("secularity" in French), establishing the separation of religion from politics. This model safeguards against any religious expressions in the public realm while protecting religious institutions from state interference. France has a longer history of separating church and state that goes back to the French Revolution of 1789, when the religiopolitical office of the Roman Christian emperor was abolished.

Article 7 of the Italian constitution affirms the separation of church and state: "The State and the Catholic Church are independent and sovereign, each within its own sphere." The fascist regime of Benito Mussolini (1883–1945) gave the Vatican formal recognition as a sovereign state, provided that the Vatican would no longer interfere in Italian politics.[2]

The US Constitution of 1788 and the Bill of Rights of 1789 guarantee the freedom of religion and the separation of the church and state, although the phrase "separation of church and state" is not used. The Constitution guarantees that no form of religion can hold any kind of peculiar privilege in the public life of the country. The Constitution remains intentionally secular in spite of the fact that those who drafted the Constitution and the majority of Americans hold strong views on religion, and many are committed to their faith. The Constitution's being secular does not mean it intends to create a secular public domain. Rather, by being secular, the Constitution guarantees that religion is free to function in the public square within the framework of freedom of thought and conscience.

The Canadian Charter of Rights and Freedoms, part of the Constitution Act adopted in 1982, guarantees political and civil rights to Canadian citizens, including the right to express their religious views. Canada, like the United States, opted for a secularized constitution that affirms the role of religion in society while separating religion from politics. The current constitution of Brazil, adopted in 1988, ensures the right to religious freedom, bans the establishment of state churches, and prohibits any relationship of "dependence or alliance" between government officials and religious leaders except for "collaboration in the public interest defined by the law."

Religious language and religious symbols, primarily Christian, still constitute an integral part of the social fabric of Western societies. Religion is not a private matter; it can be public, too, without violating the separation of church and state. Many people use their religious convictions to work for justice and equality, for the rights of the poor and marginalized. People of faith and of no faith can speak publicly, serving the common good of their nations without mixing religion and politics. The Western model promotes a pluralistic structure wherein people of various religious traditions can live and work together for the betterment of society while respecting one another's ideologies and worldviews.

---

[2]Carlo Falconi, *The Popes in the Twentieth Century* (Boston: Little, Brown, 1967), 136-45.

One of the most prominent features of Western modernization is secularization, such that freedom of thought and speech also includes freedom from traditional thinking and even religious beliefs. In a secularized world, religion(s) is granted the freedom to exist but not to dominate. Religious principles therefore do not govern economic, social, or political arenas. The secularization of Western societies during the twentieth century allowed Christianity to continue to exist but limited its influence on social and political life. Christianity was replaced by secularization in the West, in contrast to Muslim nations, in which by the second half of the twentieth century most Islamic nations adopted one form or another of political Islamism. It is imperative to view the relationship between the West and the Muslim world not so much as an encounter between Christianity and Islam but rather an encounter between Islam and secularization.

Majority-Muslim societies underwent sudden, profound social and political changes during the first half of the twentieth century. Large numbers of people were given the opportunity to influence the sociopolitical process, a privilege that had been limited to the elites in previous centuries. The nationalist movements during the first half of the twentieth century were influenced by modernist and secularist attitudes; however, during the second half of the twentieth century, traditionalist political Islamism started to challenge the legitimacy of the modernists, asserting its own legitimacy for governing. Traditionalist political Islamist organizations and various Islamic religious institutions emerged with the goal of shaping or reshaping the political trajectory of Islamic countries and communities. While secularization dominated the sociopolitical landscape in the West, the opposite process took place in majority-Muslim nations, where the pursuit of secularization was limited or restricted by the 1980s.

Islamic Modernist and Semisecular Nationalism

Most nationalist movements in the Muslim world during the first half of the twentieth century were influenced by Western political models. Some opted for the capitalistic model, whereas the majority leaned toward the socialist model, which appealed to their aspiration to establish social justice. Secular or semisecular nationalists influenced movements for independence in many Muslim countries, such as Turkey, Egypt, Tunisia, and Indonesia, during the first half of the twentieth century. Western nations have had many decades to develop their forms of government, economic structures, and cultural outlook. Majority-Muslim countries find themselves catching up in the race of modernity while they are still in the process of defining their sociopolitical structure and cultural identity. This process is further complicated by the acceleration of technological and organizational structures, which makes it even harder to catch up with the already-developed Western models.

Muslim secularists were perceived by Muslims and non-Muslims as supporting Islamic cultural norms; however, they were suspicious of traditionalist Islamists. Examples of secular and semisecular nationalists are Kemal Ataturk, the founder of modern Turkey; Gamal Abdel-Nasser and Hosni Mubarak of Egypt; Habib Bourguiba of Tunisia; Hafiz al-Assad and his son Bashar Al-Assad of Syria; Shah Ridha Pahlavi of Iran; Sukarno and Suharto of Indonesia and many others. Muslim secularists appreciated Western ideologies and promoted Westernized models of politics. They gained the support of the masses since they emerged as the saviors of their countries from Western imperialism or archaic monarchies.

Despite the secularists' early popularity, their legitimacy and credibility to govern eroded a decade or two after they took power. They carelessly imposed socialist or capitalist programs, or mixtures of the two, but failed to deliver on their promises of economic, social, and political change. Even when rapid economic growth was achieved, it benefited the wealthy elite, while most of the population continued to live in poverty and oppression. The careless implementation of economic and political programs accompanied by corruption often resulted in wasting resources that could have built stronger and more resilient economies. Most social and economic programs failed to alleviate poverty or to create significant social changes. Nationalistic ideologies and programs worked as a transitional political program after the independence of Islamic countries in the mid-twentieth century but did not provide a lasting, viable socioeconomic solution. At the same time, due to the weakness of the modernists' regimes and the failure of their economic and social programs, their resolve to maintain their grip on power through authoritarian and dictatorial governing further weakened their legitimacy.

Most Islamic regimes failed to implement democratic systems with wider participation from all sectors of society. One slogan used by rulers from Egypt to Indonesia was "guided democracy," meaning that full democracy could not be implemented and needed more time to be achieved. On the one hand, they battled traditionalist Islamists, who were and still are competing for power; on the other hand, democracy did need a stronger social and cultural base, which was lacking. Several Islamic countries adopted Western models of governing, including semidemocratic ones. Some even opted for fully secularized models of governing—Turkey, Tunisia, and Indonesia. The main difference between the Western experience of democracy and that of Islamic countries lies primarily in the relationship between religion and democracy. While the West opted for the separation of church and state, religious ideologies continued to influence democratic programs and processes in majority Islamic countries. Since there is no separation between religion and politics in Islam, Muslim scholars and politicians proposed models of democratic society based on Islamic religious principles. Many Muslim secularists used Islamic rhetoric and symbols in domestic and foreign policy to gain the support of the masses. While their main goal was appeasing traditionalist Islamists, their use of Islamic symbols resulted in legitimizing Islamism while undermining their secularized programs.

INTERNATIONAL ISLAMIC ORGANIZATIONS

One of the earlier programs adopted by semisecularist and modernist Islamists was pan-Islam or pan-Islamism. The concept was inspired by other European nationalistic ideals during the nineteenth century, such as pan-Slavism, pan-Germanism, or pan-Hellenism. By the early twentieth century, pan-Islamism developed as a reaction to Western rule over all Muslim lands and the internal corruption of Muslim leaders who cooperated with the imperialists. It is important to observe the difference between the Western models of pan-Slavism, pan-Germanism, and pan-Hellenism and the Islamic model of pan-Islamism. While the Western models were primarily nationalistic, emphasizing the national identity of a particular nation-state, the Islamic model was primarily religious from its inception.

One of the main champions of pan-Islamism was modernist Islamist Jamal Al-Din Al-Afgani, who lived in Afghanistan and Iran from 1838–1897 while traveling widely in Islamic countries. He appealed for unity among all Muslims, Sunni and Shi'ite, to create a powerful Islamic ummah (community) that could stand against outside threats and internal corruption. Al-Afgani, however, did not urge a return to the Qur'an or the hadith, as later revivalists and traditional Islamists did. He did not consider the ulama (Islamic religious leaders), most of whom he despised, as capable of fulfilling such a task either.

The concept of pan-Islamism faced many challenges in the first two decades of the twentieth century. The dismantling of the caliphate, which had no significant political power, entailed the loss of a symbolic figure that united Sunni Islam worldwide. Meanwhile, the nationalistic movements in almost every Islamic nation at the time preferred to adopt secular political agendas tailored to their own context, within which social and political identity was expressed in localized nationalistic terms rather than global ambition. The concept of a global Islamic ummah or community was replaced by localized nationalistic identity and loyalties.[3]

In response to Turkey's move to abolish the office of the caliphate, the first Pan-Islamic Congress met in Mecca in 1926 with the hope of appointing a new caliph. A World Islamic Congress met again in Jerusalem in 1931, with the same goal; it was attended by 130 delegates representing twenty-two Muslim countries. However, no agreement was reached on how to choose a new Islamic caliph. In the second half of the twentieth century, new international Islamic organizations emerged: In 1969 the Organization of Islamic Cooperation was founded, with fifty-seven member states, with the objective of being "the collective voice of the Muslim World." In 1970 the Organization of the Islamic Conference was established, with fifty-five member states, with the goal of promoting solidarity among all member states and cooperating in economic, social, cultural, and scientific endeavors. These international Islamic organizations and many others sponsor several other organizations, such as Islamic banks, economic and trade organizations, and so on. It is common for heads of Islamic states to be involved in these Islamic organizations. There is an annual Islamic Conference of Islamic states' foreign ministers. Religion and state are intertwined in Islam; it is the responsibility of the state to promote and safeguard Islamic interests.[4]

Another program promoted by secularist Islamists during the 1950s and 1960s was pan-Arabism. Gamal Abdel Nasser of Egypt was the champion

---

[3] J. Landau, *The Politics of Pan-Islam* (London: Clarendon, 1990).
[4] Abdallah al-Ahsan, *The Organization of the Islamic Conference: An Introduction to an Islamic Political Institution* (Herndon, VA: International Institute of Islamic Thought, 1988).

of the new program, with the aim of uniting other Middle Eastern countries for economic and political cooperation. Syria and Egypt formed the United Arab Republic in 1958. Other unions between Egypt, Syria, and Libya, or Egypt, Libya, and Sudan, were also considered. However, the ideology of pan-Arabism failed for many reasons. No tangible economic or political gains were achieved; the defeat of the Arab states by Israel in 1967 and fragmented political alliances seemed contradictory to pan-Arabism.[5] Furthermore, several Middle Eastern countries, such as Egypt, Syria, and Lebanon, have a much longer history and national identity that predated Arabism. While they are Arabic-speaking countries and are immersed in Arabic culture, they are conscious of their distinct nationalistic identities as being Egyptian, Syrian, or Lebanese before being Arab.[6]

Many Christians across the Muslim world participated in and encouraged such semisecularized movements that were based on nationalism rather than religion. It was the most viable opportunity to participate in the political development of their countries based on common nationality rather than religious affiliation. Many participated in drafting their countries' constitutions after independence, as in the case of Egypt, Syria, and Lebanon. Prominent Middle Eastern Christians such as Charles Habib Malik (1905–1987) of Lebanon participated in the drafting of the United Nations Universal Declaration on Human Rights in 1948.

Several Islamic countries were active participants or initiators of the nonalignment movement during the Cold War period. As many Islamic countries were not given the chance to develop their own ideology, political agenda, or social structures, they were pulled into the orbit of socialist or capitalist powers and interests. The champions of this movement were Gamal Abdel Nasser of Egypt, Josip Broz Tito of Yugoslavia, and Jawaharlal Nehru of India. The nonalignment movement provided an imaginary political alternative that never materialized.

INTERNATIONAL CHRISTIAN ORGANIZATIONS

Referencing international Islamic organizations might cause one to wonder about their Christian counterparts. While the mandate and function of these international Christian organizations are entirely

---

[5]Tawfic E. Farah, *Pan-Arabism: The Continuing Debate* (Boulder, CO: Westview, 1987).
[6]Bassam Tibi, *Arab Nationalism: Between Islam and the Nation-State*, 3rd ed. (New York: St. Martin's, 1997).

different from those of the international Islamic organizations, which combine religious activities with political and economic agendas, it is worth referencing them in this context for clarity.

During the twentieth century, various international Christian organizations were formed to promote unity and cooperation between Christians and churches globally. However, they were not associated with any political organizations or governments, nor did they promote any political or economic programs. The World Council of Churches, formed in 1948, promotes unity among churches worldwide based on a better understanding of common theology and common ministry.[7] It includes various Protestant and Orthodox churches globally; however, the Catholic Church is not a member of the council, fearing the dissolution of its beliefs and organizational structure. The World Evangelical Alliance is a global association serving the evangelical movement.[8] It is composed of several global evangelical alliances serving in 129 countries worldwide. The goal of these international Christian organizations is unity among churches and Christians while promoting the Christian faith globally. They often make statements on political issues, social injustices, the environment, and so on, but they are not political bodies, and no heads of states or political figures are active participants in these Christian organizations. They send observers to global summits such as the United Nations to voice their concern for social justice, but their capacity to influence political decisions is limited.

During the twentieth century, the Vatican assumed a prominent role in international relations. Pope John XXIII's (1958-1963) broad-minded attitudes and exposure to global issues gave him an advantage in leading the church in a critical time of social and political change. He embarked on several diplomatic initiatives in Bulgaria, Germany, France, and Turkey, which gave him wider exposure to the world of Christian Orthodoxy and Islam as well as new trends in world politics. His most remarkable contribution to the church was the Second Vatican Council (1962-1965). The council stressed, among many other topics, the urgency for unity among

---

[7]The World Council of Churches inspired the formation of several other regional ecumenical councils, such as the Asian Council of Churches, the African Council of Churches, the Latin American Council of Churches, and so on. The only regional council where the Catholic Church is a full member is the Middle East Council of Churches, which also includes a unique group of historical churches, such as the Armenian, Assyrian, and Coptic churches.

[8]The World Evangelical Alliance was called World Evangelical Fellowship before 2002, when the name was changed to its current one.

Christians while calling for better understanding and appreciation of other world religions as well as mutual understanding between Christians, Jews, and Muslims. Polish pope John Paul II (1978–2005) is well-known for his support in ending communist domination over eastern Europe. During his time, communism collapsed in his own country, Poland, as well as in other Eastern European nations. His concern for social justice led him to be critical of the excesses of both capitalism and communism. The open-mindedness of the current Argentinian pope Francis (2013–) is repositioning the Catholic Church in a way that engages contemporary culture. His passion for peace and justice led to the short-lived normalizing of relations between the United States and Cuba in 2015.

Traditionalist Islamism

During the second half of the twentieth century, traditionalist Islamists' proposals for political legitimacy started to gain momentum, challenging the preceding modernized and semisecularized models of governing. Martin E. Marty and R. Scott Appleby put it well, saying that the movement "is inspired by the belief that Islam, as a complete way of life encompassing both religion and politics, is capable of offering a viable alternative to the prevalent secular ideologies of capitalism and socialism and that it is destined to play an important role in the remaking of the contemporary world." Traditionalists' political agendas have "two distinctive but complementary dimensions: political-ideological and cultural-religious. At the politico-ideological level, neofundamentalism is engaged in a war against foreign political domination and economic exploitation and also against cultural influence and ideological intrusions of Western liberalism and Soviet Marxism" (the latter up until the 1990s). They continue, "At the cultural-religious level," contemporary traditionalist Islamic movements express themselves "in the assertion of a distinctive Islamic cultural identity and the recovery of faith based on pristine Islamic beliefs, norms, and practices," against non-Islamic cultural influences.[9]

The most influential traditionalist Islamic movement in the twentieth century is the Muslim Brotherhood (*al-Ikhwan al-Muslimun*) of Egypt. The founder of the movement, Hasan al-Banna (1906–1949), was concerned

---

[9]Martin E. Marty and R. Scott Appleby, eds., *Fundamentalisms Observed* (Chicago: University of Chicago Press, 2001), 507.

about Western influence on Egyptian society. He was equally disturbed that Jews and Christians controlled the Egyptian economy at the time. He became strongly critical of corruption and mismanagement in the Egyptian government, expressing his rejection of British domination by calling for the establishment of an Islamic political power. He saw in Western social life and its governing model a threat to Islamic principles and therefore advocated for a return to the fundamentals of Islam as a way of saving society from Western ideology and lifestyles.

He took action in the form of promoting the establishment of an Islamic state in Egypt that would be governed by the rules of the Qur'an rather than a secular constitution. He believed that Islamic shari'a had the answers for all questions regarding law and justice, advocating the restoration of Islamic law and government in response to the decadence he perceived everywhere in society. He also advocated for faithful observance of religious obligations while promoting adherence to strict moral behavior. In its early years, the movement did not attract many people; however, as the movement started responding to social and economic needs through establishing schools and medical clinics, its membership grew to half a million in the 1930s, out of the total Egyptian population of twenty-one million at the time. The movement drew its membership largely from the ranks of educated people and professionals, though it was founded in 1928 as a Muslim young men's association promoting personal piety and religious education.[10]

By the 1940s the movement became radical, sometimes violent, and its political faction became highly critical of Egyptian government, society, and culture. Al-Banna formed an Islamic political party; however, the secular government of Egypt's King Farouk was alarmed by the conservatism of the movement, prompting a ban on its activities and cracking down on its leadership. The movement resorted to violence as means to establish an Islamic state, attacking government institutions and assassinating Egypt's prime minister at the time. The government retaliated by assassinating al-Banna in 1949.

---

[10]It is interesting to note the similarities in the early function of the movement and that of the Christian organization YMCA (Young Men's Christian Association), which started in London in 1844 in response to the debilitating social conditions arising in big cities as a result of the Industrial Revolution. Both organizations advocated for better social conditions based on religious principles. While the YMCA remained a social organization and ended up being a secular rather than a religious movement, the Muslim Brotherhood became a powerful religiopolitical movement.

The Muslim Brotherhood continued under the leadership of Sayyid Qutb (1906–1966), another educator and influential writer. The movement cooperated with the Egyptian Free Officers to overthrow the monarchy and establish the republic in 1952. However, the conservative attitudes of the Muslim Brotherhood alarmed the secularist officers when in 1954 most of the leadership were arrested. Such a move angered Qutb and others, who resorted to violence against the secular government. Qutb's later writings promote the concept of jihad against oppressive regimes even if they claim to be Muslim. He draws on the writings of fourteenth-century Islamic traditionalist Ibn Tamiya (see chapter three) to press the argument that any Islamic leader who fails to apply the shari'a has thereby abandoned Islam and must be removed. Qutb was executed in 1966; however, his ideology and writings continue to influence generations of traditionalist Muslims around the globe.[11]

While the Muslim Brotherhood was flourishing in Egypt, another highly influential traditionalist Islamic movement, Jama'at-i-Islami, was emerging in India under the leadership of Abu'l A'la Mawdudi (1903–1979). Unlike Muhammad Ali Jinnah, the secularist and modernist mastermind of an independent Islamic state within an Indian federation, Mawdudi did not believe that the Muslim League was the appropriate way to establish an Islamic state. He criticized the members of the league for their Westernized habits and secularized attitudes. Mawdudi proposed the creation of an Islamic state for all Indian Muslims, regardless of their cultural background, that would be neither Westernized and secularized nor Indian. His early enthusiastic support for Gandhi faded away when he realized that Gandhi's platform was geared toward the creation of an independent India inspired by Hindu nationalism.[12]

Mawdudi stated that the current condition of Muslims resembled that of the pre-Islamic era, known as an era of *jahiliya* ("ignorance"), since Muslims had been influenced by the ideologies of various cultures such as the Greeks, Persians, Indians, and lately the Western world. He called for a return to the early time of Islam, when Muslims were illuminated by the message of the Qur'an.[13] He criticized Western political systems as flawed, describing

---

[11]Richard P. Mitchell, *The Society of the Muslim Brothers* (Oxford: Oxford University Press, 1969).
[12]Seyyed Vali Reza Nasr, *Mawdudi and the Making of Islamic Revivalism* (Oxford: Oxford University Press, 1996).
[13]Mawdudi and al-Banna's description of a "state of ignorance" is widely used by various Islamic traditionalist groups to describe the current secularized and modernized cultures.

the separation of politics and religion as a clear sign of ignorance, calling for the reversal of this misguided system. Mawdudi advocated for the creation of an ideal society that would be governed by God's law for Muslims to be free to practice their faith. He argued that practicing Islam would be compromised under any political system that did not adhere to shari'a. Much of Mawdudi's writings comprise detailed instructions regarding proper behavior, dress, and language, drawn from his interpretation of the Qur'an and the hadith.[14]

Parallel to Mawdudi's call for political Islamism, another movement emerged in India called Tablighi Jama'at ("Propagation Group"). While the goal of the movement was not exactly proselytization, it served as an organization for spiritual renewal among nominal Muslims who had been heavily influenced by Hindu culture and practices. The movement was influenced by Sufi ideologies and did not encourage participation in politics, as Sufism through history is well-known for its emphasis on spirituality and lack of emphasis on politics. The influence of Jama'at-i-Islami, in terms of political advocacy, and Tablighi Jama'at, in terms of spiritual advocacy, was instrumental in shaping the traditionalist structure of Pakistan in the following decades.[15]

Similar movements to the Muslim Brotherhood and Jama'at Islami emerged in Indonesia in the 1930s. Persatuan Islam ("Islamic Union") was a reformist movement that called for strict adherence to Islamic laws, criticizing the secularization of society. The movement was known for its uncompromising way of presenting its ideas.[16] Another Indonesian movement, Muhammadiya, was an apolitical organization that provided education, social services, and religious instructions. Nahdatul Ulama ("Renaissance of the Ulama"), an organization composed of a group of religious leaders who opposed the Westernization of Indonesia, advocated for further Islamization through education and cultural reform.[17]

The shah of Iran's implementation of Westernized governmental and educational systems angered traditionalist Muslims in the largest Shi'ite

---

[14]Kalim Bahadur, *The Jama'at-i-Islami of Pakistan: Political Thought and Political Action* (New Delhi: Chenta, 1977).

[15]Mumtaz Ahmad, "Islamic Fundamentalism in South Asia: The Jamaat-i-Islami and the Tablighi Jamaat of South Asia," in Marty and Appleby, *Fundamentalisms Observed*, 457-530.

[16]Howard Federspiel, *Islam and Ideology in the Emerging Indonesian State: The Persatuan Islam (Persis), 1923–1957* (Leiden: Brill, 2001).

[17]Greg Barton and Greg Fealy, eds., *Nahdatul Ulama: Traditional Islam and Modernity in Indonesia* (Monash, Australia: Monash Asia Institute, 1996).

country, Iran. One early critic of the shah was Jalal Ali Ahmad (1923–1969). Ahmad criticized the uncritical adaptation of Western modernization, which he called "Westoxication" (*Gharbzadagi* in Persian).[18] His ideas influenced another high-ranking religious leader, Musavi Khomeini (1902–1989). Khomeini became an open critic of the shah himself, not just the Westernization of Iran. He started questioning the lavish lifestyle of the emperor and his Westernized ideology. The shah's revival of Persian civilization and celebration of Persian historical events angered the conservative ulama, who feared that such pagan celebrations would compromise the Islamic identity of Iran.

Khomeini escaped execution due to his high-ranking religious status and was exiled to Iraq and then France, only to return in 1979 to lead the most powerful Islamic Shi'ite revolution in modern history. Within a few months, Iran was transformed from a modernized secularized state into one of the most conservative Islamic republics. Many secularized leaders, professors, and Christians were executed in the first two years of the revolution as Iran embraced Islamization of the country. According to Shi'ite Islam, the imam is the only legitimate religious and political leader. In such a theocratic political context, religion and the state are fully fused, becoming one entity. Khomeini assumed the title "Ayat Allah Ruah Allah," which means "the sign of God and the spirit of God."[19]

The Dominance of Political Islamism

Starting from the 1970s, many political Islamic groups emerged all over the Muslim world. The Iranian Revolution galvanized not only the Shi'ites but also Sunni Muslims in the mission of establishing Islam as a world political power. A new sense of pride was gained among Muslims when Iran stood its ground against the United States, and many groups were inspired to carry out jihad against injustice. A long list of perceived injustices—such as the creation of the state of Israel in Palestine while Palestinians never were able to establish their own country, the West's control of oil resources, and the mounting corruption in Islamic countries where many Muslim leaders cooperated with the West in exploiting their

---

[18]Jalal Ali Ahmad, *Gharbzadagi* [Weststrukness], trans. Ahmad Alizadeh and John Green (Lexington, KY: Mazda, 1982).

[19]Ervand Abrahamian, *Iran Between Two Revolutions* (Princeton, NJ: Princeton University Press, 1982).

resources and land—fueled the attitudes of traditionalist Islamists during the second half of the twentieth century. In response to these injustices, the most powerful Islamic organizations that had been formed decades earlier, the Muslim Brotherhood and Jama'at-i-Islami, reemerged more powerful than before, gaining new political grounds.

The Muslim Brotherhood, crushed during Nasser's era (1953–1970), was allowed to reorganize during Sadat's regime (1970–1981). Two decades later, the organization formed a political party that won 20 percent of the Egyptian parliament seats in 2005. The Jordanian branch of the Muslim Brotherhood won a quarter of the parliament seats in 2003, while the Muslim Brotherhood offshoot in Gaza, Hamas, won the Palestinian legislative election in 2006. The sweeping victories of the Muslim Brotherhood in the Middle East alarmed the semisecular leaders, who feared an Islamic takeover of the region. This prompted the cancellation of similar parliamentary elections in Egypt a few years later when the organization won more seats in the parliament in 2009. Hamas was confined to Gaza, while the Palestinian Authority continued to rule in the West Bank, with significant hostilities between the two groups. Jordan tried to appease the Islamists while crushing them when they gained more power.

The takeover of Pakistan in a military coup by Zia ul-Haq in 1977 is considered one of the most significant examples of political Islam. Although Pakistan was established as an Islamic state, the coup's objective was to create an Islamic state, based on the assumption that Pakistan was not fully Islamized. The new regime embarked on strict application of shari'a while opening a large number of Islamic schools, madrassas. As noted earlier, the number of Islamic schools increased from 900 in 1971 to 33,000 in 1988, and many became indoctrination centers for radical Islam. By the late 1980s, Pakistan became an explicitly Islamic state as many of the secularized social elites were eliminated while a large number of the military and educated people cultivated Islamic values and culture. The strict Sunni Islamization of Pakistan gained momentum as a reaction to the Shi'ite Iranian Revolution in 1979 and the Soviet invasion of Afghanistan, also in 1979.[20]

In Algeria, the Islamic Salvation Front won the 1992 legislative election. However, the military canceled the election, prompting a civil war that

---

[20]Eqbal Ahmed, *Islam: Politics and State; The Pakistan Experience* (London: Zed Books, 1985).

lasted for ten years with over 150,000 casualties. In neighboring Tunisia, the government kept the Islamists completely out of politics; however, in the 1990s the Al-Nahda (Renaissance) Islamic Party gained power and forced a coalition government with Zine Al-Abiden Bin Ali.

Even in the most secularized country, Turkey, the tide changed in favor of the Islamic party Justice and Development, which was inspired by Muslim Brotherhood ideologies. The party won the election in 2001. Since then, Reccp Tayyip, the current president of Turkey, has worked relentlessly on the Islamization of the country. His heavy measures of Islamization have created a rift with the secularists, the highly educated, and the military.

Starting in the 1970s, sociopolitical Islamism was promoted through the use of petrodollars. Several wealthy billionaires from Saudi Arabia and other Gulf states, some of whom are not associated with a particular government, took upon themselves the task of financing Islamic religious institutions worldwide. Meanwhile, several oil-rich Middle Eastern countries used oil revenues to influence political decisions and economic gains. Oil revenues became instrumental in spreading Islam globally by building mosques and Islamic institutions, sending Muslim missionaries and funding Islamic universities, subsidizing Islamic professorships in prestigious European and North American universities, and so on. The financing of such institutions resulted in promoting Islam worldwide while indirectly spreading a form of traditionalist Islam. The Saudis make no secret that they are delighted to see Wahhabi ideology spreading across the globe. They have been financing social programs promoting conservative Islam globally since the 1980s.

Many educated middle-class Muslims are torn between their advocacy for political freedom, which eventually would allow Islamists to control the political arena, and their fear of Islamist totalitarianism once they are in power. The examples of Iran, Turkey, Algeria, Egypt, Jordan, Indonesia, and Pakistan are raising serious questions about the shape and structure of political democracy according to traditionalist Islamism. Meanwhile, Western powers are pressing Islamic countries to allow for democratic process and participation, which usually results in empowering Islamists. The aftermath of the Arab revolt in 2011 is a case in point. In 2012, the Muslim Brotherhood of Egypt finally achieved its lifelong goal of controlling the country. However, a year later the Muslim Brotherhood president, Mohamed Morsi, was ousted in another mass revolution, while the organization was banned altogether.

Militant Islam: The Global Jihadi Movements

As political Islamist movements were met with resistance from various regimes across the Muslim world, a new wave of jihadi movements started to emerge. There is a difference between jihadi groups and the more organized traditionalist Islamists. Most political Islamist movements are institutionalized organizations, often using legitimate political channels such as forming Islamic political parties, competing in legislative elections, and so on to gain a platform to promote their sociopolitical programs. When such doors are shut, as in the examples mentioned earlier, jihadi movements usually emerge, trying to bring political change by force.

A prominent theoretician of jihadi ideology was Abd al-Salam Faraj, an Egyptian who wrote a short manual on jihad titled *The Neglected Duty*, which reveals the direction that Qutb, the Muslim Brotherhood leader, adopted in the later stage of his life. As the Muslim Brotherhood was crushed by the Egyptian government, Qutb came to believe that the only way to bring change in society was jihad. Following Qutb's ideology, Faraj argues that the current state of weakness and fragmentation experienced by the Muslim world is primarily due to abandoning the Islamic duty of carrying out jihad. He insists that the highest priority for Muslims should be to create the proper Islamic society that will provide Muslims the opportunity to truly practice their religion. Any social, economic, or political reform is doomed to fail if an Islamic state is not realized. Considering the current political chaos in the Muslim world, Faraj argues that the utmost priority for Muslims today is to remove the apostates who rule Islamic countries in order to establish true Islamic states. The overthrow of apostate Muslim regimes should take precedence over fighting the far-off enemy, the secularized and infidel West.[21]

Faraj's ideas inspired various militant groups in Egypt, which started attacking tourists, governmental institutions, members of the cabinet, military cadets, and Christians. His scheme was further galvanized when Sadat signed a peace treaty with Israel in 1979. It became clear that Egypt

---

[21]Johannes J. G. Jansen, *The Neglected Duty: The Creed of Sadat's Assassins and Islamic Resurgence in the Middle East* (New York: Macmillan, 1986).

had lost its Islamic compass and that the country was collaborating with the infidels, the Americans and Israel. Sadat was assassinated in 1981 by the jihadi group. The crackdown on the jihadi group revealed a long list of prominent jihadis who would play a significant role in global jihad, such as Ayman Zawahiri and Omar Abdul Rahman. Zawahiri became the second in command after Osama bin Laden, taking over the leadership of al-Qaeda in 2009, while Abdul Rahman continued his jihad mission from Sudan and later the United States. He plotted the first attack on the World Trade Center in 1992 and was sentenced to life in prison. His ideology influenced a large number of followers around the world.[22]

The Islamic jihadi movement was active at the same time in Algeria after Islamists were denied political participation in governing, as noted earlier. The trend mushroomed from that point forward, incorporating other countries and territories around the globe. Militant groups were active in Indonesia (Laskar), the Philippines (Abu-Sayyef), Nigeria (Boko Haram), Somalia (Al-Shabab), Uganda, Kenya, India, Lebanon (Hezbu-Allah), the Palestinian territories (Hamas), and so on. The apex of jihadi Islamic movements was the formation of al-Qaeda ("the Base") in Afghanistan.

Al-Qaeda and the Islamic State. The Soviet invasion of Afghanistan in 1979 drew widespread sympathy among Muslims worldwide and spurred them to join forces in defending the Afghans. The mujahideen ("those who carry jihad") responded to the call from every perceivable rank, Sunni, Shi'ites, Sufi orders, highly educated and wealthy businesspeople along with various tribal groups from within Afghanistan. The conflict attracted the interest of the United States, seeing an opportunity to weaken the power of the Soviet Union. The United States began aiding Afghani resistance while supporting the recruitment of mujahideen through Pakistan and Saudi Arabia. Omar Abdul Rahman was one such recruiter from the Middle East, while Osama bin Laden, a wealthy Saudi, took it upon himself to relocate to Afghanistan to direct the jihad against the Soviets. By the end of 1988, Soviet troops left Afghanistan, while the communist government in Kabul was overthrown in 1992. Muslims around the world celebrated the defeat of the Soviets by the consolidated effort of the ummah (community) everywhere.

---

[22]Gilles Kepel, *Muslim Extremism in Egypt: The Prophet and the Pharaoh*, trans. John Rothschild (Berkeley: University of California Press, 1985).

But the celebration did not last more than a few weeks; once the central government in Kabul collapsed, the various Afghani tribal groups started competing for power. The country descended into civil war, with over a million casualties and another five million refugees. Most foreign fighters left Afghanistan to carry out jihad in their own countries, while the United States, assessing the situation, abandoned the country altogether. In lawlessness and warfare that lasted over two years, the Taliban emerged as the savior of the country, taking control of the government in 1994. The Taliban became one of the most notorious jihadi groups. Their lack of education and rural upbringing in remote tribal regions were reflected in their policies. They applied extremely strict shari'a: women were stoned on a regular basis and were not allowed to leave their homes even when wearing the full burqa, education for girls was banned, and sports, music, watching TV, and any sort of entertainment were completely banned. Thousands of Shi'ites were massacred.[23]

Participation in the multinational jihadi forces in Afghanistan was a transformational experience for many jihadis. Many returned to carry out jihad in their own countries. Others were not able to return and were dispersed in areas where jihad was needed, such as Bosnia, Chechnya, and Kashmir. Meanwhile, another influential jihadi, Alla Azzam, a Palestinian who was disillusioned by the secularization of the Palestine Liberation Organization, ended up fighting in Afghanistan. He elaborated Faraj's call for jihad to include all territories that once were under the banner of Islam, such as Israel, Spain, and the Philippines. For Azzam, participation in jihad was the highest call for any Muslim and the decisive factor that determined whether a person was a true Muslim or an infidel. The scope of this global jihad is unlimited and can include any territory that belongs to Dar al-Harb ("the abode of war") or any group of people so far as they are labeled infidels, including other Muslims.

The success of the mujahideen in Afghanistan led bin Laden to suggest the deployment of thousands of his mujahideen to Saudi Arabia to protect his country against attacks like the one Kuwait endured in 1990 by the Iraqis. To his utmost surprise, the Saudis preferred the American military protecting their country over the Muslim mujahideen. Bin Laden was outraged that his country favored cooperating with infidels, whose presence would defile the land, contaminating the holiest Islamic sites in Mecca and Medina. Such a

---

[23]Larry P. Goodson, *Afghanistan's Endless War: State Failure, Regional Politics and the Rise of the Taliban* (Seattle: University of Washington Press, 2001).

move resulted in bin Laden turning against his own country while focusing his effort on attacking the United States. Bin Laden's statements during the 1990s indicated his belief that there was a conspiracy between the Jews, who control US policy, and the West to exploit the oil wealth of the Muslim world, with the ultimate goal of impoverishing the Muslim countries while destroying Islam itself. Accordingly, he called on Muslim jihadis to focus their effort on attacking the United States and the West rather than wasting their effort in toppling Muslim regimes cooperating with the West. The American embassies in Kenya and Tanzania were bombed in 1998, while the final blow came on September 11, 2001, with a direct attack on the United States.

The instability created in the aftermath of the American invasion of Iraq in 2003 provided ample opportunity for al-Qaeda to operate directly from within the Middle East. The trend continued in the first decades of the twenty-first century as al-Qaeda and its offshoot, the Islamic State, created havoc in Iraq, Syria, Libya, and Sinai, Egypt, while recruiting, training, and deploying jihadis to attack Europe and the United States. Between 2000 and 2017, the world witnessed an intensification of global jihad.

An Evaluation of Contemporary Political Islamism

The resurgence of Islam as a political force from the 1970s onward is a noteworthy phenomenon. Groups advocating for an Islamic revival have gained political power in many Muslim countries around the globe. They promote Islamic republics in which shari'a would be established as the law of the land. The phenomenon of global Islamic revivalism cannot be treated in isolation from larger cultural and sociopolitical issues, including economic problems, injustice, and the quest for identity and self-determination, among many others. Islamic resurgence or revival is not primarily a revival of traditionalist Islamism, although it is the most vocal variants of Islamic resurgence that attract a disproportionate amount of international attention. During the first half of the twentieth century, the modernist branch of Islamic revivalism attained considerable visibility and prominence among educated and liberal-minded Muslims long before the latter wave of traditionalist ideologies. While the voices of modernist Islamic revivalism are still influencing sociopolitical change to some extent, they are overshadowed by the more vocal voices of the traditionalist Islamists.

Islamic modernism promotes the idea of that Islam can adapt to the conditions of modern life without losing sight of its basics or fundamentals. In contrast to the traditionalists, who hold to a literal interpretation of the Qur'anic text and its laws, modernists favor preserving the spirit and intent of Islam in a modern context. Modernists share some of the same concerns as traditionalists, including the need to purify Islam from any foreign ideologies and moral behaviors that have tainted the purity and originality of the faith. However, modernists locate the core of Islamic principles in its liberal ideals of justice and reason, arguing that Islam is compatible with modern social life or at least with a version of it that adheres to the core values of Islam.

The contemporary resurgence of Islam as a political force along with Islamic revivalism springs from a number of sociopolitical concerns and historical developments. The first and foremost concern is the current predicament of the Islamic ummah (community): the subjection of all Muslim societies to foreign control; social and cultural challenges to traditional Islamic values due to modernization and secularization; the lack of advanced technology, which leads to dependence on the West; and the fragmentation of and constant conflicts within the Islamic community. One typical explanation of these predicaments is that the ummah has deviated from the untainted and original Islam, which leads to the implicit expectation that a return to Islamic purity will restore the ummah to its glorious days and rightful place on the global scene.

During the twentieth century, most of the attempts Muslim nations made to modernize their educational, political, and social systems involved Western structures and rushed technological development that were out of step with the cultural and social orientation of the masses, who remained for the most part traditional and very religious. By midcentury, such modernization programs had failed to provide any viable social or political reform in many Muslim countries. This failure was due in part to the inability of leaders to establish political institutions capable of easing the tension of moving their countries from traditional to technologically oriented societies. Complicating the problem further was the support lent to dictatorial and at times oppressive regimes by some powerful Western states. This situation resulted in raising major concerns in the Muslim mind about justice.

Religious schools were replaced by secular government–controlled institutions; however, society at large remained traditional and was not able to cope with the swift shift to secularization. Traditionalists often attribute the deterioration of moral and social life to adopting Western culture, such as movies, social media, rock music, immodest dress, and consumption of alcohol, all of which are considered signs of increased corruption in the Muslim world. Thus, wearing a veil became a sign of modesty for women, while countries such as Iran, Saudi Arabia, and others ban the mixing of genders, parties, or music. Those who break these rules are severely punished. The notion of the West as a source of moral corruption is in some respect a reaction to the colonial perceptions of Western cultural superiority, but it is also motivated by opposition to certain Western-inspired social trends that seem contradictory to traditionalists' views.

The growing wealth of the cities enhanced this image as the elite consumed Western products extravagantly and enjoyed a Western lifestyle, while the pious folk in the countryside and small villages became more and more estranged from the social elite of their societies. The growth of urban wealth, benefiting mainly the elite, increased the gap between the rich and the poor. Meanwhile, most rulers failed to address issues of social justice and equitable distribution of national resources, resulting in riots and conflicts. Social justice became a significant rallying point of Islamic revivalism from Iran to Turkey to Egypt, Algeria, Indonesia, and so on. Islamic resurgence used the concern with justice to point to the egalitarian and democratic principles associated with Islam in its original form. Desire for a return to the original Islamic tradition was used to express dissatisfaction with existing patterns of social injustice and oppressive political regimes.

Meanwhile, as many programs failed to achieve their goals of creating significant social and cultural changes, the new surge of Islamic revivalism took the form of public behaviors, such as a renewed commitment to attending mosques, wearing traditional Islamic dress, consuming only halal food, and so on as a way of asserting Islamic identity against secularization and sometimes Western modernization. Many Muslim societies saw a proliferation of religious programs in educational sectors, as well as increased Islamic publications and media programs, while charismatic preachers encouraged the masses to adhere to Islamic religious observances in daily life. On the economic level, several Islamic banks and financial institutions were established on Islamic principles. Voices calling for the implementation of Islamic shari'a were echoed globally.[24]

---

[24]John J. Donohue and John L. Esposito, *Islam in Transition: Muslim Perceptions* (Oxford: Oxford University Press, 1982).

As most semisecularized political programs failed across the Muslim world due to corruption and mismanagement, political Islam was asserted anew as the solution. Various Islamic opposition movements used the language and symbols of Islam to demand changes in their secularized governments. They adopted techniques that varied from using legal channels of competition to win parliamentary seats and advocating for sociopolitical reform to assassinating political leaders and undermining the security of the state. As John Esposito observes,

> The forms that Islamic revivalism takes vary almost infinitely from one country to another, but there are certain themes: a sense that existing political, economic, and social systems have failed; a disenchantment with and even rejection of the West; a quest for identity and greater authenticity; and the conviction that Islam provides a self-sufficient ideology for state and society, a valid alternative to secular nationalism, socialism, and capitalism.[25]

Sociopolitical developments during the twentieth century also created major cultural upheaval in many Muslim societies related to self-determinism and cultural identity. The problem of cultural identity was compounded by the drawing of modern national borders, most of which reflected the interests of Western powers rather than those living within (or divided by) the borders. Questions about identity in light of the modern concept of nationalism usually reflect the confusion between culture, religion, and ethnicity. Are all Middle Easterners Arabs? Or are they mainly Egyptians, Syrians, Iraqis, and so on? Are Egyptian Copts, Syriac, and Armenians Arabs? They speak the Arabic language and live in the Arabic culture of the Middle East, but they are also aware of their distinct ethnicities and religion (Christianity) that predate Arabism and Islamism. Religious identity within Islam in the form of the Sunni-Shi'ite divide resulted in major conflicts in Iraq, Bahrain, and Saudi Araba. The Kurdish aspiration to create a national state, Kurdistan, within the borders of Turkey, Iran, Iraq, and Syria causes constant tension in the region. Issues of nationalism and cultural identity will continue to shape and challenge Islamic politics during the twenty-first century.

Political Islamism advocates for an Islamic political structure in which shari'a would be established as the law of the land. Applying Islamic laws

---

[25]John L. Esposito, "Islamic Revivalism," in *The Muslim World Today*, occasional paper no. 3 (Washington, DC: American Institute for Islamic Affairs, 1995).

is considered a primary religious obligation if the community is to uphold to the purity and originality of the faith against any attempt to deter it in the wrong direction. The common assumption is that Islamic communities should be governed by Islamic laws religiously, socially, politically, and economically. While the interpretations and applications of such governance vary from one country to the other, there are some common practices observed across the Muslim world. Today there are several Islamic banks that apply Islamic principles in trade, finance, and commerce. There are various halal or Islamic dietary products that follow certain provisions for lawful food.

Means and methods of applying shari'a are being presented and discussed in various world contexts, including Europe and North America. While Muslims worldwide adhere to the proper format and procedures of worship, the application of other categories of the shari'a, such as criminal codes and sociopolitical laws, conflict with civil laws observed worldwide. Islamic traditionalists and many religious leaders often argue for the full application of shari'a simply because they are revealed religious laws, and thus all Muslim societies should adhere to them in order to fully comply with God's mandates for restraining evil and striving for the good of society. While theoretically that might seem to be an acceptable religious argument, practically some of these laws are hard to implement in various world contexts.

While all Muslims considered the religious text to be the highest authority for any religious or social matter, the views of Muslims on how to interpret the text in the contemporary world context vary from one context to another. Most moderate Muslims, while holding to the authenticity of the text, do not interpret it literally. The majority of Muslims uphold the validity of secular laws and contemporary human rights principles. They appreciate a social context where people can practice their religion freely. Debates on how shari'a should be applied and its compatibility with the Universal Declaration on Human Rights will take different forms and numerous interpretations across the Muslim and the non-Muslim worlds. It is an open-ended debate.

Conclusion

The twentieth century saw the continuation of divergent paths in terms of the relationship between politics and religion. While the West opted to separate politics and religion, in the Muslim world there was a surge in political Islamism by the second half of the century. Most Islamic countries tried to implement various forms of secularized or semisecularized political structures during the first half of the twentieth century. However, their rushed approach to Western modernization and secularized educational and sociopolitical programs lacked the support of the masses, who remained for the most part religiously traditional. Many of these secularized programs failed to achieve significant social changes, while corruptions and mismanagement eroded their legitimacy for governing, leading many Muslim rulers to resort to a dictatorial style of governing to maintain political power.

By midcentury, an increase in political Islamism dominated the majority of Muslim countries, replacing modernist attitudes with more traditionalist ones. Political Islamism gained steady progress in asserting its legitimacy for governing through competing in parliamentary elections and establishing Islamic political parties that responded to the socioeconomic needs of the masses. When these Islamic parties or organizations were not recognized by ruling governments, many resorted to bringing political change by force. In the latter part of the century there was a surge in jihadi movements trying to force political change through violence directed at Islamic governments as well as the West. Issues of socioeconomic hardship, lack of equality, and injustice are at the root of many political upheavals that continue intensifying in the twenty-first century.

PART THREE
RELIGIOUS BELIEFS

Patterns of interaction between Christian and Muslim communities around the globe suggest that religious orientation is key to people's perception of the other and the way they interpret the world around them. Exploring crux religious beliefs facilitates a better understanding of the core values of each religious tradition. A major focus of this section is to create an opportunity for better communication by exploring the basic theological beliefs of Islam while clarifying the core beliefs that influence Christian life and witness. Some of the key theological topics to be explored include (1) the absoluteness and relatedness of God. The Christian faith affirms a divinity that is unique in its being but at the same time open to the world, a divine capacity that out of love suffers with and for humanity. Islam traditionally affirms divine transcendence, according to which such compassion and suffering love offend its understanding of divine sovereignty. Christianity and Islam often suppose that their different understandings of theism are incompatible and contradictory. That view does justice to neither of them because both are genuinely monotheistic.

(2) While Christianity stems from a theological framework that emphasizes a personal relationship with God through the life and salvific work of Jesus Christ, Islam perceives God through his laws and the words of the Qur'an. This will lead to differing views of the person and work of Jesus Christ. (3) Christianity and Islam have common as well as divergent views on humanity and how humans relate to God. (4) We will also explore the concept of the Islamic ummah or community and how it relates to the church. Importantly, in both religions revealed Scriptures along with their interpretation provide a framework in which the community can live and interact.

Religious orientation influences one's attitude toward others and results in outward actions. People's beliefs and ways of worship influence their worldview and relationships. Exploring basic religious beliefs and worldviews can offer hope for better ways of interacting between followers of the two religions based on mutual respect and appreciation of the other.

8

GOD

Absolute, Relational

BOTH CHRISTIANITY AND ISLAM start from a strong belief in the divine. People's perceptions of God in both religious traditions provide a theological framework that shapes their attitudes, actions, ways of worship, and relationship to God and others. The focus here is on the similarities as well as the noteworthy differences between Christianity and Islam's beliefs regarding God's nature and relationship to humanity. Several topics will be explored: the Islamic belief in the absolute oneness of God (known as *tawhid*), communicated in the Islamic statement of faith, called shahada; the attributes of God according to Islam, provided in the ninety-nine names of God, in relationship to the Christian understanding of God's nature or characteristics; God's will and its effect on humanity's will; and the dialectic between God's relationality and absoluteness. The emphasis will be on how God is perceived in Christianity and Islam and how Muslims and Christians relate to God.

"There Is No God but God"

Islam revolves around the belief in one God. Five times each day, hundreds of millions of Muslims around the globe recite the same statement of faith in their daily prayer, *La ilaha illa Allah, Muhammad rasul Allah*, "There is no god but God, and Muhammad is the messenger [apostle] of God." This simple yet powerful statement of faith is the affirmation of belief. It is recited at the birth of a child, and it is the final word before death. It is the most comprehensive statement of faith among the religions of the world. As Kenneth Cragg observes, "The outsider must come to terms with what may well be considered the most God-conscious, creedally, ritually and politically institutionalized religion that history knows."[1]

The Arabic word *Allah* means "the God."[2] *Al* is the definite article "the," and *ilah* means "god." The word is derived from Semitic roots and is similar to the Hebrew (*El, Eloah,* and *Elohim*), Aramaic (*Elah*), and Syriac (*Alaha*). Arabic-speaking people in the pre-Islamic era regardless of their religious beliefs used the word *Allah*. For the pagan Arabs who believed in 360 different gods and goddesses, the word *ilah* referred to "a god," while the word *Allah* referred to the supreme and sovereign God, the creator of the universe. Prophet Muhammad's father, who died before Islam, bore the name Abdu-Allah ("servant of God"), and the main house of worship in Mecca, the Ka'ba, was called Beit-Allah ("the house of God") centuries before Islam. The pagan Arabs before Prophet Muhammad's time believed in the existence and lordship of God; they even proclaimed God's unity. So, what was new about Prophet Muhammad's message to the Arabs?

Prophet Muhammad's vital message to his people, clearly communicated in the Islamic statement of faith, "There is no God but God," was to draw attention to the one and only God. The pagan Arabs believed in the Supreme Being, Allah, but they were attached to a host of lesser gods who were far more intimately related to their daily lives. Prophet Muhammad came to challenge this polytheistic worldview, proclaiming a monotheistic faith that prohibited the worship of all lesser gods.[3]

Today there is a great deal of confusion about the meaning and the use of the Arabic word *Allah*. Some use the word in reference to the Muslim God; others use the word in reference to God in general. Arabic-speaking Christians who lived before Islam also used the word *Allah* in reference to God. All Arabic translations of the Bible through the centuries use the word *Allah*. Today, Arabic-speaking Christians use the word *Allah* in worship and prayer. But while Arabic-speaking Christians and Muslims use the same Arabic word for "God," it must be noted that their comprehension of the nature and characteristics of God differs.

---

[1] Kenneth Cragg, *The Christ and the Faiths* (Philadelphia: Westminster, 1986), 29.
[2] The equivalent of *God* (English), *Gott* (German), and *Deus* (Latin).
[3] The second half of the shahada, the statement of faith of Islam, establishes the absolute authority of Muhammad as the final apostle of God. The statement of faith in Islam is about believing in God as well as in the apostleship of Muhammad.

THE ABSOLUTE ONENESS OF GOD

The cornerstone of the Islamic faith is the absolute oneness of God. The greatness of God flows from the absolute unity and sovereignty of God. The Qur'an uses the word *ahad* ("one") to disavow the notion that God has any partner or companion associated with him. The most common word used by the Qur'an, however, is *wahid* (also meaning "one"), which highlights and affirms the absolute oneness of God. The word *wahid* implies that there is only one God to be worshiped, and he is also the Lord of the whole universe, even to those who cannot recognize him or believe in his oneness. The doctrine of divine unity, *tawhid*, is the lens through which all beliefs and practices are viewed. God's unity is the basis for divine sovereignty and defines God's transcendence (Qur'an 2:163; 6:19; 16:22; 23:91-92; 37:1-5). Since God is one, the message and messenger(s) are also unified in providing a singular revelation of guidance, primarily concerning God's oneness. That is why the Qur'an repeatedly emphasizes absolute obedience to Muhammad as the final prophet, bringing the final and complete message of oneness against Arab polytheism. The Qur'an states, "God and His apostle spoke the truth" (33:22; see also 38:84).

In light of this uncompromising emphasis on God's absolute unity, the greatest sin in Islam is *shirk*, which means associating other beings or deities with God. The Qur'an warns against the grievous sin of betraying God's oneness: "God does not forgive anyone for associating something with Him. . . . Anyone who gives God associates [partners] has invented an awful sin" (4:116). The Islamic concern with the absolute oneness of God has a historical background. When Prophet Muhammad started preaching his message of God's oneness, or *tawhid*, he found himself in a world of political, social, and religious chaos. One of his main purposes was to unite the different Arabian tribes under one social and political leadership. A unified religious belief would serve the ultimate purpose of creating a unified community. The absolute oneness of God provided the theological foundation for such a unified ummah, or community, that submits to God and follows God's straight path, shari'a.[4] In proclaiming God's oneness, Prophet Muhammad prohibited and annihilated all other forms of worship practiced by the Arabs, while at the same time creating a unified social and political force.

---

[4]The Arabic word *Islam* means "to submit."

Prophet Muhammad's call for the absolute worship of the only one God, forsaking all other idols, followed the footsteps of all the Hebrew prophets, who communicated the same message time and again. From Moses to Elijah to Isaiah and a host of other prophets, the message was for people to worship God alone (Ex 20:3; Deut 6:4; Is 45:5-6; etc.). Christians through the centuries have believed and worshiped only one God. However, their understanding and experience of the oneness of God allows for relationality in the very nature of God. Christians believe that the one God is triune in his nature and in manifesting himself to humanity: Father, Son, and Holy Spirit. The triune God is one in his essence as well as in his relationality.

Islam's affirmation of divine greatness, *Allahu Akbar* ("God is great" or "greater," since nothing can be compared to God), is a call for worshiping God alone over against the polytheistic culture that dominated pre-Islamic Arabia. It is a call to reject idolatry and worship the only and true God. That Prophet Muhammad's message of *tawhid* was influenced by earlier Judaic and Christian monotheism does not alter his basic intention of countering and eliminating *shirk*, which from an Islamic point of view was also included in these religious traditions. Only by a firm establishment of *tawhid* and final rejection of *shirk* could the sole lordship of God be realized.

Islamic monotheism does away with the notion of persons participating in divinity. The Surah of Unity, 112, declares: "Say: He alone is God, God the ever adequate.[5] He neither gives nor derives His being. Like to him there is none." The point at stake here is that divine unity requires singularity, and the greatness of God is affirmed by God's unique singularity. This faith in the absolute oneness of God is not adequately confessed in terms of number alone, that is, merely in the rejection of deities in the plural. A rigorous dissociation of God from the human realm is also entailed. The Qur'an repeatedly speaks against *al-mushrikun*, those who associate other beings or deities with God: "God does not forgive anyone for associating something with Him, While He does forgive whomever He

---

[5]The Arabic word used here is *al-samad*, which means "the one whose whole resources are within himself." The meaning of the word is very similar to Christian affirmation of God's aseity: the quality or state of being self-originated, absolute, self-sufficient, independent, and autonomous. He is not like mortals in any chain of contingency, "begetting and begotten." This is the only time the word *al-samad* is used in the Qur'an in reference to God, and it is only used in reference to God in the Arabic language.

God: Absolute, Relational

wishes to for anything else. Anyone who gives God associates (partner) has invented an awful Sin" (4:48). Against such unforgivable *shirk*, *tawhid*, the absolute oneness of God, demands the active dethroning of all false gods and the elimination of their worship.

Perceiving Christians as *al-mushrikun*, those who associate other beings or deities with God, comes from a misunderstanding of the nature and function of God's relationality. Both Christians and Muslims affirm that God is one in essence; however, they differ in their understanding of whether there can be any plurality in God's unity or oneness. Islamic monotheism, which emphasizes absolute singularity, cannot accept plurality in God's nature. Accordingly, the Christian view of God is perceived as tritheism rather than trinitarianism. As we will discuss further in chapter nine, Christians do not believe in three gods; they believe in only one God, who is relational in his nature and in manifesting himself to humanity. The Bible declares clearly: "The LORD our God, the LORD is one" (Deut 6:4). Jesus markedly makes the same statement (Mk 12:29); the apostles repeatedly emphasize the same affirmation (1 Cor 8:4, 6); and Christians through the centuries have shared the same belief and worshiped only one God.

In inviting the Arabs to worship the only and true God, the Qur'an presents several arguments confirming God's existence. The Qur'an generally uses the order of nature and the life of human beings to prove God's existence: "Verily in the heavens and the earth are signs for those who believe. And in the creation of yourselves, the fact that animals are scattered on the face of the earth, are signs for those of assured faith" (45:3-4; 51:20-21; 41:53). The Qur'an calls on those who have reasoning abilities, ears to listen, eyes to see, and mind to think to consider the obvious signs, *ayat*, that are the clear and present evidence throughout God's creation (6:96-100; 16:3-22; 27:60-65; etc.). By doing so, one is constantly confronted with one basic reality, namely that God's existence is proven through these manifestations of life and the order of the universe. Likewise, the physical, moral, and mental constitution of human beings, their history and destiny, are also evidence of God's existence. The Qur'an also uses the witness of former prophets to prove God's existence and his oneness (30:29; 21:25; 39:65; 51:50-52), affirming that *shirk* is contrary to any reasonable thinking (23:19) and is self-destructive (21:22).[6]

---

[6]Samuel M. Zwemer, *The Muslim Doctrine of God* (New York: American Tract Society, 1905), 28.

Christians share many of these views about God's natural or general revelation as evident in nature, in human history, and in the constitution of human beings or consciousness. The Bible affirms that the knowledge of God can be realized in God's creation: "The heavens declare the glory of God; the skies proclaim the work of his hands" (Ps 19:1). Paul says, "Since the creation of the world God's invisible qualities—his eternal power and divine nature—have been clearly seen, being understood from what has been made" (Rom 1:20). These and numerous other passages, such as the nature psalms, confirm that God has left evidence of himself in the created world. The Bible also indicates that God is orchestrating human history and events (Job 12:23; Ps 47:7-8; 66:7; Is 10:5-13; Dan 2:21; Acts 17:26). General revelation is also found in the human conscience, the ability to discern what is morally right and wrong. Paul speaks of a natural law that is written on the hearts of people who do not have access to God's special revelation (Rom 2:11-16). Christian theologians, however, make clear distinction between such general or natural revelation and God's final and complete revelation in Jesus Christ and his Word, the Bible.

Who Is God in Christianity and Islam?

The Islamic concept of God converges on the attributes that are essential to God's being and prove his existence. Islamic theology does not start by describing God's nature; it starts with God's attributes or characteristics, *sifat*, which mainly describe God's *will*, not *nature*. This is different from Christianity, in which theologians often speak of God's nature and who God is as the starting point of Christian theology. God's nature and characteristics cannot be examined or described in Islam. God is beyond knowledge, and only God's attributes can be observed. If God could be known, this would mean that God might also become subordinate to human inquiry, which is considered a grave sin in Islam. One might discern one's position in relationship to God's will and God's law in Islam, but one will never come to a point of knowing God. Islam addresses the issue of what God does and what God expects Muslims to do but does not answer the question, "Who is God?" God is free from personality, which is perceived to be a quality of limitation in Islam. Therefore, God is beyond any human capacity to comprehend his nature or to directly communicate with him. The essence of Islam is to obey God and to submit to his will, not to know him.

God: Absolute, Relational

In Christianity, God's revelation of himself is sufficient to enable people to have glimpses of who he is for the purpose of establishing intimate relationship with him. God is known through his encounters with people throughout human history, in establishing covenants and declaring his nature and expectations from the people he created in his own image. God's names or characteristics are significant indications of who God is in his nature and how God relates to the created world and to humanity. In Christianity, encountering God and knowing his nature and characteristics lead to informative worship of God and enjoying fellowship with him.

THE ATTRIBUTES OF GOD IN ISLAM

The typical Islamic understanding of God's attributes is derived from the ninety-nine names of God, known as *asma Allah al-husna*, or "the most beautiful names of God." While the Qur'an instructs Muslims to call God by his beautiful names, it does not provide a complete list of God's names. The only chapter in the Qur'an that mentions the phrase "the most beautiful names" and lists some of God's names is surah 59:22-24:

> God is He, than Whom, There is no other god—, who knows (all things), both secret and open; He, Most Gracious, Most Merciful. God is He, than Whom, There is no other god—The Sovereign (or The King), the Holy One, The Source of Peace (and Perfection), The Guardian of Faith, The Preserver of Safety, The Exalted in Might, The Irresistible, the Supreme (or Proud): Glory to God! (High is He), above the partners, they attribute to Him. He is God, the Creator, The Evolver, The Bestower of Forms (or Colors). To Him belong, The Most Beautiful Names: Whatever is in the heavens and on earth, doth declare, His Praises and Glory; And He is the Exalted in Might, the Wise. (see also 2:255 for a similar list of some of God's attributes)

The Qur'an does not mention a list of the ninety-nine names of God (or even mention that there are ninety-nine names). The only source that gives a detailed list of the names is the Islamic hadith, the sayings of Prophet Muhammad.[7] According to one of the most recognized collections of the hadith, Sahih al-Bukhari, "God has ninety-nine names, one hundred less

---

[7]Twenty-six of the ninety-nine names are not found in the Qur'anic text in the form accepted and circulated by Muslim scholars through the centuries. They are rather based on passages that give close meaning to the name. In recent times, some Muslim scholars have been calling for the editing of God's ninety-nine names common in Islam in order to ensure adequate alignment with the Qur'anic text as well as better explanation of their meaning.

one; and he who has memorized them all by heart will enter Paradise. To count something means to know it by heart."[8] Muslim scholars group God's names or attributes according to different categories: attributes of majesty, *jalal*, generosity, *ikram*, and beauty, *jamal*; or those of essence, *jawhar*, and those of actions, *afal*, or absolute and relative attributes.[9]

The most repeated of the divine names in Islam is the twin title *Al-Rahman al-Rahim*, (traditionally translated as "the Compassionate, the Merciful"). They are derived from the same Arabic root, *rahma*, "mercy." A better translation is "the Ever Merciful, the All-Merciful." *Al-Rahman* refers to God in his character as being merciful. *Al-Rahim* refers to the divine action of mercy. This double title of the divine is the invocation used in the beginning of every surah (chapter) of the Qur'an. It is also the invocation repeated by Muslims before saying or doing anything in their daily activities, asking for God's blessings and protection. It is a constant reminder of the most significant attribute of the divine. Another often-repeated phrase about God in Islam is *Allahu Akbar*, "God is great" (or "greater"). It is a slogan of victory usually used in a moment of triumph, success, or vindication over an enemy or unjust circumstances.

It is beyond the scope of this study to explore the meaning of every name of the ninety-nine names of God in Islam; however, it is important to touch on some of them. God is described as the creator, the provider, life-giver, the Lord of the worlds, *Rab al-alamin*. He is also described as the all-powerful, the exalted, the great, the mighty and all-wise, the real or the truth, *Al-Haqq*. God is described as peace, holy, and light. God is also described as *Al-shakur*, which means "the grateful." Muslim scholars argue that when such an attribute is used in reference to God, it refers to the fact that God accepts human thankfulness rather than God himself being thankful. Another attribute is *Al-Mu'min*, which means "the believer." Again, Muslim scholars assert that when this is used in reference to God, it refers to God being trustworthy, not to God as one who believes.[10] While the Qur'an does not describe God as love, it refers twice to God as *Al-Wadud*,

---

[8]Sahih al-Bukhari, *Tawhid*, 12:11, p. 363, no. 489. See also another collection of hadith by Sahih Muslim, Dhikr 2:4, p. 1409, no. 6475. The English translation is listed in Sahih Muslim (IV, p. 1409, no. 2912).

[9]Mohammed A. Abou Ridah, "Monotheism in Islam: Interpretations and Social Manifestations," in *The Concept of Monotheism in Islam and Christianity*, ed. Hans Kochler (Vienna: Willhelm Braumuller, 1982), 46.

[10]Kenneth Cragg, *The Call of the Minaret* (New York: Oxford University Press, 1964), 40.

God: Absolute, Relational 233

which means "the kindly" (11:90, 92), and three times to God's conditional love to those who obey him and fulfill his law (2:165; 3:31-32; 19:96).

Some of the attributes of God communicated in the ninety-nine names are titles such as *Al-mutakkber*, the proud (59:23), and *Al-muntaqim*, the avenger (30:47), "the one who leads stray whom He will" (13:27). Muslim scholars consider these attributes to be characteristics of the divine will rather than characteristics of God's nature. In other words, God is not obliged to be holy, kind, or righteous, but he wills to be so. For example, the Qur'an affirms that God "has inscribed for himself mercy" (6:12); however, God is not obliged to be merciful. What gives unity to God's action is that he wills all these characteristics, but he is not obliged to any of them. As Cragg observes, "Action, that is, arising from such descriptive may be expected, but as a matter of necessity."[11] God might be recognized by the descriptions given him, but he does not necessarily conform to any of them. Muslim scholars argue that the contradictory actions of God can be resolved in light of understanding that God may *will* contradictory actions, but his actions are beyond our reasonable capacity to comprehend them. So, God is "the One who leads astray" as well as the "One who guides." God is "the One who brings damage." God is also described as "the Bringer-down," "the Compeller," "Tyrant," or "the Haughty." All such terms have an evil sense if they are used in reference to human actions. However, in the unity of the single will of God, these descriptions coexist with those that relate to mercy, compassion, and glory according to Islam.[12]

In Islam, God's names or attributes are not descriptions of God. Early Muslim scholars concluded that a "description of God must be, at the best, inadequate and misleading, and, at the most, impossible."[13] God cannot be known, and the unity of his will might give us only glimpses of his action. God is transcendent and beyond. No human can know God or fully comprehend God's action according to Islam. The Qur'an, however, constantly speaks about a merciful and compassionate God, the one who is close to every creature (34:50; 50:16), the forgiving (5:58), and many other relational characteristics of God. So, what do we make of the many references to God's actions in relationship to humanity? The answer might

---

[11]Cragg, *Christ and the Faiths*, 41.
[12]Sayyed Hossen Nasr, *Ideals and Realities of Islam* (London: Allen & Unwin, 1966), 52. See also Cragg, *Call of the Minaret*, 37.
[13]Cited in D. B. MacDonald, "Sifa," in *The Shorter Encyclopedia of Islam* (Leiden: Brill, 1991), 545.

be found partially in the absence of historical references to God's actions. The Qur'an often makes statements about God's forgiveness or God's compassion; however, these statements are not related to or presented in a historical context where God showed his mercy or extended his forgiveness in a particular event.

It is one thing to speak of God's mercy or compassion as an abstract idea, but it is another to experience God's mercy and compassion in an actual historical context. In the biblical narrative, people usually discern God's nature and characteristics by experiencing God through historical encounters and events. For instance, Abraham, Moses, Elijah, and many others attest to God's goodness, mercy, or holiness because they experienced and encountered a holy, good, and merciful God. Jesus' disciples came to realize that God was love because they experienced firsthand a loving God. This is contrary to the Islamic view, according to which God's actions cannot be realized in human history, since God's nature cannot be comprehended by humans. The relational characteristics of God communicated in the Qur'an as well as God's relationality as affirmed and experienced in the biblical narrative might open an opportunity for dialogue between Christians and Muslims on God's nature and characteristics. Reflecting on the existential experience of God's nature: Can God's will be separated from God's nature? Can God's actions be separated from human history, and if so, how would this affect the way people perceive God and relate to him? Can people worship an unknown God?

God's Absolute Will

The attributes of God in Islam as communicated through the ninety-nine beautiful names lead into the vital theme of divine-human relations. The majority of Muslims believe that nothing exists outside God's divine order. If God wills something to happen, it happens. The Qur'an repeatedly emphasizes that the will of God is the immediate source of all reality. God has created humanity as well as their actions. God's will and determination, *qadar*, covers all reality, including the whole of human history.[14] There is nothing in the past, present, or future that has not already been

---

[14]The verb *qadara* means "to measure or to estimate." Surah 6:91: "They did not truly estimate [*qadara*] God" (see also 23:18; 17:30). The verb is used in everyday Arabic language, indicating God's absolute determinism.

determined by God from eternity. The Qur'an, however, speaks about human responsibility, which includes believing in God and God's prophets.

On the one hand, the Qur'an portrays the sovereign God as the one who orchestrates everything that happens: "Say, nothing will ever befall us save what God has written for us" (9:51). "He whom God guides is he who is rightly guided, but whom He leads astray, those are the losers. Indeed, we have created for the fire of hell [Gehenam] many of both jinn and men" (7:178). "Had we so willed we should have brought every soul its guidance, but true is that saying of Mine: I shall assuredly fill up hell [Gehenam] with jinn and men together" (32:13). God may also be responsible for human disbelief (10:99), ignorance (6:35), disunity (5:48), and even associating other beings with God, shirk, the most unforgivable sin in Islam (16:35-36).

According to the Qur'an, human actions do not affect God. "And he who turns back on his heels, not the least harm will he do to Allah, and Allah will give reward to those who are grateful" (3:144). As some Muslim scholars have emphasized, "When God rewards the pious, that is pure kindness and when He punishes the sinners that is pure justice, since the piety of humans is not useful for God, nor does the sinner do Him any harm. It is He who causes harm and good."[15] According to the ninety-nine beautiful names of God, God is perceived as the "deceiver" (*al-mudill*; 4:88; 13:27). God is also described as "the best of Schemers" (4:143). Twenty times the Qur'an attests that God leads people astray (7:178; 32:13; 4:88; etc.).

The idea that God carries out acts of deception raises significant concern about the nature of God and God's role in relating to people. One of the issues that Muslims struggle with is how one might distinguish between God's acts of guiding to the right path and God-ordained deception. If God ordained the believing of believers and the disbelief, ignorance, and shirk of others, how can God punish people for actions he ordained for them?

On the other hand, God requires submission and human response in faith. "Whatever of good happens to you is from God; whatever evil happens to you is from yourself" (4:79). One of the most frequently quoted verses to support this argument is, "God does not change what has to do with a people until they change what has to do with their own souls," but it adds, "if God has willed evil to a people, then none can turn it away" (13:11-12). The contrasting approaches to divine-human relations portray God as the

---

[15] Andrew Rippin and Jan Kinappert, *Islam* (Manchester: Manchester University Press, 1986), 133.

forgiver, the one who out of his compassion forgives those who ask for it (40:3; 2:173, 182, 192, 199, 218, 225-26, 235); the returner (opposite of forsaker; 2:37, 54, 160, 187; 5:39, 71; 9:117-18), who is willing to "transform the very lapses of those who genuinely repent into goodness"; and the one who might mislead or withhold forgiveness.[16] Since God is absolute and his nature cannot be known, it is hard to predict God's action. God has absolute sovereignty in granting forgiveness or not, in being compassionate or not.

The Qur'an emphasizes that individuals have a degree of autonomy (7:178-82; 13:29; 42:15). However, such autonomy is only granted within the overall will of God (10:99-100; 81:29; 82:7-8). Since God's sovereignty is absolute, humans have no autonomous will outside God's overarching will. One early Muslim scholar, Al-Ash'ari (873–936), tried to reconcile this overpowering image of God's will with that of human free will by suggesting that God works within the will of the human doer to "acquire" the will to do certain actions. Such acquired (*iktisab* in Arabic) human will enables a person to fulfill religious obligations, to live a good moral life, and to do other desirable actions that will result in saving one's moral responsibility and accountability. Since God willed the deed in the will of the doer, God's sovereignty is kept intact, while humans remain accountable for their actions. This suggestion neither negates nor affirms that there is such a thing as human free will.[17]

The unresolved duality of the divine and human wills, a major theme in Islam, has been the focus of theological discussion through the centuries. Early Muslim scholars who supported the concept of free will, known as *al-qadariyya*, were eventually suppressed, while the more orthodox belief in the predestination and supremacy of God's will has dominated throughout the history of Islam. In the eleventh century the great Muslim theologian Al-Ghazali (1059–1111) noted:

> God wills the unbelief of the unbeliever and the ill-religion of the wicked and without that will, there would neither be unbelief nor a relation. All we do, we do by His will. . . . If one should ask why God does not will that people should believe, we answer, "we have no right to inquire about what God wills or does. He is perfectly free to will and to do what he pleases."[18]

---

[16] Fazlur Rahman, *Islam* (Chicago: University of Chicago Press, 1979), 34.
[17] Quoted in Kenneth Cragg, *The Dome and the Rock* (London: SPCK, 1964), 163.
[18] Al-Gazali, *The Disintegration of the Philosophers*, cited in *Medieval Islamic Civilization: An Encyclopedia*, ed. Frank Griffel and Josef W. Meri (New York: Routledge, 2006), 265.

According to the dominant belief in Islam, expressed in statements such as that of Al-Gazali, everything that happens, whether good or evil, human actions, thoughts, or behaviors, has been foreseen and determined by God from eternity. The common phrase used by Muslims to reference this fundamental concept is, "It has been prescribed or written for you" (*maktub*), based on surah 9:51. Humanity therefore lives in a state of constant compulsion under the sovereignty of God, with limited power to change current or future circumstances. Such an understanding of God's will has detrimental consequences for how people view and react to events and circumstances. If God is the ultimate author of whatever happens in human history, there is no need for humanity to interfere or contribute to change what already has been determined. Humans have limited responsibility to avoid disastrous events, accidents, or socioeconomic downfall; they must accept them, submitting to God's will. Such ideology influences many cultures and might explain the current socioeconomic circumstances of many communities around the world today.

Humanity therefore stands under the divine authority, submitting to God and God's will in total obedience. *Islam*, or "submission," is the only appropriate relationship between humanity and God. The most characteristic description of the human status before God is *abd* ("servant" or "slave"), a term that is frequently used in Muslim names. Entering into this relationship is also perceived to be by God's permission. The belief or disbelief of a person, which distinguishes Muslims from non-Muslims, is also determined by God. Within the relationship of submission, worship and behavior are the two forms by which the sovereignty of God is acknowledged in Islam.

Being utterly independent of his creation, God has no direct relationship with the people he created. Therefore, God does not reveal himself directly to his creation. God reveals his will and law only through angels and prophets. As Kenneth Cragg puts it,

> The revelation [speaking of the Qur'an] communicated God's law. It does not reveal God Himself.... The genius of Islam is finally law and not theology.... The sense of God is a sense of Divine command. In the will of God there is none of the mystery that surrounds His being. His demands are known, and the believer's task is not so much exploratory, still less fellowship, but rather obedience and allegiance.[19]

---

[19]Cragg, *Call of the Minaret*, 52.

The Islamic belief that God is God alone cannot be adequately articulated in the theological sense without the application of Islamic law. As Muslim scholar Fazlur Rahman observes, "To accept or conform to the laws of God is *Islam*, which means to surrender to God's law."[20] The Islamic statement of faith, "There is no God but God," should be fully realized theologically, socially, and politically.

The Islamic perception of God's absolute sovereignty should provide an opportunity for reflection on the dialectic between God's sovereignty and humanity's free will. Submission to God might not be possible or even necessary if a degree of free will is not guaranteed. Affirming God's sovereignty should not negate humanity's free will. To the contrary, God's sovereignty ought to inspire mature fellowship and worshiping hearts. The idea that God's sovereignty requires unquestionable submission might compromise God's greatness, as it may imply that God's sovereignty is dependent on human submission. God's sovereignty is manifested when God allows humans to be humans, capable of making their own decisions freely, making good and bad choices, even rejecting God and sinning against him. Growth and maturity happen when people commit mistakes and learn from them, not when they are constrained, having no choices. God's laws should be observed out of free will and the desire of the heart, not force. God is truly worshiped and obeyed if he is loved from the heart, mind, and soul. The ultimate goal of worship ought to be fellowship with God, not just submission.[21]

God's Will or Plan in Christianity

The Christian faith stresses the unity of God's intention and actions as governed by consistency and purpose. God's will or plan in Christianity is derived from an experiential awareness of who God is, what he does, and why; it is the overarching reality that encompasses all of existence. The Bible speaks of God's design, which includes the concept of purpose (Job 38:2; 42:3; Ps 139:16; Is 22:11; 37:26; Jer 49:20; 50:45; Acts 4:28; Rom 8:29, 30; Eph 1:5, 11; and many other references). God's plan is from eternity and is manifested in the creation of the world and human beings (Gen 1–2; Is 22:11), in the establishment of several covenants with Noah (Gen 9),

---

[20]Fazlur Rahman, "The Message and the Messenger," in *Islam: The Religious and Political Life of a World Community*, ed. Marjorie Kelly (New York: Praeger, 1985), 43.

[21]The concept of absolute submission to God influences the structural fabric of many Muslim societies, where absolute submission to authorities as well as in the family is expected.

Abraham (Gen 12; 17) and Israel (Ex 4; Deut 28). God's plan reflects God's eternal sovereignty in orchestrating human history, based on God's desire to have fellowship with the people he created and loves (Ps 139:16, Job 14:5). God's plan includes the well-being of his children and all his creation in full view of his manifest goodness, provision, and protection (Ps 27:10-11; 37; 65:3; 91; 121; 139:16; Dan 12:1; Jon 3:5, 10).

God is constantly portrayed as the one who delivers his people from the bondage of sin, with its resulting alienation and disobedience to God, opening new opportunities for people to worship and have fellowship with him (Is 43:9-27; 25:7-10; Lam 3:21-25), a plan that ultimately includes his redemptive work in Christ (Gal 3:8; 4:4-5). He chose us "before the creation of the world" (Eph 1:4; see also Eph 3:11), "before the beginning of time" (2 Tim 1:9), and God manifests his purposes within history (2 Tim 1:10). God's plan is "good, pleasing, and perfect" (Rom 12:2; see also Eph 1:5), and everything that happens is part of God's good intentions for his children (Rom 8:28; Eph 1:11-12).

God's plan is efficacious: what God has purposed from eternity will come to pass, and his purposes will be accomplished (Job 42:2; Is 14:24-27; 46:10-11; Jer 23:20; Zech 1:6; 1 Cor 12:18; 15:38; Col 1:19). God's all-inclusive divine purposes will be realized in human history; nothing can deter or frustrate his purposes. He "works out everything in conformity with the purpose of his will" (Eph 1:11; see also Prov 21:30-31; Jer 10:23-24). God's plan or purpose is manifested in the fulfillment of prophecies (Mt 1:22; 2:15, 23; 4:14; 8:17; 12:17; 13:35; 21:4; 26:56; Jn 12:38; 19:24, 28, 36; Acts 2:23; 4:27-28).

The psalmist is comforted, not threatened, by God's provision because he knows that God is good. He exclaims, "How amazing are your thoughts concerning me" (Ps 139:17 NIV 1984). Such confidence in God's goodness leads to worship: "I praise you because I am fearfully and wonderfully made; your works are wonderful, I know that full well" (Ps 139:14). God's plan is not compulsory: God does not force his plans over his creation. God's greatness and sovereignty are manifested in granting free will to his creation to respond to God's pleasing purposes either by accepting his provision of grace or rejecting it. God does not force humans to act in certain ways but gives them the freedom to act according to his purposes. The ultimate purpose of God's plan and the whole creation is God's glory (Rev 4:11; Eph 1:12). God's plan is the deepest reflection of who God is; the holy, loving God who loves and cares for his creation and leads every aspect of its existence for the purpose of his glory. God's plan reveals and demonstrates what God does in preserving, directing, and redeeming the world he created and loved.

The major difference between the Christian understanding of God's will and that of Islam is that human free will is not mutually exclusive of the divine will. The freedom given to humanity at creation is an expression of God's love. That humanity misuses the gift of freedom, which has resulted in human misery under sin and alienation from God, does not change God's intention to establish fellowship with humanity. The Bible portrays the history of the God-humanity relationship as a series of initiatives taken by God to reestablish relationship with undeserved and rebellious people. The Christian understanding and experience of God's will affirms that an all-wise, all-powerful, loving, and good God is directing human history toward his pleasing and perfect will.

God's greatness and sovereignty are expressed in the dynamism of human history, in which people are given the freedom to relate to God and to worship him freely. God's greatness is manifested in giving his worshipers the status of being God's children, according to which they freely call him "*Abba*, Father" (Rom 8:15).

As Cragg rightly observes, "Salvation from misunderstanding of the divine-human inter-will situation does not arise merely from sound analogies or intellectual truth. It is the heart of Christian witness that in Christ and his cross we find a path of life in which our wills are more fully ours for being made over to Him. The love of God within becomes the condition of the law of God without."[22] Human history is not moved by blind fate but rather by a loving God with whom we relate and in whom we have our being. We may look forward, then, with confidence toward the good and pleasing purposes of his will, aligning our lives with his good will: "Your will be done, on earth as it is in heaven" (Mt 6:10).

God's Nature in Christianity: "Who Is God?"

The starting point in Christian theology and Christianity in general is the question, "Who is God?" One's view and experience of God is the

---

[22]Cragg, *Dome and the Rock*, 170.

framework within which one builds one's faith, lives one's life, and has relationship to others. The attributes of God in Christianity refer to the very characteristics of his nature. We come to know God only as he reveals himself to us. While God's revelation is complete and accurate, it is not exhaustive, simply because God is beyond any human capacity that can fully comprehend him. There will always be an element of mystery and the unknown about who God is. As humans, we perceive God through our mental capacities and experiences in life. We express our thoughts and our understanding of reality through vocabulary and concepts that are governed by cultural contexts. We use terminology such as *king, father, sovereign, absolute, relational*, and many other words to express our experiences of God. While such expressions are helpful in articulating our understanding of God, they are limited to human capacities of comprehending and are not fully exhaustive in grasping the fullness of God's nature. We also need to be aware that our knowledge of God is not simply derived from human conceptions projected on him; God's attributes as communicated to us through his self-revelation are objective characteristics of his very nature.

Personal. In contrast to Islam, according to which God is unknown and cannot be perceived in terms of relationality or personality, the biblical narrative portrays a personal God, with self-consciousness and will, capable of feeling and having reciprocal relationships with other social beings. God's relationality/personality is expressed through God's name and God's actions. When God calls Moses in the wilderness of Sinai, he calls Moses by his name and identifies himself as the God of Abraham, Isaac, and Jacob. He is a personal God who has been in personal relationships with his people for generations before, extending his mercies and goodness (Gen 26:2-5; 28:13).

In response to God's calling him to deliver the Israelites, Moses asks God about his name. It is a personal encounter and an intimate request, as Moses desires to be acquainted with the God who is calling him and sending him out. God identifies himself as Yahweh ("I AM WHO I AM"; Ex 3:14) and affirms that his name is eternal because he is an eternal God (Ex 3:15). God reveals himself to Moses as both an eternal and sovereign God and an intimate God who is currently present and can be approached: "I will be with you" (Ex 3:12). In this encounter God demonstrates that he is not an abstract, unknowable being or a nameless force. Abraham carried on a deep conversation with and even questions God, and God gladly responds to his concerns. In fact, it is God who initiates the dialogue, which concludes with Abraham coming to a point of knowing God in his holiness, love, mercy, and justice (Gen 18).

In the Scripture, the relational God is portrayed in various names that reflect his loving and compassionate nature. In addition to the common name Elohim, "God" (Gen 1:1, 17:7; Jer 31:33), and El-Shaddai, "God Almighty" (Gen 49:24; Ps 132:4-5), God is known as Yahweh or Jehovah (Deut 6:4; Dan 9:14), which reflects immediacy and closeness. Yahweh is present, accessible, near to those who call on him for deliverance (Ps 107:13), forgiveness (Ps 25:11), and guidance (Ps 31:3). There are a host of such names that reflect God's care and relationality: Yahweh-Jireh, "the Lord provides" (Gen 22:14); Yahweh-Rapha, "the Lord who heals" (Ex 15:26); Yahweh-Rohi, "the Lord is shepherd" (Ps 23:1); Yahweh-Shammah, "the Lord hears and is present" (1 Sam 1:20; Ezek 48:35); Yahweh-Shalom, "the Lord our peace" (Judg 6:24).

God's personality/relationality is also manifested in his actions. God takes the initiative to approach people. After creation, God comes and talks with Adam and Eve, apparently as a regular and common occurrence (Gen 3). He takes the initiative to call Abraham and to reveal himself to Moses, empowering Moses to liberate his people. God's promise to Moses, "I will be with you," is fulfilled, and Moses' life and mission attested to that every step of the way. God's promise to deliver his people from bondage in Egypt is fully realized, and they are overjoyed by his presence among them (Ex 15). God speaks and communicates through various prophets and historical events to reveal himself to his people. His promises and warnings come to pass exactly as he said. God's complete and final revelation of himself, in the coming of Christ, manifests the love of God to redeem humanity (Rom 5:8). Karl Barth writes, "The personal God has a heart. He can feel."[23] God as a person communicates, acts, relates to humanity, and can be approached. He can be spoken to, and in turn he speaks. A personal God who loves

---

[23]Karl Barth, *Church Dogmatics*, ed. G. W. Bromiley and T. F. Torrance (Edinburgh: T&T Clark, 1957), II/1:370.

and cares can be approached in prayer, where he is eager to hear the cries of his children and enter into fellowship with them. Prayer is the deepest awareness of God's sovereignty and relationality: in prayer, people come to experience the fullness of his grace, realized in the good pleasure of his will. Because God is a person, our relationship with him has dimensions of warmth, love, acceptance, understanding, and respect.[24]

Spirit. God is a Spirit (Jn 4:24; 1 Tim 1:17; 6:15-16), which means that God has no physical body or nature, is not composed of any matter, and is not limited to a geographical or spatial location or time as we comprehend them. Several passages in the Bible suggest that God has physical features such as eyes, hands or feet, attempting to describe God through human analogies (anthropomorphism). There are also times where God appears in physical form (theophany, e.g., Gen 18). Such temporary self-manifestations of God do not negate, contradict, or affect his very nature as being that of spirit. God chooses to manifest himself in ways humans can comprehend and relate to. God's ultimate and complete revelation comes through the incarnation of Jesus Christ.

Holiness. One of the most significant attributes of God's nature, which runs throughout Scripture, is holiness. Its significance is reflected in its numerous occurrences and the force with which it is expressed. Isaiah speaks of encountering God's holiness in the temple, where "the doorposts and thresholds shook," and the seraphim cried out, "Holy, Holy, Holy is the LORD Almighty" (Is 6:3-4). When God touched Mount Sinai, the whole mountain was in flames and "trembled violently" (Ex 19:18). The Hebrew word for "holy," *qadosh*, means "to separate, consecrate or sanctify"; it also means "marked off" or "withdrawn from ordinary and common use." The word denotes a significant characteristic of God, manifested in the purity of fire that cleanses and sanctifies, as in the coming of the Holy Spirit on the day of Pentecost (Acts 2). The ultimate purpose of encountering God's holiness, as fearsome as it is, is to sanctify and transform people's lives. Those who encounter God in his holiness (e.g., Moses, Isaiah, or the early disciples) are empowered to take on new responsibilities of ministering to their people and the world.

---

[24]This is different from some of the common perceptions about God, according to which people perceive God as the great unknown or as a vending machine that is ready to solve their problems and answer whatever need they might have.

God's holiness reflects God's absolute purity and goodness. "Your eyes are too pure to look on evil; you cannot tolerate wrongdoing" (Hab 1:13). The proper response to God's holiness is awe, purity, and praise: "Let them praise your great and awesome name—he is holy" (Ps 99:3). God's holiness is the standard of Christian moral character. Scripture constantly emphasizes that believers are to be like God in his holiness: "I am the LORD your God; consecrate yourselves and be holy, because I am holy" (Lev 11:44; see also Lev 1:3, 10; 3:1, 6; 4:3). When people encounter God in his holiness, they realize their sinful nature and inadequacy (Is 6:5; Lk 5:8). At the same time, they are transformed to attain purity and holiness in their lives. Paul calls the believers in Corinth, a city that was indulging in a sinful lifestyle, to separate themselves from such practices and strive for holiness (2 Cor 6:14–7:1; see also 1 Thess 3:13; 4:7). Likewise, Paul calls the church of Christ in Ephesus to be holy and blameless.

Glory. Related to God's holiness is God's glory. Expressions of the exaltedness, loftiness, and splendor of God are correlated with holiness: "Who is like you—majestic in holiness, awesome in glory, working wonders?" (Ex 15:11). God's holiness and glory are not just titles given to God; rather, they are expressed and experienced through encountering God in his actions and self-manifestation.

In contrast to the biblical theme of God's holiness and glory, the concept of God's holiness is not clear in Islam. God is given the title "holy" only twice in the Qur'an. Surah 59:23 mentions the title "holy" along with a list of other titles as part of the most beautiful names of God, "God is He, than whom there is no other God-the king [Sovereign], the holy one." Surah 62:1 follows the same pattern: "Whatever is in the heavens and on earth declares the praise of God, the king, the holy, the exalted, the wise." The Qur'an refers to the "Holy Spirit" four times, three times in reference to Jesus: "To Jesus the son of Mary, we gave him signs and strengthen him with the Holy Spirit" (2:253; the same phrase is repeated in 2:87; 5:110). The fourth time, the title "Holy Spirit" is used in reference to God's revelation to Prophet Muhammad: "Say, the Holy Spirit has brought the revelation from the Lord" (16:102). Abdullah Yusuf Ali explains that the Holy Spirit is "The title of the angel Gabriel, through whom the revelation came down."[25] In addition to these references, the Qur'an uses the word *holy* twice in

---

[25] Abdullah Yusuf Ali, *The Meaning of the Holy Qur'an* (Brentwood, MD: Amana, 1992), 664.

describing the location where Moses received God's revelation, "the holy valley of Tuwa" (20:12; 79:16).[26] The absence of the concept of God's holiness poses concern about the nature of God and has an effect on the moral behavior of people. There are no historical references to times or events when someone encountered God's holiness, and neither is there mention that God requires people to live a holy life.

Righteousness and justice. God is perfect and right in his nature as well as in his actions. God's righteousness is expressed in God's laws, which are as perfect as God is (Ps 19:7-9). God commands only what is right and perfect, a reflection of who God is in his nature. God's righteousness affirms that his actions are consistent with the law he himself has established (Jer 9:24). The standards of choosing between right and wrong are not arbitrary; God establishes and adheres to standards that are as perfect as his nature.

Not only does God act according to the laws he establishes, but he also expects people to follow his rules. His righteousness is reflected in ethical conduct (Lev 19:36; Deut 25:1). God's righteousness establishes the framework for his justice, the way in which his laws are administered. God's justice means that he administers his laws fairly and justly, not haphazardly. When the Bible speaks about the consequences of sin and the rewards of the righteous, it makes clear that God's justice will be administered without favoritism or partiality. God's warning to Adam and Eve, that "you must not eat from the tree of the knowledge of good and evil, for when you eat from it you will certainly die" (Gen 2:17), comes to pass justly and fairly when Adam and Eve are punished for their disobedience.[27] God punishes sin because he is a holy and righteous God. Sin disrupts the very structure of the divine order, which requires holiness, justice, and righteousness; therefore, this disruption has to be dealt with justly (Deut 7:10; Ps 58:11; Rom 12:19). God's justice is manifested in rewarding the righteous, those who live according to his will and follow his

---

[26]Some English translations of the Qur'an use the word *holy* to translate the word "pure" (*taher*) or "prohibited" in Arabic (i.e., surah 80:14; 98:2). The word *holy* (*qoduos*) in the original Arabic Qur'an is only used twice in reference to one of God's titles, while the phrase "Holy Spirit" (*Al-Ruah Al-qodis*) is used three times in reference to Jesus and one time in reference to revelation, as mentioned before.

[27]The Qur'an speaks of Adam and Eve as forgetting God's command, not disobeying God. There is no mention of sin against God. The Qur'an states that God extended forgiveness to Adam and Eve not because they had committed any sin but for forgetting God's command (see surah 2:35-38).

commands (Deut 7:9; 28:1-14; Ps 1:1-3; 37:10-11, 29; Is 12:1-6). God also expects people to administer justice on earth through fair and just judgment (1 Sam 8:3; Amos 5:12).

The theme of God's justice is frequently mentioned in the Qur'an, especially in relationship to punishing the wicked and unbelievers while rewarding believers and those who do good deeds. The word *taqwa* ("fear of the Lord") is sometimes translated "righteousness" (74:56), and the phrase "good deeds" is often translated "good righteousness." However, the biblical concept of God's righteousness, which upholds consistency in God's nature, laws, and actions, has no parallel in Islam since there is no concept of God's righteousness being fulfilled through works of redemption where God's justice and grace are being fully realized.

Faithfulness. God's faithfulness indicates that God constantly and faithfully fulfills his promises. The promise to Abram that he would have a son was fulfilled years later, despite all circumstances that suggested otherwise (Gen 21:1-8). God's promise that the Israelites would inherit the land (Gen 15:18-20) was fulfilled four hundred years later despite their unfaithfulness and constant disobedience. God's promise of the coming of a redeemer in Genesis 3:15 was fulfilled centuries later in the coming of Christ (Gal 4:4). Speaking of God's faithfulness, one of the Hebrew prophets asks: "Does he speak and then not act? Does he promise and not fulfill?" (Num 23:19). Paul constantly reminds the Christians of God's faithfulness (1 Cor 1:9; 2 Cor 1:18-22; 1 Thess 5:24; 2 Tim 2:13). Divine faithfulness implies that God will never change, either in his nature or in his promises; what God says is truthful and precise. God "does not lie or change his mind" (1 Sam 15:29; see Titus 1:2; Heb 6:18). God neither uses deception nor leads people astray (cf. surah 2:106; 14:4; 6:125). A God of faithfulness and truth expects people to be faithful and truthful. Paul reminds the Christians to be truthful in their words and deeds: "We have renounced secret and shameful ways; we do not use deception, nor do we distort the word of God" (2 Cor 4:2; cf. surah 4:88, 143; 13:27).

Love. Love is the very nature of God, a definition of who God is. "God is love" (1 Jn 4:8). God's love is expressed in communion within the Trinity before the creation of the world. The Father declares, "This is my Son, whom I love" (Mt 3:17). Jesus says of the Father, "I love the Father" (Jn 14:31). The relationship between God and those who experience God's love is expressed in an intimate, reciprocal relationality of love (1 Jn 4:16). The apostle Paul speaks of "the God of love and peace" (2 Cor 13:11).

God's love for his people is evident throughout Scripture (Deut 7:7-8; Mal 1:1-2). God's unconditional love was fully manifested in the self-giving of Christ (Jn 3:16). God's love was not motivated by humanity's prior love for God. God extended his love to humanity while we were still sinners and God's enemies (1 Jn 4:10; Rom 5:6-10). God's love is not an abstract concept; it is demonstrated in his actions, in the sending of the Son, in his redemption of sin. Divine love constantly seeks to reconcile people with God (2 Cor 5:18), seeking them out (Lk 15).

Jesus draws a contrast between the master-servant relationship and that of God and his children (Jn 15:13-15). The relationship between the loving God and believers is like that between a father and his children (1 Jn 3:1). The Father-child relationship with God (in contrast to the Lord-servant relationship in Islam) corresponds to our being created in God's image. According to Islam, it is degrading to call God a father simply because such a concept might trigger the notion of God entering into a marital relationship in order to have children (6:101; 72:3). The Qur'an also cautions against the concept that any creature might resemble God in any form (112). But Christians share the same concern, and when Scripture speaks of being children of God, it speaks about being adopted into God's family in spiritual and not biological terms. Being created in the image of God does not refer to divine features appearing on humans but rather spiritual qualities of holiness, righteousness, love, and communication. It is dignifying to humans to be created in the image of God and reflects God's awesome attributes.

Grace and mercy. God extends his love to humanity through grace, mercy, and compassion. God's compassion and mercy are shown in practical ways and are not simply an abstract description. God had compassion and extended mercy to the Israelites living under bondage in Egypt (Ex 2:24; 3:7; 34:6). Jesus had compassion for the people when he saw them helpless and harassed; he touched them and healed their sicknesses (Mt 9:35-36; 14:14; Mk 6:34). God's mercy is the manifestation of God's unconditional love to save and redeem undeserved humanity. "The kindness and love of God our Savior appeared . . . not because of righteous things we had done, but because of his mercy" (Titus 3:4-5; see Titus 2:11). Paul uses rich language to illustrate the lavish love of God extended through his glorious grace to unmerited people: "In love he predestined us for adoption to sonship through Jesus Christ, in accordance with his pleasure and will—to the praise of his glorious grace, . . . in accordance with the riches of God's grace that he lavished on us" (Eph 1:4-8). God's mercy is not limited to those who believe in him and submit to his laws (surah 3:30-32); his mercies are extended to the whole human race. He "causes his sun to rise on the evil and the good, and sends rain on the righteous and the unrighteous" (Mt 5:45; see also Ps 145:16; Mt 6:26, 28; 10:29; Acts 14:17). God inherently loves his creation, provides for it, and extends his mercies to every living creature.

The difference between God's grace and God's mercy is not clear in Islam. While God is called a "merciful God" over two hundred times in the Qur'an, the Qur'an less often reminds people of God's grace bestowed over believers as well as the people of Israel (1:7; 2:47, 122). God's mercy and compassion in Islam are primarily viewed in the context of the forgiveness of sins, earthly blessings, or in being a Muslim, one who follows the straight path of Islam. "The path of those upon whom you have bestowed favor, not of those who have evoked [your] anger or of those who are astray" (1:7). According to surah 16:18, "And if you should count the favors of Allah, you could not enumerate them. Indeed, Allah is Forgiving and Merciful." The Qur'an refers to the conditional love of God in a way that implies that God's love and mercy are synonymous. "Say, [O Muhammad], 'If you should love Allah, then follow me,' [so] Allah will love you and forgive you your sins. And Allah is Forgiving and Merciful. Say, 'Obey Allah and the Messenger.' But if they turn away—then indeed, Allah does not like the disbelievers" (3:31-32; see also 5:54).

According to Islam, God loves those who fear him (3:76; 9:4), trust in him (3:159), and fight for his cause (61:4). But God does not love unbelievers (3:32), evildoers (3:57), the proud (16:23), or prodigals (7:31). Muslim theologians understand God's love in a metaphorical way: God loves believers in that he wants to reward them for their obedience, to forgive their sins, and to honor them in the hereafter.[28] In Islam, God's love is largely defined as a response to people's obedience. It results from their submission. The dominant theme in Islam is God's mercy, not God's

---

[28]Fakhr-ul-Din Razi, *Al-Tafsir al-Kabir* (repr., Beirut: Dar al-kutub al-ilmiyya, 1990), commentary on surah 85:14; hadith 16:31, p. 112.

love. Mercy illustrates God's divine will, not his nature. God extends mercy to those who deserve mercy (4:97-100). Mercy, not love or grace, is the expression of divine favor. God "grants mercy to whom He pleases" (9:27). However, God is not obliged to love or to extend mercy to anyone; it is his prerogative to bestow mercy on some and to withhold it from others. God choses to be lenient and forbearing, *al-Sabur* (3:155), annulling sin for those he wants to forgive and reward (3:134, 140). That God does not love sinners is repeated twenty-four times in the Qur'an (e.g., 3:37; 4:107).

The Islamic understanding and experience of God's mercy and love is different from the unconditional love of God in Christianity. God's love in Christianity is the fullness of his revelation, extending redemption and salvation to unworthy sinners whom he loved while they were still sinners. The love of God shows the heart of God, not merely a prerogative of his will. Divine love epitomizes the relationality of God, expressed in communion with humanity. It signifies God's intention toward creation, which he cares about, and humanity, which he loved to the extent of giving himself (Jn 3:16; Rom 5:5-8; 1 Jn 4:10). God has "poured out" his love (Rom 5:5), manifested ultimately in the sacrificial death of Christ for humanity's sin and transgression.

God's love is indicative of God's participation in humanity's suffering. The anguish of Christ in Gethsemane (Mt 26:36-42) and his suffering at Golgotha (Mt 27:33-50) express God's loving nature and his participation in human history. The atoning work of God in Christ is an expression of God's greatness that is expressed in God's love. God's compassion and mercy are fully realized in the cross of Christ. God is relational and exists in interrelationship; he is not the unknown, remote, "unmoved mover" who has no passion toward his creation. Unlike Islam, according to which God is excluded from participating in any human realm, God's forgiveness in Christianity is both the work of God and a revelation of his nature.

This participatory divine love invites a response. The God who showed his love to us and initiated the work of salvation, the one who loved us first, also calls people to respond to his love. Loving God with all one's heart and mind and soul (Mt 22:37) can only happen as a response to God's unconditional love. Only those who have experienced God's love and forgiveness can extend God's love and forgiveness to others

(1 Jn 3:15-16). Forgiveness of sin is granted only because God's love is complete in his justice. God's justice requires that there be payment of the penalty of sin. In atonement for sin on the cross, God's justice and God's love have been fulfilled. God's love is the framework of his justice, and the atonement is the deepest manifestation of God's love fulfilled through his justice.

Those who accept God's love and grace extended through the work of atonement are those who receive forgiveness of sin. Forgiveness of sin is not a merit that God simply bestows on those who submit to him and follow his laws. The idea of responding to God's guidance with devoted submission to God in anticipation of God's forgiveness of sin is an offense to the very nature of God, who in his love acts justly. Sin is a serious offense against God that requires redemption; it is not simply the mistakes humans commit. God cannot contradict his nature by overlooking the sin of humanity and simply extend a hollow forgiveness. The fullness of God's love is manifested in his self-giving to redeem humanity in order to satisfy his justice. God is both righteous and loving and has himself given what he demands.[29]

Our perception and experience of God are the lenses by which we relate to God and to one another. Loving others stems from God's love. Trusting others and having compassion on them is an expression of God's mercy and faithfulness. If such attributes are missing or mitigated in the very nature of God, it might be impossible for people to attain to such characteristics by simply trying to be loving, merciful, or trusting. The concept that God rejects those who do not submit to his laws while disliking unbelievers has a significant psychological impact on how people relate to God and to each other, and is different from God's unconditional love, mercy, and grace extended to undeserved humanity according to Christianity.

Immanence and transcendence. God's immanence and transcendence refer to the ways in which God relates to the created world. They are not simply attributes of God; they are the overarching indicators of how God relates to the world. Immanence refers to God's presence and relationality, while transcendence refers to God's sovereignty and distance from the created world. It is important to keep these two dialectical dimensions in

---

[29]William G. T. Shedd, *Dogmatic Theology* (repr., Grand Rapids, MI: Zondervan, 1971), 1:377-78.

balance. Emphasizing one over the other risks losing God's relationality or absoluteness.

The biblical narrative emphasizes God's presence and relationship to the created world (Gen 1:2), and with humanity in particular, which was created by God breathing his Spirit (Gen 2:7; see also Is 63:11; Mic 3:8). The indwelling of God's Spirit or the breath of God is the source of life that sustains all human beings (Ps 104:29-30; Job 27:3; 33:4; 34:14-15). God's Spirit dwells among his people (Hag 2:5), and God's presence is realized throughout the whole universe (Jer 23:24). Quoting Greek philosophers, Paul declares to the Athenians, "For in him we live and move and have our being" (Acts 17:27-28). God is also recognized as a personal God who initiates personal encounters and relationships, establishing covenants with Noah (Gen 9:8-17), Abraham (Gen 17:1-8), and Israel (Ex 19; Deut 28). God's immanence is fully realized in the incarnation of Christ, who discloses the fullness of God's glory, grace, and truth as God's wisdom, the Logos, dwells among us (Jn 1:14). God is a relational God who fully reveals himself in Christ, whom we can see with our eyes and touch with our hands (1 Jn 1:1). This does not mean that "God in Christ" has become fully apprehensible, and we have come to fully comprehend God. Paul reminds the Romans,

> Oh, the depth of the riches of the wisdom and knowledge of God!
> > How unsearchable his judgments,
> > and his paths beyond tracing out!
> "Who has known the mind of the Lord?
> > Or who has been his counselor?"
> "Who has ever given to God,
> > that God should repay them?"
> For from him and through him and for him are all things.
> > To him be the glory forever! Amen. (Rom 11:33-36; see also Is 55:9)

God's transcendence is realized in his greatness, power, and knowledge as well as his goodness and holiness. The great and exalted God is also the one who seeks to establish relationship with his people. The one who created the world also cares for and sustains the world (Is 57:15).

Many Christian theologians have tried to explain the relationship between God's immanence and transcendence, or God's relationality and absoluteness. Karl Barth (1886–1968) emphasizes God's transcendence over any human speculation about God, asserting that God is distinguished from humanity by an *infinite qualitative distinction*.[30] Søren Kierkegaard (1813–1855), who influenced Barth's concept of God's transcendence, affirms "God's qualitative distinction and dimensional beyondness." God is qualitatively different from humans; he cannot be extrapolated from human ideas, personality, or character, being in a different dimension of time and space altogether.[31] Jürgen Moltmann's *Theology of Hope* articulates a comprehensive model in which God is realized not only through historical encounters and events but also through eschatological and futuristic modes.[32] While these contributions are helpful in articulating the relationship between the absoluteness and the relatedness of God, they are not complete or inclusive. God is absolute and exalted, he is beyond and majestic, yet he is relational; he delights in establishing fellowship with the people he has loved from eternity.

Concluding Remarks

While Christians and Muslims might have different approaches to letting God be God, they long to worship him and to exalt his name. They recognize his transcendence and glory, and they also experience his nearness in their daily lives. Although the Islamic view of God's transcendence results in forcing God outside the realm of comprehension, Muslims are constantly reminded of God's mercy and compassion. When Muslims go on pilgrimage, known as hajj, they circle the Ka'ba with their hands open to receive God's mercy, saying: "Here I am, Lord! Here I am!" Five times a day, Muslims around the globe pray to God, asserting *Allah Akbar* ("God is great"). It is a constant cry of reaching out for God, hoping that God is listening to their prayers. Muslims fast for thirty days every year during the month of Ramadan, seeking God's forgiveness of their sins. It is the desire of their hearts to worship God, to please him, and to submit to his will.

God is near, as surah 34:50 declares: "It is He Who hears all things and is [ever] near" (see also 50:16). Christians and Muslims need to discern the meaning of God's nearness and how it influences their relationship

---

[30]Barth, *Church Dogmatics*, I/1:188-90.
[31]Søren Kierkegaard, *Concluding Unscientific Postscript*, trans. D. F. Swenson and W. Lowrie (Princeton, NJ: Princeton University Press, 1941), 369.
[32]Jürgen Moltmann, *Theology of Hope* (Minneapolis: Fortress, 1991), 37-71.

with God. Muslims are constantly reminded in their daily prayers and invocations of God's mercy, *rahma*, as they frequently recite the words, "God is the Most Merciful Compassionate." Will experiencing God's mercy and compassion along with God's nearness lead to grasping glimpses of God's loving and caring nature? The Qur'an also speaks of God's practices as unchanging: "Such has been the practice of *sunna* [meaning 'standard'] of Allah in the past, no change wilt thou find in the practice of Allah" (67:3). Can this imply that God's unchanging nature points to God's unchanging faithfulness and goodness, to a God who is consistent in his nature and actions, who is holy and just? The greatness of God is truly manifested in giving people the opportunity to worship him freely and to love him from their hearts. The deepest desire of the human heart is to know God, to worship him, and to glorify his name.

9

JESUS CHRIST

A Prophet

CENTRAL TO THE CHRISTIAN understanding and experience of God's nature and relationality is the person of Jesus Christ, who epitomizes God's final and complete revelation to humanity. The nature and work of Jesus Christ takes us to one of the most controversial topics between Christianity and Islam. The Bible and the Qur'an offer different accounts of Jesus' life and function, his relationship to God, and his place in the history of divine guidance or salvation. They portray different perspectives on the purpose of his mission, death, and resurrection. The heart of the Christian faith, the incarnation of God in Christ, is unthinkable in Islam because God is infinitely transcendent. The Christian belief that Jesus Christ is the Son of God is blasphemous according to Islam. God cannot have a Son and cannot be described as a Father because he is absolute and above finite humanity. Surah 112 negates the Nicene Creed by asserting that God is "unbegotten, unbegetting." Perceiving Jesus Christ as a savior has no place in Islam either, since humans have no need for a savior. The death of Christ on a cross to redeem humanity contradicts the Islamic understanding of God's sovereignty and justice. A just and powerful God would never allow his prophet to die such a shameful and humiliating death. The Christian notion of Christ proclaiming a gospel of salvation that includes forgiveness of sin and reconciled relationship with God does not fit the portfolio of Jesus according to Islam.

Jesus, according to Islam, is a prophet of God who proclaimed the gospel as a guide to his people, the same way Prophet Muhammad was instructed to proclaim the message of the Qur'an. According to the Qur'anic account of Jesus, the performing of miracles is a sign from God for people to believe and has no further purpose, such as establishing the reign of God through healing and forgiveness. There is no mention of Jesus forgiving sins or casting out demons in the Qur'an because there is no concept of redemption of sin or understanding of an evil power that opposes God's kingdom. The Qur'an constantly cautions against the Christian belief in a Trinity, which is perceived as shirk (associating other beings or deities with God), the gravest sin in Islam. God made his word a book from heaven, not a person. Books are all that prophets proclaim, and they are the only means of guidance. As Kenneth Cragg observes, "Islam and Christianity will never be at one about Jesus. . . . In the one 'the Word is made flesh,' in the other 'a word is born.'"[1] Exploring these topics from Islamic and Christian perspectives is vital to understanding how Christians and Muslims perceive the nature and mission of Jesus Christ and how such perceptions influence their lives and relationships.

The Islamic perception of Christ's nature and the purpose of his mission is the focus of this chapter, including the portrait of Jesus in the Qur'an, the hadith (Islamic tradition), and the reflections of Muslim scholars in early Islam as well as today. The following chapter will present the biblical narrative of the life and ministry of Jesus the Christ and his work of salvation. The discussion of the nature and work of Christ will lead to exploring the relational understanding and experience of God in Christianity. The climax of God's revelation in Christianity is the incarnation of Jesus Christ, who fully manifested the nature and character of God, extending forgiveness of sin and reconciliation. Simultaneously, the Christian encounter with God's revelation in Christ and the coming of the Holy Spirit leads to the understanding that God is trinitarian in his very nature as well as in his relationship to humanity and the world.

Jesus According to the Qur'an

Jesus Christ has a special status in Islam. Muslims honor Jesus as one of God's greatest prophets who has the same status as Abraham and Moses.

---

[1]Kenneth Cragg, *The Christ and the Faiths* (Philadelphia: Westminster, 1986), 39.

The Qur'an refers to Jesus in ninety-three verses of fifteen surahs (chapters). While the name Jesus is mentioned briefly in several lists of prophets, some surahs give quite detailed accounts about his life and mission, and other references to Jesus are simply a repetition of what was mentioned in other surahs.[2] Muslims usually consider the portrait of Jesus depicted in the Qur'an to be the most authentic account.

The announcement and birth of Jesus. According to the Qur'an, the angels told the Virgin Mary that she would give birth to a son (3:42-51; 19:16-21).[3] "Behold! The angels said: 'O Maryam! God gives you glad tidings of a Word from Him: His name will be *al-Massih* [Messiah] *Isa* [Jesus], son of Maryam, held in honor in this world and in the age to come, and he will have his place among those who are brought near [to God]" (3:45). The Qur'an affirms the virgin birth of Jesus in surah 19:16-21, which is titled "Maryam" (named after Mary):

> Then we send to her [Mary] our spirit *ruhuna*[4] and he appeared to her as a man in all respect. She said: "I seek refuge from you to the Most Gracious if you fear God." He said: I am only a messenger of thy Lord to announce to you the coming of a faultless[5] son. She said: how can I have a son when no human has touched me, neither have I been unchaste? He said: thy Lord said: "it is easy for me, and that we may make of him a revelation for mankind and mercy from us, and it is a thing ordained."

The surah goes on to elaborate the story with a host of other events unfamiliar to the biblical account. It says that Mary gave birth to Jesus in

---

[2]Kenneth Cragg, *Jesus and the Muslims: An Exploration* (Oxford: One World, 1985), 18-32. See also in Arabic Mounir Khawwam, *Al-Masih fi Al-fikr Al-Islami wa fi Al-Masihiyya* [Christ in contemporary Islamic thought and in Christianity] (Beirut: Khalifa, 1983).

[3]The Qur'an presents Mary (or Miriam, according to the Qur'an) the mother of Jesus as the daughter of Imran ("Amram," according to the biblical record) the father of Moses and Aaron (Ex 6:20). There seems to be a confusion between Miriam, the sister of Moses and Aaron, and Mary the mother of Jesus. The biblical account presents Mary as a descendant of the tribe of Judah (Mt 1:3-16), not Levi. According to Surah 3, which is titled *Al 'Imran* ("The household of 'Imran"), Mary was entrusted to Zechariah, who was a priest in the temple of Jerusalem. Mary grew up in the temple under the care of Zechariah, who would often find her with food that God had provided for her (3:35-37). The biblical account refers to Mary visiting the house of Zechariah and Elizabeth for three months, after which she returned to her own home, but it never says that Mary lived with them (Lk 1:39-40, 56) or at the temple in Jerusalem. According to the Jewish tradition, no women ever lived in the temple.

[4]English translations use the word *angel* instead of "our spirit." The original Arabic word is "our spirit," not "angel."

[5]The Arabic word is *zakii'n*, which also can be translated as "good" or "smart."

unbearable pain under a palm tree, which lowered its branches to feed her while a spring of water miraculously appeared to her (19:23-26). The Qur'an notes that Mary had to travel to a place far away from Nazareth; however, there is no mention of Bethlehem, while Joseph is never mentioned as part of these events. The Qur'an affirms that Jesus came to the world as God breathed his Spirit into Mary. "And [remember] her who guarded her chastity: We breathed into her Our Spirit [*ruhuna*], and we made her and her son a Sign for all people" (21:91; see also 66:12).

Jesus spoke in the cradle. According to the Qur'an, when Mary returned to her family with a newborn son, she was accused of adultery. "Truly an amazing thing has you brought. O sister of Aaron!⁶ Thy father was not a man of evil, not thy mother a woman unchaste!" (19:27-28). But Mary pointed to her child, while her accusers asked, "How can we talk to one who is a child in the cradle?" At this point the Qur'an asserts that Jesus spoke in the cradle, defending his mother and declaring, "I am indeed a servant of God. He has given me revelation and made me a prophet. And he has made me blessed whenever I be and instructed me with prayer and almsgiving as long as I live" (19:30-31).

Titles given to Jesus in the Qur'an. The Qur'an uses several titles in reference to Jesus. The most common name is *Isa*. The word is a transliteration of the Greek Ἰησοῦς (*Iēsous*), which is the equivalent of the Hebrew יֵשׁוּעַ (*Yeshua*), meaning "God saves."⁷ It is used twenty-five times in the Qur'an, and on sixteen of these occasions in the phrase *Isa ibn Maryam* ("Isa the son of Mary"). Referring to Jesus as the "Son of Mary" may be understood in the context of seventh-century Christianity, when Mary had assumed a significant place in the tradition. It is contradictory to the Arab custom to name a person according to the mother's line of descent. For the Qur'an to call Jesus "Son of Mary" affirms the extraordinary fact that he had no earthly father, and more significantly his humanity, which disavows any aspect of divine nature: Jesus is the son of Mary, not the Son of God.

Jesus is also given the title *al-Massih* ("the Messiah") eleven times. However, this is more of an honorary title, one that does not refer to a

---

⁶The Qur'an affirms in this verse that Mary the mother of Jesus is Miriam the sister of Moses and Aaron.

⁷The Arabic word for Jesus used by Arab Christians before and after Islam is not Isa but يسوع (Yasu). It is not clear whether the Qur'an is avoiding the use of the common Arabic word for Jesus in order to eliminate any reference to his redemptive function.

functional role of being a savior or the anointed one; such concepts have no place in the Qur'an. There are a multitude of important titles given to Jesus, such as "the Word of God" and "the Spirit of God" (4:169-71), "the Speech of Truth" (19:34-35), a "sign unto men," "mercy from God" (19:21), and "faultless" (19:24). Such titles are mainly honorary and are not indicative of Jesus' nature or ministry. Several Christian commentators on the Qur'an have tried to make theological assumptions out of such titles, claiming that the Qur'an supports Jesus' divine nature and his saving ministry. However, such claims are not affirmed in Islam and are not supported by the Qur'anic text.[8]

Jesus' calling and ministry. The sending of Jesus into the world, according to the Qur'an, was an act of mercy and a sign from God to all people (19:21). God instructed Jesus in the "Books, wisdom, Torah and *al-injil* [the gospel]" (3:48; 5:110). Jesus, however, was entrusted mainly with the gospel, which he preached to the people of Israel (3:49). As a faithful servant or apostle of God, his main message was to call the Israelites to worship God (3:50; 19:36; 43:64). Those who followed Jesus are described as those who have hearts full of compassion and mercy (57:27). Jesus set an example for others to follow (43:57, 59) and was blessed by God wherever he went (19:31). The Qur'an, however, never refers to Jesus as a teacher and never mentions any of his teachings. Jesus is the only prophet mentioned in the Qur'an who is empowered by the Holy Spirit (2:87, 253; 5:110), and the only reference to the Holy Spirit in the Qur'an is related to Jesus' ministry.

The Qur'an upholds that Jesus' preaching of the gospel came as an affirmation of God's previous revelation in the Torah: "We send Jesus the son of Maryam, confirming the Torah that had come before him. We send him the Gospel: in it were guidance and light, and confirmation of the Torah that had come before him: a guidance and admonition to those who fear God" (5:46; see also 3:3). However, the following verses, while confirming the messages of both the Torah and the gospel, instruct Prophet Muhammad to follow the latest book, the Qur'an, because it contains the truth (5:47-48). Jesus is also given the power to override some of the prohibitions mentioned in the Torah (3:50), a precedent to be followed in Islam as well.

---

[8]Some writers make a contrast between Jesus, who never sinned and is portrayed as faultless in the Qur'an (19:18), and Muhammad, who prays for forgiveness on several occasions (40:55; 80:1-10).

Jesus' ministry as supported by signs in order for people to believe. Several Qur'anic texts indicate that Jesus was supported by signs (*bayyinat*) in order for the people of Israel to believe in his ministry. According to the message delivered to Mary,

> And God will teach him the books and the wisdom, the Torah and the gospel and [appoint him] an apostle to the children of Israel [with this message]: "I have come to you with *a sign* from thy Lord, in that I make [create] for you out of clay, as it were, the figure of a bird, and breathe in it, and it becomes a bird by God's decree; and I heal those born blind and the lepers, and I raise the dead by God's decree, and I declare to you what you eat and what you store in your houses. Surely therein *a sign* for you if you believe." (3:47-49; see also 5:110)

The emphasis here is not on what Jesus has been doing as much as on the fact that such extraordinary acts are signs from God to support Jesus' ministry. While the Qur'an repeatedly refers to Jesus healing the blind and the lepers as well as raising the dead, no account of any specific miracles is mentioned in the Qur'an.[9] Surah 5:110 speaks of Jesus being supported by the Holy Spirit while repeating the words mentioned in surah 3:47-49. It starts by reminding Jesus of God's favor over him, which was primarily in strengthening his ministry by the Holy Spirit. "O Jesus the son of Maryam! Recount my favor to you and your mother as I strengthened you with the Holy Spirit so that you speak to the people in your cradle and as an elder. Behold I taught you the books, the wisdom, the Torah, and the gospel. And behold you make out of clay, as it were, the figure of a bird by my decree."

Speaking of Jesus creating birds from clay and breathing into them might give the impression that Jesus is a creator, an act only ascribed to God. In fact, the Arabic word *khalaqa*, which means "to create," is exclusively used in the Qur'an in reference to God's activity in creation. The Qur'anic accounts of Jesus' creating birds go further to indicate that he used clay (*teen* in Arabic), the exact substance used by God in creating human beings. It even uses the verb related to God breathing life (*nafakha*) as an indication that Jesus breathed the breath of life into what he has created.

---

[9] The biblical narrative gives specific details on how and why Jesus healed people and raised the dead, which will be discussed later. However, the Bible never refers to Jesus creating birds from the clay or speaking in the cradle. Such claims are found in apocryphal writings such as the Infancy Gospels, which were widely circulated at the time of Muhammad among the Christians of Najran.

Several Christian apologists have used such Qur'anic accounts to argue that Jesus' divinity is mentioned in the Qur'an; however, a deeper look at the Qur'anic text suggests the opposite. The Qur'an affirms that Jesus could perform miracles, but at the same time it negates the Christian belief in Jesus' divinity by affirming that such miracles were not proof of his divinity; they were primarily done by "God's decree." God decreed such miraculous acts, and Jesus was simply a tool used by God. In response to the Christians of Najran, who communicated to Prophet Muhammad their belief in Jesus' divinity rather than Muhammad's apostleship by citing Jesus' performance of miracles, surah 19:21 says, "They argue that he is God because he used to raise the dead, and heal the sick, and declare the unseen; and make clay birds and then breathe into them that they flew away; and all this was by the command of God Almighty" (19:21).

Surah 5, which is titled *al-Ma'ida* ("The table"), draws its title from an episode in which Jesus, at the request of his disciples, asked God to send down a table from heaven in order to satisfy their hearts and to confirm Jesus' authenticity, which God answered by providing such a sign for them (5:112-15). This episode may remotely refer to the feeding of the multitudes mentioned in the Bible. However, the text gives the impression that the disciples were testing Jesus by asking him for such a sign. That is why Jesus answers them by saying, "Fear God." The concluding statement by God implies a harsh punishment for those who do not believe.[10]

The Qur'an constantly affirms that any miraculous act performed by Jesus was primarily a sign from God to prove his ministry to the people of Israel. The Qur'an also states that Moses performed miracles for the same purpose (43:46). The Qur'an, however, indicates that Prophet Muhammad's most significant miracle was revealing the Qur'an. Speaking of this, the Qur'an

---

[10] "And behold I inspired the disciples [the Arabic Qur'an never uses the word *disciples*; the word in Arabic is *al-hiwarun*, which means 'the conversers'] to have faith in me [in God] and my messenger [Jesus]. They said: we have faith and do bear witness that we are Muslims. [According to the text, Jesus' disciples called themselves Muslims, meaning 'submitting to God.'] Behold! The disciples said: O Isa the son of Mary! Can thy Lord send down to us a table from heaven? Isa said: fear God if you are believers. They said: we only want to eat from it and satisfy our hearts, and to know that you have indeed told us the truth, and that we ourselves may be witnesses to the miracle. Isa the son of Mary said: O God our Lord send us from heaven a table set as a solemn festival for the first and the last of us. And a sign from thee and provide for us our sustenance for you are the best sustainer. God said: I will send it down unto you but if any of you after that resist faith I will punish [torment] him with a penalty [torture] such as I have not afflicted on anyone among all people" (5:111-15).

uses the phrase "it was brought down by God's decree" (2:97), similar to Jesus' miraculous acts, while the Qur'anic revelations are also described as "signs" from God (2:110) like the signs that supported Jesus' ministry.

Jesus' crucifixion denied. One of the greatest areas of controversy between Christianity and Islam revolves around the way Jesus departed this world. Against all biblical affirmations and historical records that uphold Jesus' death on a cross, the Qur'an makes a strong claim that Jesus was never crucified. The Qur'anic account of the end of Jesus' life on earth is as much blanketed in mystery as his birth. In a context where the Qur'an is strongly condemning the Jews for repeatedly breaking their covenant with God, it makes a strong statement that God would never allow the Jews to put Isa ibn Maryam, God's apostle, into such a shameful death on a cross. Surah 4:153-59 sets the context for the argument that Jesus was never crucified. It contains a strong polemical argument against the Jews, who are accused of breaking God's covenant, breaking the Sabbath, slaying God's prophets, dishonoring Jesus' mother by making false accusation against her, and boasting in their claim that they have crucified Jesus.[11] The Qur'an strongly defends Jesus' apostleship and affirms God's justice by refuting the biblical account that Jesus was crucified while making a noteworthy statement that the Jews had no such power to kill God's prophet:

> That they said "we killed *al-Massih* Isa in Maryam, the messenger of God," but they killed him not nor crucified him, but so it was made to appear to them, and those who differ therein are full of doubts, with no [certain] knowledge but only conjecture to follow. For surety they killed him not. Nay, God raised him up unto himself and God is exalted in power, wise. (Surah 4:157-78)

Muslim commentators offer various interpretations of what took place in this event. They all agree that the Jews plotted to kill Jesus by crucifying

---

[11] "The People of the Book [Jews and Christians] ask you [Muhammad] to cause a book to descend on them from heaven. Indeed, they have asked Moses for greater than that, for they said: Show us God in public [face to face]. But they were dazed [punished] for their presumption by thunder and lightning. Then they worshipped the calf even after clear signs had come to them. Even so we forgave them and gave Moses manifest proofs of authority. And for their Covenant we raised over them *Al-Tour* [a reference to Mount Sinai] and we told them enter the gate kneeling. And we said to them: 'transgress not in the matter of the Sabbath' and we took from them a solemn Covenant. [They have incurred divine displeasure] in that they broke their Covenant, that they disbelieve the signs of God, that they slew the messengers in defiance of right, that they, 'their hearts are the wrappings [not circumcised].' God has set the seal on their hearts for their blasphemy, and little is it they believe. That they said, 'we kill *al-Massih* Isa ibn Maryam, the apostle of God, but they killed him not.'"

him. The Qur'an affirms, "They [the Jews] plotted or 'planned a scheme' and God also plotted for God is the best of plotters [schemers]" (3:54). The Qur'an also states that such a plan failed. Based on the phrase "it was made to appear to them" (*shubbiha lahum*), the common interpretation is that God made someone else to resemble Jesus, who was mistakenly crucified instead of Jesus. Several suggestions are given as to who that person might have been: some commentators resolve that it was Judas Iscariot, while others suggested that it was Simon of Cyrene or someone else.[12] The view that Judas replaced Jesus on the cross was reinforced in the Muslim mind by the pseudo Gospel of Barnabas, which was written in the sixteenth century (this is different from the pseudo epistle of Barnabas written in the first century), claiming that Jesus was never crucified and that Judas Iscariot took his place on the cross. Such an interpretation, while saving Jesus from death on the cross, presents an alarming concern about God's nature considering the Islamic understanding of God's justice. It simply implies that a just God allowed an innocent person to die instead of God's prophet in order to save his apostle.

The Qur'an refers to a state of "doubt" and "conjecture" surrounding the crucifixion event. Such a reference indicates awareness of heretical beliefs such as docetism, which claimed that Jesus never had a real physical body but only an apparent or spiritual body and that his crucifixion was only apparent. (Docetist Christians had to escape from areas under the control of the Byzantine Empire to avoid persecution, and some ended up living in Arabia before Islam.) The Qur'an in surah 4:157-58 is making a point that Christians disagree among themselves and therefore their beliefs are not certain. "And those differ therein are full of doubts, with no [certain] knowledge but only conjecture to follow."

According to surah 4:158, Jesus was "lifted up" by God, which gives the impression that he did not die but was taken up to heaven. The concluding verse about this event, surah 4:159, states, "There are none of the People of the Book [the Christians and the Jews] who will not believe in him [Jesus] before *his* death. And on the Day of Judgment he will be a witness [*shahid*] against them." According to the interpretations given by several Muslim scholars, this verse has two possible explanations. If the pronoun *his* refers to the death of an individual Christian or a Jew, then this means that Jews

---

[12]Geoffrey Parrinder, *Jesus in the Qur'an* (New York: Barnes and Nobles, 1965), 111.

will come to believe that Jesus is God's prophet, while Christians will come to believe that Jesus was not the Son of God. In other words, both Jews and Christians will come to believe in Jesus as he is portrayed in the Qur'an. If "his death" refers to the death of Jesus, this means that before Jesus dies at the end of time (since he has not yet died), Christians and Jews will believe in him the way Muslims do. Either way, the following words negate any hope as a result of such a belief since Jesus "will be a witness against them."[13]

The traditional Islamic understanding of how Jesus was rescued from the cross is based on only one account, in surah 4, which asserts that God "lifted him up to himself." Many Muslims believe that since Jesus did not die, he will come back to earth to complete his mission, and then he will die a natural death. However, surah 3:55 offers a different answer; it indicates that Jesus in fact died and then was lifted up: "Behold! God said: O Jesus! I will cause you to die [*mutwaffika*] and raise you to myself and clear you [or cleanse you] of those who blaspheme; I will make those who follow you superior to those who reject faith [blasphemers] to the Day of the Resurrection." Surah 5:117 also confirms that Jesus died using the same word. While the Arabic word *mutwaffika* has only one meaning, "causing one to die," and it is a common Arabic verb used throughout the centuries until today to speak of death, some commentators argue that in that context it refers to God calling Jesus to himself. Others believe that Jesus continued to live in hiding until he died a natural death and that he will be raised on the day of the resurrection like the rest of humanity.[14] Looking beyond the end of Jesus' earthly ministry, the Qur'an affirms that "on the Day of Judgment, he [Jesus] will be a witness [*shahid*] against them" (4:159), that is, against the People of the Book, who indulge in the conjectures of human doubt (4:157) instead of holding to "the statement of truth" (19:34), by which the Qur'an confirms Jesus as a prophet in the historical and eschatological sense. Surah 19:33 records Jesus saying, "Peace be upon me the day I was born, the day I die, and the day I shall be raised up to life."

Whatever the explanation of what happened to Jesus, the Qur'an maintains a consistent argument that Jesus was never crucified, which aligns with the Islamic belief that there is no salvation through sacrificial death. The Islamic concern about saving the life of a godly prophet like Jesus

---

[13]Fakhr-ul-Din Razi, *Al-Tafsir al-Kabir* (repr., Beirut: Dar al-kutub al-ilmiyya, 1990), 6:11, 78-83.

[14]Mounir Kawwam, *Al-Masih fi Al-fikr Al-Islami wa fi Al-Masihiyya* [Christ in contemporary Islamic thought and in Christianity] (Beirut: Khalifa, 1983), 351.

resonates with Peter's reaction when Jesus spoke about his suffering. This topic will be discussed in chapter ten.

Jesus' ministry as twisted/misunderstood by his people. The Qur'an frequently alludes to the fact that Jesus was constantly challenged by his people. Although God accredited Jesus through many signs, not many people believed in him (43:63; 61:6, 14). Even when Jesus performed miracles, the blasphemers or the unbelievers said, "This is nothing but evident magic" (5:110). Those who believed in him are called the supporters of God (*ansaru Allah*; 3:52). According to the Qur'an, many Israelites rejected his message, and the climax of their rejection was manifested in their failed attempt to kill Jesus by crucifying him, as noted earlier.

The most detailed Qur'anic texts referring to Jesus' life and mission usually conclude with harsh condemnation concerning how his followers (particularly Christians) have twisted his words and misunderstood his nature and his mission. After arguing that Jesus was not crucified, surah 4:171 makes a strong statement against Christian belief in the Trinity, "O People of the Book do not exceed in your religion nor say of God but the truth, *al-Massih* Isa ibn Maryam [was no more] than a messenger of God and his Word which he bestowed on Maryam and a Spirit proceeding from him. So, believe in God and his messenger. Say not 'Three' desist." The Arabic word used in the Qur'anic text is *thalatha*, "three," not the Arabic word for "Trinity," which is *Al-Thalouth*. Obviously, Christians do not worship three Gods but a trinitarian God.

A similar argument is presented in surah 5 after the detailed account of Jesus' ministry of healing people and creating birds from clay. It states, "And behold! God will say: O Jesus son of Mary! Did you say unto people worship me and my mother as gods in derogation of God? He will say: Glory to thee! Never could I say what I have no right [to say]. . . . Never had I said to them except what you did command me to say, 'Worship God, my Lord and your Lord'" (5:116-17; see also 2:113-21; 3:52; 19:34-35).

Jesus in the Hadith

References to Jesus in the hadith (Islamic tradition) reaffirm many Qur'anic accounts while expanding on other aspects not covered in the Qur'an.[15] The

---

[15]Hadith (*ahadith*, plural) are the oral traditions narrated on behalf of Prophet Muhammad on various occasions concerning almost every conceivable aspect of the Muslim community. They are believed to be the narrative account of what the Prophet Muhammad said, did, or approved of.

hadith asserts the honorary titles given to Jesus in the Qur'an, such as *al-Massih*, "Word of God," "Spirit of God," and so on. The hadith also elaborates on Jesus' characteristics, teachings, and mission. Bukhari, for example, asserts that Prophet Muhammad narrated that Jesus was the only child who was never touched by Satan at birth.[16] The hadith depicts Jesus as a poor ascetic prophet, almost like the Buddha. One hadith tells of Jesus walking barefoot, accepting small portions of daily food while crossing his feet in prayer from sunset until sunrise. The hadith asserts that Jesus "was an ascetic in this world longing for the next world and eager for the worship of Allah."[17]

While the Qur'an never mentions anything about Jesus' teachings, the hadith expands on this topic and gives several accounts of what Jesus supposedly taught. These include several parables mentioned in the Bible as well as Jesus' teachings on the forgiveness of enemies and the need for a new birth. Furthermore, the hadith expands on the topic of Jesus performing miracles, including some extraordinary activities. While the Qur'an mentions that Jesus raised the dead without a reference to any particular event, the hadith narrates that Jesus was able to bring back to life Shem, Noah's son, from the grave in order to elaborate on his preaching.[18] Tabari cites a long tradition about Jesus raising a king's son, a son of a widow, and a sheep and a calf.[19] Another account mentions that Jesus slaughtered a gazelle, roasted it, and then raised it back to life to frolic away in the wilderness. Some hadith use biblical stories to speak of miraculous acts performed by Jesus. Of particular interest is the hadith about Jesus turning desert sands into gold and then poisoning some onlookers who attempted to steal it.[20]

They also include further explanation and expansion on Qur'anic verses. The Arabic word *hadith* means "conversation." It is believed that a chain of reliable companions of the Prophet and their successors transmitted such oral traditions or conversation. The *ahadith* were collected by reliable writers, transcribing them for further reference 150 years after Muhammad's death (seven generations). The two most reliable collections are al-Bukhari (d. 870) and Muslim (875). Bukhari, for example, has 3,460 hadith under 97 chapters. During the last twenty years or so, some Muslim scholars have called for the editing of the controversial *ahadith* on the basis that some of the *ahadith* are not reliable. However, most Muslims consider the oral tradition transmitted in the hadith as a second authentic source on religious matters and beliefs after the Qur'an.

[16] Alfred Guillaume, *The Traditions of Islam* (Beirut: Khayats, 1966), 149.
[17] The hadith is attributed to Ka'ab al-Akbar, cited in Jane Dammen McAuliffe, *Qur'anic Christians: An Analysis of Classical and Modern Exegesis* (New York: Cambridge University Press, 1991), 131-32.
[18] Razi, *Al-Tafsir al-Kabir*, 2:451-52; Zamakhari, 1:653.
[19] Abu Ja'far Muhammed Tabari, *Jami 'l-bayan 'fi ta'wili l-Qur'an* (repr., Cairo: Dar al-Ma'arif, 1968), 5:110.
[20] Cited in Arthur Jeffery, ed., *A Reader on Islam* (The Hague: Gravenhage, Mouton, 1962), 204.

While the Qur'anic text is open to several interpretations as to what happened to Jesus at the end of his life on earth and whether he died before being raised to God or not, several ahadith affirm that Jesus did not die and that he will return again before the day of judgment. Speaking of God sparing Jesus from the cross, Al-Tabari explains surah 4:157 by commenting on the words *shubbiha lahum* ("it appears to them") with a detailed account of what happened that day. He narrates that Jesus went into a house with his companions, but when the Jews surrounded the house to arrest Jesus, God made all of them to look like Jesus. So, when the Jews burst into the house to capture Jesus, all they saw were duplicates, resulting in the threat of killing them all. In this stressful moment, Jesus asked his companions which of them would purchase paradise for himself that day. One of them volunteered and went out and said that he was Jesus, so they took him and crucified him.[21] A hadith by Zamakhari narrates similar account with various details, including a reference to the Last Supper and Jesus' washing the disciples' hands (not feet) and then asking them whether one of them could die instead of him (Zamakhari 2:783).

The hadith's affirmation that Jesus did not die leads to another significant aspect of his mission, his eschatological function at the end of time. The hadith explains the raising of Jesus to heaven as a preface to his role at the end of time, which includes his role as the final judge. According to Ibn Kathir, at the end of time Jesus will return to earth, appearing at the white mosque in Damascus.[22] Tabari further explains Jesus' mission when he returns as including the destruction of *al-dajjal* ("the deceiver"), then breaking crosses, killing pigs, and abolishing the jizya (the poll taxes paid by non-Muslims in the Islamic state).[23] This hadith makes a strong statement about how Jesus will judge Christians, the primary recipients of his wrath. Destroying crosses and killing pigs are indications of Jesus' disapproval of their misguided religious beliefs and behaviors. This suggests

---

[21]Tabari, 3:133. See also Razi, 4:250.
[22]Ibn Kathir, 4:594. It is not clear why Jesus will return to the white mosque in Damascus. The white mosque in Damascus is considered the fourth holiest site in Islam after the great mosque in Mecca that hosts the Ka'ba, the prophet mosque in Medina where Prophet Muhammad is buried, and Al-Aqsa mosque (the Dome of the Rock) in Jerusalem. The last two sites indicate Islam's superiority over Judaism and Christianity. Al-Aqsa mosque was built on the site of the Temple Mount, while the white mosque in Damascus used to be the church of St. John the Baptist, which was turned into a mosque after the Arab invasion in the seventh century.
[23]Tabari, 17:69; see also Razi, 4:426.

that the Christians have been misguided in their belief that Jesus died on a cross, which has led to their constantly using the sign of the cross in their daily lives. It also alludes to their misbehavior in eating pigs, which is prohibited according to Islam.

Abolishing the jizya is an indication that there will be no need for it, since there will be no more disbelief by Christians as Jesus will explain to them that they should become faithful worshipers of the true God (i.e., Muslims), calling them to renounce their blasphemy in believing in Jesus as the Son of God.[24] During that time, Jesus will marry, have children, and live for some time until he becomes an elderly person. Eventually Jesus will die and will be buried next to Prophet Muhammad in Medina.[25] According to the hadith, Jesus' return to earth at the end of time validates the Islamic claim that Jesus was never crucified; hence, he has to return in order to complete his mission. His natural death and burial uphold the Islamic claim that he is not divine and is like any other human being.

Surah 17:1 makes a reference to one of the most significant events in Islam: Prophet Muhammad's experience of being taken at night from the holy mosque in Mecca to the furthest mosque (Al-Aqsa) in Jerusalem, where he was caught up through the seven heavens into the very presence of God.[26] The Qur'an does not give many details on the event; it says only, "Glory be to Him who carried his servant by night from the holy mosque to the furthest mosque, the surroundings of which we have blessed, that we might show him some of our signs" (17:1). The hadith, however, gives further details on this night journey and Prophet Muhammad's encounter with other prophets, particularly Jesus. One hadith mentioned by Tabari states that Prophet Muhammad passed through the heavens, being greeted by several famous prophets as a fellow prophet. Finally, he reached a higher heavenly layer, where he met Abraham, Moses, and Jesus.[27] Other hadith place Jesus in the second, third, or even fourth heaven, while still others indicate that Prophet Muhammad did not specify where each prophet was situated. One of the most noteworthy outcomes of meeting Abraham, Moses, and Jesus is

---

[24] In fact, the jizya (taxes paid by non-Muslims) was abolished in 1926 when the last Islamic caliphate, the Ottoman Empire, was dismantled.

[25] This hadith is attributed to Ibn al-Jauzia, in *Kitab al-Wafah*, quoted in Muhammad Ataur-Rahim, *Jesus: A Prophet of Islam* (London: MWH, 1979), 228.

[26] Al-Aqsa mosque was first built in AD 705 on the site of the Temple Mount when the Arabs conquered Jerusalem, seventy-three years after the death of Muhammad.

[27] Tabari, 15:2-14.

recounted in the conversation between them about their knowledge of the end of time or the final hour. While Abraham and Moses have not been informed about the end of time, Jesus knows about the final hour.[28] Another hadith refers to the fact that Jesus' return will usher in the beginning of the end of time. They all refer to surah 43:61, which says "He [Jesus] is indeed the knowledge for the hour."

The ultimate message of the hadith is that Prophet Muhammad is superior over Jesus, and Islam is superior over other religions. While the hadith initially portray Jesus as a prophet, his prophethood is limited to a particular time and people, the nation of Israel. To the contrary, the message of Prophet Muhammad, being the seal of the prophets, supersedes all previous prophets and applies to all times and places. The hadith affirms that Jesus is the closest prophet to Prophet Muhammad; according to Bukhari, Prophet Muhammad said, "I am nearest of men to the Son of Mary. Between Jesus and me there has been no prophet."[29] In another hadith it is narrated that Prophet Muhammad affirmed that he was "most akin to Jesus among the whole humankind."[30] Jesus is portrayed as one of the greatest prophets, given titles that are only bestowed on him, supported in his mission by signs and miracles. He is also the only prophet associated with the end of time. However, he remains a human being, and his role is limited in comparison to that of Prophet Muhammad.

The hadith constantly affirms Prophet Muhammad's superiority over Jesus and takes the Qur'anic portrait of Jesus' humanity further. Jesus waits with Abraham and Moses beneath the throne of God to welcome Prophet Muhammad to heaven during his night journey. One hadith asserts that Jesus foretold the coming of Prophet Muhammad. Another hadith tells of a man asking different prophets about salvation. When he reaches Jesus, Jesus directs him to Prophet Muhammad, indicating that Muhammad was the seal of the prophets and that God "has forgiven his former and later sin."[31] The Jesus of the hadith became more limited in his role and more subservient to Prophet Muhammad. The portrait of Jesus in the hadith greatly influences the contemporary image of Jesus in Islam. It also aligns perfectly with the larger

---

[28]Hadith attributed to Abd Allah ibn Masoud, narrated by Tabari, 15:12.
[29]Quoted in Geoffrey Parrinder, *Jesus in the Qur'an* (Oxford: Oxford University Press, 1977), 39.
[30]Hadith narrated by Abu Hurairah and cited in Abdul Rahim Alfahim, *The Two Hundred Hadith* (Makkah, Saudi Arabia: Makkah, 1990), 177.
[31]Hadith narrated by Abu I'Laith al-Samarkandi in *Tanbih al-Ghafilin*, cited in Jeffery, *Reader on Islam*, 227.

perception of the nature and characteristics of God as well as the role of his prophets according to Islam. Jesus does not reveal anything about God's nature, and he has no soteriological role to play; he cannot offer salvation from sin. He is simply another great prophet among many others who preceded him.

JESUS IN FORMATIVE ISLAM

The portrait of Jesus in formative Islam (eighth century AD, the first century of Islam) is framed in the context of the Islamic perception of God's oneness and transcendence. Jesus is presented as a great prophet of God who preceded Prophet Muhammad, a great human teacher to be emulated. While his mission and lifestyle are highly regarded, he is not the main focus of Islamic reflection and inquiry; his role is marginalized by the advent of the Qur'an and constantly presented in light of the final message of Prophet Muhammad.

One early Islamic writing on Jesus is that of Ibn Ishaq (704–767). Living in a world dominated by Christians and Jews, he proposed that Islam was a continuation of Judaism and Christianity. He envisioned Jesus as someone preparing the way for the final message delivered by Prophet Muhammad, emphasizing the humanity of Jesus against the claim that he was the Son of God. According to Ibn Ishaq, Jesus came first as a prophet to the Jews, then fled to Yemen, where he died. After his death, Jesus was made an angel to be able to live in heaven before his return to earth as the Mahdi who will rescue the righteous and judge the wicked. Ibn Ishaq's ideas are presented in his book, *Sirat Rasul Allah* ("The biography of the apostle of God"), where he details the life of Muhammad and other prophets beginning with Abraham.[32]

A similar legendary text was written by Al-Tha'labi (d. 1036), *Qisas al-Anbiya* ("Stories of the prophets"), which blends Qur'anic and biblical accounts with a host of apocryphal legends. He uses Ibn Ishaq's writings, weaving portions of them with hadith to formulate a continuous narrative. These stories of the prophets include an extensive account of Jesus. Al-Tha'labi starts with a genealogy of Jesus, asserting that Jesus and Mary were sinless. Soon after Jesus was born, he was entrusted to a carpenter named George, who later brought him to the temple and introduced him to Joseph,

---

[32] Alfred Guillaume, *The Life of Muhammad: A Translation of Ishaq's "Sirat Rasul Allah"* (Oxford: Oxford University Press, 1955). The Arabic text used by Guillaume was the Cairo edition of 1937 by Mustafa al-Saqqa, Ibrahim al-Abyari, and Abdul-Hafiz Shalabi, *Ibn Ishaq's "Sirat Rasul Allah"* (Cairo, 1937).

who facilitated Jesus and Mary's escape to Egypt. Al-Tha'labi refers to Jesus' unusual childhood, during which he was able to impress his teachers by knowing the true meaning of the alphabet and the content of their lectures. As a youth, Jesus used to create birds from clay and breathe into them. In one instance when Jesus detected the evil plans of the children playing with him, he turned them into pigs. Jesus is also portrayed as an impoverished ascetic who lived most of his life as a homeless man.[33]

In *Qisas al-Anbiya*, Jesus is described as a great teacher who instructed people to be "born twice" and reminded them that the "sick do not need a physician." Jesus is also credited with teaching that this materialistic world has no value: "Mud and gold were alike for him." When asked whether anything could be built with permanence from brick or stone, he replied, "A house built on the waves of the sea cannot stand." Jesus also performed several miracles, according to Al-Tha'labi, in one of which he fed the multitudes for forty days, and those who ate this food were cured from any diseases, which resulted in people believing in Jesus as a prophet. In reference to Jesus' creating birds from clay, Al-Tha'labi explains that those birds died right away in order to make a distinction between God, the only creator, and Jesus, who was simply performing miracles for people to believe in him.

Al-Tha'labi also explains that Jesus used to recite certain formulas, such as, "O Living, O Eternal One," before raising the dead, affirming that God was the one who raised the dead. Al-Tha'labi refers to the Lord's Supper, where Jesus washed the feet of his disciples. He also narrates that at the end of Jesus' life on earth, Jesus began to sweat drops of blood when he prayed for God to keep his disciples safe. Three hours after Judas was crucified, Jesus was lifted up to heaven, returning seven days later, and he gathered his disciples and instructed them to go and summon people for God. Al-Tha'labi also refers to the hadith that confirms that Jesus resides in paradise until his return to earth as the appointed ruler (caliph) over the Muslim community. He will make war against all false religions, breaking crosses, killing all pigs, and abolishing the jizya, poll taxes paid by non-Muslims.[34]

Such a detailed account of Jesus' life and role reflects some familiarity with the Christian account of Jesus. Most of it does not reflect the biblical

---

[33]Cited in Jeffery, *Reader on Islam*, 573-75.
[34]Cited in James Robson, *Christ in Islam* (London: John Murray, 1929), 44-74.

view of Jesus but rather represents the many legends available at the time. The issue at stake here is that such early writings became an authority for explaining religious beliefs and therefore contributed to the shaping of the Islamic view of Jesus through the centuries.

JESUS ACCORDING TO ISLAMIC THEOLOGY (*KALAM*)

As the Muslim community started to grow and gain control over large Christian territories that extended from Spain to India, theological interpretations of the Qur'an and the hadith became crucial. Muslims encountered various cultural traditions representing Persian, Hellenistic, and Roman thought, among many others. By the ninth century, Muslim scholars found themselves in a context where they needed to rationalize and express their religious beliefs to the larger Christian community that was still dominant at the time. The early period of Islamic theologizing (ninth to twelfth century), which was influenced by the dominant culture of the Christian Hellenistic world, allowed for rationalization of the faith and the use of philosophy in establishing categories for theologizing. However, once Islam became the dominant religion across the region, rationalization was restrained, and the later Muslim scholars were restricted in their theological deliberation.[35]

Between the ninth and the twelfth centuries, several notable Muslim theologians presented comprehensive theological works that influenced Muslim scholars for generations to come. Many of them are considered the authority on religious matters, and their work still influences the beliefs of Muslim communities up to today. Islamic theologians such as Al-Tabari, Ibn Hazm, Al-Ghazali, and Al-Razi commented on the nature and mission of Jesus in the larger context of explaining Islamic theology or *Kalam* by interpreting the Qur'an and the hadith.[36] Their work was presented in the context of refuting Christianity and therefore served as the standard Islamic apologetic rhetoric back then and continues to do so today.

Persian theologian and historian Al-Tabari (838–923) is well-known for his devotional material on the lives of the prophets. His most celebrated

---

[35]Muslim scholars, such as Ibn Taymiya (1262–1327) and Ibn Khaldum (1332–1406), were instrumental in their interpretation of Islamic law, jurisprudence, and a host of other topics.

[36]The Arabic word *kalam* means "speech," "statement," or "argument" and is used in reference to Islamic theology or religious deliberation.

work is a comprehensive commentary on the Qur'an (*Jami al-bayan fi tafsir al-Quran*), which is held as a classic reference in Qur'anic exegesis due to its detailed references. Al-Tabri stated that the gospel of Christ had been corrupted and popularized the view that the Christian Scriptures were flawed beyond recognition. According to Al-Tabari, Jesus was a rabbi who taught that outward action must be congruent with inward motivation, a great preacher advocating godliness through asceticism. Al-Tabari asserts that Jesus was granted the ability to perform miracles, such as opening the eyes of the blind and raising the dead. However, he argues that Jesus' power was inferior to that of Muhammad. He cites an illustration from one of Prophet Muhammad's companions to prove his point:

> Ibn Abbas said they [the disciples] were fishermen who were catching fish. Jesus passed them and said, "What are you doing?" They replied, "We are catching fish." He said to them, "Will you not come with me that you will catch men?" They replied, "What do you mean?" He said, "We will summon men to God." They replied, "And who are you?" He said, "I am Jesus, Son of Mary, God's Servant and Apostle." The disciples asked, "Are any of the prophets above you?" Jesus replied, "Yes, the Arabian Prophet."[37]

Al-Tabari is also credited with popularizing the substitution theory regarding Jesus' crucifixion, which claims that Jesus was saved from the cross by a substitute from one of his disciples. Al-Tabari's main portrait of Jesus is focused on what he calls "Jesus' incorruptible witness," always pointing to the one God and his apostle Muhammad.

The Andalusian Ibn Hazm (994–1064) is known for his strict interpretation of the Qur'an and the Hadith (*hazm* means "strict" in Arabic). He was an Islamic traditionalist who dedicated four volumes to refuting the reliability of the Bible. Like Al-Tabari, Ibn Hazm advocates that the Christian Scriptures have been corrupted. He argues that at first there was only one *Injil* (Gospel) revealed to Jesus, but subsequently unfaithful scribes produced four Gospels. Therefore, according to Ibn Hazm, the current Gospels are not the true message of Jesus. He lists scores of biblical accounts pointing to discrepancies in names and dates, claiming that Christians have corrupted the Bible, which resulted in the rise of many sects within Christianity.

---

[37] Al-Tabari, *The History of the Prophets and Kings* (repr., Cairo: Dar al-Ma'arif, 1976), 2:14.

Ibn Hazm focuses his criticism of Christianity on what he describes as the flawed nature of the Bible and the Christian claim of the divinity of Christ. He argues that Jesus was a great prophet of God, upholding the Qur'anic account of Jesus while sharply criticizing the biblical record. He contends that belief in the incarnation of God is a mockery of religion. For him it is profane to say that Jesus enabled God to fulfill the work of salvation. He makes several arguments against the divinity of Christ, which he considered the most blasphemous heresy the Christians came up with. He asks: If Jesus were God, how could God pray to himself? He cites John 8:40, asserting that Jesus refers to himself as only a man. Furthermore, he argues that the God of love in Christianity contradicts the God of the Hebrew Scripture, which enforces his stance that the whole Bible is corrupted.[38] Ibn Hazm's ideology is widespread across the Muslim world today, and his critiques of the Bible and Christian beliefs are frequently used to refute Christianity.

Al-Ghazali (1058–1111), also known as "the Great Imam," is considered the most original thinker in Islam. He was a great historian, theologian, jurist, and mystic. He was able to reconcile orthodox Islam with its mystic Sufi tradition, legitimizing both Sunni Islam and Sufism and bridging the gap between Islamic spirituality and intellectualism. As a Sufi, Al-Ghazali argues that one's knowledge of God can be based on active participation in the will and work of God, which will lead into communication with God (such a concept has no place in Sunni Islam). Inner experience and intellect, according to Al-Ghazali, lead to deeper knowledge of God and the purification of the human soul. He even argues that salvation can be attained by faith.

In light of these unfamiliar statements in Islamic theology, Al-Ghazali argues that Jesus demonstrates a passion for the divine through his active participation in God's will and work, a model that all human beings should emulate. Al-Ghazali sees in Jesus a great model for humanity, emphasizing Jesus' humanity against the Christian belief in his divinity. Al-Ghazali argues that Jesus is respected by Muslims because he is considered a great model for humanity, not divine. He even affirms biblical statements such as Jesus' declaring, "I and the Father are one," arguing that such statements

---

[38]Camilla Adang, Maribel Fierro, and Sabine Schmidtke, eds., *Ibn Ḥazm of Cordoba: The Life and Works of a Controversial Thinker* (Leiden: Brill, 2012).

express the intimate relationship between Jesus and God, which others might strive for (while Sufiism accepts this interpretation, such an idea is considered blasphemy in orthodox Islam). Al-Ghazali argues that the biblical record should be read as metaphoric poetry, which would allow for accepting some Christian claims.

While Al-Ghazali affirms that Jesus was a great prophet, he categorically denies that any divine characteristics should be associated with Jesus. In his famous work, *Al-radd ala iluhit Isa bi sharh al-injil* ("Answering Jesus' divinity by explaining the gospel"), he devotes large sections to discrediting Christian belief of the incarnation, questioning the divinity of Christ on several biblical accounts. Like Ibn Hazm, Al-Ghazali wonders how Jesus could be God and still pray to God. He also questions Jesus' prayer in Gethsemane, stating that Jesus' will and God's will seem to be different. He refutes the Christian belief that Jesus, as God, could be crucified and bleed, and he considers the burial of Jesus the stupidest idea ever presented. He comments, "By Allah! There is no stupidity to be found more foul, than of those who believe that the God of the world has been buried.... Verily, the one whom God misleads has no right guide."[39]

Al-Ghazali stumbles upon reading John 17:22, "I have given them the glory that you gave me," which he considers to be a major proof of the corruptibility of the Bible. He questions, "Is it possible for divinity to be given?" For Al-Ghazali, Jesus was a great prophet who could turn clay into birds, but he was not divine and cannot transform humanity destined for hell into children of God, bestowing God's glory on them.

Al-Razi (1149–1209), a Persian poet and notable theologian, sought to integrate Greek and Persian philosophy into the Islamic context. Al-Razi considers Jesus to be a great moral example for humanity. He makes a comparison between Prophet Muhammad's mission, which started at the age of forty, and that of Jesus, who started his ministry at thirty. He states that Jesus' mission lasted for three years, three months, and three days before he was lifted up to heaven. Al-Razi is noted for his emphasis on Jesus' humanity; he claims that Jesus will return to earth to destroy *al-dajjal* ("the deceiver"), marry, have children, die, and then be buried next

---

[39] Windrow J. Sweetman, *Islam and Christian Theology: A Study of the Interpretation of Theological Ideas in the Two Religions* (London: Lutterworth, 1947), 2/1:297. See also R. McCarthy, trans., *Deliverance from Error: Five Key Texts Including His Spiritual Autobiography al-Munqidh min al-Dalal* (Louisville, KY: Fons Vitae, 2000).

to Prophet Muhammad in Medina. Al-Razi is also known for his view that God entrusted Jesus with the judgment of the world because of his purity.[40]

The early centuries of Islamic theologizing are crucial in establishing the framework for interpreting the Qur'an and the hadith while setting them as the ultimate sources of Islamic theology, literature, politics, jurisprudence, and social life. These theological findings became the norms for authoritative religious interpretations for generations to come and up until today. The Islamic perception of Jesus is depicted through the Qur'anic record, which is considered superior to the biblical one. The notion that the Bible has been corrupted, and therefore Christians' view of Jesus has been distorted, was fully established at that time. While there is no specific time given as to when this corruption took place, or by whom, the notion of the corruptibility of the Bible has been a common theme throughout the history of Islam. The Qur'an is affirmed as the standard pillar of God's revelation and the final and complete message. Any other scriptures that differ from or contradict the style, content, or core message of the Qur'an are deemed corrupted. Since the Qur'an is perfect, its portrait of Jesus, like anything else, is the only complete and valid account. These views have been strongly reaffirmed through the centuries and are firmly established today.[41]

JESUS IN CONTEMPORARY ISLAMIC THOUGHT

On one account, the portrait of Jesus introduced by early Muslim scholars continued through the centuries and is widely circulated today by many traditionalist Muslim scholars. On another account, several later, more moderate Muslim scholars present a broader outlook on the function and the nature of Christ, reinterpreting the traditional Islamic views while presenting new perspectives on the topic. One prominent traditionalist voice is that of Sayyed Qutb (1906–1966), the founder of the Muslim Brotherhood. He argues that the prophetic message of Jesus became

---

[40]Cited in F. Peters, *Judaism, Christianity and Islam: The Classical Texts and Their Interpretation* (Princeton, NJ: Princeton University Press, 1990), 2:174.

[41]The Qur'an makes several references to the fact that previous scriptures (the Torah and the Injil) were inspired by God (surah 5:45-47). Other verses, however, hint at the concept of biblical corruptibility, indicating that the Jews and the Christians have been changing and twisting God's message in the Gospels and the Torah (surah 2:79, 87, 89, 109). Surah 2:106 argues that God's revelation can be abrogated or changed by God's decree: "None of Our revelations do We abrogate or cause to be forgotten, but We substitute something better or similar; don't you know that Allah has power over all things?"

corrupted and in the end contributed to the current imbalance and confusion in the West. He further explains,

> The Jews resisted Jesus and his message inviting people to gentleness, peace, spiritual purification, and renouncement of ritual formalities which do not bear on faith. They . . . attempted the murder of Jesus by crucifixion. But God alone ordained the time of his death and raised Jesus to Himself. We do not know the manner of Jesus' death, as there is no definite injunction in our Qur'an or Tradition regarding this.[42]

South African Islamic apologist Ahmad Deedat (1918–2005) states that Jesus, as a great prophet, is respected in Islam more than in Christianity. In his book *Christ in Islam*, a collection of his debates, he makes several comparisons between the Qur'anic and the biblical accounts of Jesus, emphasizing that Jesus' prophetic message was corrupted. He clarifies, "According to the Qur'an, the first miracle performed by Jesus was speaking in the cradle declaring that he is a prophet of God while in the Bible the first miracle attributed to Jesus was turning water into wine!" Astonished at this contrast, Deedat further comments that Jesus as the Word of God was instructed to speak God's word, not to make wine.[43] Stressing the humanity of Jesus, charismatic Muslim preacher Mutwali Al-Sha'rawi (1911–1998) misinterprets Jesus' parable in Matthew 25 as claiming that Jesus had five wives.

Moderate Muslim scholar Al-Akkad (1889–1964) is well-known for his volumes *The Genius of Mohammed* and *The Genius of Christ*. Al-Akkad's *Genius of Christ* extolls Jesus, whose life and teachings form the foundation of the Christian faith. He regards Jesus as one of the most esteemed of a long line of prophets, who was called by God to be the bearer of divine revelation to the Jews. The book virtually ignores the Islamic literature about Jesus and instead draws almost exclusively from the New Testament, especially the four Gospels.[44]

According to contemporary Western Muslim scholar Mahmoud Ayoub, the Qur'an refutes the event of Jesus' death on a cross in order to deny the Jews, representing humanity as a whole, the ability to defeat God's will,

---

[42]Sayyed Qutb, *Islam: The Religion of the Future* (repr., Cairo: Dar Al-Shoroq, 2005), 34.
[43]Ahmad Deedat, *Christ in Islam* (Durban, South Africa: Islamic Propagation Center International, 1987), 53.
[44]Abbas M. Al-Akkad, *Abqariat Al-Massih* (Cairo: Dar al-Hilal, 1945). English translation by Abbas Mahmoud al-Akkad and F. Peter Ford Jr., trans. and eds., *The Genius of Christ* (New York: Sunny, 2001).

embodied in Jesus as God's *kalima* ("word") and *ruh* ("spirit"). He states, "The claim of humanity (here exemplified in the Jewish society of Christ's earthly existence) to have this power against God can only be an illusion." The Qur'an, Ayoub concludes, passes "an accusation or judgment against the human sin of pride and ignorance."[45]

Ayoub's observation reflects the deep Islamic concern for God's power in protecting his messengers, but at the same time, as a Shi'ite scholar he sees a purposive value in human suffering. Ayoub goes beyond traditional Islam in accepting the concept of redemption, which he sees as a motif running throughout the history of religions, including the suffering of Shi'ite imams such as Ali and his two sons Hassan and Hussein, who were massacred in Karbala by Sunni Muslims. Ayoub argues that there is a redemptive efficacy in remembering those godly and faithful people who strived in their suffering to uphold justice and peace. According to Ayoub, Jesus was not the only unique means of redemption but a convincing demonstration of its universal reality.

Another contemporary Muslim scholar, Ismail al-Faruqi, declares that Jesus was a preacher of monotheism and an example of universal ethical values. According to al-Faruqi, Jesus and his message were inseparable, for he modeled in life what he preached. Jesus' message comprises the highest moral values of truthfulness and chastity, which lead to peace in the spiritual sense. Al-Faruqi argues that creation is not inherently evil, nor is human nature inherently sinful. The possibility of living peacefully in relationships is demonstrated by Jesus' life, which shows others how to conduct themselves in relation to the world and others. Jesus' life and message, according to al-Faruqi, exemplify the meaning of redemption, which is not something that can be achieved by a single act in Jesus' life such as coming to the world or dying on a cross.[46]

Algerian French Muslim scholar Ali Merad portrays Jesus as a theomorphic being. He notes that the Qur'an nowhere applies to Jesus the Arabic term *bashar* ("earthly, mortal being") and argues that the term *abd* ("servant"), by which the Qur'an introduces Jesus' life and ministry,

---

[45]Mahmoud Ayoub, "Towards an Islamic Christology: An Image of Jesus in Early Shi'i Muslim Literature," *Muslim World* 66 (1976): 163-88; Ayoub, "Towards an Islamic Christology II: The Death of Jesus, Reality or Delusion," *Muslim World* 70 (1980): 91-121.

[46]Ismail Al-Faruqi, *On Arabism: Urubah and Religion: A Study of the Fundamental Ideas of Arabism and Islam as its Highest Moments of Consciousness* (Amsterdam: Djambatan, 1962), 58-120.

"expresses not the notion of humanity but of service to God." Based on this interpretation, Merad does not hesitate to recognize in Jesus "an exceptional nature" or to speak of him as a prophet of "surpassing dignity," although this remains short of "sharing in the divine essence."[47]

Another moderate Islamic perspective on the life and mission of Jesus is found in the writings of Indian-British scholar Hasan Askari. He sees in Jesus the symbolization of the dialogical way in which God communicates with humanity. In this way, the Word of God and the human word maintain their "dialogical character," symbolized in Jesus, in whom "the Person is the Word." Jesus represents the dialogical character of divine-human relationship. Askari interprets this relationship as a dialectic between Christianity's prevailing concept of the "Word as Person" and the Islamic dominant perception of the "Word as Book":

> Their separateness does not denote two areas of conflicting truths, but a dialogical necessity. When the Qur'an rejects the incarnation of God in Christ, it corrects the idolatry of the Person as Word of God, and this it does by establishing the supremacy of Speech (*Kalam*) as Revelation. But when the Qur'an narrated the events of the life of Jesus . . . it invokes the supremacy of the Person of Christ as Word (*Kalima*) of God.[48]

The perspectives of modern Muslim scholars on the person and work of Jesus are helpful in establishing mutual respect and constructive dialogue between Christians and Muslims. Such contributions are vital in building bridges between the two communities, yielding hope for more peaceful coexistence.

Concluding Remarks

Whereas conservative Muslim thinkers reinforce the early Islamic portrayals of Jesus, moderate Muslim intellectuals express openness in terms of expanding their understanding of the nature and function of Christ while maintaining traditional Islamic views concerning his humanity. The overall Islamic perception of Jesus can be summarized as viewing Jesus as a great prophet of God among other prophets. Islamic terminologies describing Jesus as the Word of God and as the Spirit of God, as well as referring to

---

[47]*Encounter: Document for Muslim-Christian Understanding* 69 (November 1980), 1-17.
[48]Hasan Askari, "Dialogical Relationship Between Christianity and Islam," *Journal of Ecumenical Studies* 9, no. 3 (1972): 477-87.

Christ's surpassing greatness and his exceptional nature, assert the Islamic view of him as an honored prophet of God but not a divine person. Jesus is highly regarded as one who lived what he taught, providing a great model for humanity to emulate. Jesus is considered a model of higher ethical standards but not one who offers forgiveness of sin.

The historicity of the crucifixion and Christ's suffering will probably remain an issue of differing views among Muslims and between Muslims and Christians. The reason for the Islamic denial of the crucifixion has nothing to do with the historical event as such; rather, it exemplifies the Islamic concern for maintaining God's sovereignty, which transcends the human condition. It exhibits a concern for establishing God's justice while saving true prophethood from humiliation and disgrace; such a fate for one of God's messengers cannot be tolerated. Considering the Islamic view on humanity, Jesus' function is perceived from the lens of his being a great prophet of God, since humans are not sinners by nature and in no need of a savior.

10

JESUS CHRIST

The Savior

AFTER SURVEYING THE ISLAMIC portrait of Jesus according to the Qur'an, hadith, and Islamic thought, it is imperative to explore the biblical account of Jesus to provide an opportunity to engage Christians and Muslims in better understanding and dialogue on the person and function of Christ.

The biblical narrative gives a reliable account of the person and function of Jesus as documented by eyewitnesses who personally encountered Jesus and witnessed firsthand the events surrounding his life and ministry. It is an authentic record, unlike legend and oral traditions that circulated centuries after the events. It is imperative to explore the Christian account of Jesus by examining the record of the eyewitness who lived with Jesus, those who personally interacted with him on various occasions, listened to his teachings, saw his miracles, witnessed his death on the cross, and encountered him after his resurrection. The New Testament presents a detailed and comprehensive account of Christ and his ministry. One of those reliable eyewitnesses, Luke, asserts in the opening of his Gospel, "Many have undertaken to draw up an account of the things that have been fulfilled among us, just as they were handed down to us by those who from the first were eyewitnesses. . . . Since I myself have carefully investigated everything from the beginning, I too decided to write an orderly account for you" (Lk 1:1-3).

One of Jesus' close acquaintances, John, writes about Jesus, "That which was from the beginning, which we have *heard*, which we have *seen* with our eyes, which we have looked at and our hands have *touched*—this we proclaim concerning the Word of life" (1 Jn 1:1). Peter, another close disciple of Jesus, asserts, "We did not follow cleverly devised stories when we told you about the coming of our Lord Jesus Christ in power, but we were *eyewitnesses* of his majesty" (2 Pet 1:16).

The Bible presents a reliable historical account of Christ's teaching, ministry, sacrificial death on the cross, and victorious resurrection. It views the incarnation of Christ and his life and ministry as a fulfillment of previous prophecies. It clearly explains the purpose of Christ's incarnation, his redemption of humanity, and the hope in his second coming.

The Incarnation of Christ

The Gospel according to John states that Jesus preexisted from eternity, before incarnating and taking a human body. "In the beginning was the Word, and the Word was with God, and the Word was God" (Jn 1:1). Jesus is the originator of existence ("through him all things were made"; Jn 1:3) and the source of life ("in him was life"; Jn 1:4). The eternal Logos took on human flesh and incarnated: "The Word became flesh and made his dwelling among us" (Jn 1:14). Matthew explains that the incarnation of Christ was a fulfillment of previous prophecies indicating the presence of God with his people: "'They will call him Immanuel' (which means 'God with us')" (Mt 1:23).

Matthew and Luke give detailed accounts of the coming of Christ to the world. Luke emphasizes Gabriel's announcement to Mary that she will have a son and that "you are to call him Jesus. He will be great and will be called the Son of the Most High" (Lk 1:31-32). The angel's message affirms the participation of the triune God in the work of salvation through the incarnation of Christ. "The Holy Spirit will come on you, and the power of the Most High will overshadow you. So the holy one to be born will be called the Son of God" (Lk 1:35). The description given to Jesus applies only to God, "the holy one . . . will be called the Son of God" (see also Mt 1:18-20). Luke gives specific historical context as to when Jesus was born (during the Roman census ordered by Caesar Augustus) and where (the town of Bethlehem). He also mentions the names of every governor ruling over that region (Lk 2:1-4).

The Gospel account of Jesus' incarnation explains the purpose of his coming to the world: to save humanity. "Today in the town of David a

Savior has been born . . . ; he is the Messiah, the Lord" (Lk 2:11). It is good news of great joy to all people that God is saving humanity from sin and death. A righteous and devout man by the name Simeon is able to attest to this fact when he sees the newborn Jesus in the temple: "For my eyes have seen your *salvation*" (Lk 2:31). Speaking on the timing and the purpose of Christ's incarnation Paul affirms, "But when the time had fully come, God sent his Son . . . to redeem those under the law" (Gal 4:4-5).

This person who preexisted from eternity, incarnated in a human form, lived in a particular place and in a particular time in history, became the very center of the Christian faith. His life, teaching, sacrificial death on a cross, and resurrection are understood by Christians to be God's final and complete answer to humanity's predicament: sin and death. Putting Jesus in the context of the Christian faith, we need to answer his fundamental question: Who is he? How does Jesus relate to God, and how does he relate to the rest of humanity?

Jesus identifies himself as the bread of life (Jn 6:35), the light of the world (Jn 8:12), and the way, the truth, and the life (Jn 14:6), as well as the resurrection and the life (Jn 11:25). Jesus declares himself equal with God, using one of the most significant phrases in the Hebrew Scriptures, "I am." "Very truly, I tell you . . . before Abraham was born, I am!" (Jn 8:58). This phrase recalls God's words to Moses, "I AM WHO I AM" (Ex 3:14). Jesus' hearers unmistakably understand what he means, picking up stones to kill him.[1]

Titles Given to Jesus as Indicative of His Nature and Function

Titles given to Jesus in the biblical account are neither honorary titles nor replicated ones; they are indicative of his nature and function. Titles such as Savior and Messiah assert a functional Christology within the framework of salvation-history (*Heilsgeschichte*), defining the function of Christ. These designations of Christ's work are also perceived through the lenses of the ontological passages speaking about his nature. The title "Messiah" or "Christ," Χριστός (*Christos*) in Greek, is the equivalent to the

---

[1]There is also a very similar correlation between the Greek of Jn 8:58 and the LXX rendering of Is 43:10. The LXX translates Ex 3:14 as "I am the being" rather than "I AM WHO I AM." Greek-speaking Jews may have made as strong a connection with Is 43 as with Ex 3 when hearing Jesus' words in John.

Hebrew מָשִׁיחַ (*mashiakh*) or "messiah," which means "anointed one." This is not just part of a name, Jesus Christ; rather, it is an interpretative title that explains his function. It signifies the eschatological expectation of Israel in the coming of the Messiah as well as the Christian interpretation of what was fulfilled in the life and work of Christ.

Peter's declaration "You are the Christ" (Mt 16:16) places Jesus in the context of Jewish expectation. The anointed one was expected to establish justice among the people and destroy oppressors, ushering in a period of economic prosperity and political stability. Peter is anticipating a victorious Messiah, not a suffering one (Mk 8:32). Peter's concern about God's justice and God's power resonates with the Islamic concern; that is why the Qur'an refutes the fact that Jesus was crucified.

Considering the sociopolitical confusion that surrounded the title Messiah, Jesus avoids using this title while accepting others' referring to him as such. Jesus constantly refers to himself as the Son of Man—one who forgives sins (Mk 2:10), has power over the Sabbath (Mk 2:28), has no place to rest (Mt 8:20 and many others).[2] The title also refers to the sufferings of the Son of Man (Mk 8:31; 9:31; 10:33-34; etc.) as well as the exaltation of the Son of Man at the end of time (Mk 13:26; 14:62). When Jesus is asked by the high priest whether he is the Christ, he gives an answer that uses the term "the Son of Man" instead of "Christ." However, Jesus uses the phrase in its apocalyptic context, referring to the expected end of time and the coming of the reign of God (Mk 14:62).[3] While avoiding calling himself the Christ because of the term's political implications, Jesus places himself at the center of Jewish apocalyptic expectations, affirming that he is that expected Son of Man. His hearers understand him clearly; that is why, upon hearing Jesus' statement, the high priest concludes, "You have heard the blasphemy" (Mk 14:64). The transition from hope in the Messiah to the expectation of the Son of Man was fused into a single, unified vision of the futuristic

---

[2]This function of the Son of Man is in line with the prophecies of Ezekiel, who as the Son of Man is filled by the Holy Spirit (Ezek 2:2) in order to announce God's word (Ezek 2:3-4) to people who are described as not hearing or seeing (Ezek 12:2-3).

[3]In this context, Jesus is referring to himself as the Son of Man according to Daniel's vision: "There before me was one like a son of man, coming with the clouds of heaven. He approached the Ancient of Days and was led into his presence. He was given authority, glory and sovereign power; all nations and peoples of every language worshiped him. His dominion is an everlasting dominion that will not pass away, and his kingdom is one that will never be destroyed" (Dan 7:13-14).

role of Jesus the Christ as the eschatological hope. The title "Son of Man" indicates that Jesus holds together divine and human characteristics; he is the eschatological fulfillment of God's kingdom and at the same time the representative of humanity. He brings both God's grace and God's judgment.

The concept of the Son of Man lived on in Paul's understanding of the nature and function of Christ under the phrase "second Adam" or "last Adam." The two figures are contrasted: while through Adam humanity has fallen into sin and death, the second or last Adam, Christ, brought salvation from sin and death (Rom 5:12-19). According to Paul, both Adam and Jesus are representative figures: Adam accounts for the universality of sin, while Jesus accounts for the restoration of life. Pauline Christology further unites the preexistence of Christ, salvation through the cross, and the exaltation of Christ, merging Christology within the framework of soteriology. Jesus Christ, who existed from eternity in the essential form of God, who chose to empty himself κένωσις (*kenōsis*) to the extent of suffering death on the cross, is being exalted as the Lord Κύριος (*Kyrios*; Phil 2:6-11).

The Gospels assert that Jesus Christ is the Son of God (Mk 1:1; Lk 1:35), "the Son of the Most High" (Lk 1:32), emphasizing Jesus' unique nature in being the "one and only" Son of God (Jn 3:16). Jesus constantly refers to himself as "the Son of Man," but he is fully aware that he is the eternal Son of God (Jn 17:1). The use of these seemingly contradictory expressions indicates the nature and function of Jesus the Christ. He is a representative of humanity while at the same time holding a unique and unparalleled relationship with God as his Father. Jesus refers to God as his Father (Mk 14:36; Jn 20:17) and has a special sense of the fatherhood of God (Mt 11:27), addressing him with a word of peculiar intimacy, *abba* (Mk 14:36).[4] Jesus shares the same identity as the Father: "I and the Father are one" (Jn 10:30).[5] His nature as the Son is inseparable from his

---

[4]Jesus makes a distinction between his relationship to God as his Father (Mt 11:25; Mk 14:36) and the disciples' relationship to God "your father" (Lk 6:36; 12:30, 32) or "your Father in heaven" (Mk 11:25; see Mt 23:9). He also says, "I [will go] to my Father and your Father" (Jn 20:17). Jesus never includes himself with his disciples by saying "our Father." The Lord's Prayer is sometimes used mistakenly to make such an assumption; Jesus, however, makes a clear statement, "This . . . is how you should pray: Our Father . . ." (Mt 6:9; see Lk 11:2).

[5]The word ἐσμεν (*esmen*), translated "are," is actually a first-person plural verb. More accurately, Jesus' statement reads, "I and the Father, *we* are one."

mission and authority, and all authority has been given to him (Mt 28:18).[6] Other significant titles such as Logos, God's Word or Wisdom (Jn 1:1, 14), are used to explain the nature of Christ in the Hellenistic context. In his life, teaching, sacrificial death on the cross, and victorious resurrection, Jesus was able to combine and even give a new meaning to unrelated titles: Messiah, Son of Man, Son of God, Logos, Christ, Lord, last Adam, and so on.

Jesus' Ministry: Ushering in the Reign of God

In his earthly life, Jesus had a holistic ministry with significant purpose: establishing the reign of God. His ministry included teaching and preaching, healing the sick, casting out demons, and forgiving sins. Jesus' public ministry started with his baptism and concluded with his sacrificial death on the cross, followed by his resurrection. Jesus did not need to be baptized, having no sin to repent of; his baptism was a public declaration that he had accepted the mission to be "the Lamb of God, who takes away the sin of the world" (Jn 1:29). His baptism is God's affirmation of who Jesus is and what he will do: "This is my Son, whom I love" (Mt 3:17; see Mk 1:11; Lk 3:22). Jesus' baptism is followed by a time of fasting in preparation for his ministry. At the conclusion of this period, Jesus is tempted by the devil to fulfill the role of the Messiah according to the Jewish expectations of the time instead of offering himself as a sacrifice to redeem humanity.[7]

In his first preaching at the synagogue in Nazareth, Jesus makes it clear that Isaiah's prophecy, "The Spirit of the Sovereign Lord is on me, because the Lord has anointed me to proclaim good news to the poor" (Is 61:1), has been fulfilled in his own life and ministry: "Today this Scripture is fulfilled" (Lk 4:21). Jesus' teaching and ministry are consistently described as good news because Jesus came to proclaim a new reign of God's kingdom where the oppressed would be set free, the blind would see, and peace would be proclaimed. He was sent to the world to liberate people from their sins. His words are not simply inspired by God; Jesus' words

---

[6] Jesus as the eternal Son of God makes us in turn the children of God (Rom 8:14-17; Gal 3:26; 4:5). In him God "has predestined [us] to be conformed to the image of his Son" (Rom 8:29).

[7] The Gospel narrative indicates that Jesus could have accomplished each one of these expectations. However, his messiahship was fully realized not in political power, economic prosperity, or religious reformation but through redemption of sin through sacrificial death on the cross.

are God's words (Mt 24:35). Jesus is not an earthly prophet like other prophets who came to proclaim God's word (Ex 8:1; 1 Kings 20:13; Is 28:14; Jer 19:15; and many others); he is God's Word himself. He teaches with authority (Mk 1:22; Mt 7:29), and his authority extends over the law and the Sabbath (Mk 2:28).

Jesus' proclamation of the good news of the kingdom is fully realized through "healing every disease and sickness among the people . . . those suffering severe pain, the demon-possessed, those having seizures, and the paralyzed" (Mt 4:23-24). Jesus' miracles are not great performances to prove his power or to impress people (Jesus rejects performing miracles for such reasons; see Mt 12:38-39). Rather, they are God's manifestation of the restoration of broken and helpless humanity. When Jesus saw the crowds, "he had compassion on them, because they were harassed and helpless" (Mt 9:36). God's mercy and compassion are not abstract concepts; God's compassion is fully realized in Jesus' actions of delivering people from their misery, healing them, and restoring their humanity. Such proclamation of the good news of God's kingdom includes the most significant dimension of Jesus' ministry: forgiveness of sins. Jesus extends his forgiveness to people before healing them (Mk 2:5; Lk 7:36-50; Jn 8:1-11). Upon hearing Jesus' offer of forgiveness, people often mumble among themselves, accusing him of blasphemy. Jesus as God incarnate has the authority to extend forgiveness of sin. Jesus' ministry fulfilled God's ultimate purposes for the salvation of humanity; it was a comprehensive ministry that ushered in healing, restoration, and forgiveness.

Jesus' Sacrificial Death

The climax of Jesus' ministry is his sacrificial death on the cross. The Gospel accounts give significant details of his suffering, while the New Testament narrative as a whole envisions God's salvation of humanity through Christ's sacrificial death. Through the centuries, the cross became central to the Christian faith, a symbol that identifies Christianity and the Christian life. The Christian faith revolves around knowing Christ in "the power of his resurrection and *participation in his sufferings*" (Phil 3:10).

In the Roman and Jewish contexts of Jesus' time, the cross was the most humiliating method of death. According to the Jewish law, dying on a cross signified absolute rejection from the community and God's extreme punishment for blasphemy. "Cursed be everyone who is hung on a pole" (Gal 3:13; see Deut 21:23). Crucifixion, as a means of punishing dangerous criminals and rebels in the Roman Empire, was not something that nobles and elites would be associated with, and even mentioning criminals' crucifixion was not considered good manners in the presence of respectable people.[8] Worshiping a "crucified God," to use Martin Luther's terminology, was considered totally unacceptable and inappropriate in the Jewish and Roman world. A religion of the cross had no respect in such a context. The Islamic concern that God's justice and power should not have allowed for his prophet to die such a shameful death was expressed in other religious traditions and cultural contexts centuries before Islam. Not only this, but Isaiah declares in his prophecies that the crucified Christ has "no beauty or majesty to attract us to him" (Is 53:2). A crucified Christ is "a stumbling block to Jews and foolishness to Gentiles" (1 Cor 1:23). Why the cross, then? Why have Christians through the centuries been adamant about stressing the significance of Christ's death on a cross? Why does Paul, a highly respected Jewish leader and a Roman citizen, declare: "May I never boast except in the cross of our Lord Jesus Christ" (Gal 6:14)?

Dying on the cross was Jesus' main purpose in coming to the world. Oftentimes, the events that led to Jesus' crucifixion give the impression that Jesus died a humiliating death as a victim of religious and political conflict that somehow could have been avoided. While it is true that Jesus' preaching and lifestyle put him in conflict with various religious groups, he constantly spoke about his death on a cross as a future event that he had full control over. It was the ultimate purpose of his coming into the world. Obviously, Jesus' preaching on the imminence of the unconditional grace of the kingdom, his association and full acceptance of sinners and tax collectors, and his constant pronouncement of forgiveness of sin have evoked the anger of different religious groups. However, Jesus makes it clear that he came in order to die for the world's sin (Jn 3:14-15). He fully explains the kind of death he is going to endure (Jn 12:32-33).

Jesus' statements about his death are shocking to his audience and contradict their expectation that the Messiah would remain forever (Jn 12:34). Jesus' statement that he will go to Jerusalem, will suffer and die, and three days later will be raised to life (Mt 16:21) is astonishing to his disciples.

---

[8]William E. Dunstan, *Ancient Rome* (Lanham, MD: Rowman & Littlefield, 2010), 53.

Peter responds by saying, "Never, Lord!" ... "This shall never happen to you!" (Mt 16:22). Peter, like the rest of the disciples and all of Israel, was anticipating a victorious Messiah, not a suffering one. Peter's perception of God's power and justice, which echoes that of Islam, would not allow for such a humiliating death of God's Messiah. Jesus' disciples find it difficult to accept such a teaching, and they are deeply troubled when Jesus repeatedly emphasizes his coming sufferings (Mt 17:22-23), not fully comprehending his words (Mk 9:32; Lk 18:34).

However, for Jesus, the source of life, experiencing death was the way to restore life. Jesus was never surprised by the cross, and he constantly taught his disciples about it (Mt 16:17-22; Mk 8:31-33; Lk 9:21-22, 33-35), declaring its costly significance on several occasions (Jn 3:14-17; 12:32-34). He is intentional about going to Jerusalem in order to be crucified: "As the time approached for him to be taken up to heaven, Jesus resolutely set out for Jerusalem" (Lk 9:51). He gives a full description of what exactly will take place there.[9] When Jesus teaches about his suffering, he concludes by inviting the disciples and all Christians to deny themselves, take up their cross, and follow him (Mt 16:23-24; Lk 9:23-25). Fellowship with Christ includes participating in his suffering (Phil 1:29; Col 1:24).

Jesus had full control over his life, including his determination to be crucified. Jesus voluntarily and freely gives up his life. He asserts, "I lay down my life—only to take it up again. No one takes it from me, but I lay it down of my own accord. I have authority [power] to lay it down and authority to take it up again" (Jn 10:17-18). When Jesus died on the cross, "He ... [freely] gave up his spirit" (Jn 19:30). His willingness and choosing to die on the cross must be understood in contrast to other occasions when Jesus faced serious threats of being killed by the crowed, instances where people desired to harm him but were unable to. On those occasions he simply left the crowd and went on his way (Lk 4:29-30; Jn 8:59; see Jn 10:31, 39-40), indicating that he had full control over his earthly life.

The Bible gives significant details and a reliable account of Jesus' suffering and crucifixion. Jesus was fully aware of what would take place

---

[9]"Jesus took the Twelve aside and told them, 'We are going up to Jerusalem, and everything that is written by the prophets about the Son of Man will be fulfilled. He will be delivered over to the Gentiles. They will mock him, insult him and spit on him; they will flog him and kill him. On the third day he will rise again'" (Lk 18:31-33).

before the cross; the severity of the coming pain and suffering is reflected in his anguished prayer in Gethsemane to the extent that "his sweat was like drops of blood" (Lk 22:44; see Mt 26:36-46; Mk 14:32-42; Lk 22:39-46). As an eyewitness of the event, John gives a noteworthy account with vital details, describing the encounter between those who were sent to arrest Jesus and his disciples. This account negates any claims that Judas or someone else was mistakenly arrested instead of Jesus. "Jesus, knowing all that was going to happen to him, went out and asked them, 'Who is it you want?' 'Jesus of Nazareth,' they replied. 'I am he, Jesus said" (Jn 18:4-5). John explains, "When Jesus said, 'I am he,' they drew back and fell to the ground" (Jn 18:6). This encounter portrays Jesus in his full nature, the eternal Son of God, the "I AM," the holy and powerful God, and the Son of Man who took on a human form to save humanity.

Following this encounter, there are noteworthy encounters between those who come to arrest Jesus and the disciples. One of Jesus' disciples, Peter, reacting to what happened, "struck the high priest's servant, cutting off his right ear." John adds, "The servant's name was Malchus" (Jn 18:10). John gives details about which ear was cut as well as the name of the person. There is no room here for confusion. Meanwhile, Jesus affirms once again that it is his choice to die: "This is your hour—when darkness reigns" (Lk 22:53), and that he does not need the help of anyone to defend him: "'Put your sword back in its place,' Jesus said to him [Peter], 'for all who draw the sword will die by the sword. Do you think I cannot call on my Father, and he will at once put at my disposal more than twelve legions of angels? But how then would the Scriptures be fulfilled that say it must happen in this way?'" (Mt 26:52-53; see Jn 18:11).

The Gospel accounts give full details of the places and names of those who tried Jesus, the accusations presented against him, and the words exchanged between Jesus and the various religious and political leaders. His religious trial at the Sanhedrin, the highest religious court, is carefully documented (Mt 26:57-64). Similar to Jesus' religious trial, his encounter with Pilate in his political trial is not only about the details of what took place but the significant phrases used and their implications (Jn 18).

Christ's surrender of himself to the abandonment of death reveals the depth of God's nature, the depth of the relationality of the triune God. The Son dies in a state of forsakenness by the Father, being cursed for the sins of the world, taking the wrath of God on himself. At the same time, the

Father suffers the death of his own beloved Son in the unending pain of love. "There is no remoteness from God which the Son in his forsakenness did not suffer, or into which his self-giving did not reach," affirms Jürgen Moltmann.[10] But at the same time, the Son is always one with the Father, and the Father is always with him. Christ's giving of himself to death on the cross while enduring the severity of abandonment also manifests the depth of fellowship that unites the Father and the Son. The reason Christians are so proud of the cross of Christ is that it is God's ultimate manifestation of his love to sinners. Through the cross, God's redemption of sin and death is finally realized.

Remarkable events that followed Christ's death on the cross. The eyewitnesses of Jesus' death on the cross report a number of notable events surrounding his death. The Gospels report that complete darkness descended from the sixth hour to the ninth hour of the day (noon to 3 p.m.; Mt 27:45; Mk 15:33; Lk 23:44) as an indication of the intensity of the evil and darkness that surrounded this significant event in history. As God in Christ took upon himself the suffering of this world, the darkness of the evil power along with sin and death was on full display. The gospel reports that at the end of this darkness, Jesus "gave up his spirit" (Mt 27:50), crying out, "Father, into your hands I commit my spirit" (Lk 23:46), as an indication that at this moment, Jesus decided to give up his Spirit on his own terms (Jn 10:17). Jesus' final words before giving up his Spirit are "It is finished" (Jn 19:30), signifying that the work of salvation has been completed once and for all.

"At that moment the curtain of the temple was torn in two from top to bottom" (Mt 27:51). This event indicated that reconciliation between God and humanity had been completed. The curtain that separated God's holiness, as represented in the holy of holies in the temple, was torn apart because the final sacrifice to redeem humanity had fully been accepted in the death of Jesus the Christ. "The earth shook, the rocks split.... When the centurion and those with him who were guarding Jesus saw the earthquake and all that had happened, they were terrified, and exclaimed, 'Surely he was the Son of God'" (Mt 27:51, 54; see Mk 15:39). He added, "Surely this was a righteous man" (Lk 23:47). The crucifixion of Christ was not a simple event that can be ignored or dismissed. Its

---

[10]Jürgen Moltmann, *The Church in the Power of the Holy Spirit* (London: SCM Press, 1980), 95.

remarkable significance was reported in detail by several eyewitnesses, including not only those who loved him and followed him but even those who crucified him. The Roman authorities and politicians who witnessed his death could not help but make statements such as, "He was the Son of God." The cross of Christ is the most significant event in history, an occurrence that changed the course of history forever.

THE POWER OF JESUS' RESURRECTION

The life and ministry of Jesus the Christ, and the whole Christian faith, does not end at the cross; it reaches an apex at Christ's victorious resurrection. The resurrection of Jesus as a historical event was observed by many witnesses and became the focal point of the church's witness. In his sacrificial death, Jesus willingly offered his life for the redemption of humanity. His resurrection established God's power in putting an end to the power of sin and death, bringing justification and reconciliation with God (Rom 4:25). Jesus' resurrection from the dead signified that the one who is "the resurrection and the life" (Jn 11:25) was able to conquer death by experiencing death himself, vanquishing the power of death because death has no power over him. The issue at stake here is not whether God was able to rescue his prophet from the cross in order to prove his power and justice. Rather, God's majesty, power, and love are profoundly manifested through Christ's sacrificial death and victorious resurrection. The Creator of the universe, the source of life, experienced death in order to redeem humanity from sin and death. God's power in the resurrection of Christ overcomes death, giving eternal life (Heb 2:14-15).

The historicity of the resurrection is documented by many eyewitnesses who also expressed their astonishment about the event. It is not a fabricated story where events were put together to create a fairy tale or legend. The Roman soldiers guarding Jesus' tomb were the first to encounter the resurrection event (Mt 28:2-4; never in history do we know of a situation where a dead person was guarded by armed soldiers). The narrative of what the guards experienced is noteworthy because they had no interest at stake in making up such a story; the fact that the tomb they guarded ended up being empty put them in danger (Mt 28:11-14).

While these events were taking place, a group of devout women who had followed Jesus and supported his ministry encountered the same reality that Jesus was risen. The Gospel asserts, "Trembling and bewildered, the women went out and fled from the tomb . . . because they were afraid" (Mk 16:8). This is a true and real reaction to an unusual and unexpected event. Even when the women went and told the rest of the disciples what had happened, "Their words seemed to them like nonsense" (Lk 24:11). The Gospel reports that Peter and John went to the tomb to find out for themselves what had happened. As eyewitnesses of the empty tomb immediately after Jesus' resurrection, they gave a detailed account of what they had seen (Lk 24:12; Jn 20:6-9). John gives a full description, indicating that no one had taken the body of Christ since the burial linens were intact and looked like the body was there but without anything inside. John comments, speaking about himself in the third person, "He saw and believed" (Jn 20:8-9).

Several times the risen Christ appeared to the disciples (Mk 16:14; Lk 24:36; Jn 20:19), assuring them that he was alive, showing them his wounded body as a sign that he was risen (Lk 24:39-40; Jn 20:19), inviting them to touch him (Jn 20:27). Jesus shared meals with his disciples after his resurrection (Lk 24:41; Jn 21:10-13; Acts 1:4), he entered into lengthy discussions with them (Lk 24:13-27; Jn 21:15-23), and he spoke about the kingdom of God for forty days (Acts 1:3). Years later, Paul reports that "he appeared to more than five hundred . . . , most of whom are still living" (1 Cor 15:6); "he . . . gave many convincing proofs that he was alive" (Acts 1:3).

Jesus' disciples, as eyewitnesses of his death and resurrection, went through a lengthy journey of interpreting what they had seen and experienced, which in many ways was contradictory to their expectations. On the road to Emmaus, two of the puzzled disciples, speaking about Jesus' crucifixion, express their struggle and frustration, asserting, "He was a prophet, powerful in word and deed before God and all the people. The chief priests and our rulers handed him over to be sentenced to death, and they crucified him; but we had hoped that he was the one who was going to redeem Israel" (Lk 24:19-21).

Jesus' death on the cross was shocking for his disciples and followers. It was totally against their expectations. Only through encountering the risen Christ did they come to realize that this man, Jesus of Nazareth, was not simply a great prophet of God but both Lord and Savior. They came to recognize that God's power and justice were not realized through the destruction of their enemies (Lk 9:54-56) but rather through suffering on a cross. They came to know that God reveals his power in powerlessness. The transcendent God can suffer and participate in the suffering of his people. In Christ's death and resurrection, we do not encounter an absolute but a relational God, the God who extends his mercy, passion, and love to his created world. Only in encountering the risen Christ are people able to know the extent of God's love for them. In his resurrection, Christ overcame the power of sin and death. "Death has been swallowed up in victory" (1 Cor 15:54). The hope of Christians is fully realized in believing Jesus' words, "I am the resurrection and the life. The one who believes in me will live, even though they die; and whoever lives by believing in me will never die" (Jn 11:25-26).

The Glorified Christ

The Bible relates a comprehensive account of the nature and function of Christ, culminating in his heavenly existence and glorious second coming. A glimpse of the glorified Christ is portrayed in the Gospel accounts during Jesus' incarnation on earth: "There he was transfigured before them. His face shone like the sun, and his clothes became as white as the light" (Mt 17:2; see also Mk 9:1-2; Lk 9:29). John gives a similar description of the glorified Christ: "The hair on his head was white like wool, as white as snow, and his eyes were like blazing fire. His feet were like bronze glowing in a furnace, and his voice was like the sound of rushing waters. . . . His face was like the sun shining in all its brilliance" (Rev 1:14-16). The book of Revelation gives a powerful image of Christ's glorified heavenly existence, as praise and worship are being constantly offered to the Lamb seated on the throne (Rev 5:12; see Rev 4:11; 5:13-14). It portrays the glorified Christ as the Lamb who was slain or the one who suffered death (Rev 1:18; 5:12), affirming that the glorified and exalted Christ is the one who redeemed humanity through his sacrificial death. At the same time, the biblical narrative asserts the second coming of the glorified Christ (Acts 1:11; see Rev 1:7) to judge the world (Rev 21:11-15).

According to the Christian faith, Jesus is not simply a prophet among many others; Jesus is God incarnate, who redeemed humanity from the power of sin and death through his life, sacrificial death on the cross, and victorious resurrection. This Christ event is fully articulated in the words of an early statement of faith:

> Who, being in very nature God,
>> did not consider equality with God something to be used to his
>>> own advantage;
> rather, he made himself nothing
>> by taking the very nature of a servant,
>> being made in human likeness.
> And being found in appearance as a man,
>> he humbled himself
>> by becoming obedient to death—
>> even death on a cross!
> Therefore God exalted him to the highest place
>> and gave him the name that is above every name,
> that at the name of Jesus every knee should bow,
>> in heaven and on earth and under the earth,
> and every tongue acknowledge that Jesus Christ is Lord,
>> to the glory of God the Father. (Phil 2:6-11)

As the early Christians continued to reflect on the nature and function of Jesus Christ, they came to realize that he was a unique being who was both divine and human while at the same time having a unique relationship with God. For the disciples and those who encountered Jesus, there could not be the least doubt concerning the true humanity of Jesus. They had known Christ "according to the flesh." They were eyewitnesses of his teaching and ministry, his suffering on the cross, and subsequent death. At the same time, the disciples came to realize that Jesus Christ was not just an ordinary human being. They knew full well that Jesus was also divine. They had encountered Christ, who extended forgiveness of sins and taught with authority, who had authority over nature and raised the dead by his power.

They also encountered the glorious, resurrected Christ, who was victorious over death. Encountering the risen Christ reaffirmed their belief in the earthly Jesus, who had an authority different from everything they had experienced before. The early Christians regarded Jesus as God incarnate and addressed him as such. This is evident from the fact that they pray in the name of Jesus. They believed in the divine nature of Christ and his preexistence (Gal 4:4; Col 1:19), being the Son of the Father before his incarnation. His sonship is eternal and predates his earthly birth. They affirmed Jesus' two modes of being: his earthly existence as a human being and his heavenly existence from eternity (Rom 1:3-4), having "equality with God" (Phil 2:6).

THE TRINITARIAN GOD

Encountering God in Christ and the power of his Holy Spirit led Christians to believe in a trinitarian God. There seems to be an inherent contradiction between Christianity and Islam concerning God as Trinity. The notion of a trinitarian God is categorically rejected in Islam based on the Islamic belief in the absolute unity and oneness of God. The Qur'an repeatedly refutes belief in tritheism composed of God, Mary, and Jesus (5:116), rebuking Christians for believing that God had a partner, Mary (making Mary a goddess), who gave birth to a son, Jesus. Obviously, Christians have never believed in such a tritheism. The Qur'anic perception might reflect a misunderstanding of the Christian belief in a Trinity due to the extreme veneration of Mary during the sixth century.

Muslims are alarmed by biblical expressions such as the "only begotten" Son of God (Jn 1:18; see Jn 3:16), an expression that was affirmed and expounded by the early Christian creeds and all Christians through the centuries. The biblical phrase is mistakenly interpreted by Muslims as meaning that God physically married a human female, begetting a child. As a result, Muslims think that Jesus was a third God in addition to God and Mary, being part of a three-God council. Thus Christians are branded polytheists (*mushrikun*: those who associate other beings or deities with God). Commenting on the phrase "only begotten," Muslim apologist Ahmad Deedat states, "God does not beget because begetting is an animal act. . . . We do not attribute such an act to God." He further explains that begetting is equivalent to creating, and "God cannot create another God."[11] As Muslim scholar Abdu 'L-Ahad Dawud puts it, "The Christian belief concerning the eternal birth or generation of the Son is blasphemy."[12]

Nowhere in the biblical narrative do we encounter the idea of God physically marrying or giving birth to children. Christ's eternal sonship does not imply physical generation or creation by the Father but rather reveals an eternal, intimate relationship expressed by the concept of Father

---

[11]Cited in Anis A. Shorrosh, *Islam Revealed* (Nashville: Thomas Nelson, 1988), 254.
[12]Abdu 'L-Ahad Dawud, *Muhammed in the Bible* (Kuala Lumpur: Pustaka Antara, 1979), 205.

and Son. Jesus Christ was not made a God by Christians; he is God eternal, incarnated in a human form. In other words, he added human nature to his divine nature, not the other way around.

Unfortunately, the Qur'an leaves no room for Muslims but to denounce this perceived blasphemy against God. As the Qur'an states, those who claim that God is three are in erroneous infidelity against the truth: "They do blaspheme who say, God is one of three in a tritheism: for there is no God except God" (5:76). The Qur'an goes another step further, stating that such oneness of God was asserted by Jesus, who denounced any association with a triadic God: "And behold! God will say: O Jesus the son of Mary! Did you say unto men, worship me and my mother as Gods in derogation of God? He will say: Glory to thee! Never could I say what I had no right [to say]" (5:116). A deeper look at the Qur'anic text reveals that what the Qur'an is disapproving of tritheism, not Trinity. As mentioned earlier, the Arabic word used in the Qur'anic text is *thalatha*, "three," not the Arabic word for "Trinity," which is أَلثَّالُوث (*Al-Thalouth*). Christians, however, do not worship three Gods but a trinitarian God.

The Christian belief in a trinitarian God was not the result of a corrupted biblical record or the speculations of Christians in later times, as some Muslim scholars argue. It has its roots in the biblical narrative and the experience of the early Christians, who encountered God in his atoning work through the incarnation, death, and resurrection of Jesus Christ and further experienced the power of the Holy Spirit, who transformed their lives and mission. Christian belief in the Trinity accounts for the reality that constitutes the heart of the gospel; the death and resurrection of Christ manifest the very nature of God and God's relation to humanity. The early Christians tried to find meaningful terminology to express their belief in the God who manifested himself as trinitarian and therefore used the Latin word *Trinitas* to express this reality.

Oftentimes Christians refer to the trinitarian nature of God as a mystery. The *mysterium logicum* of Christian theology, however, is based on encountering a God who revealed himself as Father, Son, and Holy Spirit. Finite humans might not comprehend "the depth of the riches and wisdom and knowledge of God," acknowledging the mystery of the divine nature of his "unsearchable" judgments and paths that are "beyond tracing out" (Rom 11:33). Yet, Christians can attest to the God they encounter in his self-revelation in Jesus Christ and in their experience of the empowering of his Holy

Spirit. In the biblical narrative we constantly encounter a God who is both beyond and yet intimate, transcendent, absolute, and infinite yet approachable and relational. It may not be possible to explain the triune nature of God in all its dimensionality; however, Christians should be able to explain the relevance of encountering the triune God who transforms their lives.

In responding to Muslim apologists who demand an explanation of the Trinity, it is self-contradictory to explain the Christian belief in the trinitarian nature of God apart from a thorough understanding and experience of God's relationality encountered in the biblical narrative. The Trinity cannot be grasped based on some logical formulas or metaphoric analogies, which often result in misleading ideas and confusion. Comprehending God's trinitarian nature must be viewed in the larger context of God's relationality as manifested in his redemption and sanctification.

The unity of God's oneness expressed in the trinitarian nature of God implies that God's unity is complex and not simplistic. Divine unity is greater than the limited human understanding of oneness without distinction. It is not a matter of arithmetic, of relating one and three. God is not an abstract reality but a relational, loving person involved in the world he created. Christians affirm that God has revealed himself as loving Father, approachable through the Son, and accessible through the life-giving Holy Spirit. The Father is eternally alive in his spirit and perfectly made known in his Son Jesus Christ. The Father, Son, and Holy Spirit are eternally united in a joyful communion of love.

The Trinity reveals God's very nature and relationality to humans. The Trinity reveals the very nature of God as well as God's relationality to humanity and the world. We do not encounter an abstract ideal but a relational God. The nature of God as love is fully expressed in the trinitarian relationship of God the Father, Son, and Holy Spirit. While Islam casts aside the work of salvation accomplished by God in Christ as an offense to the nature of God's oneness, in Christianity, the cross of Christ epitomizes a tremendous unity between the Father, Son, and Holy Spirit in their mutual willingness to be identified with one another and with humanity, even to the extent of enduring affliction and experiencing death. God the Father and God the Holy Spirit grieve over the sins of the world and suffer the giving of God the Son in the darkness of Calvary.[13] The love of the

---

[13]Jürgen Moltmann, *The Trinity and the Kingdom* (London: SCM Press, 1980), 30-35.

triune God was fully manifested on the cross of Christ. On the cross, God the Father reconciles divine love and mercy with divine holiness and justice. Through his death on the cross and victorious resurrection, Christ overcame the power of sin and death, giving new hope for eternal life.

Likewise, the Holy Spirit is the divine breath (*ruakh*) creating and sustaining life (Gen 1:1-2). The Spirit is a Spirit of truth, who guides individuals (Ps 143:10) and instructs them (Neh 9:20). The Spirit gives gifts to believers (1 Cor 12:1-12), brings fruit of character into their lives (Gal 5:22-23), and empowers them for witness (Acts 2:4; 4:8, 31; etc.) The Spirit is described as a comforter and an advocate (Jn 14:15-29). The Spirit also grieves over the sins of people (Is 63:10) and convicts them of their sin (Jn 16:8-11). The life-giving, divine Spirit enables human faith to respond to the provision of salvation (2 Cor 3:18). God the Holy Spirit actualizes the work of salvation into the realm of Christians' personal and communal experiences, enabling them to worship and to live for the glory of God (Jn 4:24; 1 Cor 6:19). The Holy Spirit, who was active in creation, is also active in restoring creation, which is groaning and travailing under the power of sin, bringing healing and deliverance. Muslims often find it difficult to comprehend a Trinity including the Holy Spirit as understood and experienced by Christians, since there is no clear understanding of that phrase in Islam. In Islam, the term *Holy Spirit* is mainly associated with the angel Gabriel, whose function is communicating revelation from God (19:17).

A proper understanding of the Trinity leads to proper understanding of the nature of God, which in turn influences how we relate to God and others. Theological reflection on the work of the atonement might give the impression that God the Father was not involved in the work of atonement, that it is only the Son. The Father is portrayed as the judge who punishes the guilt of sinful humanity through the death of his Son in order to satisfy God's judgment over sin. The Son participates in the judgment of sin while offering redemption through his sacrificial death. The Father experiences the suffering of the death of his Son while judging the sins of humanity. Likewise, the Holy Spirit grieves over the sins of humanity and works in their hearts to sanctify them. The biblical narrative constantly portrays God as one who is involved in human suffering and misery, who grieves and is saddened over humans' sin (Gen 6:6), the one who took the initiative to redeem and restore, establishing new covenants when humans failed to keep God's laws and promises (Gen 3:21; 9:9; 17:2; Deut 12:32, 28;

and many others). The biblical God is not aloof and indifferent to human need and suffering.

A deeper look at the nature of the triune God and the close relationship within the Trinity reveals the depth and magnitude of God's love and care for humanity. God the Father is not far removed from humanity; to the contrary, he is loving and compassionate to the extent of sending his only Son to redeem humanity (Jn 3:16). It is not only Jesus who suffers our suffering, but the triune God is fully involved in the work of redemption and sanctification. The eternal God reveals himself in the incarnation of Christ and the indwelling of the Holy Spirit, presenting the dynamic relationality of God that enters into the spatial and temporal horizons of the human experience. In Islam, God's interaction and revelation is a past and completed moment; in Christianity, it is an active, ongoing working of God to reveal and restore humanity to himself.

The Trinity's essence and relationality. According to the Christian faith, the three members of the Trinity are distinct persons or modes of being, yet they are one in essence. So, while the Father, Son, and Spirit are identical within the one Godhead, they are "relatively" distinct from one another. As Karl Rahner explains, "There is one power, one will, one self-presence. . . . There is not a moment which distinguishes the divine 'persons' one from the other, even though each divine 'person,' as concrete, possesses a self-consciousness."[14] There is only one outward activity of God. When certain functions are attributed to one of the three persons rather than the others, all participate to some degree in what is being done. While redemption for example is the primary work of the incarnate Son, the Father and the Spirit are also involved. Similarly, sanctification is primarily the work of the Holy Spirit; however, the Father and the Son are involved as well. Thus, when certain activity is attributed to one of the persons, it is also implicitly attributed to the other two persons and in this sense only *appropriated* to the one person.[15]

The three members of the Trinity are distinct persons, but they are one in essence. The Trinity is a communion of three persons, modes of being, or centers of consciousness, who exist and always have existed in union with one another. They are related to one another in *agapē* love, which

---

[14]Karl Rahner, *The Trinity* (New York: Harder & Herder, 1970), 75-76.
[15]Rahner, *Trinity*, 76.

unites them in the most intimate of relationships, wherein each is conscious of what the other is conscious of. There is complete equality of the three and a mutual glorifying of one another. There are certain functions that primarily belong to one of the persons; however, all participate in the function of each. In his incarnation, the Son subordinates to the Father, but this is a functional rather than essential state. While we encounter the trinitarian God as Creator, redeemer, or sanctifier, the Trinity cannot be reduced to formulas such as "God the Creator, God the Redeemer, God the Sanctifier." This formula reduces the Trinity to a functional Trinity tending toward modalism, eliminating the eternal nature of the triune God, which is the very nature of God regardless of whether there was a created world that needed redemption or not. In other words, the three members of the Trinity are distinct persons or beings assuming different roles, and each person is revealed to us in distinction from the others while they constitute the very same one God.

Concluding Remarks

The Qur'an appeals for a common ground between Christians and Muslims: "Say: 'O People of the Book, come to common grounds between us and you. That we worship none, but Allah. That we associate no partners with Him. That we do not take from among ourselves Lords and patrons other than Allah'" (3:64). While Christians fully endorse the threefold appeal made in this Qur'anic statement, their experience of God's oneness also includes relationality in God's nature and manifestation of himself to humanity. Christians believe in and worship only one God, but their monotheism is *trinitarian*, whereas Islamic monotheism is *unitarian*.

The Christian belief in Christ as God does not make a god of the man Jesus; instead, it recognizes that God fully revealed himself in Jesus Christ in order to save humanity. Jesus Christ did not become God; he is God from eternity. The incarnation of Christ was the addition of human nature to his divine nature. Jesus accepted certain physical and spatial limitations, but he never lost his divine nature (Phil 2:6-7). "In Christ all the fullness of the Deity lives" (Col 2:9). The incarnation of God in Christ did not undermine God's oneness, his transcendence, or any of his attributes. God's self-revelation in Christ provides historical evidence of his compassionate heart and unconditional love for humanity while not compromising his holiness, justice, and sovereignty. The way God manifested his love, compassion, and forgiveness in Jesus Christ leads to a deeper sense of God's greatness and majesty, resulting in worshiping God with hearts full of praise and thanksgiving.

Encountering God in Christ and experiencing the power of the Holy Spirit prompted a larger question about the very nature of God. Thus Christians came to the realization that God is a triune God. The trinitarian God of Christianity is different from the tritheistic formula that the Qur'an rightly criticizes. Christians do not worship three Gods: God, Jesus and Mary. Rather, Christians worship only one God, who in his nature is Father, Son, and Holy Spirit. The Trinity is a community of three modes of being or existence, who exist and always have existed in union with one another.[16] They are bound to one another with *agapē* love, which unites them in the most intimate of relationships. Humanity is able to attest to this sacrificial love in Jesus Christ through his life and work of salvation, showing glimpses of God's surpassing love.

The church throughout the centuries has worshiped God as Trinity because through the atoning work of Christ people have been redeemed from sin and death and came to acknowledge Jesus as Lord and Savior. Their lives have been transformed by the power of the Holy Spirit so that they live a life pleasing and glorifying to God. Those who have been reconciled to God by the atoning work of Christ and sanctified by his Holy Spirit are enabled to address God as "our Father." This fellowship, *koinōnia*, is the very nature of the church; it is a sign, instrument, and foretaste of what God intended for all humanity.

---

[16]No human concept or terminology is adequate to describe the nature of God's being or existence. Terminology such as *person* usually leads to confusion.

11

HUMANITY AND SALVATION

CHRISTIANITY AND ISLAM VIEW the relationship between God and humanity from different lenses based on their differing understanding of the nature of human beings. Christianity asserts that humans are created in the image of God (*imago Dei*), while Islam cautions against any resemblance between humanity and God. According to Islam, God created human beings for the purpose of worshiping him and submitting to his law. That Adam and Eve disobeyed God's command does not lead to human nature being sinful or original sin, as emphasized in Christianity. Instead, their sin was forgiven and their actions did not affect the rest of the human race. Therefore humanity needs guidance from God provided through prophets and revealed Scripture(s), not a savior to redeem them from sin.

THE ISLAMIC CONCEPTION OF HUMAN NATURE AND SIN

According to Islam, humans were created in a state of purity or innocence (*fitrah*). They eventually committed mistakes and made wrong decisions. Such actions are not considered to have been sin against God. Surah 2 indicates that after creation Adam and Eve were placed in the garden and were commanded not to eat from a particular tree (a nameless tree). They mistakenly disobeyed God's command.[1] Their disobedience is described

---

[1] "We said (God): O Adam dwell and thy wife in the Garden and eat from the bountiful things therein; but approach not this tree, otherwise you will be committing injustice [*fa takuna min al-zalimin*]. Then Iblis [Satan] humiliated them [made them slip] from the Garden and got them out

as being in a state of injustice or committing an unjust act. Despite some general similarities between the biblical and Qur'anic accounts of the fall, there are notable differences between the Christian and Islamic interpretation of humanity's transgression. While in Christianity humanity's fall is considered a serious offense against God that resulted in breaking the most intimate relationship and therefore affected the whole human race, in Islam, Adam and Eve's actions are viewed as a mistake that happened out of ignorance, an isolated event that has no bearing on the rest of humanity. The Christian understanding that a sinful nature permeates all humanity, individually and collectively, because of the fall stands in stark contrast to the Islamic interpretation of what took place in the garden. According to Islam, Adam's mistake, or slip, was forgiven when he received guidance from God.[2]

Several Qur'anic texts give the impression that Adam and Eve's disobedience was basically out of ignorance rather than intentionality (20:115-23). Muslims tend to focus on Adam's forgetfulness rather than his disobedience. Since Adam is considered the first prophet in Islam, and God's prophets are protected from committing major sins, the Islamic scholar Kausar Niazi asserts, "To call Adam a sinner . . . is unbelief."[3] The following verses, however, give a different account: "Adam rebelled against [or disobeyed, *asa*] his Lord and went astray [*faghawa*]" (20:121). The appeal for forgiveness in surah 7:22-23, "If thou forgive us not and have mercy on us, we shall certainly be the losers," indicates awareness of the magnitude of their action and their sense of hopelessness without God's mercy. Adam and Eve take responsibility for their disobedience, stating, "Our Lord! We have wronged ourselves [*zalamna anfousna*]."

Viewing humans' transgression as a result of ignorance rather than deliberate disobedience is supported by the larger Islamic concept that humans were created innocent. "Set your face to the religion as one of the pristine faith [*hanif*], the state of natural purity [*fitrah*] in which He created people" (30:30). According to the Islamic hadith, Prophet Muhammad commented on this verse by saying, "No child is born except in the state of natural

---

of where they have been. We said [God]: Get ye all down with enmity between yourselves. On earth will be your dwelling place and pleasure for a while" (2:35-36; see also 7:19).

[2]Muslims usually interpret the phrase "Adam received words from his Lord" as accepting a special revelation from God, since Adam is considered the first prophet in Islam.

[3]Kausar Niazi, *Creation of Man* (Karachi: Ferozoono, 1975), 63.

purity [*fitrah*] and then his parents make him Jewish, Christian, or Magian."[4] Since Islam is the natural, pure religion, every human being is born Muslim or innocent (without sin). Another hadith, however, indicates the contrary: "No child is born but the devil hath touched it, except Mary and her son Jesus."[5] The concept of human purity needs to be reconciled with the various accounts of humanity's awareness of their transgression against God, expressed in the words of the first human beings, and its dreadful effects on the whole human race as stated by the Qur'anic narrative.

Similar to the biblical account, the Qur'anic text attributes the reason for such transgression to Adam and Eve being tempted to seek a higher level of existence. Yet the reason differs greatly in the two accounts. In the Bible, the temptation is to become "like God, knowing good and evil" (Gen 3:5). In the Qur'an, the temptation is to "become angels or . . . immortals" (7:19-20). However, according to several Qur'anic accounts, it seems that humans already have a higher status than angels. Surah 2:32-33 states that God requested the angels to bow down to Adam, while the angels could not attain the same knowledge as Adam. Somehow the seriousness of the act of transgression is lost, since seeking to become like angels or immortals is not really a sinful act. Furthermore, the Qur'anic explanation of the consequence of eating from a nameless tree, "committing injustice [*fa takuna min al-zalimin*]" (2:35; 7:19), is remarkably different from God's warning in Genesis 2:17, "You must not eat from the tree of the knowledge of good and evil," and the explicit consequence, "You will certainly die."

Contrary to the Qur'anic account, in which human sin is perceived as seeking to become immortal, in the biblical account God prohibits Adam and Eve from eating from the tree of life as a consequence of their sinful act, not the other way around. Adam and Eve had the opportunity to eat from the tree of life and not die; this, however, is not considered a sinful act according to the Bible. Prohibiting Adam and Eve from eating from the tree of life after sinning was not a punishment but rather an indication of God's provision to limit the effect of sin so that humanity would not live in a state of sinfulness forever. As God laments, "The man has now become

---

[4]Muhammad Muhsin Khan, trans., *Sahih al Bukhari: Arabic-English* (Beirut: Dar Al Arabia, 1985), 6:284.
[5]Khan, *Sahih al Bukhari*, 298.

like one of us, knowing good and evil. He must not be allowed to reach out his hand and take also from the tree of life and eat, and live forever" (Gen 3:22). The contradiction in the two accounts explains the major difference between the Christian and Islamic understandings of human nature and the seriousness of disobeying God.

The Bible indicates that Adam and Eve had a sense of shame as a result of their actions (Gen 3:7), while the Qur'an indicates that Satan was the one who disclosed to them their shame (7:21-22; 20:119-21). The Qur'anic account stops at Adam and Eve's sewing leaves to cover themselves. Since their transgression was simply out of ignorance, there is no need for God's intervention except to offer forgiveness. The biblical record, however, proceeds to affirm, "The LORD God made garments of skin for Adam and his wife and clothed them" (Gen 3:21). This action constitutes the first sacrifice made to atone for their sin. It exemplifies God's love, care, and protection of sinful and undeserving humans.

According to both the biblical and Qur'anic accounts, Adam and Eve were expelled from the garden as a consequence of their transgression (Qur'an 2:35; 7:24-25). But if their action was out of ignorance and they were forgiven, there was no reason for them to be expelled from the garden. Muslims believe that Adam and Eve were placed in the garden for a trial period to examine their inclinations before being sent down to earth.[6] Muslim scholar Niazi explains, "Adam's ejection from the Garden has been interpreted by small-minded people as a sort of punishment. . . . However, the order 'get ye down' was mentioned after pardon has been granted, in order to dispel the notion that the Fall resulted from a sinful act. . . . Adam was created as God's viceroy 'khalifa.' . . . He had to have come down to this world to manage it."[7]

What is sin in Islam? According to the Qur'an, sin is disobeying God's will, mainly revealed in God's law. This disobedience is due to either ignorance of God's law or the inherent weakness of human nature (4:28). The gravest sin in Islam is associating other beings or deities with God, shirk (4:48; 18:58; 20:82; 40:3; 42:25, 30, 34). Only the person who commits an

---

[6]Some Muslims believe that the garden was a place outside planet Earth. Some Muslim scholars believe that when Adam and Eve were expelled from the garden, they were placed (landed) in Mecca, where the Ka'ba is. That is why the Ka'ba has a significant place in Islam. Such claims are not backed by any Qur'anic references.
[7]Niazi, *Creation of Man*, 66-68.

act of sinful behavior will bear the consequences of their actions, as "no liability of one soul can be transferred to another" (6:164; 17:15; 35:18; 39:7; 53:38). This is why Adam's transgression is perceived as having no repercussions for the rest of the human race.[8] God's law is communicated throughout the Qur'an and can also be detected in the form of previous covenants made with Adam, Noah, Abraham, Moses, and Jesus (2:77-84; 5:7-10; 20:114-15; 33:7). Humans are expected to fulfill all covenants mentioned in the Qur'an carefully. The Qur'an also teaches that good deeds usually outweigh evil ones (4:40; 6:160; 10:27).

While the concept of original sin is foreign to Islam, the Qur'an speaks extensively about humanity's condition, indicating the sinfulness of human nature. Humanity is described as sinful (ungrateful or unjust; 14:34-37), ignorant or foolish (33:72), forgetful (39:8), weak (4:28), rebellious (96:6), boastful (11:9-13), and quarrelsome (16:4). The Qur'an also indicates that "the soul has an inward inclination towards evil" (12:53) and that "if God were to punish men for their wrongdoing, he would not leave on earth a single creature" (16:61-63). Surah 95 gives a disturbing account on the condition of humanity created by God: "We have indeed created man in the best of form [state], Then we abase him to the lowest of the low."

Throughout the history of Islam, several Islamic scholars have struggled to explain the sinful nature of humanity. Ibn Hanbal (780–855), the founder of one of the strictest schools of law in Islam, related that the companions of Prophet Muhammad indicated, "We have no control over our hearts."[9] Ibn Hazm (AD 994–1064), a champion of fundamentalist doctrine, affirms that the human soul spontaneously inclines to dishonesty.[10] One of the most common Islamic phrases describing the condition of the human heart is *al-nafs al-ammara bil-so'a* ("the uncontrolled appetitive soul toward carnal desires"). This phrase is frequently used by Muslims to describe human sinfulness. If this is the condition of humanity, will right guidance be sufficient to enable people to attain to God's law? Is there a need for a radical solution from such human predicament?

---

[8]Ismail Faruqi, *Islam and Other Faiths*, ed. A. Siddiqui (Leicester, UK: Islamic Foundation, 1998), 120.
[9]Kenneth Cragg and R. Marston Speight, *Islam from Within: Anthology of a Religion* (Belmont, CA: Wadsworth, 1980), 90-91.
[10]R. Arnaldez, "Ibn Hazm," in *Encyclopedia of Islam*, 2nd ed. (Leiden: Brill, 1960), 265.

The Christian Conception of Human Nature and Sin

The Christian understanding of human nature and sin is linked to God's nature and standards. Since God is holy and pure, he expects humans to be holy and pure, and any deviation from God's standards is considered a serious offense against God. The Bible uses a wide variety of terms to describe sin, each emphasizing a different dimension of the magnitude of sin. Sin is characterized as rebellion against God (Is 1:2; Deut 21:18; Ps 78:8; Ezek 2:3), stubbornness and disobedience (Rom 1:30, 2 Tim 3:2; Heb 11:31; 1 Pet 3:20), transgressing God's command (Num 14:41-42; Deut 12:31; 18:9-12; 26:13; Jer 34:18; Dan 9:11; Hos 6:7; 8:1), and missing the mark, indicating the human failure to attain to God's standards (Lev 24:15; Is 53:12; 1 Cor 3:16-17).

According to the Bible, sinful actions and motivations stem from human sinful nature or sinfulness, an inherent inner disposition inclining to wrong acts and thoughts (Rom 7:18-19). We are not sinners because we sin; we sin because we are sinners. Sin is a state of human beings, while sinful thoughts and actions are the results of such a sinful nature—not the other way around. Sin is failure to live up to what God expects of humans in thought, action, and being. Jeremiah declares, "The heart is deceitful above all things and beyond cure. Who can understand it?" (Jer 17:9; see also Mk 7:20-22).

The biblical narrative indicates that sin is universal, and all human beings have sinned against God since the beginning of creation. It also asserts that sin affects God, since God is a personal and relational God who cares about the humans he created and their actions. In the time of Noah, "The LORD saw how great the wickedness of the human race had become on the earth, and that every inclination of the thoughts of the human heart was only evil all the time" (Gen 6:5; see also Gen 8:21). This disastrous condition of the human race affected God: "The LORD regretted that he had made human beings on the earth, and his heart was deeply troubled" (Gen 6:6). God's response was to blot out the whole human race along with all living creatures (Gen 6:7). This action signifies the magnitude of sin as well as God's grief over sin. It was very painful for God to annihilate his "very good" creation. Human sin had a far-reaching impact on the whole of creation: "Now the earth was corrupt in God's sight and was full of violence" (Gen 6:11). David describes the magnitude of humanity's corruption: "They are corrupt, their deeds are vile.... There is no one who does good, not even one" (Ps 14:1, 3, see also Rom 3:23).

That includes all prophets and godly people. Although Scripture refers to Noah as "a righteous man, blameless among the people of his time" (Gen 6:9), Noah was not a perfect person (Gen 9:20-27). Abraham was a man of great faith, also called to be "blameless" (Gen 17:1), yet he had his shortcomings (Gen 12; 16; 20). Moses was truly a man of God who demonstrated an enduring kindness and patience with the Israelites; nonetheless, his temper resulted in his being prevented from entering the Promised Land (Num 20:10-13). David was a man after God's own heart (1 Sam 13:14), yet his sins were grievous (2 Sam 11; 24). Jesus' disciples had their own shortcomings as well. While Peter exhibited an unprecedented faith by walking on water (Mt 14:28-29) and expressed his love for Christ to the extent of offering to die for him (Mt 26:35), his sins resulted in several rebukes by Jesus (Mt 16:22-23; 26:69-75; Lk 22:24-27). The biblical record does not hide the sins of godly people and prophets; it exposes them in order to teach us the extent and seriousness of sin, how greatly it has affected the whole human race. The Bible constantly and accurately presents righteous and godly people who yet remain sinners.

The effect of sin on the human race is disastrous according to the biblical record. The penalty of sin is death (Gen 2:17), which permeates humanity because of sin (Rom 3:23; 5:12-19; 6:23). The Bible refers not only to physical death, which is a very apparent result of sin, but also to spiritual death, which is separation from God. Death affected the whole human race because of Adam's sin. Humanity was present collectively in Adam since we inherited our physical and spiritual essence from our first parents. We were present in Adam; therefore, we all have sinned in Adam. Through Adam's sin, all humanity has received a corrupt nature and therefore is considered guilty of sin in God's sight. People become responsible for their sins once they reach the age of moral responsibility, when they are consciously able to discern what is good and what is evil, activating what is already inherited in their sinful nature.

The Bible speaks, however, of a remedy or a way out of this dilemma of sin and its consequences of death and alienation from God. In the same passage where Paul asserts that sin and death entered the human race through Adam, he also affirms that "God's abundant provision of grace and

... righteousness reign in life through ... Jesus Christ" (Rom 5:17). God's grace as manifested through the work of salvation presented by Christ is sufficient to remedy the effect of sin, which is death. Through Christ's sacrificial death, death is exchanged for life (Rom 5:18-19). The prayer in the first surah of the Qur'an is a plea for God to "show us the straight path" (1:5). The straight path starts from a changed heart. What is needed is a renewed relationship with God: "Create in me a pure heart, O God" (Ps 51:10).

THE ISLAMIC VIEW OF SALVATION

The term *salvation* is not used by Muslims and seems foreign to the language of the Qur'an and Muslim scholars. Humans are not fallen, and they have no need for a savior. Humanity's essential problem is not sinning or rebelling against God but primarily weakness and forgetting. According to Islam, humans are by nature good or innocent and remain so until they commit wrongful deeds. Because humans are weak and forgetful, they cannot follow God's will as manifested in God's law; therefore, guidance and constant reminders are needed. Such guidance is offered through God's prophets and revealed scriptures.[11]

Regardless of what humans do, God will never be affected by human actions. Correspondingly, salvation consists of every Muslim's desire to be granted forgiveness and entry into paradise at the day of judgment, which may be attained through performing religious obligations and good deeds. Muslim scholars present a host of explanations of such religious obligations and good deeds. One of the most quoted verses in the Qur'an, identifying the basic tenets of faith (*iman*) is surah 4:136: "O Believers, Believe in God and his Apostle [Muhammad], and in the Book [the Qur'an] which He has sent down upon His Apostle and in the Book [the Bible] He sent down before. Whoever disbelieve in God, and His Angels, His Books, and His Apostles, and in the Last Day, has surely gone into far error" (see also 57:28; 61:10-12). What distinguishes the believer (*mu'min*) from the unbeliever (*kafir*) is belief in these basic tenets of faith: God, God's apostle(s), angels, God's books (the Qur'an and the Bible; however, since Muslims believe that the Bible has been corrupted, the emphasis remains on believing in the final and ultimate message of the Qur'an), and the last day,

---

[11]Bardu D. Kateregga and David W. Shenk, *Islam and Christianity: A Muslim and a Christian in Dialogue* (Grand Rapids, MI: Eerdmans, 1980), 16-18.

including believing in God's final judgment of humanity. Corresponding to these five categories of faith are the five religious pillars of Islam, which are required for all Muslims in order to obtain God's favor:

1. The recital of the Islamic *shahada* or statement of faith: "I bear witness that there is no God but God, and that Muhammad is the Apostle of God."
2. Ritual prayer (*salah*), which should be performed five times a day, along with communal worship during the Friday noon prayer.
3. Almsgiving (*zakat*), according to which Muslims are expected to donate 2.5 percent of their income annually for Islamic religious charities.
4. Fasting (*sawm*) of Ramadan for thirty days from sunrise to sunset.
5. Pilgrimage to Mecca (*hajj*), which is required at least once in a lifetime if the person is physically and financially able.
6. Some Muslims also include jihad as a sixth religious pillar, whereby Muslims are called to fight a holy war for the cause of God. The Qur'an praises those who give their lives "to earn the pleasure of God" (2:207).

Muslims are required to observe such religious duties carefully in order to maximize their chances of gaining God's favor and the possibility of gaining entry into paradise.[12] Entry into paradise also requires good deeds, which go hand in hand with observing religious obligations. The Qur'an affirms, "To those who believe and do deeds of righteousness has God promised forgiveness and a great reward" (5:10). The Qur'an uses the image of a scale to illustrate God's judgment. "Those whose good works outweigh their bad works will go to paradise, whereas those whose bad works outweigh their good works will go to hell" (23:102-3; cf. 7:8-9; 101:6-8).

Entry into paradise, according to Islam, is entirely dependent on God's final judgment. While observing religious obligations and performing good deeds will certainly maximize the chances of one's entry into paradise, God is the one who will finally decide the fate of all humanity. The Qur'an and Muslim scholars have varying perspectives on humanity's future prospects. On one hand, God is perceived as "the best of those who forgive" (7:155). God's mercy, compassion, and forgiveness are extended for all sins (39:53).

---

[12]Muhammed Abdul Rauf, *Islam: Creed and Worship* (Washington, DC: Islamic Center, 1974), 24.

God's mercy is even shown in changing the evil of a person into good upon repentance (25:70), and rewarding good deeds by multiplying them tenfold while punishing bad deeds only by equal proportion (4:40; 6:160).

On the other hand, God is not bound by the obedience or disobedience of his creatures. As the absolute and sovereign God, he grants forgiveness to "whom he pleases, and punishment to whom he pleases" (2:284; 3:129; 5:18, 40; 48:14). God's mercy is categorically based on divine prerogative and favor even for believers who have sincerely fulfilled all religious obligations. God's mercy and forgiveness, along with the hope for paradise promised by the Qur'an, are eschatological; they will only be revealed on the last day. There is no assurance of eternal life in Islam since God is not obliged to grant paradise for anyone; God may deny such a privilege even for the most devout. Muslims do not consider such lack of assurance problematic. To the contrary, they see it as a motivation for continued obedience to God's law and his will. Ismail Faruqi states, "There is nothing (one) can do which would assure him or her of salvation. . . . The scale of justice itself is infinite, and there is no point at which Muslims may carry their titles to Paradise, as it were, in their pockets. Everyone strives, and some strive more than others."[13] It is considered an act of unbelief or arrogance for anyone to say that they have assurance of eternal life in Islam.[14]

The Christian View of Salvation

Contrary to the belief that humans are not inherently sinful and therefore have no need of salvation or a savior, Christianity emphasizes that all humans have sinned against God and need to be saved from their sin. Because of God's holiness and justice, sin has to be punished and redemption has to be offered in order for people to be forgiven their sins. In Christianity, God is the author of our salvation, which was accomplished through the atoning, sacrificial death of Jesus Christ and his victorious resurrection (1 Pet 3:18). God's love and God's justice were mediated on the cross of Christ (Rom 3:25-26; 5:8; 1 Jn 4:10). The good news of the

---

[13]Ismail Faruqi, *Islam* (Niles, IL: Argus Communications, 1984), 5.

[14]The Qur'an gives different indications as to who might find favor with God and gain entry into paradise. Earlier surahs suggest that Jews, Christians, and those who do good deeds will find favor with God and may be granted entry into paradise (2:62, 111-12). The later surahs restrict such privilege to Muslims who believe in the oneness of God, while Jews and Christians are considered infidels due to their grave sin of shirk, or associating other beings and deities with God (4:150-51; 5:75).

gospel is that the judge of the world is at the same time the savior who redeems humanity (Is 12:2; Rom 8:31-34). Salvation in Christianity answers the dilemma implicit in God's pardoning sinners without practicing his justice or condemning them without showing his mercy. The cross of Christ manifests God's mercy as well as his justice. It points to God's love for sinners as well as satisfying God's justice in punishing sin without compromising the seriousness of sin. God hates sin, not sinners.

The Christian understanding of salvation is more comprehensive than forgiving sins; the cross of Christ not only redeemed humanity from sin and death but also won the battle over the evil power itself (Eph 1:19-22). The problem of evil is not addressed in the Qur'an, and it remains unresolved in the Muslim mind. To the contrary, the Bible affirms God's victory over the evil power, which was displayed through the death and resurrection of Jesus Christ. Christ's victory is the source of hope for humanity because it manifests God's sovereignty over creation and the destiny of human beings.

Contrary to the view that no one can be guaranteed God's favor or entry to paradise, the biblical narrative gives assurance of redemption, resulting in hope, peace, and joy (Rom 5:1-2). Good works are natural outcomes of a life-changing experience; they are not means for salvation (Gal 5:22-23; Eph 2:10). The Qur'an promises God's favor and entry to paradise to "those who believe and work righteousness" (2:25; 3:15, 195; 4:57; 5:85, 119), while "those who oppose God and His Apostle" will be punished in the blazing fire of hell (9:63, 68; 39:70-75). The overarching message of the Qur'an is about God's eternal retribution, which results in a state of uncertainty as to what a person might face after this life. The fear of hell is very real since God is waiting to punish people's wrongdoing and misbehavior (9:68; 12:107). By contrast, the biblical narrative of salvation is about God's redemptive love to undeserving humanity, as God's justice and God's love met on the cross of Christ (Rom 5:8). If God's judgment were based on his justice alone, no one would have been saved (Rom 3:10). God did not wait for people to do anything in order to save them simply because there is nothing they could have done to save themselves. The gospel points to God's salvation, offered through faith in a savior, Jesus Christ. The promise of eternal life is for all who put their trust in his redemptive work (Eph 2:8-10).

While Christianity and Islam emphasize a form of existence beyond this earthly realm, they differ in their understanding of its functionality and purpose. Paradise in Islam is a place of intensified earthly pleasures, and those who have access to it will enjoy gardens full of fruit, rivers and springs, sexual pleasure, and comfortable life, among many other rewards (2:25; 9:21-22; 10:9-10; 18:31; 37:40-47; 56:12-40; 88:8-16). In contrast, heaven according to the Christian faith is about being in God's presence, enjoying fellowship with him through praise and worship (Rev 7:9-17; 21:1-8).

Concluding Remarks

The fundamental difference between the Christian and Islamic understandings of salvation finds its roots in the contrasting interpretation of the nature of God and the nature of humanity. In Islam, people present themselves before a merciful God with their own moral record, hoping for God's favor. Speaking of God in Christ redeeming humanity offends Muslims' sense of God's greatness and majesty. Humans are distant from God and unworthy of the sovereign Lord getting involved in their misery. To the contrary, the Christian experience of salvation enables the Creator of the world to enter human history and become God with us, Immanuel. Redemption shows how God's sovereignty, mercy, and justice have been mediated to undeserving humanity. Salvation is about God's greatness being displayed in his suffering love. The promise of eternal life is not simply about a paradise full of gardens, plentiful food, and other pleasures; it is about enjoying God's presence and having fellowship with him. Humans are incomplete when they are not in relationship with the Creator God. Salvation is about enjoying God's peace, which stems from the assurance that God loves us, that our sins have been forgiven, and that we are assured of being with him in eternity.

12

COMMUNITY

The Ummah and the Church

Since Christianity and Islam are the leading religions of the world today, making up over 60 percent of the world's total population, interactions between followers of the two religions are a daily reality that affects almost every community on the planet. One topic that is vital for Christians and Muslims globally is their perception and experience of community and how each religious tradition views and interact with the other. Even though Christians and Muslims have differing religious worldviews and a complex history of encounters, examples of forgiveness, reconciliation, and acceptance of the other can offer us hope for peaceful coexistence and mutual respect in the future.

Perceptions

Christian-Muslim encounters are often viewed through the lens of the perception of the other. The way each community perceives the other results in certain attitudes and actions. The early Islamic community had many encounters with the Christians of the sixth century. Arab merchants, including Prophet Muhammad and many of his companions, encountered Christian communities in various places in and around Arabia through their trading expeditions. Like many travelers, they were welcomed in monasteries, where they observed the lifestyle of Christians. Meanwhile, the first Muslim community related to several Christian groups living in Arabia before Islam who were part of the cultural fabric of the Arabian society. However, the Qur'an and early Islamic writings give the impression that the early Islamic community's view of Christianity was mainly influenced by various Christian heretical groups that broke out from mainline Christianity and ended up living in Arabia, where they found a safe haven from possible persecution by the Byzantine Empire.[1] Unfortunately, interactions with such groups did not result in an accurate representation of Christianity in its biblical and orthodox tradition.

Since the Qur'an is considered the very word of God, its view of Christianity is the standard for understanding and relating to Christians throughout the centuries. While the earlier surahs of the Qur'an portray a favorable image of Christians, the later ones convey harsh criticism of their disbelief and the corruption of their faith. The earlier surahs of the Qur'an affirm, "Those who believe and those who are Jews and the Christians and the Sabians, whoever believes in God and the Last Day and acts uprightly, they have their reward from their Lord" (2:62). As Prophet Muhammad encountered serious criticism from the Jews of Medina, a somewhat later surah contrasted Christians with Jews: "You [Muhammad] will indeed find the most hostile of people to the believers are the Jews and the idolaters. You will indeed find the closest in affinity to the believers are those who say, 'We are Christians.' That is because among them are priests and monks, and they are not proud" (5:82). This openness toward Christians also reflected the kindness shown to a group of Muslims who fled to Christian Ethiopia for fear of persecution in Mecca.

Surah 57:27, while still speaking favorably of Christians, criticizes the monastic tradition, indicating that such practices will not be accommodated in Islam. Other surahs indicate an awareness of the conflict between Christians and Jews as well as divisions among Christians, stating that the contrasting claims of Jews and Christians negate the authenticity of both religions (2:113). Surah 5:14 refers to division among Christians while hinting to the corruptibility of their faith. It indicates an awareness of the division and conflicts among sixth-century Christians.

---

[1] The Qur'an, for example, reprimands those Christians who worship Jesus and Mary instead of God (5:116), an indication that the veneration of Mary was common practice among some Christians in Arabia. The Qur'an also uses the apocryphal Gospel of Peter to claim that Jesus used to create birds from clay (3:49).

The later surahs of the Qur'an offer harsh criticism of both Jews and Christians for not accepting the prophethood of Muhammad and for claiming that the truth was exclusively theirs (2:135; 3:64-101). The text signals a transition from appealing to Christians and Jews, seeking their acceptance of Islam, to establishing Islam as superior to both religions while tracing its roots directly to the untainted faith of Abraham.[2] The later harsh criticism of the Christians is not about their lifestyle as much as their corrupted religious beliefs from an Islamic point of view. Christians are criticized for believing in the divinity of Christ: "They do blaspheme who say: 'Allah is Christ the Son of Mary'" (5:72, 73; see also 5:17 and several other texts). Christians are also criticized for believing in Christ's crucifixion (4:156-58) and tritheism (4:171; 5:116). According to the Qur'an, Christians received a revealed Scripture (*Injil*, the Gospel) through the prophethood of Jesus, and therefore they deserve being called "the People of the Book." However, the Gospel became corrupted, and Christians deviated from believing in the oneness of God. Prophet Muhammad brought the truth about the worship of only one God through the message of the Qur'an, yet Christians refused to believe in him or his message.

Christians' allegedly misguided beliefs became the established perception of Christianity and Christians. While the earlier, favorable surahs are usually used in interfaith dialogue and in promoting amicable relationships between Muslims and Christians, Muslims also view Christians as blasphemous since they associate other beings or deities with God, the gravest sin in Islam. The message of the Qur'an gives the impression that Christians should be viewed and treated based on the final arguments presented in the later surahs, which point to the disbelief of the People of the Book (3:64-120) while asserting, "If anyone desires a religion other than Islam, never will it be accepted" (3:85). The Qur'anic views of Christianity and Christians are further elaborated in the hadith as well as various interpretations through the centuries.

Obviously, there is no biblical text concerning Muslims and Islam, since Islam came centuries after Christianity. However, Christians who came

---

[2]"They say, 'Be Jews or Christians and you will be guided.' Say [to them] No, but the creed of Abraham as a *hanif* [the one who holds the untainted and true faith] was not of idolaters" (2:135).

under the dominance of Islamic empires found themselves in a context where they had to defend their faith against Islamic criticism of their religious beliefs while dealing with the sociopolitical systems of the Islamic state. Christians' perception of Islam has been shaped by Islamic criticism of its core beliefs in the divinity of Christ and the Trinity. Several Christian apologists through the centuries tried to explain their faith while clarifying the basic Christian beliefs in Islamic context. While such endeavors limited antagonism between the two communities, they hardly convinced Muslims to follow Christianity.

THE ISLAMIC COMMUNITY, UMMAH

A key Islamic religious principle calls for the establishment of an Islamic community, ummah. The Qur'an declares, "You were the best *Ummah* [community] manifested to mankind, demonstrating what is right and prohibiting what is wrong, and believing in Allah" (3:110; see also 2:143). Throughout the centuries, Muslims have tried to keep the ummah as pure, religious, and as strong as possible. This necessitates total submission to God, which also requires submission to God's law, shari'a. Muslims differ, however, in their view of the basic principles that characterize the ummah. They also differ in how they interpret Islamic laws and customs that govern the ummah. While moderate and more secularized Muslims accept a multifaith form of society, traditionalist Islamists envision a religiously homogeneous community where Islamic principles and ethos dominate. Moderate Muslims argue that Islamic laws are open to various interpretations that might suit different cultural settings and historical eras, and therefore they might mean different things in different times and places. Traditionalist Islamists, to the contrary, argue that submission to God requires literal interpretation and fulfillment of whatever is considered religiously authoritative and obligatory.

The ummah according to traditionalist Islamists. The desire to establish an Islamic society or ummah based on religious principles led to the fusion of social and political structures, resulting in creating Islamic states such as Pakistan ("the land of the pure") in 1947 and the Shi'ite system in Iran in 1979. These political models inspired traditionalist Islamists from the Middle East to Africa and Southeast Asia, calling for the establishment of Islamic societies according to Islamic ethos and principles. During the second half of the twentieth century, political Islam gained momentum worldwide, and its dominance stemmed not so much from its military power but rather from the power of a strictly literal interpretation of religious texts and Islamic laws. The surge in establishing Islamic communities based on religious principles inspired large numbers of average Muslims and gave them a sense of identity and purpose more powerful than the previous socialist and nationalistic ideologies of the first half of the twentieth century. In many Muslim nations, politicized religion has been systematically adopted by various groups as means of ideological mobilization simply because these societies lack any other convincing sociopolitical ideologies. The end result is an ambiguous concept of a state and society where Islamic notions are interwoven with modern and even secular concepts of governing.[3]

The process of establishing an Islamic ummah or community carried out by various Islamic traditionalist groups during the second half of the twentieth century varied from one context to another; the underlying methodology, however, was the same. There was an emphasis on the comprehensive and universal nature of Islamic ethos, based on a strict interpretation of religious obligations, while adopting an exclusivist and literalist interpretation of religious texts, calling for a rigorous pursuit of moral, social, and political reconstruction of society. Traditionalists succeeded in promoting a holistic concept of Islam where religion, politics, and social life are interdependent entities that form the structure of the society under the banner of Islam and its religious principles. As a young Kuwaiti woman put it, "Islam influences the way I think, the way I interact with people, the way I dress, the kind of food I eat, the way I perceive the whole reality and my own existence." The pattern of Islamizing societies that dominated various Islamic countries during the second half of the twentieth century remains a relatively significant force worldwide today.

Traditionalist Islamists' plan to establish an Islamic ummah reached an apex during the first decade of the twenty-first century. Immediately after it started to lose its appeal to the masses. Radical groups such as the Islamic State, which attracted a large number of young Muslims from

---

[3]John J. Donohue and John L. Esposito, *Islam in Transition: Muslim Perceptions* (Oxford: Oxford University Press, 1982).

around the world, were hoping to bring about the territory of Islam or submission globally. They called for the eradication of modern state borders often created by Western powers and the establishment of a unified Islamic state, as in the case of dissolving the borders between Syria and Iraq by ISIS in 2011. Such extreme traditional versions of political Islamism resurfaced as a postmodern phenomenon in response to cultural disillusionment as well as socioeconomic and political destabilization. These young Muslims saw themselves as the champions of a lost, glorious historical narrative in which Islam conquered and defeated the pagan cultures of the ancient world, replacing "the state of ignorance" and disbelief with pristine faith. They envisioned a global Islam that dominated every land and culture with the one true worship of Allah. However, the movement lost momentum, resulting in a reversal of attitudes among the majority of Muslims worldwide. More moderate, inclusive attitudes toward Islamic governing and the concept of the Islamic ummah prevail today.

Issues of social equality, freedom of expression, and freedom of worship must be addressed in the context of contemporary social and cultural interaction globally. How does the concept of the Islamic ummah relate to and embrace other cultural norms and religious beliefs in the many global contexts of the world today? Coexistence with and within Islamic societies may be influenced by the Islamic ethos that perceives a divided world of Islam or submission, war or unbelief. Islamic voices on these topics vary significantly. They range from the very conservative and even fanatical to the more liberal and secular. Faced with many sociopolitical uncertainties, various traditionalist Islamists resolve to literally interpret Islamic laws as their way of envisioning a true Islamic ummah. It is their way of asserting their social and religious identity in a fast-changing world of political and economic upheaval.

The ummah according to moderate Muslims. Attitudes held by moderate Muslims on what constitutes an Islamic ummah or community during the first half of the twentieth century are re-emerging globally starting from the second decade of the twenty-first century. Cultural relativism as affirmed by moderate Muslims has contributed to better understanding, mutual respect, and cooperation between Muslims and other religious traditions. This form of Islamic cultural relativism is primarily concerned with promoting religious principles while giving equal consideration to others' religious ideologies and ethos. Contributions made by Islamic modernists such as Abdullahi an-Na'im, a contemporary, moderate Muslim scholar on human rights and the status of non-Muslims in the Islamic societies, are helpful and promising. He argues that all people, regardless of their religious orientation, should have rights such as equal citizenship in their countries, emphasizing the worth of many ways of life and affirming the values of other cultures.[4] Such moderate Islamic attitudes are consistent with universal standards of human rights. In *Islam and the Secular State*, An-Na'im argues that the state is territorial, not Islamic. He emphasizes that there should be a separation between Islam and the state while recognizing that there will be a connection between Islam and politics.[5]

Islamic modernist Soheib Bencheikh, a Muslim imam from Marseille, France, holds up secularism as means of protecting the rights of all minorities, including Muslim minorities in Europe. He argues that secularism safeguards against religious discrimination while allowing various religious traditions to coexist harmoniously in modern societies. He affirms the Qur'anic notion that belief or disbelief is ordained by God, indicating that no human can challenge such provisions (10:99-100). Bencheikh's approach marks a significant shift in Islamic modernist attitudes toward secularism, which had been considered a threat to Islam by many Muslim thinkers, even modernists.[6] An-Na'im's work further affirms and clarifies the role of religion, primarily Islam, in the secularized world context.

One topic related to the Islamic concept of ummah is the Islamic affirmation of separation between Muslims and non-Muslims. The Qur'an identifies distinct categories of faith and unfaith, the household of Islam (Dar al-Islam) and the household of war (Dar al-Harb), and the inseparable unity of religion and state (*din wa dawla*). Such divisions, when interpreted literally, create an atmosphere of inequality and separatism. While the ultimate goal is the establishment of a pure, unified, and strong Islamic community, others might find it impossible to participate and

---

[4] Abdullahi An-Na'im, "Religious Minorities Under Islamic Law and the Limits of Cultural Relativism," *Human Rights Quarterly* 9, no. 1 (1987): 1-18. See also Abdullahi, *Towards an Islamic Reformation: Civil Liberties, Human Rights and International law* (Syracuse, NY: Syracuse University Press, 1990).
[5] Abdullahi An-Na'im, *Islam and the Secular State* (Cambridge, MA: Harvard University Press, 2008).
[6] Interview with Soheib Bencheikh, "Islam and Secularism," Qantara.de, April 2004.

integrate in such a community. Surah 3:110 concludes with the remark, "If only the People of the Book had faith, it would have been better for them. Among them are some who had faith, but the majority are perverted transgressors." The literal application of such religious structure almost guarantees that the relationship be always unequal. It allows for the survival of non-Muslims, but hardly for equal engagement or active participation. In many parts of the world, Muslim and Christian communities share the same cultural values except their religious faith. The two communities have similar attitudes about family values, improved life conditions, and hope for a better future. The concern, however, is about the quality of that shared future.[7]

The voices of modernist Muslims reemerging today are promising, as they call for a holistic approach to how the ummah should be structured. They use Qur'anic accounts where coexistence between the conflicting territories of Dar al-Islam and Dar al-Harb might be welcomed and accommodated. Surah 109, titled *Al-Kafirun* ("The infidels"), declares, "Say: O ye that reject faith [infidels], I worship not that which you worship. Nor will you worship that which I worship.... To you be your way [or religion] and to me mine [religion]." The Qur'an presents differing views on how the Muslim community should relate to the world. While it calls for bringing about God's submission, it also allows others to practice their own religious beliefs without forcing them to accept Islam: "Let there be no compulsion in religion, the Truth stands out clear from the error" (2:256). The Qur'an also indicates that it is God's will that not all humanity will become Muslim. "If it had been the Lord's Will, they all who are on earth have believed. Will you then compel mankind against their will to believe?" (10:99). "No Soul can believe except by the will of Allah" (10:100). If this is the case, fighting non-Muslims is a pointless endeavor that goes against God's will.

The future coexistence of Christian and Muslim communities depends primarily on the willingness of both communities to respect the differing religious views they hold. The Muslim community has a responsibility to

---

[7]A couple of scholarly works on this issue are important to mention here: David Little, John Kelsay, and Abdelaziz Sachedina, eds., *Human Rights and the Conflict of Culture: Western and Islamic Perspectives on Religious Liberty* (Columbia: University of South Carolina Press, 1988); Bassam Tibi, *Islam and the Cultural Accommodation of Social Change*, 2nd ed. (Boulder: University of Colorado Press, 1991).

tolerate and accept Christians as equal and genuine partners in society. This in turn depends on the willingness of contemporary Muslims to interpret Islamic religious laws according to the principles of human rights, dignity, and religious freedom. The Christian community has a responsibility to encourage mutual respect and dialogue with the Muslim community. Christians should encourage and promote inclusive forms of political structures, education, and social life. Christian communities in many parts of the world have contributed to the establishment of various social and educational institutions that serve the whole community regardless of their religious or ethnic background. Many Christians and Muslims play significant roles in promoting equality and freedom; such a high calling of mutual respect and cooperation should continue to be the ultimate objective of Christians and Muslims around the globe.

Muslims and Christians in the Islamic Ummah

Christians and Muslims have lived and interacted within the Islamic ummah in many parts of the globe for as many as thirteen centuries. The history of coexistence and interaction between the two religious communities is long and rich, carrying layers of memories and events. Some of those memories are painful and discouraging; others are hopeful and promising. Christians and Muslims have often enjoyed friendly relations and respect for each other. Christian communities living in predominantly Muslim nations coexist in a context where self-definition and self-determination are attained within the political and cultural framework of Islamic rule.

Isolation. In many cases, and despite such a long history of coexistence, each religious community has little actual contact with the other, and their knowledge of each other's religious tradition is minimal. While Christian and Muslim communities usually interact on the social and economic levels, the communities have existed in a relationship of mutual isolation when it comes to understanding and appreciating each other's religious traditions. In many parts of the world, Christian and Muslim communities were and still are not able to take seriously the other's view of reality. Even in semisecularized state systems, in which the modern concept of equal citizenship under a common civil law has been established, communal separation and cultural isolation persist.

This voluntary religious-ideological isolation characterizes the relationship between Christian and Muslim communities across various regions of the world. Isolation often leads to misconceptions on both sides. In an ideologically isolated community, what is true and acceptable is what the larger society upholds as such, whether in terms of religious beliefs, rituals, or values. Since Christians living in predominantly Muslim societies hold to religious beliefs and values that differ from and even contradict what the community at large considers to be the norm, they are often viewed with suspicion. As a result, Christians living in predominantly Muslim countries often end up creating their own communities within the larger society as their way of maintaining their religious beliefs and values against Islamic criticism and sometimes forced conversion. Such hibernation becomes the only way to survive while upholding a historical identity and culture that otherwise would be engulfed by the larger society.

Christians and Muslims need to actively take others' worldviews seriously if they desire to overcome such a state of ideological isolation. Interfaith dialogue, which is happening around the globe, should be encouraged and promoted not just for scholars and religious leaders but among people in the community at large so that various sectors of society can listen to and appreciate one another's religious worldviews, aspirations, frustrations, and hopes. Many Christians are not able to grasp the Islamic concern for God's oneness and its implications for worship and social and cultural life. Likewise, Muslims are confused about Christians' beliefs and practices. The majority of Muslims have never been introduced to the Christ of faith that Christians treasure and uphold. They are not cognizant that Christians are not worshiping three different Gods but only one trinitarian God. In listening to each other, Christians and Muslims will be surprised at how much they have in common when it comes to their social and cultural lives.

Hostility. Religious-ideological isolation has been the most common type of relationship between Christians and Muslims for most of their history, but hostility often erupts as a result of confusion and mistrust. Differences in religious beliefs and social values are often perceived as a threat to the existence of the other. Religious tensions are gripping the global community with fear and anxiety. Reacting to Western colonization and domination over Islamic territories, many Muslims perceive political decisions and interaction with the West from the lens of an Islamic-Christian struggle over world resources and territories, not accounting for the substantial secularization of the West. Some Muslims even perceive the Western agenda as a deliberate offense against Muslims and Islam. While Western societies often welcome Muslims as an integral part of society, tensions between Muslims and others in the West are increasing due to conflicting cultural and religious values, resulting in increased tension and anxiety.

The rhetoric of hostility is usually fueled by upholding certain religious beliefs that seem contradictory to the worldview or well-being of the other. A hostile atmosphere results in a competitive relationship as both communities stress their differences rather than acknowledging their many similarities. The only way forward in combating hostilities is to openly address concerns rather than ignoring them or pretending that they do not exist. The notion that Christians and Muslims share the same religious beliefs will not help in overcoming tension. An honest dialogue acknowledging religious differences and worldviews is the way forward. Mutual respect and appreciation of the other is usually established on solid ground that recognizes the differences as well as the value of the other while allowing the other the opportunity to express themselves freely.

Irrational reactions. In a rapidly changing world of social conflict and political and economic instability, feelings of distress sometimes result in irrational reactions, a reality that often colors daily encounters between Christians and Muslims. In the assertion of Islamic identity against socioeconomic and political upheaval, Christian-Muslim relations usually suffer. While Christians and Muslims living in predominantly Islamic societies are facing the same sociopolitical problems and economic strains, Christians sometimes become targets for attacks as a way of venting Muslim frustration. Meanwhile, Muslims living in predominantly non-Muslim nations are sometimes viewed with suspicion in terms of their loyalty to and support of secular state systems and social structures.

Religious differences might also be interpreted as a challenge to the core values of the other. The very presence of the other community is perceived and interpreted as a challenge to that which is most sacred in the community's religious beliefs and practices. The threat of the other may be real but most probably is imagined. Whatever the validity of the perceived threat, the theological response is clear: the other community is framed as on the wrong side of truth.[8]

Religious violence is a serious threat to peaceful coexistence. In many cases, friendly relations in the community are shattered, and even after the violence has subsided, matters can never be quite the same again. It only takes a rash of fanaticism to create such a situation. During the second half of the twentieth century and up until the 2010s, the world witnessed several violent episodes of religious conflict. The aftermath of the Balkan war of the 1990s resulted in the division of former Yugoslavia into fragmented, smaller nation-states. Majority former Yugoslavians are either Christians or Muslims, and they are working hard to reclaim their great history of peaceful coexistence. Terrorist attacks in Europe and North America created unnecessary anxiety and fear among people. Unless there is a genuine willingness to find ways of coexistence and acceptance based on forgiveness and reconciliation, Christians and Muslims in the Balkans, Nigeria, the Middle East, Indonesia, central Asia, Europe, and North America are all vulnerable to more conflicts and violence.

Positive trends. During the golden era of Islam, in the eighth and ninth centuries, Christians were instrumental in the overall development of society. Their administrative skills were much needed and appreciated. In contrast, when the power and the prestige of the ummah was challenged during the Crusades, a call for jihad against Christians was sounded, resulting in the massacre of thousands of Christians across the Middle East, reducing their numbers and influence from majority to a minority status. Even during this lowest point of intolerance, there were calls to extend God's love to Muslims rather than fighting them, and some Muslim leaders responded positively to such gestures.

There are many positive signs in terms of coexistence and mutual respect between Muslims and Christians around the world. The majority of Muslim states tolerate their Christian population and allow Christian worship. Christian clergy and leaders often have amicable interactions with their Muslim counterparts across the Middle East and south Asian countries. Many share a meal together commencing the break of the fast during the month of Ramadan. Many Gulf states, such as the United Arab

---

[8]John Esposito analyzes this topic extensively in his books *The Islamic Threat: Myth or Reality* (Oxford: Oxford University Press, 1992) and *Islam and Democracy* (Oxford: Oxford University Press, 1996).

Emirates, Bahrain, Oman, and Kuwait, have donated land for church buildings. In Egypt, when fanatics burned and destroyed churches and Christian institutions in 2012, the government took the initiative to rebuild these churches. Saudi Arabia is advocating for new social and cultural reforms with the goal of an inclusive society where various religious traditions are tolerated. In 1996, when the bishop of Oran, Algeria, was assassinated by extremists, thousands of Muslims attended his funeral and mourned the man they called "the bishop of the Muslims." In many African nations, Christians and Muslims enjoy friendly relations and work harmoniously for the betterment of their societies.

The Community of the Kingdom

The concept of a Christian community is so central to the biblical account. Various terms are used to identify and describe the nature and function of the community. The most common term to describe the Christian community is *church*. Jesus said, "I will build my church, and the gates of Hades will not overcome it" (Mt 16:18). It is understood that through Jesus' redemptive work of salvation, Christians—who are called by God, redeemed by Christ, and empowered by the Holy Spirit—are called to be God's people, or the church. Peter further elaborates on Jesus' words by emphasizing that Christians "are a chosen people, a royal priesthood, a holy nation, a people belonging to God" (1 Pet 2:9 NIV 1984). The Bible and the Qur'an refer to Christian and Muslim communities, respectively, as a distinct community with specific characterizations and functions. Both communities are described as unique and special: "best *Ummah* [community] manifested to mankind" (3:110) and "chosen people, a royal priesthood, a holy nation, a people belonging to God" (1 Pet 2:9 NIV 1984). While the Islamic concept of ummah emphasizes the purity and power of the community, the biblical account highlights its holiness and relationship to God. The Islamic ummah includes the integration of religious, political, and social life as interdependent entities governing society under the banner of Islam and its religious principles. In Christianity, the ultimate nature and function of the community of the church is not so much political or economic but rather missional and communal for the purpose of worshiping God. It is often reflected in living for God's glory and extending God's redemptive work of salvation.

The biblical narrative speaks of a community that is often defined and understood in relation to the idea of the kingdom of God. Prior to Jesus' time, people were anticipating the coming of God's kingdom, in which God's reign would usher in a time of peaceful existence, the establishment of justice as well as economic prosperity. Several, including Jesus' disciples, expected in Jesus' life and mission the establishment of such a reign of God on earth. However, on many occasions Jesus made it clear that his kingdom was not about establishing a sociopolitical or economic structure but about a kingdom established through his life and sacrificial death to redeem humanity to God. Jesus was concerned with the human condition under sin and alienation from God, which resulted in such social, economic, and political misery. He tackled the source of the problem rather than fixing the apparent consequences.

Jesus' messianic mission of forgiveness of sin and restoring relationship with God ushered in God's kingdom. Jesus points to the kingdom as the purpose of his coming; he explicitly defines his mission as proclaiming the kingdom of God through teaching and healing using expressions such as "The kingdom of God has come near" (Mk 1:15). The basic idea of the kingdom is that God in Christ entered human history and confronted evil and destruction, restoring life with his redemptive power. Entering the kingdom requires repentance and acceptance of God's forgiveness of sin. Jesus constantly emphasized God's acceptance of sinners, divine forgiveness, and grace. Those who have been reconciled with God and experienced God's love and grace through the sacrificial death of Christ have a responsibility to extend God's love, forgiveness, and reconciliation to others. The new community of forgiven sinners have a responsibility to live in a way that glorifies God.

The ethos of the community of the kingdom is based on healed and restored relationships that are expected to embrace others in fellowship. "There is neither Jew nor Gentile, neither slave nor free, nor is there male and female, for you are all one in Christ Jesus" (Gal 3:28). All are equal, and to all God has extended his mercy and grace. The community of the kingdom is expected to extend God's love and acceptance to all: "But I tell you, love your enemies and pray for those who persecute you" (Mt 5:44). Christians' calling is to embrace the enemy, not to destroy others (Lk 9:54-56). Before Jesus ascended into heaven, the disciples bewilderedly asked him, "Lord, are you at this time going to restore the kingdom . . . ?"

(Acts 1:6). His reply was that through their life of witness to Christ's redemption and reconciliation, people and nations would be ushered into the kingdom (Acts 1:8).

The church has a responsibility to proclaim the kingdom and to point people to the person of Christ, who is able to transform people and communities, giving them the opportunity to experience God's forgiveness and reconciliation. Christians usually refer to the kingdom as a reality that is experienced in the here and now but that will be fully realized in the future, when Christ returns at the end of time. The early Christians fully realized that they were sojourners in this world; however, in their life and witness they rose above the state law and were able to serve their communities faithfully. They kept the balance between being committed citizens while anticipating the fulfillment of God's kingdom in eternal life.

While not all Christians have fully grasped or lived out the realities of the kingdom as intended by Christ, there are many examples of those who were and are able to live the ethos of the kingdom. In our global context today, Christians have greater opportunities as well as responsibilities to live and witness to the love of Christ that redeems and embraces. They are called to live and embody the ethos of God's kingdom through their lives and sacrificial witness.

Toward Better Ways of Coexistence and Mutual Respect

Christian communities living with or within Islamic societies are constantly faced with the inherently theological nature of Islam and its vociferous insistence on institutionalized theism. The cry *Allahu Akbar* ("God is great") is both a theological statement and a way of life. Those who truly acknowledge and believe that God is great have also a responsibility to live like it. The theological statement calls for political action; in the context in which Islam originally developed, this meant the eradication of all pseudo worship and the destruction of any idols. Believing in the oneness of God, *tawhid*, demands the active dethroning of false gods and the elimination of false worship. The call to bring people under God's rule was taken to be a political responsibility, to be achieved through power. The verb *aslammna*, from which the word *Islam* is derived, has a double meaning: it refers to both surrender to God and submission to prophetic and caliphal rule (49:14).

The contemporary version of this Islamic vocation often takes the form of a call for desecularization, the establishment of an Islamic society, and the application of Islamic law, shari'a. The issues that need to be addressed in our contemporary world context include: In what sense can and should the state institutionalize God's will? How do reason and revelation interact? What is sacred and God-given, and what is culturally relative and temporary? The meaning and application of *Allahu Akbar* ("God is great") and *aslammna* ("surrender to God") need to be understood in relation to a world of cultural diversity and sociopolitical and economic realities. The establishment of the oneness of God over all aspects of life needs to be interpreted and reconciled with the Islamic concept of God the All-Merciful, *Al-Rahman Al-Rahim*, so that the sovereignty of God will not be imposed but loved and wanted. One noteworthy phrase attributed to God in the Qur'an is *Rab Al-Alamin* ("the Lord of the world") or *Rab Al-Nas* ("the Lord of the people"). It is a major theme that runs through the Qur'an and is its concluding word: "Say, I seek refuge with the Lord and cherisher of the people. The king of the people. The God of the people" (114). While the Muslim people were originally addressed here, the concept might be extended to include others whom God has created, being "the Lord of the whole world, the Lord of all people."

This notion of God being the God of all people might open new horizons for how Muslims and Christians should relate and interact. God cannot be understood as present to and concerned with only one group of people or with only one particular religious tradition. The expression and affirmation of the divine must come to be understood as the expression of the activity of a God who cares for and loves the whole world. The future coexistence of Christianity and Islam depends on bringing together what Islam means by *Allahu Akbar* ("God is great") and what the New Testament understands by "God in Christ." To see the task this way does not mean being naive about the sharp contrast between the two concepts. On the contrary, it requires recognizing that this is the heart of the relationship, without which there will be no real meaning to interaction between the two religions.

The Christian faith affirms a divine capacity that is unique in its oneness but at the same time open to the world, a divine capacity that out of love suffers with and for humanity. Islam traditionally affirms divine transcendence, according to which such compassion and suffering love are offensive to the idea of divine sovereignty. Christianity and Islam often suppose that their understanding of theism is incompatible and contradictory. That view does justice to neither of them because both are genuinely monotheistic. Theism is neither plural nor competitive but rather relational. The Christian understanding of God is fundamentally oriented toward moving forward to a better future with God. It is the future that has come in Jesus Christ, which may and should interpret reality and guide present action.

Both Christianity and Islam are striving toward the same aim of letting God be God. Both religions want to establish the recognition of divine lordship over all aspects of life, but they differ on how to make this happen. The Islamic ultimate vocation of bringing all aspects of life under God's sovereignty needs to be assessed in relation to other religious traditions. The notion that there is no difference between establishing the oneness of God theologically and the sovereignty of God politically, economically, and socially needs to be considered in light of the complexity of contemporary world structures, in which politics and economics are bound to a global system. Human interactions should be established on mutual recognition and collaboration whereby each in the community contributes to the enrichment and appreciation of others' traditions and ways of life. A modern state system should allow diversity of religious thought and practice to be integrated in the fabric of society.

Religious beliefs should give meaning to life, enabling people to work for peace and justice, contributing to the advancement of society. A process of self-evaluation is essential to determine how religion can be a source of peace, love, and grace, contributing to the well-being of all people. Religious values are meant to bring hope amid despair and fear, peace and comfort instead of violence and persecution. Relationship with God is meant to bring unity and harmony in life, to give people the power to live and achieve their potential.

Concluding Remarks

In the context of globalized Christianity and globalized Islam, religious experiences differ from one culture to the other, and living faith as expressed and experienced by a group of Christians or Muslims varies widely. Christianity and Islam differ greatly in their religious and cultural outlook. Such diversity should be a source of celebration and admiration.

Christians and Muslims ought to be inspired to uphold the unity and integrity of their communities. They equally have a responsibility to better relate to and interact with each other while responding to challenges facing the global community. What we see today on the world scene is not just religious tension supported by religious principles and differing worldviews; it is a world in turmoil, a world in a constant state of crisis, crying for help. Religious tensions are an expression of frustration, disillusionment, and meaninglessness experienced by alienated humanity. Christians have a responsibility to extend God's unconditional love to hurt and confused people. The narrative of God's good news can break through that vicious cycle of hatred and tensions, redeeming humanity from sin and alienation. God's redemption is not a collection of abstract ideas or a set of religious formulas. It is a liberating power that brings hope and peace.

At the heart of the Christian witness is a capacity for suffering, "For it has been granted to you on behalf of Christ not only to believe in him, but also to suffer for him" (Phil 1:29). Life in Christ is a call for faithfulness unto death. As religious violence increased during the last decades, many Christians around the world paid the ultimate price for following Christ by being martyred for their faith. As many Christians in the Middle East were put to death at the hands of religious extremists, the continual response was extending forgiveness to those who murdered their loved ones. It is a Christian calling that might inspire other Christians around the world to be faithful followers of Christ unto death.

Being faithful witnesses, Christians not only suffer for Christ but also hope for a glorified future with God. Our understanding of hope is both historical and transhistorical. If we view history, with its conditions and potentialities, as open, we come to realize God's liberating power, which transforms history and creates new opportunities for better future. God's transforming power is active in imminent historical processes and events as well as in the future coming of his kingdom, transcending history. The liberating power of God's kingdom is both a potentiality and a responsibility. Christians have a responsibility to make this liberating power of God's kingdom a reality. The hope we have in Christ will be actualized when people are reconciled with God and communities are reconciled with one another so that God can receive all glory.

GENERAL INDEX

Abbasid Caliphate or Dynasty, 21, 22, 27, 28, 32, 35, 36, 45, 60, 81, 82, 104
Abbasid Caliph(s), 23, 24, 25, 27, 31, 60
Afghanistan, 4, 131, 182, 183, 203, 212, 215, 216
   and Afghans, Afghani, 130, 182, 215, 216
Africa, xi, xiii, 3, 30, 65, 83, 84, 85, 86, 88, 97, 98, 105, 106, 108, 110, 112, 113, 114, 134, 140, 153, 169, 172, 177-79, 318, 326
   and African Christianity, 63
   and East Africa, 108, 109, 111, 112, 134
   and North Africa, xiii, 3, 5, 6, 9, 10, 11, 12, 22, 24, 25, 27, 44, 45, 46, 54, 68, 69, 74, 80, 81, 84, 98, 99, 107, 108, 110, 114, 125, 126, 128, 149, 172, 176, 191
   and North African Christians, 44
   and sub-Saharan Africa, 25, 109, 110, 177
   and West Africa, 108, 109, 110, 111, 134, 139
Al Azhar Islamic University, 46, 141, 142, 171, 185
Aleppo, 56, 60, 61, 64
Alexandria, 4, 5, 10, 11, 16, 26, 36, 39, 126, 172
Algeria, 22, 45, 69, 109, 128, 172-76, 191, 212, 213, 219, 326
Americas, 79, 83, 84
   and Latin America, 86, 87, 111, 123, 196
   and North America, xi, 88, 114, 115, 120, 121, 122, 124, 135, 143, 144, 193-96, 213, 221, 325
   and South America, 84, 85, 87, 111, 114, 123
Antioch, 4, 5, 10, 11, 39, 49, 50, 56, 77, 156
Anatolia, 49, 57, 78, 127, 136, 137, 151, 154, 155, 158
Arab(s), 14-16, 21, 24, 30, 35, 36, 38, 43, 52, 57, 101, 103, 104, 105, 108, 109, 111, 149, 153, 162, 165, 174, 226, 227, 267
Arabia, xii, 13, 14, 15, 16, 19, 25, 35, 43, 74, 99, 138, 139, 153, 162, 168, 153, 213, 215, 216, 219, 228, 262, 314, 315
   Arabian king, 165
   Arabian nights, 24
   Arabian Peninsula, 16, 168
   Arabian Prophet, 272
   Arabian tribes, 227
Asia, 60-62, 64, 65, 81, 82, 84, 86, 88, 98, 105, 107, 112, 113, 114, 133, 140, 153, 164, 169, 187
   and Central Asia, 4, 17, 25, 26, 45, 57, 59, 61, 64, 65, 68, 74, 96, 97, 103, 104, 105, 131, 150, 186
   and Southeast Asia, 60, 85, 97, 106, 107, 108, 132, 133, 183, 184
Asia Minor, 5, 25, 37, 47-49, 50, 54-57, 74, 77, 78, 81, 98, 155, 158
   See also Turkey
Armenia, Arminian(s), 4, 5, 9, 47, 57, 65, 77, 101, 136, 137, 151, 155, 158, 166, 220
Assyrians, 151, 161, 162, 164, 166
Assyrian Church or Syriac Church, 4, 9, 22, 25-27, 36, 57, 64, 77

Baghdad, 22, 24, 26, 29, 31, 32, 34, 60-62, 64, 72, 81, 162
Bangladesh, 104, 132, 180-82
Balkans, 40, 78, 84, 98, 102, 129, 130, 137, 147, 148, 149, 187, 189, 190, 325
Britain, 3, 121, 127, 130-34, 148, 150, 153, 154, 155, 159, 170, 176, 180, 184, 187
British, 88, 105, 108, 111, 121, 121, 166, 127, 129, 131-34, 137, 139, 140, 142, 148, 149, 151, 153, 154, 164, 165, 168, 169, 170, 176, 179, 180, 191, 199, 208
   and British Isles, 84
Bulgers, 14, 41, 42
Bulgaria, 59, 78, 129, 130, 189, 206
   and Bulgarian church, 42
Byzantium, 7, 13, 14, 43, 49, 76, 77, 84
Byzantine Christendom, xiv, 7, 9, 11-13, 36, 38, 39, 40, 52, 54, 158
Byzantine Empire, xii, xiii, 9, 11-14, 17, 21, 30, 38, 39, 43, 45, 47, 47-49, 51, 55, 57, 76-79, 81
Cairo, 45, 46, 72, 109, 141, 185
Calvin, John, 93
Carthage, 5, 16, 39
Catholic Church, 47, 52, 58, 87, 88, 94, 95, 110, 114, 120, 123, 196, 200
   and Catholic Missions, 123
Charlemagne, 13, 25, 37, 39-41
Charles Martel, 17, 39
China, 17, 25, 26, 43, 44, 57, 59, 60, 64, 65, 68, 81, 84, 85, 86, 105, 106, 108, 119, 133, 149, 186, 187
Colonization, xii, 83, 85-88, 114, 123, 127, 144, 323
Constantine, 5, 6, 8-10, 36, 40, 52, 53
Constantinople, 7, 10, 11, 14, 36-38, 48, 49, 51, 55, 76, 78, 79, 96, 98, 189
   See also Istanbul
Crusades, Crusaders, 45-57, 62, 65, 67-69, 72, 73, 76, 77, 81, 113, 325
Damascus, 17, 18, 22, 60, 72, 73, 165, 266
Dar Al-Islam, 18, 25, 44, 56, 62, 63, 72, 78, 81, 132, 153, 320, 321
   and Dar al-Harb, 132, 216, 320, 321
Dhimmi(s), 18, 19, 20, 39, 63
Dominicans, 67, 75, 87
Dutch, 107, 108, 111, 133
Eastern Christianity, 21, 36, 38, 39, 46, 52, 56, 79, 98
Edessa, 49, 50, 56, 77
Egypt, 4, 5, 8, 11, 12, 14-16, 21, 28, 45-47, 50-52, 56, 57, 60, 62, 68, 71, 74, 80, 99, 101, 108, 111, 112, 126, 127, 134, 139, 141, 142, 166, 170-72, 185, 201-5, 207-9, 213, 214, 217, 219, 242, 248, 270, 325
   and Upper Egypt, 5, 36, 63
Egyptian Church or Christians (Coptic Church) 9, 22, 36, 56, 57, 62, 63, 172, 220
   and Copts 4, 22, 46, 172

Elm Al-Kalam, 34, 271, 278
England, 4, 26, 41, 48, 50, 69, 96, 122, 127, 131, 178, 191, 193, 199
Enlightenment, 116-18, 120, 122, 124
Ethiopia, 4-6, 14, 63, 111, 112, 134, 172, 178, 315
Ephesus, 56, 77, 78, 244
Europe, 3, 17, 25, 40-45, 47, 48, 49, 53-55, 59, 61, 63, 66, 68, 69, 71, 72, 74-76, 79, 81, 82, 84, 88-90, 92-95, 97, 98, 101, 102, 109, 113-17, 119, 120, 124-26, 128, 130, 135, 136, 140-44, 147-48, 154, 157-58, 162, 172-74, 187-93, 196-97, 207, 217, 221, 320, 325
    and Eastern Europe, 13, 41, 58, 59, 79, 82, 83, 98, 99, 102, 113, 114, 117, 125, 130, 136, 187-90, 196, 207
    and European Christendom or European Christianity, 13, 38, 39, 40, 43, 52, 53, 54, 58, 79, 81, 82, 93, 94
    and Northern Europe, 13, 25, 41, 43, 95, 96
    and Southern Europe, 3, 5, 10, 11, 43, 95
    and Western Europe, 40, 45, 47, 53, 59, 60, 67, 72, 76, 102, 117, 130, 190-93
Fatimid Caliphate or Dynasty, 45-47, 54, 56, 81
France, 4, 5, 17, 25, 39, 40, 48, 50, 51, 53, 54, 63, 66-69, 91, 96, 121, 123, 128, 130, 148, 150, 153-55, 160, 166, 172, 173, 175, 177, 191, 193, 199, 206, 211, 320
Francis of Assisi, 55, 67, 68
Franciscan(s), 58, 59, 65, 67, 75, 87
French, 88, 111, 123, 126, 127, 128, 129, 131, 134, 141, 151, 165, 166, 172, 174, 277
General Baybars, 57, 62, 63
Germany, 6, 39, 40, 48, 59, 69, 90, 92, 96, 119, 130, 131, 134, 148-51, 191, 199, 206
    and Germans, 120, 149
Greece, 4, 37, 45, 71, 78, 79, 129, 155, 158, 189
    and Greeks, 101, 155
Hadith, 19, 29, 73, 135, 141, 231, 255, 264-72, 275
Hejaz, 45, 138, 149, 153, 168
Hidden Imam, 137, 138, 140, 161
Holy Land, 47, 48, 51, 52, 54, 55, 68, 80, 81
Holy Roman Emperor, 13, 37, 40, 50, 96
Hungary, 59, 98, 102, 148, 149
Iberian Peninsula, 52, 79, 84, 86-88, 97
Ibn Taymiya, 73, 74, 209, 271
India, 4, 5, 17, 18, 22, 24, 27, 57, 62, 65, 66, 83, 84, 85, 86, 88, 97, 98, 103, 104, 105, 106, 108, 112, 114, 125, 131, 132, 142, 152, 179-82, 191, 209, 210
Indonesia, 88, 106-8, 133, 153, 183, 184, 197, 201, 202, 203, 210, 213, 215, 219, 325
Injil (or Al-Injil), 258, 272, 274, 316
Inquisition, 67, 75, 95
Iran, 4, 66, 99, 103, 104, 114, 125, 127, 130, 131, 132, 136, 137-38, 151, 159-65, 168, 169, 170, 202, 203, 210-11, 220
    and Iranians, 129, 131, 159, 160, 161, 182, 211, 213, 219, 318
    See also Persia
Iraq, 4, 22, 25, 27, 102, 127, 136-38, 149, 151, 153-55, 158, 160-66, 170, 211, 217, 220, 319
    and Iraqis, 216, 220
    See also Mesopotamia

Islamic Empire, 22, 23, 24, 26, 27, 30, 31, 43, 44, 45, 47, 58, 62, 64, 72, 74, 81, 98, 146
Islamic reformers, 140-43
Istanbul, 78, 98, 101, 137, 155, 157, 189
    See also Constantinople
Italy, 5, 25, 40, 66, 69, 79, 84, 90, 128, 134, 172
    and Italians, 128, 175
Jamal Al-din Al- Alfghani, 141, 142, 203
Japan, 27, 85, 86, 177, 187
John of Damascus, 17, 31
Jerusalem, 14, 16, 17, 18, 46, 47, 49-52, 54, 56, 204, 266, 267, 287, 288
Jihad, 16, 55, 63, 99, 134, 153, 172, 174, 175, 182, 190, 209, 211, 214-17, 221, 310, 325
Jizya, 18, 19, 100, 266, 267, 270,
Ka'ba, 14, 15, 18, 226, 266, 305
Kazakhstan, 25, 105, 131
Kenya, 111, 112, 134, 178, 215, 217
Kyrgyzstan, 105, 131, 186
Kurds, 151, 155, 158, 162-64, 166
Lebanon, 64, 127, 154, 161, 166-68, 205, 215
Levant, 45, 46, 57, 64, 74
Libya, 4, 109, 128, 172, 176, 177, 205
Luther, 90-92, 113, 141
Mali, 109, 134, 177
Malysia, 106-8, 133, 184, 185
Mameluke(s), 27, 52, 56, 57, 60, 62, 63, 65, 74, 81, 99, 111, 112, 126
Mecca, 15, 18, 99, 109, 195, 204, 216, 226, 266, 305, 315
Medina, 15, 18, 99, 216, 266, 315
Mesopotamia, 12, 15, 16, 21, 25, 28, 32, 64, 71, 80, 99, 162, 164, 165
    See also Iraq
Middle East, 3, 4, 5, 24, 25, 30, 45, 56, 57, 60, 61, 62, 63, 64, 79, 81, 82, 94, 99, 114, 125, 126, 128, 153, 159, 160, 166, 167, 168, 169, 170, 172, 175, 177, 194, 196, 197, 205, 212, 213-15, 217, 220, 318, 325, 331
    and Middle Eastern Christians, 44, 56, 64, 65, 205
Mission, missionaries, 4, 65, 68, 69, 82, 86, 87, 115, 122, 123, 124, 143, 144
Modernity, Modern Age, 74, 115, 116, 117, 118, 120, 124, 135, 140
    and modernization, 115, 116, 125, 135, 136, 137, 139, 141, 143, 144
Monasticism, (monasteries), 5, 12, 21, 26, 28, 41, 46, 56, 59, 63, 66, 67, 69, 75, 77, 164, 172, 314
Mongols, Mongolians, 29, 45, 57-65, 72, 73, 74, 81, 97, 98, 104, 105
Morocco, 17, 22, 45, 80, 97, 99, 107, 110, 128, 172-75
    and Moroccans, 84
Mughal Dynasty of India, 84, 98, 103-5, 114, 125, 132, 142
Muslim Brotherhood, 74, 157, 171, 207-10, 212-14, 275
Napoleon, 40, 126
    and Napoleonic Wars, 128
Netherlands, 88, 96
    and Netherlands Indies, 152, 183
Nigeria, 109, 110, 134, 139, 178, 215, 325

General Index

Nubia, 4, 5, 63, 108, 111
Orthodox Churches, 42, 79, 96, 100, 187-89, 206
  and Eastern Orthodoxy, 96, 187-89
Ottoman Empire, xiv, 61-62, 81, 97-103, 105, 113, 114, 125, 126-30, 135, 136, 138, 149, 153, 156
  and Ottoman Caliph, 126, 135
  and Ottoman Sultan, 78, 99, 100, 101, 130, 135, 140, 149, 153
  and Ottomans, 78, 79, 82, 84, 97-104, 107, 112, 113, 125-30, 132, 135-37, 140, 147, 149, 153, 155
Pakistan, 17, 22, 104, 132, 179-82, 191, 210, 212, 213
Pan-Arabism, 171, 176, 177, 204, 205
Pan-Islamism, 142, 150, 153, 203
Palestine, 45, 49-51, 57, 60, 99, 126, 127, 154, 164, 165, 213
  and Palestinian Christians, 154
  and Palestinians 167, 213
People of the Book, 19, 20, 33, 55, 74, 261, 262, 316, 321
Persia, Persian, 4, 14, 16, 22, 23, 24, 60, 64, 71, 80, 84, 102, 103, 105, 106, 130, 137, 156, 159, 161, 164, 186, 209, 211, 271, 274
  and Persian Empire, xiii, 12, 13, 14, 16, 30, 39, 43
  See also Iran
Philippines, 106-8, 133, 185, 186
Poland, 41, 59, 188, 207
Pope Urban II, 48, 49, 53
Portugal, 79, 83, 85, 87, 107, 110, 134
  and Portuguese, 84, 85, 86, 87, 88, 106, 107, 108, 110, 112, 113, 123
Qajar Dynasty of Iran, 131, 132, 137, 138, 159
Qajar shah(s), 137, 159
Reformation, 83, 88, 89, 91, 92, 93, 94, 95, 96, 97, 101, 114, 116, 117, 120, 136, 140
  and reformers, 90, 91, 93, 94, 95, 113
  and reformed theology, 93, 95, 96
Renaissance, 74, 75, 82, 89, 90, 116, 141, 176
Revival movement, 115, 121, 122, 143, 144
Roman Empire, xii, 3-7, 9, 12-14, 16, 30, 37, 43, 57
Romania, 59, 98, 130, 189
Rome, 7, 9-11, 14, 25, 26, 36-40, 47, 54, 69, 75, 92
Russia, Russians, 13, 42, 57, 58, 59, 60, 66, 79, 96, 97, 98, 106, 119, 128, 129, 130, 131, 136, 137, 150, 187-89
  and Russian Orthodoxy, 187, 188
  See also Soviet Union
Safavid Dynasty of Persia, 98, 102, 103, 104, 105, 114, 125, 130, 131
Saladin, 45, 50, 55, 57
Saudi Arabia, 30, 45, 138, 139, 153, 168, 169, 325
Scandinavian (Vikings), 42, 96
Secularization, 75, 115, 116, 125, 143-46
  and secularist Islamists, 202, 204
Senegal, 109, 134, 139, 177
Serbia, 98, 129, 130, 189, 190
Shari'a, 24, 29, 73, 100, 122, 132, 135, 136, 139, 140, 159, 169, 175, 178, 179, 180, 185, 208, 209, 210, 212, 216, 217, 219, 220, 221, 227, 317, 328
Sharif Hussein of Hejaz, 153, 154, 162, 165
Shi'ite(s), 16, 17, 22, 28, 45, 102, 103, 131, 132, 137, 159-63, 166, 167, 170, 181, 182, 194, 203, 211, 212, 215, 216, 220, 277, 317

Sicily, 45, 52, 56
Silk Road, 4, 17, 26, 59, 65, 66, 105
Slavs, Slavonic, 13, 41, 42, 101, 129
  and Pan-Slavic, 129
Somalia, 111, 134, 178, 215
Soviet or Soviet Union, 131, 160, 150, 157, 160, 182, 183, 186, 188, 189, 207, 212, 215
  See also Russia
Spain, 6, 9, 17, 18, 22, 25, 27, 32, 39, 43, 44, 52, 54, 56, 67, 68, 70, 79, 80, 81, 85, 86, 87, 103, 107, 110, 133, 216, 271
Spanish, 84-88, 107, 113, 123, 128, 133, 174, 198
  and Spanish Reconquista, 45, 54, 79, 80, 84, 97, 98
Sudan, 4, 45, 108, 111, 134, 139, 140, 215
Sufi, Sufism, 28-30, 73, 138, 139, 210, 215, 273, 274
Sunni(s), 16, 17, 28, 30, 45, 102, 127, 132, 137, 138, 142, 161-63, 167, 170, 182, 194, 203, 204, 211, 212, 273, 277
Switzerland, 91, 93, 96
Syria, 5 11, 12, 14-17, 21, 22, 26, 36, 45, 46, 47, 49, 50, 57, 64, 65, 68, 73, 80, 99, 101, 126, 127, 151, 153, 154, 155, 158, 161-67
Tajikistan, 4, 25, 105, 106, 186
Tawhid, 225, 227, 228, 328
Thomas Aquinas, 29, 53, 67, 70
Timothy, Patriarch of the Assyrian Church, 25, 26, 31
Trinity, 9, 30, 31, 32, 70, 124, 247, 255, 264, 295-301, 317
  and trinitarian, xv, 229, 255, 264, 295-301, 323
Turkey, 5, 37, 45, 47, 55, 62, 73, 74, 84, 129, 154-59, 163-65, 191, 197, 201, 202, 204, 206, 213, 219, 220
  and Turks, 49, 50, 51, 54, 55, 56, 76, 77, 79, 98, 100, 101, 103, 104, 105, 113, 127
  and Seljuk Turks 47, 74, 77, 79, 98
  See also Asia Minor
Turkmenistan, 4, 25, 105, 131, 186
Tunisia, 5, 16, 22, 45, 51, 80, 128, 172, 173, 175, 176, 201, 202, 213
Uganda, 178, 215, 217
Ulama, 29, 101, 135, 136, 138, 142, 159, 160, 161, 175, 204, 210, 211
  and Muslim religious leaders, 101, 125, 126, 135, 138, 142, 159, 160, 161
United States, 121, 122, 133, 148, 159, 160, 170, 176, 183, 187, 190, 193-95, 200, 207, 211, 315-17
  Umayyad Caliphate or Dynasty, 15, 17, 18, 20-22, 31
  Umma, 55, 142, 203, 204, 215, 218, 223, 227, 314, 317-22
  and United States Declaration of Independence, 121
  US Bill of Rights, 200
  US Constitution, 200
Uzbekistan, 4, 25, 61, 105, 131, 186
Wahhabi Movement, 74, 138, 139, 168
Western Christianity, xiii, 36, 39, 115, 116, 120, 122
Yemen, 4, 14, 25, 171
Xinjiang 106, 150, 186

Finding the Textbook You Need

The IVP Academic Textbook Selector
is an online tool for instantly finding the IVP books
suitable for over 250 courses across 24 disciplines.

ivpacademic.com